# WOMEN HEALING/
# HEALING WOMEN

**BibleWorld**
Series Editor: Philip R. Davies, University of Sheffield

BibleWorld shares the fruits of modern (and postmodern) biblical scholarship not only among practitioners and students, but also with anyone interested in what academic study of the Bible means in the twenty-first century. It explores our ever-increasing knowledge and understanding of the social world that produced the biblical texts, but also analyses aspects of the Bible's role in the history of our civilization and the many perspectives – not just religious and theological, but also cultural, political and aesthetic – which drive modern biblical scholarship.

**Published:**
*Sodomy: A History of a Christian Biblical Myth*
Michael Carden

*Yours Faithfully: Virtual Letters from the Bible*
Edited by: Philip R. Davies

*The Apostle Paul and His Letters*
Edwin D. Freed

*The Morality of Paul's Converts*
Edwin D. Freed

*The Origins of the 'Second' Temple:*
*Persian Imperial Policy and the Rebuilding of Jerusalem*
Diana Edelman

*Israel's History and the History of Israel*
Mario Liverani

**Forthcoming**
*History, Literature and Theology in the Book of Chronicles*
Edited by: Ehud Ben Zvi

*Symposia: Confrontations in Biblical Studies*
Roland Boer

*Sectarianism in Early Judaism*
Edited by: David J. Chalcraft

*Linguistic Dating of Biblical Texts*
*An Introduction to Approaches and Problems*
Ian Young and Robert Rezetko

*Vive Memor Mortis*
*Qoheleth and the Wisdom of his Day*
Thomas Bolin

# WOMEN HEALING/ HEALING WOMEN

### THE GENDERIZATION OF HEALING IN EARLY CHRISTIANITY

## ELAINE M. WAINWRIGHT

LONDON   OAKVILLE

Published by

UK: Equinox Publishing Ltd
Unit 6, The Village,
101 Amies St.,
London, SW11 2JW

US: DBBC,
28 Main Street,
Oakville, CT 06779

www.equinoxpub.com

First published 2006

**British Library Cataloguing-in-Publication Data**
A catalogue record for this book is available from the British Library.

**Library of Congress Cataloging-in-Publication Data**
Wainwright, Elaine Mary, 1948-
  Women healing/healing women : the genderization of healing in early Christianity /
Elaine M. Wainwright.
      p. cm. -- (BibleWorld)
  Includes bibliographical references and index.
  ISBN 1-84553-134-5 (hb) -- ISBN 1-84553-135-3 (pbk.)
  1. Bible. N.T. Gospels--Socio-rhetorical criticism. 2. Healing in the Bible. 3. Bible.
N.T. Gospels--Feminist criticism. 4. Women in the Bible. 5. Women healers--R ome.
I. Title. II. Bible world (London, England)
  BS2555.6.H4W35 2006
  261.5'6108209015--dc22
                                2005032075


ISBN   1-84553-134-5   (hardback)
         1-84553-135-3   (paperback)


Typeset by CA Typesetting, www.sheffieldtypesetting.com
Printed and bound in Great Britain byLightning Source UK Ltd., Milton Keynes
and Lightning Source Inc., La Vergne, TN

I dedicate this book
to
healing women through the ages
and in particular
to my friend, Mary,
healer and transformer of bodies and e/Earth

# CONTENTS

## LIST OF PLATES

# Acknowledgements

Women healing captured my imagination some years ago and the investigation undertaken in this study has been supported and encouraged by many people whom I wish to acknowledge here.

I thank first all those students who have explored the topic with me and become excited by the findings which were emerging. The participants in the 2002 Maryknoll Summer School were the first to experience some of the developed insights and they brought their rich experience of cross-cultural ministry to the topic. Students in the Brisbane College of Theology and the School of Theology at the University of Auckland have become excited with me as the work developed. And many women's groups with whom I've shared my finding have raised new and challenging questions for me. I am grateful for the insights which each of them have brought to my explorations as these have shaped my thinking in multiple ways.

My research was significantly advanced by a Catholic Biblical Association Visiting Scholarship at the École Biblique in Jerusalem in the first half of 2001. Even though the wonderful library was boxed during renovations, sufficient resources were still accessible for me to undertake the ground work for the project. A month prior to this in the British Library and the Wellcome Trust Library, London, gave me access to a wide range of both contemporary and historical material that gave shape to my approach. I thank each of these institutions for their extraordinary support for scholarship generally and this work in particular.

Dialogue with one's colleagues makes a significant contribution to the development of ideas and the undertaking of this project has been no exception in this regard. I have presented papers at the Society of Biblical Literature annual meeting on at least three occasions and at the annual meeting of the Australian Catholic Biblical Association. The very positive support for the topic and the critical comments for its development have been very much appreciated and I thank all those too numerous to name. I want to thank, in particular, Anne Elvey and Veronica Lawson who read an all but final draft of the manuscript and whose feedback has certainly enhanced the final product.

The taking up of a position of Head of the School of Theology at the University of Auckland meant that the project had to be placed on hold for some time as I discovered the requirements of a new role. A University Staff Research Grant has been most helpful, therefore, in ensuring that the project has been able to be completed. The grant made possible my engaging a research assistant and without the assistance of Sarah Hart who functioned in this capacity for almost eighteen months, I would never have been able to bring this work to conclusion. Joan Parker proofread the final draft and for this I am most grateful. And to the office staff in the School of Theology, especially Pervin Medhora and Lorraine Noda who have taken up a number of additional tasks to enable me to do the final production of the text, my sincere thanks.

My final thanks go to my family and friends who are always patient with the amount of time I spend in my office and whose interest and encouragement never flags.

During the course of my research I have published the following articles which represent insights along the way and I wish to acknowledge them here. Insights from them are, no doubt, scattered throughout the text.

'"Your Faith Has Made You Well", Jesus, Women, and Healing in the Gospel of Matthew', in Ingrid Rosa Kitzberger (ed.), *Transformative Encounters: Jesus and Women Reviewed* (Biblical Interpretation Series, 43; Leiden: E.J. Brill, 2000), pp. 224-44.

'The Matthean Jesus and the Healing of Women', in David E. Aune (ed.), *The Gospel of Matthew in Current Study: Studies in Honor of William G. Thompson, S.J.* (Grand Rapids: Eerdmans, 2001), pp. 74-95.

'Not without my Daughter: Gender and Demon Possession in Matthew 15.21-28', in Amy-Jill Levine with Marianne Blickenstaff (eds.), *A Feminist Companion to Matthew* (Sheffield: Sheffield Academic Press, 2001), pp. 126-37.

The article below, however, was necessary for the integrity of the fourth chapter of the work and I thank Orbis Books for their permission to include some segments of it.

'The Pouring Out of Healing Ointment: Rereading Mark 14:3-9', in Fernando F. Segovia (ed.), *Toward a New Heaven and a New Earth: Essays in Honor of Elisabeth Schüssler Fiorenza* (Maryknoll, NY: Orbis Books, 2003), pp. 157-78.

Finally, I recognize that the book would have been poorer if it did not include some of the images of the clay and stone that have preserved the memories of women healing from antiquity. I thank the National Archaeological Museum, Athens, Bildarchiv Foto, Marburg, and the Musei Vaticani for their permission to include the plates of a number of artifacts.

Auckland
1 September, 2005

# ABBREVIATIONS

| | |
|---|---|
| *ABR* | *Australian Biblical Review* |
| *Aff.* | *De affectionibus* (Affections), Hippocrates |
| AGJU | Arbeiten zur Geschichte des Spätjudentums und Urchristentums |
| *Agr.* | *De agricultura* (Agriculture), Cato |
| *AJP* | *American Journal of Philology* |
| *ANRW* | *Aufstieg und Niedergang des römischen Welt: Geschichte und Kultur Roms im Spiegel der neueren Forschung* |
| *Ant.* | *Jewish Antiquities*, Josephus |
| *Arch* | *Archaeology* |
| BAGD | W. Bauer, W.F. Arndt, F.W. Gingrich and F.W. Danker, *Greek-English Lexicon of the New Testament and Other Early Christian Literature*. 2d ed. Chicago, 1979 |
| BCE | Before the Common Era |
| BETL | Bibliotheca ephemeridum theologicarum lovaniensium |
| *Bib* | *Biblica* |
| *b. Ketub* | Babylonian Talmud *Ketubbot* |
| *b. Sanh.* | Babylonian Talmud *Sanhedrin* |
| *BTB* | *Biblical Theology Bulletin* |
| *BR* | *Biblical Research* |
| BZNW | Beihefte zur Zeitschrift für die neutestamentliche Wissenschaft |
| C | Century |
| *Cat. Maj.* | *Cato Major* (Cato the Elder), Plutarch |
| *Caus. plant.* | *De causis plantarum*, Theophrastus |
| CE | Common Era |
| *CIL* | *Corpus inscriptionum latinarum* |
| CSJH | Chicago Studies in the History of Judaism |
| *Deipn.* | *Deipnosophistae*, Athenaeus |
| *Descr.* | *Graeciae description*, (Description of Greece), Pausanius |
| *Epid.* | *Epidemiae* (Epidemics), Hippocrates |
| EPRO | Etudes preliminaries aux religions orientales dans l'empire romain |
| *ExAud* | *Ex auditu* |
| FF | Foundations and Facets |
| Gal | Galen |

| | |
|---|---|
| *Gyn.* | *Gynaecology*, Soranus |
| HSM | Harvard Semitic Monographs |
| *HTR* | *Harvard Theological Review* |
| *Hor* | *Horizons* |
| *IEJ* | *Israel Exploration Journal* |
| *IGRR* | *Inscriptiones Graecae ad res Romanas Pertinentes* |
| *Il.* | *Ilias* (Iliad), Homer |
| *JBL* | *Journal of Biblical Literature* |
| *JSHJ* | *Journal for the Study of the Historical Jesus* |
| *JSNT* | *Journal for the Study of the New Testament* |
| JSNTSup | Journal for the Study of the New Testament: Supplement Series |
| JSOTSup | Journal for the Study of the Old Testament: Supplement Series |
| *Jusj.* | *Jus jurandum* (The Oath), Hippocrates |
| LCL | Loeb Classical Library |
| *Leg.* | *Leges* (Laws), Plato |
| *List* | *Listening: Journal of Religion and Culture* |
| *Loc. hom.* | *De locis in homine* (Places in Man), Hippocrates |
| LXX | Septuagint |
| *Med.* | *De medico* (The Physician), Hippocrates |
| *Med.* | *Medea*, Seneca |
| *Morb.* | *De morbis* (Diseases), Hippocrates |
| *Morb. sacr.* | *De morbo sacro* (The Sacred Disease), Hippocrates |
| *MTSR* | *Method and Theory in the Study of Religion* |
| *m. Zab.* | Mishnah *Zabim* |
| *Nat.* | *Naturalis historia* (Natural History), Pliny the Elder |
| *Nat. hom.* | *De natura hominis* (Nature of Man), Hippocrates |
| *Neot* | *Neotestamentica* |
| *NovT* | *Novum Testamentum* |
| NTOA | Novum Testamentum et Orbis Antiquus |
| *NTS* | *New Testament Studies* |
| OBT | Overtures to Biblical Theology |
| *OCCL* | *The Oxford Companion to Classical Literature* |
| *Od.* | *Odyssea* (Odyssey), Homer |
| *Resp.* | *Respublica* (Republic), Plato |
| *RevExp* | *Review and Expositor* |
| *SBLSP* | *Society of Biblical Literature Seminar Papers* |
| SBLSymS | Society of Biblical Literature Symposium Series |
| *SJT* | *Scottish Journal of Theology* |
| SNTSMS | Society for New Testament Studies Monograph Series |
| SSEJC | Studies in Early Judaism and Christianity |
| *ST* | *Studia theologica* |
| *TD* | *Theology Digest* |
| *Theaet.* | *Theaetetus*, Plato |
| Tob | Tobit |

| | |
|---|---|
| *Vict.* | *De victu* (Regimen), Hippocrates |
| v.(v). | verse(s) |
| WBC | Word Biblical Commentary |
| WUNT | Wissenschafliche Untersuchungen zum Neuen Testament |
| ZNW | *Zeitschrift für die neutestamentliche Wissenschaft und die Kunde der älteren Kirche* |

# INTRODUCTION

*Woman Heal Thyself*, the engaging title of Jeanne Elizabeth Blum's book,[1] came to my attention when the seeds of this present project were but germinating. Her provocative play on the Lukan text 'Physician, heal thyself' (Lk. 4.23) brought into focus two seemingly conflicting worlds. It was not at all surprising, in the dying years of the twentieth century, that 'woman' would be invited to heal.[2] Indeed, over the course of that century, increasing numbers of women have engaged in all aspects of healing.[3] The decentring effect of Blum's text lay elsewhere. It was the insertion of 'woman' into the Lukan gospel command to heal. Suddenly I realized that despite the widespread language of healing in the Second Testament and the significance of the commissions to heal given by Jesus, that no women are specifically named as healers in these early Christian texts or are among those explicitly commissioned by Jesus to heal.

This is a significant lacuna at the very time when women are becoming more aware of the ways in which texts from the past, and reconstructions of that past, shape both the present and the future;[4] and when more and more women are becoming engaged across the spectrum of healing, seeking their genealogies but also critically examining the very construction of healing.[5] The reading of our past, therefore, is not a thing of the past. It does not shape the past but it shapes the present and the future. It constructs a consciousness, it provides genealogies, and it functions rhetorically to shape meaning. Decades now of women doing history and decades of feminist historiography have changed both the present and the future for many women. This particular work takes its place within that stream of historical research whose focus has been and is women's agency in human history as it turns attention to women healing in the Graeco-Roman world generally, and in early Christianity in particular.

Health is a key concern for human kind. Currently it is at the forefront of contemporary Western culture and society as major Western powers struggle with the spiralling costs of the biomedicalization of health. These costs, in their turn, are placing enormous pressure on their health care systems. In the two-thirds world, on the other hand, most people lack even basic health care facilities and resources and so for them too, health is a key concern. Also in the Western world, health and health care are moving beyond the biomedical into the fields of natural therapies and medicines. Witness the rise of health stores, and the vast expansion of practitioners engaged in therapies such as chiropractice, massage, reike, aromatherapy and many others. Boundaries between these fields blur also as professional health workers trained in the biomedical model incorporate natural medicines and therapies in their treatment of patients or as those whose foundation is in the natural therapies acquire biomedical skills, often applying them in new ways and in new contexts. Also people are generally taking much more responsibility for their own health care thus moving health and healing into the popular arena beyond the purely professional.

Further boundaries blur as practices like yoga and meditation, whose origins lie within religious traditions, are assimilated into the expanding field of therapies and health care. Ancient and indigenous practices of healing are also recognized as bearing a wisdom that has been lost beneath the weight of science and biotechnology. Health and healing within contemporary Western culture is, therefore, no longer considered a field which belongs solely to professional biomedical practitioners. It is multidimensional, incorporating not only the somatic but the psychological and the spiritual/religious. The genderization of contemporary Western health care is also shifting as women emerge as particularly visible within the natural therapies and are becoming increasingly so across the range of specialities within the biomedical field of health care.[6] Standing at the opening of the twenty-first century, therefore, we are in a unique position to consider healing and health care anew and, from these new perspectives, to *read* history.

In light of the above, one of the initial considerations for this project will need to be the understanding of healing and health that informs it. The project began with a focus on women healers. It was evoked by the recognition, noted above, that women are not commissioned to heal within the narratives of the Second Testament and yet it is commonly claimed that women are generally healers and that early Christianity was a religion of healing. How might one explain these seeming disjunctions? I believed initially that a search for women healers in antiquity and early Christianity would uncover women's agency. During the course of the research, however, the focus has broadened to 'women healing', a term which will function in a multidimensional way in this study to include women's agency not only as healer but also as the one being healed within the context of health care and its gendering in early Christianity.

While gender is a key factor informing the study, it will not remain the sole perspective. Recent challenges from women beyond the field of Western feminism have drawn attention to the limitations of gender as a category of analysis. It is always intertwined with other areas of difference such as class, race, ethnicity, education, religion and spirituality. As an Australian of Anglo-Celtic origin, I stand in the tradition of the colonizers of the land of my birth and am conscious of the very ready construction of 'the other', whether Aboriginal or more recent arrival within that context. The incorporation of a postcolonial perspective into my hermeneutic will be a significant factor for consideration in this project so that the colonization of women's healing within history may be uncovered and the agency of those colonized may be revealed. Recognition of this multidimensionality of historical women will challenge tendencies to see and to construct indigenous and non-English speaking background women's healing in an Australian context as monolithic, denying difference and the multiple subjectivities of these women in relation to health care.[7]

As a woman, however, I carry in my body the marks of my colonization by Western traditions generally and by Christianity within that tradition in particular. Bringing a feminist perspective into dialogue with the postcolonial will ensure that neither gender nor actual historical women are obscured as other areas of domination come into focus. Also, standing with the human community at the dawn of a new century, my heart is moved by the plight of this planet called Earth which cries out for healing, that its agency might be restored within human consciousness and praxis. A reading of healing within history that does not continue or augment the silencing or obscuring of Earth's agency will need to interweave an ecological perspective with the feminist and post-colonial reading positions indicated above as necessary for this project.

The first chapter will, therefore, be given to a consideration of the field of research, namely healing, and the establishing of the ground or the space on/in which the understanding of healing particular to this study can play. The development of a reading perspective or hermeneutic will be shaped by both the location/context of this particular reader and the scope of the topic as established by the understanding of healing. Within this emerging context of reading, choices will be made regarding the particular methodologies which will best facilitate this project of reading women healing in early Christianity. I use the word methodologies advisedly as the sources or texts for this study will be multiple including literary texts such as classical authors and Christian evangelists; artefactual material including grave inscriptions and statuary; and material texts which encompass spatial and geographic locations and other elements of the body's environment together with the body itself. The methodologies will need therefore to be literary, socio-cultural, historical and material.

It is not surprising that the increased focus on health and healing in the contemporary world has brought with it what seems to be a renewed attention to the history of healing. I use the word 'renewed' explicitly since the story of healing in the ancient world has already begun to be told.[8] In the late-nineteenth and into the first half of the twentieth century we find titles like Maurice Albert's *Les médicins grecs à Rome*,[9] Clifford Allbutt's *Greek Medicine in Rome*,[10] Louis Cohn-Haft's *The Public Physicians of Ancient Greece*,[11] together with those works which specifically addressed women's participation within this history – Sophia Jex-Blake, *Medical Women: A Thesis and a History*,[12] Mélanie Lipinska's *Histoire des femmes médicins depuis l'Antiquité jusqu'à nos jours*,[13] Kate Campbell Hurd-Mead's *A History of Women in Medicine: From the Earliest Times to the Beginning of the Nineteenth Century*,[14] and Walther Schönfeld's *Frauen in der abendländischen Heilkunde: Vom klassischen Altertum bis zum Ausgang des 19. Jahrhunderts*.[15] As the titles suggest, these works were general surveys based on the author's interpretation of classical texts and ancient inscriptions. Little attention was given to the context of the texts and its shaping of the text itself or to the reading location of the historian/interpreter of those texts.

Studies of this general nature still persist,[16] but historians of ancient medicine are calling for a much greater attention to context. Vivian Nutton states very clearly that '[t]he study of the social history of medicine in Greece and Rome shows, above all, the pitfalls of wide generalization'.[17] Helen King[18] reviews two recent works which set the study of ancient medicine in its socio-cultural context, namely *Ancient Medicine in its Socio-Cultural Context*,[19] and *The Western Medical Tradition: 800 B.C. to 1800 A.D.*[20] She asks: '[w]hat of the future for those who seek to understand ancient medicine by putting it into its socio-cultural context?'[21] In answering her own question, she goes on to assert that '[m]uch of the impetus for new work on ancient medicine has come from those studying the role of women in the ancient world, who have mined the medical texts in search of evidence both for ideology and for practice'.[22] But she adds further that 'new agendas are entering the field, old issues are being addressed through new methodologies, and attempts are being made to bring together the different disciplinary skills necessary and to develop a greater sensitivity to the sources'.[23] This study belongs along such a trajectory as it brings together not only a feminist but postcolonial and ecological perspective to the study of women healing in antiquity and combines methodological tools from across literary, social scientific and historical approaches. It is these which will facilitate a reading of its unique combination of sources.

In a second and third chapter, using the multidisciplinary and interactive hermeneutical and methodological approach established in the first, women healing/healing women in the Graeco-Roman world will be explored. This is the world in which women healing within early and emerging Christianity is located and in which it can be analyzed and understood. As King indicated above, the sources may not be new[24] but they will be read from new perspectives in an attempt to give greater subjectivity to women's healing and richer or denser contextuality to the gendering of healing. These chapters will begin to explore the interconnectivity of professional and folk medicine together with other material aspects of women healing.

Within the Graeco-Roman world of popular and folk medicine and within Hellenistic Judaism, healing was not only, nor even predominantly, a human task but one that brought humanity into contact with divinity. From the fifth century BCE through to at least the fourth century CE, Asclepius, the male god of healing, was virtually synonymous with healing within the Graeco-Roman religious world.[25] Hygieia seems to have been relegated to daughter and helper status. Isis' association with the restoration of life renders her healing prowess great but this is not her sole function in the symbolic world of Graeco-Roman religion. As early Christianity developed, Jesus and the tradition of healing associated with him as Divine Physician began to rival that of Asclepius. Like the human world of healing, the divine was highly gendered. The second half of Chapter Three will bring women healing into dialogue with the symbolic universe of divine healing. It will give particular attention to gender and the religious and spiritual experiences of women within their constructions of religious worlds. Although this will be the particular focus of this section, these issues will need to be engaged during the course of the study.

Accompanying the renewed focus on medicine and healing in antiquity has been an expansion of studies of healing in early Christianity. John Wilkinson's *The Bible and Healing: A Medical and Theological Commentary* represents a more traditional study that seeks to understand references to sickness and disease in the biblical texts from a medical or biomedical point of view and healing within a theological context.[26] The work of Hector Avalos[27] and John Pilch,[28] especially that which focuses on the Christian Scriptures, represents a shift in approach. As John Pilch's subtitle indicates, the disciplines of medical and cultural anthropology are brought to bear on the study of healing within early Christianity. As with the study of ancient medicine, therefore, significant attention is given to the broad socio-cultural context of healing and newer disciplines like that of medical anthropology enable the meaning of healing to emerge with richer texture in its original context. This study seeks to intervene within this more recent approach to healing, however, to highlight its lack of significant attention to gender, to the materiality of Earth and to other categories of difference which feminist studies are rendering visible.

Subsequent chapters will examine women healing within the synoptic gospels. A feminist, post-colonial, ecological hermeneutic will inform the multifaceted methodological approach combining literary, socio-cultural, and material readings of Christian texts. Attention will be given to the language of healing within the dynamic of the literary texts but also to the function of this language within socio-cultural and material contexts. This section of the study is the crux of the work whose impetus arose from the realization noted above that women are not commissioned to heal within the context of the Second Testament and yet it will be shown that women have traditionally been healers.[29] Initial explorations of the Gospel of Mark will be undertaken in detail. Because most of the stories are shared by the evangelists, subsequent chapters will focus more on the changes or emphases particular to each of the gospels of Matthew and Luke. Since women healing are virtually absent from the Johannine gospel, except perhaps for the brief account of Mary of Bethany pouring ointment over the feet of Jesus, this study will focus only on the synoptic gospels.[30]

This project could be continued into other texts of the Second Testament as well from the second and third centuries of the Common Era. This, however, is to enter a space where scholarly opinions differ in relation to healing generally and where the evidence is sparse. I leave the development of this ongoing history to others, hoping that the approach developed and the insights gained in this study will encourage further exploration.

My goal is that this work will participate with other feminist, postcolonial and ecological readings of history and readings of biblical texts and contexts to shape a renewed present and a new future in which difference and 'otherness' can be respected and celebrated not only for the transformation of the human community but for the transformation of human-Earth relationships toward the survival of our planet. The particular way in which it is envisaged that this work will contribute to such a transformation is by its attentive reconstruction of a past that may provide new genealogies for the present and into the future.

# Chapter 1

## WHERE THEORY AND PRACTICE MEET:
## A WAY TOWARD TRANSFORMATION

It is usually at the edges where the great tectonic plates of theory meet and shift that we find the most dramatic developments and upheavals. When four tectonic plates of liberation theory – those concerned with the oppressions of gender, race, class and nature – finally come together, the resulting tremors could shake the conceptual structures of oppression to their foundations.[1]

[P]erhaps it is at the margin, not at the center, where we can find authorization to work out alternatives that can remake experience, ours and others. In that sense, I suppose, the margin may be near the center of a most important thing: transformation. Change is more likely to begin at the edge, in the borderland between established orders.[2]

This chapter is concerned with theory, the development of a framework to shape analysis of the subject matter – women healing. It will, therefore, consider the interrelationship of these 'great tectonic plates' that Plumwood acknowledges – gender, race, class and nature – in the development of a lens for reading. It also prepares the methodological ground for the interpretation of the wide range of texts and text-types that constitutes this study.

Such a movement between theory and practice is not simply a move from hermeneutic to methodology. As Beverley Skeggs acknowledges,

[m]ethodology is itself theory. It is a theory of methods which informs a range of issues from who to study, how to study, which institutional practices to adopt (such as interpretative practices), how to write and which knowledge to use. These decisions locate any knowledge product within disciplinary practices and enable and constrain engagement with other theoretical and political debates.[3]

The task is one of naming the ground or space of this investigation, not in a rigid way that would stifle exploration, but in a way that will enable creative praxis as sources are chosen and new interpretations undertaken.

As this study begins, I am aware that its scope needs to be clearly articulated. The arena of consideration, healing, is vast, as has already been indicated in the introduction. The theoretical discussion of this chapter will enable the range of this particular study to be established in terms of the topic itself, the perspective of this particular interpreter,[4] and the tools and approaches which will enable a particular reading or readings to emerge. Initially the very topic must be explored in order to determine the field in which this study will move and it is to this that I now turn.

### Scoping Healing

Even a quick glance at dictionary definitions of the verb 'to heal' indicates that its usage belongs to a number of fields. One would expect the most basic definition, 'to restore to health or soundness',[5] which links it primarily with the field of human health, illness, sickness and restoration to wholeness. The second definition given in this same text is '[t]o set right; repair...the rift between us' and hence includes human relationships. A third definition is to 'restore (a person) to spiritual wholeness'. What this definition draws to our attention is that healing is not concerned only with the intra-human or inter-human but can encompass the other-than-human, a point which will be taken up later in this study.

The Encarta Dictionary likewise gives the first two of its definitions to the medical aspect of healing, the making of a person or an injury healthy or whole.[6] The third refers to the inter-human healing and a fourth to the getting rid of some 'evil' which goes beyond the scope of the previous categories.

A recognition of the multifaceted aspects of these dictionary definitions draws attention to the tendency today, particularly in the West and in a world dominated by the West, to focus healing only on the biomedical: a healing of a particular disease which has affected a particular part of a human body. Cure the disease and healing has been effected. Sargent and Brettell point to some of the causes of such a focus:

> This medicalization occurs through such phenomena as language, the technological domination of the body, the subordination of alternative sources of knowledge and experience that are not derived from biomedicine, and the influence of market forces on medical practice.[7]

As a result of this, other possible understandings of the healing of the human body and the curing of diseases, in other eras and other locations, that took or take account not only of the body but also of the mind and the spirit have been marginalized in the thinking of the West.[8] This study's focus on healing in the Graeco-Roman world and early Christianity will need, therefore, to be attentive to the breadth of possible understandings of healing in those worlds, understandings that transgress the biomedical. As interpreter, I will need to allow aspects of healing other than the cure of disease to emerge in seeking to understand women healing in another time and another place.

Medical anthropology is an important contributor to our establishing of the scope of 'healing'. This relatively new discipline has made clear that healing is, in the words of Coyle and Muir, 'more than a clinical event'.[9] Medical anthropological studies have shown that healing is a *process* which includes making meaning of life's lesions.[10] As such, its ambit is not only healer and patient but rather these actors within a socio-cultural context. A study of women healing will need, therefore, to give attention not only to women healers and women patients but also the meaning-making process in which they are engaged in a socio-cultural context where gender plays a very significant role in the construction of meaning.

Meaning-making has, in many eras and many societies both ancient and contemporary, significant links with religion, and the Graeco-Roman world was no exception.[11] While Hippocratic medicine may have distanced itself from the religious dimension of that society in order to develop a more 'scientific' approach, certainly in the society at large, such a distancing was inconceivable. And so, even as the dictionary definition would indicate, healing of the body in this project will be placed within the meaning-making system of the particular era and social group under consideration that will include the religious dimension even when these are in tension. Where women and gender intersect with these tensions and compatibilities will be of significance to this study.

Just as the contemporary discipline of medical anthropology provides significant insight into the establishing of the dimensions of healing appropriate for this study, so too does that of ecology. The language of healing, making whole and establishing or re-establishing wellbeing within the entire ecological system is one which is becoming more and more familiar in our day. Elias and Ketchman, for instance, use such language when they speak of the call '[t]o right the imbalance, fix the brokenness, heal the wounds, and become whole again',[12] reminiscent of aspects of the definitions of healing evoked above. Those engaged in what Zana Daysh has established as the field of 'health ecology' extend or perhaps make more explicit what has begun to emerge even in dictionary definitions, namely that 'health in its broadest sense' can be understood 'as a matter of energy, upheld by a spiritual force which necessarily encompasses all aspects of life of individuals and communities, and their environments'.[13] Morteza Honari likewise emphasizes, in the same collection of essays, the significance of placing healing 'at the centre of human and environmental interactions'.[14]

Some of the issues raised here will receive more detailed development within the hermeneutical section of this chapter. For the present, however, they have contributed to the establishment of the scope of healing particular to this study. Healing will not be considered as simply somatic, limited to a focus on a specific dis-ease and its cure and those engaged in that process as healer and/or healed. It will also be explored as socio-cultural, concerned with human meaning-making in particular contexts, and as ecological or environmental in its location in material worlds.

### Si[gh]ting Gender

It has been demonstrated above in scoping the field in which this study will play, that the material world of bodies, their physical/biological wholeness or malfunction, their environment, and the socio-cultural world of meaning-making are intricately interwoven. There is no 'out-there' definition of healing that can be separated from the world-view/s of those who would define it. As a result, feminist anthropologists and historians have drawn attention to the gendering of healing, as material and as socio-cultural, in the past as well as in the present.[15] Both women and men have been engaged in the healing process but often in quite different ways depending on how gender functioned within the meaning-making processes in their contexts.[16] Recognition of such gendering gives rise to the specific focus of this study. Explorations of healing within early Christianity have taken little or no account of gender and so have not only skewed the resultant readings of this history but have contributed to the normalization and thereby the authorization of male-centredness in this particular aspect of life. They have participated, therefore, in the construction and maintenance of what Val Plumwood calls the 'master' paradigm of Western consciousness.[17] It will be argued that, for the sake of women and the Earth, a study of the gendering of healing in early Christianity is not only opportune but urgent. Below, some of the factors that contribute to both the rationale for, and the scope of, a gendered study of healing will be made clear.

First, the gendering of healing in the past as in the present has been and is political. Medicine is a significant arena for the interplay of power in a society.[18] The participation of women in health care systems both as healers and active patients has been and continues to be a source of women's liberation.[19] History, however, provides a more pervasive perspective, namely, that medicine and the health care system in which the process of healing is embedded have been among the most oppressive arenas of women's lives across history. A study of the gendering of healing will need to be one which takes account of power but in a way which does not construct and maintain a dualistic oppression/liberation model. Rather the multiple nuances of this power will be more explicitly explored in the hermeneutical section below. A new reconstruction of women healing, taking account of the power dynamic, will enable the rich texture of ancient women's participation in the fields concerned with healing in their societies to emerge in all their diversities.

A second factor which colours the study of the gendering of healing is that across contemporary societies, women are actively engaged in myriads of ways, depending on contexts, with 'new creativity and passion', Christina Feldman says,[20] in the healing of wounds of gender, ethnic, racial and colonial oppressions as well those of the planet. The particularity of this engagement from standpoints of women's historical, social and cultural experiences, enables them to reconstruct, remap or revision women healing in a way that is not only significant for a vision of the past but will shape a different present and future. Women's participation in this healing of wounds is not to be seen as a result of their greater affiliation to healing in a way that essentializes them.[21] Rather, they contribute, as do men, as gendered historians of healing. This results from their engagement with the challenges of contemporary healing from the perspectives of their reflection upon their particular experiences of ecological, postcolonial, or gendered oppression and discrimination. It is women's location as particular subjects which makes possible their particular reading of healing.

Hence, si[gh]ting gender in a study of healing cannot lead simply to an add women/add gender and stir approach. Rather, it will shape both what will need to be studied, giving particular attention to the dimensions of healing explored above, and the way in which it will need to be studied. It is this second aspect which now demands attention as some of the hermeneutical issues already raised and the way in which they will shape this study are explored.

### *Chan[g/c]ing Lenses – Shaping Vision*

#### *Feminist*
As a critical feminist scholar seeking transformation or healing of human-human and Earth-human relationships, I am aware that I stand at this

point in history. I am, therefore, conscious of 'a globalized world increasingly interconnected and multilayered with meaning'.[22] Such a location necessitates the construction of a hermeneutic for this reading of ancient women healing that is responsible and responsive to the complex issues of that world. Mary John, however, has raised some radically challenging questions in relation to first-world, Western women's attempts to articulate their reading positions in response to the critiques that have emerged in contemporary feminist literature regarding the extension of gender analyses to include attention to race, ethnicity, class and other axes of difference. She advocates a more thorough *questioning of our positionality* than Haraway's 'situated knowledge' would suggest.[23] Indeed, she points to the need for feminists to continually historicize both reading positions and knowledge even in the face of the frightening prospect 'that the culture she was raised in may embody nothing worth saving'.[24]

For the feminist scholar of early Christianity who stands within the contemporary Christian tradition, such a possibility may, indeed, be frightening since the tradition being studied is not just a historical artefact but the living tradition that may have nurtured her spirit and in aspects of whose gospel tradition she may continue to find meaning.[25] It is, however, a necessary stance if re-articulations of the Christian tradition and its history are not to serve a continuation of the oppressions inherent in the 'master' paradigm in which it was forged and which it embraced/embraces in different ways throughout its history. A transformative vision for a more holistic future for both humanity and the Earth community may not, however, readily emerge from a reading of the tradition and its historical documents.[26] In order not to impose such a vision, I find myself informed by Anne Elvey's continual re-articulation of the 'not-yet' which she says needs to characterize an eco-feminist reading of the Christian tradition.[27] The unfinished nature of feminist, postcolonial and ecological dismantlings of the 'master' paradigm that is implicated in all our knowledge and our histories means that this 'not-yet' character needs to continually inform all our reading practices.

Clarke and Olesen borrow the metaphor of 'diffraction' from Donna Haraway using her definition to characterize what I am calling a feminist reading practice for transformation. They point out that '[d]iffraction is an optical metaphor for the effort to make a difference in the world…a device for considering how to make the end [of the millennium] swerve'.[28] For them as for this project, the swerve is a decentering of health and medicine from its biomedical model and its male-centredness and hence a re-visioning or a re-mapping/re-reading. As Clarke and Olesen indicate, the term 're-visioning' is limited because of its very optical allusion. The task is more multidimensional and, in the case of this project, seeks not only to see anew but to hear, to map and to read women healing in all their complexity and heterogeneity so that women of antiquity whether Greek, Roman, Jewish or Christian may be heard, seen, evoked into subjectivity.[29]

Just as Elvey recognized the 'not-yet' nature of the world in front of the text which an eco-feminist reading may open up, Joshel and Murnaghan on the other hand, acknowledge the *silences* in the very texts or sources and in the world/s behind those texts when the focus is women in antiquity.[30] But they also sound a warning, alerting us to the danger of creating what they call 'more noise' in the process of seeking the subjectivities of women of antiquity that could, indeed, further obscure these ancient women. They alert us to the difficult and delicate path that must be followed to enable women's agencies and subjectivities to emerge in as much particularity as possible even in the face of the paucity of not only sources but also data within those sources. This project will be, therefore, an intervention, a reconstruction, re-mapping, re-reading which shares with all other such reconstructions of antiquity a highly provisional quality. In this, it participates with other similar studies which intervene in and resist the totalizing effect of most reconstructive studies of Greek, Roman and early Christian healing within the master paradigm.

As a study, therefore, women healing within early Christianity and within the Graeco-Roman world cannot be comprehensive. It will be partial because of both the limitations of the sources and the particular reading perspective I am constructing here. A feminist reading which seeks to take account of variables and differences in the lives of women beyond those created by gender is, however, of necessity characterized by complexity. In order that these complexities not simply create the 'noise' Joshel and Murnaghan warned of, general clarifications here may free the later textual and source analyses of this possibility.

This study will consider the gendering of healing over a period of approximately three centuries from the Hellenistic period through to the end of the first century of the Common Era. It will range over a geographical area that skirted the Eastern Mediterranean from Alexandria in the south to Rome and its environs to the north, following the coastline both east and then west. The understanding of gender is significant, therefore, in relation to both the temporal, physical and socio-cultural variables that its range entails. This study considers *gender* not as an unchanging construct to be discovered and named but rather as a process both temporally and culturally contingent, always under construction and reconstruction.[31]

Gender will not, therefore, emerge in this study as a fixed object[32] but will need to be considered in relation to other variables in the lives of both women and men healing. As attention is given to gender roles, relations and ideologies, this must be extended to include their intersection with geographic location, socio-cultural meaning-makings, and political processes.[33] Since gender is not, therefore, constructed by men for women but worked out in the very process of interaction in socio-cultural and political contexts, women's agency within its construction in the context of healing will be of significance.

This study will not, therefore, focus simply on where women were visible in the health care system or on the oppression of women by the medical system. Rather it will open a space in which attention can be given to women's participation within the world of healing, both as healer and as patient, and to the *agency or power* which women exercised from both subject positions and the consequent contribution they made to meaning within the system. This is based on an assumption established above and shared with Helen King that the health care system was such that 'men and women both had some power, and within which women as patients could become active agents in their own diagnosis and treatment.[34] King goes on to say that '[t]his suggests that the interplay between women and men is rather more subtle'.[35] Such a nuanced approach is a necessary one, as will be seen below, when a reading framework is established which seeks to deconstruct not just the gender dualism but the interlocking web of dualisms which characterize the 'master' paradigm. If the new paradigm is to relate women and men to nature as well as to culture then this 'subtle interplay' will be a necessary element along this path of transformation.

A term introduced above and which has become commonplace in feminist critical theory is that of '*subjectivity*'. Beverley Skeggs has explored this most recently in relation to experience in order to show that 'we are all produced as subjects with subjectivity, through our experiences, through the interpretation of these experiences and through time'.[36] To seek to reconstruct the subjectivities of ancient women healing will be a difficult task because our access to them and their experience is only by way of their representations in sources which are most often male generated. To raise questions regarding the construction of their subjectivities as multidimensional, it will be necessary to listen and to read for the intersections of gender, race, class and religion in historical, socio-cultural and material circumstances as these may have contributed to the representations which we have and as these may point to possible experiences of women in those worlds. This, too, adds to the 'provisional' nature of such a project but attentiveness to this provisionality also critiques similar projects which claim objectivity and certainty.

Questions regarding women's agency and subjectivities also alert us to the possibility of *resistance*. It is generally understood that in all historical periods while some women have identified with the male hegemony of the 'master' paradigm, others have resisted. This study will seek for evidence of such resistance in relation to healing. In this, as interpreter, I will heed Ortner's advice that 'whatever the hegemonic order of gender relations may be – whether 'egalitarian', or 'male dominant', or something else – it never exhausts what is going on. There are always sites, and sometimes large sites, of alternative practices and perspectives available, and these may become the bases of resistance and transformation'.[37] In historical research, however, resistance is generally not large scale but rather hints which indicate that the 'master' paradigm is being subverted in the most subtle of ways. This aspect of the project shares, therefore, the perspective of Judith Okely who looks not for 'organised protest, or sustained mass movements viewed over time' but for 'moments where resistance crystallises in isolated individual acts or gestures'.[38] This is, of course, even more difficult with regard to ancient texts because we do not see the 'individual acts or gestures' but must look for clues in a word or phrase in a text or perhaps the absence of indicators of the 'master' paradigm.

*Postcolonial*

The above dialogue with contemporary feminist critical theory, has provided a nuanced feminist critical reading perspective for my task as biblical interpreter and historian of early Christianity, focusing on:

> positionality,
> silences,
> gender,
> agency and power,
> subjectivity, and
> resistance.

It is, however, incomplete, especially for this interpreter who is very aware of her location in a socio-cultural and political context shaped by colonialism. This has constructed my consciousness in subtle ways of which I have little or no awareness. As I begin a research project into women healing in early Christianity, I am cognizant of the rich histories and traditions of healing which are carried in the memories of the Australian and New Zealand indigenous populations, of the multicultured members of those populations, and in particular of the women of these groups. In developing a postcolonial perspective that will function interactively with the feminist, I seek to develop categories of analysis which will enable the multicultural aspects of women healing in the Graeco-Roman world and early Christianity to emerge. In their turn, these recognitions will challenge any possibility of presenting this account of women healing as a universal one which could function as a new genealogy for all Australian or New Zealand women or indeed for all women. It is envisaged also that the very process of attending to differences as these have come to be understood in postcolonial discourse will lead to a greater sensitivity to these differences in women healing in my Australian and New Zealand contexts as well as my global context.

At the outset of this discussion, it is important to call attention to Rajeswari Sunder Rajan and You-me Park's understanding of what they call 'postcolonial feminism'. For them it is not just a 'sub-set' of either postcolonial or feminist studies. Rather, they say it is an 'an intervention that is changing the configurations of both postcolonial and feminist studies. Postcolonial feminism is an exploration of and at the intersections of colonialism and neocolonialism with gender, nation, class, race, and sexualities in the different contexts of women's lives, their subjectivities, work, sexuality, and rights'.[39]

One of the key aspects of this intersection is the recognition of the *construction of the other*. Just as women have been constructed to serve the 'master' paradigm by their very negation so too has 'the native', 'the primitive', the colonized. In this act of negation, the colonizer or master is defined. A feminist postcolonial approach needs, therefore, to take account of some elements of the dualistic structure of Western thought which Val Plumwood draws to our attention.[40] Those dualisms which have serviced a colonial consciousness are, in addition to the male/female: self/other, master/slave, civilized/primitive [native], public/private.[41] Such dualisms are not a discovery of feminist, postcolonial or ecological studies. They were forged and shaped, at least in their origins, in the very Graeco-Roman world that is the object of this study. Attention to their manifestations in the sources and world views of that era and a reading against their grain in order to allow the diverse subjectivities of the women of this study to emerge will not only break the colonial perspective on that history but also contribute to unseating its current hegemony. What this will mean for a study of healing women in antiquity who were colonized by political, gender, cultural and religious hegemonies will be that this study will seek to avoid the tendency to essentialize and universalize them as is the challenge in relation to colonized women today.

A second category to which feminist postcolonial studies have drawn attention is '*hybridity*'. As a result of colonialism, subjectivities are forged from multiple processes and experiences: those of being colonized, those of one's indigenous culture, those of operating as subject within the colonial culture, those of a new, a different person in a different socio-cultural and political space. Gyatri Spivak warns, using a variety of interpretations of Indian *sati*, of too readily thinking that we can give voice to this hybridity of colonized subjects. Rather, she advocates an attentiveness to the heterogeneity 'breaking through' what she sees as 'skeletal and ignorant accounts'.[42] This is particularly pertinent to a construction of historical women healing when the accounts we have are likewise 'skeletal and ignorant' in many instances. Her warning shares with that of Joshel and Murnaghan above about creating noise or, in her instance, creating voice.[43]

One result of such attention to hybridity is, however, the recognition of a new space created by colonial processes. It is here that one hears the 'vitality of the emergent traditions that marginalized peoples have created in recognition of their exclusions'.[44] It is here that peoples construct what Lamphere, Ragoné and Zavella call a 'pastiche' of their old and their new cultural forms in order to 'preserve their cultural heritage within changing contexts'.[45] If women and women healing were colonized in antiquity and in early Christianity in particular, what indicators do we see of the creation of a 'pastiche' woven together by women as they drew on traditions of healing which belonged to their ancient genealogies as women and on elements of healing in the colonizing culture of professional medicine and emerging Christianity? Can we get any glimpses of what was emerging? If attention is not given to this, then it is easy to miss the differences, the particularities of women healing in antiquity.

An image has emerged in postcolonial studies in relation to this place or this space where something new develops for those who speak with many voices, those of the colonizers and the colonized. It is that of the '*border*' or the '*borderlands*'.[46] This is not a place of equality but rather it is here that the creative resistance considered above can emerge and be recognized in its heteroglossial nature.[47] For this project the development of this image by Gloria Anzaldúa is particularly pertinent because for her the image of borderland provides a way of thinking about healing, in particular healing the divisions among peoples. She says:

> at some point, on our way to a new consciousness, we will have to leave the opposite bank, the split between the two mortal combatants somewhat healed so that we are on both shores at once, and at once see through the serpent and the eagle eyes.[48]

She raises for me a question about this study of women healing in antiquity from a postcolonial feminist perspective. Can this very work itself be
a work of healing, of bringing healing women into the centre of a historical re-reading so that the male/female, culture/nature and other such
divides begin to be shifted, tectonic though these shifts may need to be?

## *Ecological*

> We are not alone. Nonhuman materialities, like all kinds of human organ-
> izational endeavors, configure our situatedness both in front of us and
> behind our backs.[49]

What these words of Clarke and Olesen bring starkly to our attention is an
often forgotten element, not only in studies of processes and products of
oppression and hegemony, but in all studies and indeed in human consciousness generally. They address our absolute embeddedness in other-
than-human materiality as well as its independent integrity. But as Clarke
and Olesen go on to say, and as exploration of this third element in my
reading perspective will establish, such a forgetting is being challenged.
One of the areas where this challenge or this shifting of attention will be
most significant is that of healing for here the material body is central.[50]
While Clarke and Olesen stress the impact of attention to the material on
'retheorising women health and healing', I would add that it will also
profoundly affect the emerging reconstruction of the history of women
healing, their memory, their genealogies. It should also be recalled here,
at the outset of this exploration, what was noted above in establishing the
scope of healing, namely that for the health/human ecology movement 'the
health of human beings is contained in the nature of relationships to
whatever surrounds them; the environment as totality – all there is'.[51] It
seems therefore, that the significance of an ecological perspective for
reading women healing in antiquity is not an optional but a necessary
feature. What follows is the establishing of just how such a perspective
may function in this study and how it can function interactively with the
feminist postcolonial hermeneutic developed above.

One point which it is important to establish at the beginning of this
exploration of the significance of the material is that while its independent
integrity is affirmed, in relation to a meaning-making system such as
healing, it will always be interconnected with the socio-cultural aspects of
life.[52] It is, by its very nature, therefore, interactive with the processes
explored above in relation to gender and colonization. It was perhaps Kaja
Finkler who brought this most forcefully to my attention. For her '[t]o
isolate an individual's life's lesions' which she sees as constitutive for

understanding health and healing, 'we must place that person's existence in its material and ideological settings'.[53] And so for her it is not just the constructions of culture but also the material realities of women's actual lives which are essential for an understanding of their health and healing.[54] *Attention to the material*, to the actualities and the shifts and changes in the physical realities of women's lives in antiquity will, therefore, be an essential component of this study. As with other aspects of the historical study of women already noted earlier, access to this type of information will indeed be limited. We do not know with certainty women's actual location in houses, their access to the market place and city streets or to resources for healing such as herbs and other *pharmaka*, the health hazards that affected particular geographic locations and their import for women, and, most importantly, the impact of illness on a variety of aspects of women's physical location/s. An interpretation of sources such as inscriptions, references to women healing in medical texts, and stories of women healed in gospel texts will, however, be undertaken in dialogue with the expanding body of research which has provided insight into the material aspects of women's lives in antiquity.[55] In this way, attention to the material can be enacted and can be shifted from the margins of our consciousness to the centre.

Such a shift in consciousness turns us to dialogue with Val Plumwood's oppressive dualisms that she uncovers through a careful analysis of Western culture. The effects of this web are, on the one hand, that human dependency on nature and the material is denied and, on the other, that the independence of nature in relation to the human is obscured.[56]

For the purposes of this study, what is essential to highlight from Plumwood's excellent analysis is that the construction of the other in terms of gender, race, and colonization is intimately connected to the construction of nature as inferior to the human. These processes are not just masculinized. What she claims is at issue is that they are 'linked to a concept of the "master" who is white, Western and dominant...the multiple, complex cultural identity of the master [is] formed in the context of class, race, species and gender domination'.[57] Given that the master is the 'man of reason', the reason/nature dualism is a significant one to shift. In a study of women healing, it would be possible, therefore, given the scientific biomedicalization of healing that has its roots in antiquity but which has reached an unprecedented apex in our day, to focus simply on women's engagement with the curing of diseases, their insertion into the developing 'master' system. Such a reading would, in its turn, continue to maintain and even further develop the reason/nature dualism and hence would

continue to support the network of dualisms which underpins the patriarchal domination of women and all constructed 'others' in multiplicative
ways.

This study will not take this path since I share Plumwood's concern
that the dismantling of this system of oppressive dualisms is absolutely
urgent.[58] And yet the path of change is a difficult one to negotiate. Having
learnt much from decades of feminist dismantling, Plumwood warns
against the simple reaffirmation of an identification of women with nature
in a way that does not touch on the dualistic system, hence simply re-
inscribing that very system in new projects.[59] She also cautions against the
dissolving of identity and hence of difference and diversity which has been
part of the postmodern project and which would deny or silence the rich
diversities and subjectivities of beings in the world of nature and of women
just as these are beginning to be attended to with recognition and respect.
For her the pathway through to an affirmation of the identity and centrality of the material as of women entails attention to both continuity and
difference. An ongoing and critical analysis of any manifestations of the
dualistic system is essential as the system continues to function and to
shape the consciousness even of its critical analysts. This, however, must
work interactively with a recognition and affirmation of the rich diversities
of the material world.[60] To stand in this place of attention to continuity
and difference is to occupy a borderland, a place which deals with the very
tensions that such a stance involves and which does not allow for a simple
reduction of perspective to either a supposed demolishing of the prison of
the 'master' paradigm or a re-inhabiting of it, an image that Plumwood
herself uses.[61]

The critical eco-feminist approach developed by Plumwood is, therefore, one which aims to associate both women and men with nature and
culture, but not in an undifferentiated way which essentializes relationships and interactions. Rather, it is a 'move to a further stage in their
[women's] relations with nature, beyond that of powerless inclusion in
nature, beyond that of reaction against their old exclusion from culture,
and towards an active, deliberate and reflective positioning of themselves
*with* nature against a destructive and dualising form of culture'.[62] Such
a move, she suggests, will be one which will entail moving across the
dualisms in a way which draws together various liberationist projects and
hence the interaction of feminist, postcolonial and ecological perspectives
being developed for this project.[63]

One of the outcomes of such an ecological approach in relation to
healing is *attentiveness to Earth* which supplies the material resources for

healing. A shift to natural remedies and the availability of traditional Chinese medical prescriptions in the West has brought a greater awareness of this at the same time as laboratory manufacture of *pharmaka* today by way of test-tube manipulation contributes further to a false consciousness of human independence of Earth's resources.[64] Such attentiveness will ensure that this study is not informed by a 'denial of dependence' in a way contrary to the Hippocratic medical system in which human sufferers were seen in a much more global context:

> The following were the circumstances attending the diseases, from which I framed my judgments, learning from the common nature of all and the particular nature of the individual, from the disease, the patient, the regimen prescribed and the prescriber – for these make a diagnosis more favourable or less; from the constitution, both as a whole and with respect to the parts, *of the weather and of each region; from the custom, mode of life, practices and ages of each patient...* (Hippocrates, *Epid.* 1.23; emphasis mine)

This is attention to the material which has already been considered earlier. The further questions which this study will address are whether female physicians brought a particular perspective to this materiality as a result of their socio-cultural and physical locations within their contexts; and whether the attention to the material was simply in terms of its relationship with, its impinging on the human or whether it may have been recognized as independent. In relation to the above text, for instance, this would entail a consideration of whether male and female physicians were attentive to the material aspects of male and female patients in different ways. It would also ask if the Hippocratic perspective shaping this attentiveness was already participative in the construction of the 'master' paradigm in that the material was simply contributive to the human, or if it suggests other possibilities. The extreme difficulty of answering such questions in relation to antiquity is clearly recognized but attention to the questions may enable new glimpses to be gained of ancient data and experience.

While attentiveness to Earth can be seen to be connected to healing, even more so is an *attentiveness to the body*. Already 'the body' has been a significant area of exploration in critical feminist theorizing.[65] Mary Mellor is one who brings this theory into dialogue with an ecological approach, demonstrating that human embodiment is intimately connected not only to socio-cultural processes but also to ecosystems. For her,

> Ecofeminists start from the importance of human embodiment (as reflecting biological existence) and embeddedness (within the surrounding ecosystem) and direct their attention to the impact of both on women. The

case ecofeminism is making is that women represent the dilemma of human
embodiment in a sexed and gendered society. Human embodiment, in turn,
represents the fact that human beings live not only in an historical and
social context, but also an ecological and biological one. The needs of
human embodiment have to be met within an encompassing ecosystem.
Differences in the historical and social position of human beings mean that
their relationship to their ecosystem may be very different.[66]

This attentiveness will need to take place within the context of a critical
ecofeminist approach as outlined above when considering Val Plumwood's
analyses. It was noted there that the new space within which ecofeminists
can practise a different association of women, men and nature can be conceived as a borderland. Sherry Ortner uses this same metaphor in her
consideration of the significance of the body when combining ecofeminist
and postcolonial perspectives.[67] Like Plumwood, she too is insistent that
while the body is a significant site for new readings to take place, account
must be taken of the many nuances that must accompany this so that
woman is not simply associated with body and nature anew to the continued exclusion of herself from two other significant elements of human
consciousness, namely history and culture.[68]

Mary Mellor grapples with some of the nuances of this in dialogue with
the work of Rosi Braidotti and others who advocate what they call 'a
radically differentiated female-embodied materialism'.[69] The two terms
that she holds in tension are the embodiment of women and men in both
physical and socio-cultural realities in all their diversities and the embeddedness of these in ecosystems. It is the bodies of women and men that
bleed and which are healed just as it is the bodies of women and men
which are the instruments of healing. What the ecological perspective
brings to a re-reading of healing in antiquity, therefore, is a recognition of
the embeddedness of this embodiment within not only socio-cultural but
ecosystems and this in a way which seeks to pay attention to the body and
its materiality and the materiality which characterizes its context. Such
attentiveness will not only enrich the texture of a reading of women
healing but like other aspects of this project, seek to change the consciousness of its readers.

A final consideration before leaving these reading perspectives and their
interconnectedness is *space*. Like the earth and the body, space is mapped
in the meaning-making process and needs, therefore to be re-mapped
when new meaning-making, new *poiesis* is at stake. The colonization and
the gendering of space has been a significant one in the development of
the 'master' narrative. Ancient Greece and Rome participated in such

mappings of space. It will be of particular significance, therefore, how we interpret space. Do we simply maintain the conventional gender mapping of public space in this new reading or can women's presence in the public arena be interpreted as an instance where we see resistance to the gendered and colonized appropriation of public space to the 'master'?

This project is concerned with reading, mapping, visioning women healing in early Christianity. What this section on theoretical perspectives or chan[g/c]ing lenses has made clear is that a reader concerned about the effects of contemporary readings or re-visionings of history on the maintenance of the 'master' paradigm is immediately aware of her embeddedness in the interconnective web of gendered, racial, colonial and environmental dominations. This section has woven together a new map for reading. It has shaped a new vision or perspective from some of the finest feminist, postcolonial and ecofeminist theorists that will guide a revisioning of women healing in the Graeco-Roman world, formative Judaism and early Christianity. The reading itself will be material and textual shaped by the theory but engaged as a practice. It will be from the 'borderland' where tensive elements such as body and mind, woman and man, and tensive practices like continuity and difference cross over, creating a new space from which healing of the rifts between them can take place. It is from here that this project seeks to tell a new story of women healing in early Christianity. It will be a story from 'subordinated and ignored parts of western culture', from 'sources other than the master'.[70] It will be undertaken with care but also with a new imagination that seeks to allow the richly textured diversities of women, the colonized, the earth, the body and space to emerge or to be waited upon in their pluralities and their otherness. It will no longer be a changing of the lenses but a chancing of the new lenses which of themselves are multidimensional.

*Collecting Tools*
The sources for this study are multiple – references to women healing in classical texts of predominantly male authors; accounts of women healing on stelae or in gospel stories; inscriptions engraved in stone on tombstones extolling women healing; geographic locations of material realities such as texts and tombstones and of the lives of the women whom they narrate; as well as other material and socio-cultural indicators which enable the exploration of the embeddedness of women healing. As a result, the study will need to take its place methodologically at the interface of many disciplines for reading such a variety of sources.[71] This is not surprising, however, given the chan[g/c]ing of lenses outlined above and the recogni-

tion of the intersection of hermeneutic and methodology. In terms of a reading of history and medicine or healing, Helen King too notes this intersection when she says that 'medical history often fails to appreciate the nature of its sources, and of itself, as 'text'; as culturally specific constructs, the form of which influences the meanings which they present'.[72] Thus sources, interpretive perspective/s and methodological approaches will all need to be multidimensional.

In relation to sources and a contemporary reading of them, Page duBois offers the timely warning that the civilizations of antiquity differ radically from the present and that access to them is shaped by discontinuity. They are, she says, 'fragmentary and contaminated by centuries of interpretation and loss'.[73] From new reading locations, however, especially those which seek to dislodge the dualisms of patriarchy and other manifestations of domination, these sources can be read anew. Such readings will not destroy the gender and other dualisms which characterized antiquity. Given, however, the agency of women, of the colonized, and of nature, this study will not be confined to a reiteration of the ancient dualisms only. As du Bois says, '[w]e cannot *will* our way past gender or past individual subjectivity, but we can theorize, historicize, and imagine a future beyond domination'.[74]

It is the active quality of the sources which will enable such a historicizing. We have already noted in relation to women, and even more so the environment, the seemingly deafening silences of sources. Steven Johnstone makes clear in his study of women and slaves in antiquity that the silences do not function simply to render the marginalized invisible. Rather, it is by these silences and marginalizations that they are actively constituted. He draws on Joan Scott who notes that '[i]t is not individuals, who have experiences but subjects who are constituted through experiences' to argue for the active power or function of sources in the creating of the subjects of history.[75] He advocates, therefore, a 'confronting of the gaps in the evidence', a process which Elisabeth Schüssler Fiorenza has long promoted in relation to the reconstruction of early Christianity from a feminist perspective.[76] It is the multidimensional reading of some of the gaps in the sources as well as the sources themselves that is the particular contribution that this project can make.

### Socio-Rhetorical Approach[77]

Since many of the sources in this study are literary, whether they are written upon papyri, parchment or stone, a literary approach is foundational. Considerations in the development of reading perspectives above have, however, made it clear that such literary sources function to construct socio-cultural and material aspects of women healing in antiquity. The particular literary approach taken will, therefore, be rhetorical in that it will facilitate analysis of the effect of the text, the world which it constructed and in turn the world which its contemporary reading constructs, and the human consciousness which such readings shaped and shape. Careful attention will be given to those literary aspects of each text that are appropriate to it. In a narrative account of healing in a gospel text or on an Asclepiean inscription, attention to characterization may be significant. In another, it may be the direct speech given to a character or the language used to describe the healed state. And in yet another, the question of the voice of the implied author and his/her ideological world view may be central. It will then be a question of considering the effects of these literary features in their socio-cultural and material contexts in order to effect a multilayered construction of women healing.

A number of the texts for consideration such as accounts of healings in the Asclepieia as well as the gospel healing stories are not just literary texts in the sense of written record but they also have a prior oral history. The gospel stories at least, from among these, continued to be transmitted in an aural/oral context after being committed to writing.[78] These texts, therefore, need to be analyzed in a dynamic historical and socio-cultural contextuality in order that questions of their changing effects may be given due attention especially in light of the need established earlier of being attentive to shifts and changes in time, in locations, in communities of reception and other variable factors.

A particular aspect of the rhetorical effect of texts that will inform this study is intertextuality, which is concerned with the way texts intersect or the presence of several texts within a text. Both writers and readers are engaged in the processes that give rise to intertextuality. In this study whose concern is with rhetoric and the function of texts, attention will be given to the ways in which readers may have made meaning of particular texts as a result of the intertexts they recognized and which shaped their understanding of women healing.[79]

Both texts and intertexts function within a broader socio-cultural context of healing and the health care system/s of antiquity. The literary analyses of this study will need to be accompanied by an anthropological approach that will enable an exploration of such socio-cultural contexts. It is the particular field of cultural anthropology which has proven most clearly of assistance in studies of healing in early Christianity. In this study of women healing, however, this will be nuanced by way of dialogue with feminist/medical anthropology. This will enable a mapping of the texture of the society in which women participated in healing in a way that can be attentive to the socio-cultural meaning-making processes, implicated as they are in the construction of gender, the colonized and the material.

Recently, biblical scholarship has focused attention on the semantic and hermeneutical aspects of the medical anthropological model and this too will be important for a study that is particularly concerned about meaning-making within material and social contexts.[80] Medical anthropologist Arthur Kleinman has been a particularly significant contributor to this hermeneutical perspective and since aspects of his work will be used to inform the socio-cultural analysis within the methodology employed in this project, further discussion of his approach is appropriate here.

He has repeatedly reiterated that the focus of his work has been and is on the 'clinical'. This aspect of healing, he describes as the 'beliefs, expectations, norms, behaviors, and communicative transactions associated with sickness, health care seeking, practitioner-patient relationships, therapeutic activities, and evaluation of outcomes'.[81] Indeed, from this it becomes clear that Kleinman provides a framework for considering healing within an entire cultural system, the health care system,[82] which in its turn intersects with other cultural systems like religion within any given context. For this study, the intersection of the two systems, namely the health care and the religious will be a significant one. What Kleinman reminds us of is that the health care system, like the religious system, is a construction of the researcher on the basis of the 'beliefs, expectations, norms, behaviours' and other elements within the system as these have been observed in a particular context as well as how people '*act* in it and *use* its components'.[83] It is always, therefore, interactive with context, both the context being studied as well as the context of the interpreter. If this is constantly reiterated and remembered, then, Kleinman indicates, such an understanding of health and healing can be 'used across cultural, historical, and social boundaries'.[84] It can, therefore, provide a working framework for this study which seeks to uncover the differences and particularities of women healing in the antiquity of early Christianity.

Another significant aspect of Kleinman's construction of the health care system is that while he acknowledges his constructionist approach,[85] and while his primary focus is on social and symbolic reality, both of which are constructs, he acknowledges their relationship with biological and physical reality.[86] Indeed, he goes on to discuss what he calls the 'ecology of health care systems' which includes, as he says, 'political, economic, social structural, historical and environmental determinants'.[87] He does not seem to give very specific attention to the historical and environmental determinants in his own research, but his system is such that it allows for the attention to these external and material aspects of healing with which this eco-justice reading of healing is concerned.

Kleinman's constructionist or hermeneutic approach has been particularly significant in recent studies of healing in the biblical world. There is, however, a lacuna in the work of scholars such as Avalos and Pilch beyond their static understanding of gender.[88] The important shift to the semantic which Pilch and others demonstrate in their interpretations of biblical healing, creates the impression that all illness realities are 'fundamentally semantic' in a way which obscures the physical, material or environmental aspects except as constructions. Also, by considering all healing as basically 'hermeneutic or interpretive activity', aspects such as 'the patient's symptoms and identified illness' are seen to 'represent personal and group values and conceptualisations and not simply mere biological reality'.[89] This shifting of attention away from the purely biomedical to the semantic, which has been an important move, carries within it the potential to deny the biological. In this way, the biological and the material are relegated to an inferior position within the master paradigm and subsequent interpretations fail to shift human consciousness to an interactive relationship with the biological and the material in a way which will be transformative of that consciousness.[90] Use of Kleinman's constructionist model and dialogue with those scholars of healing in early Christianity who have been influenced by it will, therefore, need to be nuanced by a very specific attention to the material but in a way which eludes a simple return to a biological or biomedical understanding of healing. Attention to gender as socio-cultural meaning-making process will likewise add to this nuance.[91]

In order to read accounts of women healing in antiquity, as healers or healed, in the context of meaning-making within the complexity of particular socio-cultural contexts, I have found Kleinman's modeling of healing within a health care system to be particularly helpful.[92] In *Writing at the Margin*, Kleinman indicates that he himself has moved away from the use of 'models' because they imply 'too much formalism, specificity, and authorial certainty'[93] and that he has become much more aware of 'differences, absences, gaps, contradictions, and uncertainties'.[94] The use of Kleinman's modeling as a way of seeking the meaning of healing narratives in this study of women healing will not, however, be at the service of 'authorial certainty' but rather as a path which may open into women's subjectivity in the healing process which, in its turn, will be nuanced by the feminist concern for difference and particularity and its location in

complex socio-cultural and material contexts as has already been discussed above. Kleinman's categories of analysis will be used as a tool to
guide initial questions which will be raised in relation to the socio-cultural
realities constructed in and by the text to which other hermeneutical
questions can be addressed to develop the analysis. The formalism which
Kleinman rejects need not characterize the use of his categories of analysis
in this study and a brief description of these below will already demonstrate where nuances particular to this study will be brought into play.

The first category in Kleinman's map is *institutional setting* which
focuses on the location within the various sectors of the health care
system. Kleinman highlights three: the popular, the professional, and the
folk.[95] He notes, however, that the lines are blurred between them and an
exploration of women healers will demonstrate that female gender can
function to further blur such neat distinctions. It will be argued that
women inhabit, perhaps more so than men, the 'borderland' areas, the
overlapping sections. This model enables us to focus there in accordance
with the hermeneutical perspective established above.[96] While Kleinman's
institutional setting locates healers and healed within the social sectors of
the health care system, this analysis with its attentiveness to the material,
will also need to look to the material setting, the space of encounter and its
intersection with the social.

The second category, *characteristics of interpersonal interaction*, considers the number of participants in the healing episode; its time quality or
whether it is episodic or continuous; the quality of the relationship; and
the attitudes of participants to healing. This will be an area in which a
study of women and men healing will enable genderization to emerge.
*Idiom of Communication* is the third category and includes the mode of
communication as well as the particular explanatory model operative in
the communication – how the illness is named and described together
with its effects and other related elements. It is here that attention to the
body, the material and its place in understandings of illness will receive
attention. The 'beliefs, expectations, norms, behaviors, and communicative
transactions associated with sickness' constitute the fourth category of
*clinical reality*. The multidimensionality of the reading perspective will
find play here as gender, religion, hybridity and borderland status intersect.
*Therapeutic Changes and Mechanisms*, the fifth category of analysis,
enables attention to be given to the language descriptive of the illness and
also of the healed state, and gender differences certainly emerge in some
sources in this regard.[97]

Interactive with the health care system as cultural system are the various other cultural constructs of a given society. Brief mention was made

above of religion. Another is honour/shame. Julian Pitt-Rivers describes the system of honour and shame in this way. Honour is 'the value of a person in his own eyes, but also in the eyes of his society. It is his estimation of his own worth, his claim to pride, but it is also the acknowledgment of that claim, his excellence recognised by society, his right to pride.'[98] Shame, on the other hand is described as 'a sensitivity to the opinion of others'.[99] And for Pitt-Rivers, such a system is highly genderized: 'honour derives predominantly from the father, whereas in its aspect of shame it derives predominantly from the mother'.[100] It is not surprising, therefore, that for Pitt-Rivers, the intersection of the honour/shame and health care systems is likewise genderized.

> ...the distinction in powers relates clearly to the moral division of labour which is visible in every context, and especially in those where the physical person, the human body, is the centre of attention. Thus methods of curing are clearly defined as to sex; those employing practical techniques and acquired skill, the bone-setters, and manipulators, are always men. Those requiring natural knowledge, herbalists, are indifferently men or women, while all magical cures are effectuated by women since they depend upon the quality of 'grace' which is a female attribute uniquely. This moral division of labour is reproduced, as one might expect, in the realms of witchcraft. Men bewitch by using a book of magic and invoking thereby the Devil, evil spirits and poltergeists... Female witchcraft operates in quite another way; through as it were, a negative use of grace assisted by charms and spells which are not written down.[101]

While this study will give particular attention to the function of honour/ shame and its intersection with health, a feminist reading attentive to the shaping of socio-cultural constructs as process/es will not simply accept such a genderization of health care. Rather, it shall explore the very constructions of gender, honour/shame, other cultural codes and indeed the health care system itself for aspects of contestation and intervention which will challenge assumptions of static cultural givens.

Ortner and Whitehead similarly consider what they call the 'prestige structure' of a society to be of almost central significance in seeking to give some order to the variety of socio-cultural variables, but their study also recognizes the genderization of the system/s and they take much more account of the ongoing process of construction. They alert readers to what they call possible 'tensions between a formally instituted prestige arrangement and those components of the productive system essential to its maintenance'.[102] In this regard, Ortner's cultural study, *Making Gender*, is particularly helpful for this project which needs to grapple with issues such as the way in which maleness as status defining within healing in antiquity was intersected by women physicians of varying marital status in this sex-gender defined domain. On the one hand, she warns that a study of 'texts' as constructive of identities and subjectivities is incomplete without attention to the material ways in which such texts imposed themselves on 'real people' in 'real time' (and she raises the question of which people and in which time, not in generalities but in their particularities). On the other hand, she calls attention to the ways in which what might be constituted as concrete or material acts of resistance or negotiation need to be analyzed in the context of the meaning-making structures which seek to constrain agency.[103] Gendered and ecological readings of prestige structures need, therefore, to be both material and hermeneutical, attentive to text and context and their continual intersection. It is a socio-rhetorical reading as laid out above which will facilitate such an attentiveness.

But it is not only cultural anthropology which enables an exploration of the rich texture of context but also history as an active process of giving coherence and meaning to the past, a shaping of memory in order that it has meaning.[104] But the discussions of the hermeneutical frameworks above and their categories of analysis, which in fact will be tools for this historical work, indicate that constructions of the past are never separate from perspectives of the present. Lerner cites Dilthey in this regard as saying that '[t]he power and breadth of our own lives and the energy with which we reflect on them are the foundation of historical vision'.[105] The very act of doing this history, then, continues the work of feminist and postcolonial theorists of bringing categories such as 'gender' and 'subjectivity' into question not just as categories which functioned historically but which continue to function and have meaning. It also moves beyond those poststructuralist approaches which would limit knowledge to textual representations of events.[106] The feminist ecological aspect of this project seeks to give value to the material context in a retelling of the story of women healing and to trace the interconnectivity of text and material context.

A desire to attend to the heterogeneity of ancient women's historical voices and subjectivities as well as the heterogeneity of perspectives and approaches, makes the new historicism a significant dialogue partner in the construction of this methodological approach. Feminists have critiqued a new historicism which fails to take account of gender, but given all of the nuances to reading perspective and methodology already undertaken above, it could be claimed that Veeser's summing up of aspects of the new historicism demonstrates its affiliation from an historical perspective with much of the construction of hermeneutic and methodology which has emerged so far in this chapter:

- that every expressive act is embedded in a network of material practices;
- that every act of unmasking, critique, and opposition uses the tools it condemns and risks falling prey to the practice it exposes;
- that literary and non-literary 'texts' circulate inseparably; and
- that no discourse, imaginative or archival, gives access to unchanging truths nor expresses inalterable human nature.[107]

I close this section on a socio-rhetorical reading which combines literary, feminist medical anthropological and feminist critical historical approaches with these words of Elisabeth Fox-Genovese which speak to the necessity for the intersection of the rhetorical, the cultural and the historical/contextual in a re-reading of women healing.

> No more than the author can the text escape history, although history herself [*sic*] assures some texts the power to speak compellingly to more than one historical moment. No more than the author can the text claim political innocence, although a sophisticated politics invariably presents itself as comprehensive world view. The history that informs even the most abstract text is ultimately political in privileging a particular distillation of common experience. Craft and talent play their roles, as does audience response, in permitting the production and dissemination of texts and thereby in establishing their influence... Ultimately to insist that texts are products of and participants in history as structured social and gender relations is to reclaim them for society as a whole, reclaim them for the political scrutiny of those whom they have excluded, as much as those whom they have celebrated, for all of those in whose names they have spoken or claimed to speak. And it is to reclaim them for our intentional political action, and ourselves for political accountability.[108]

### Theological Meaning-Making – an Outcome

The goal of this project, namely the mapping or re-mapping/re-visioning of women healing in early Christianity and the interpretation of Second Testament texts in terms of their contemporary rhetorical effect in the context of historical reconstruction, seeks to cross what I have experienced as constructed divisions between theology and religious studies – to stand in a borderland. This study will be historical reconstructive as well as feminist theological. Standing within the ecofeminist, postcolonial reading perspective developed above and employing as necessary the tools identified, this study will attend to the subjectivities of early Christian women healing as these may emerge. It will listen for the Christian story-telling they and others engaged in that may have constructed a gospel vision of healing transformation that functioned rhetorically/theologically within different communities of reception in early Christian contexts. It will also be attentive, on the one hand, to their symbolic representation of divinity and healing in their religious/theological world of meaning-making and, on the other, to the Earth, the body and space as the material ground for understanding healing but also as material ground which calls for attention. Such a study will not only reconstruct worlds behind and in the texts being studied but, being theological/rhetorical, it will shape a world in front of the text for contemporary readers. In this respect it seeks to be critically vigilant to its own rhetorical functioning so that this reading is responsible to women and men, the colonized and the colonizer as well the Earth community in their multiple subjectivities.

To claim a theological outcome as a goal of this study in the final paragraphs of this chapter is not to make it pivotal, central, ultimate or to render it an afterthought. Rather, it is to recognize that the very web of processes that constitute this study participate in theologizing. To undertake a feminist critical theology of early Christian healing just as to reconstruct early Christian women healing is to engage in the dynamics of the interpretive task as outlined above.

This chapter has engaged in theory toward practice. Like the space from which that interpretive practice will take place, it too has been a 'borderland'. Stances, categories of analysis, elements of what have been dualistic constructions and methodological tools have been crossed over and engaged in this 'borderland'. As a result, the unfolding of this one particular story of early Christian women healing which follows will be a new story. It will engage as rigorously and critically as possible with the nuanced and interactive approach constructed above. On the other hand, it will also seek to free the creative imagination without which no new story is possible. Its goal will be a transformative healing of at least elements of the gendered, colonial and Earth-denying consciousness and resultant relationships that cry out from almost every corner of our globe.

## Chapter 2

## WOMEN HEALING/HEALING WOMEN:
## A NEW LISTENING TO ANTIQUITY

The past *claims* us, and we are accountable to that claim – otherwise why
engage in the rewriting of history.[1]

*Our sources of knowledge* about women doctors in antiquity are fragmentary...[y]et even from these fragments we can piece together some sort of
picture, and the most important feature to emerge is simply that these
women *existed*.[2]

The next two chapters read/listen for and imagine into subjectivity, on the
basis of the scant evidence available to us, the women of antiquity and
their engagement with healing and with aspects of the health care systems
operating in their contexts. The many questions raised in the opening
chapter will be addressed to the variety of sources available, fragmentary
though they may be, in order that the shadowy female figures engaged in
healing either as healers or as healed might emerge with richer texture to
their lives and to the socio-cultural and material contexts in which they
lived. In many instances, we may find ourselves frustrated because the data
which would enable us to answer the questions posed is simply not available.[3] At other times, new questions and new categories of analysis may
enable a new story to emerge from sources which have been seemingly
tried and tested. Holt Parker draws the conclusion that '(w)omen physicians, though undoubtedly only a small percentage of the medical personnel, were an everyday part of the ancient world'.[4] He does not ask how they
were a part of this ancient world that was highly gendered nor whether
their activity supported or challenged this genderization process as well as
other cultural codes of their society. Such questions can give new insights
into both the life and world of ancient women healing.

Some scholars have already begun aspects of the task of these chapters.
Jukka Korpela examined the social status of some women healers honoured in inscriptions as well as possible economic data that might be able
to be drawn from particular types of inscriptions.[5] Nancy Demand brought

new questions to a number of lekythoi and grave stelae depicting women giving birth. She questioned whether they were in fact funerary memorials to women who died in childbirth – the usual interpretation – or whether they remembered and honoured the midwife who is depicted with the birthing woman hence honouring her occupation also.[6] The genderization of Hippocratic medicine has been given very specific attention in recent years by scholars such as Lesley Dean-Jones[7] and Helen King.[8] I will dialogue with these works to establish the network of associations which this study seeks to analyze. Like the ancient sources it will be viewed through the cracks which a feminist, postcolonial and ecological perspective opens up on the ancient world.

What will be covered in this chapter and the next does not represent an entire reconstruction of medicine in the Graeco-Roman world. Rather, the focus is much more specific – women healing/healing women in this context. What emerges will not be a synthesis but rather a 'kaleidescope' that Nutton suggests can give expressions to the 'workings of change'.[9] For women healing as for medicine generally, it needs to be clear that 'Athens was not Alexandria, Rome was not Pergamum',[10] as Nutton suggests. In this same vein, I could add that third century BCE and its story of Agnodike was not the first century CE that honoured many midwives and female doctors. Also, Antiochis of Tlos whose father Diodotus was a doctor and who was recognized by the city for her skill in healing was not Secunda, slave to the imperial household of Livilla, who is honoured simply as *medica*.

One of the challenges in a survey such as this which will cover an array of different types of material across a broad geographical area and time frame is how to organize the data so that particular attention can be paid to the differences in the lives of the women who emerge as well as to the shifts and changes in power dynamics, genderization and other cultural processes. I have chosen to use a chronological framework as the foundation and to allow other factors like geography, familial location, social and economic status, changes in physical environments and sex/gender dynamics to intersect with the foundational framework in a variety of ways. Literature and public documentation like inscriptions are the sites where the negotiation of cultural factors such as gender and honour becomes visible and the shifts and changes resulting from this negotiation will likewise intersect with the chronological frame.

Another organizing frame will be Kleinman's three-fold structuring of a health care system as popular, folk and professional.[11] He suggests that the largest sector is the *popular*. In Kleinman's own words, this is the 'lay, non-professional, non-specialist, popular culture arena in which illness is first defined and health care activities initiated'.[12] In antiquity, when professional medicine was in its infancy, this was certainly the main arena of healing but because of its very nature as popular and non-professional, it is the area for which we have least surviving data. It is also the arena in which women are more likely to have been practitioners as well as patients because of its location in the home or familial and kinship groupings. This study will, therefore, be ever attentive to whatever glimpses may be gained into this area by way of new questions and new lenses of investigation.

Of much smaller proportions are the other two sectors – the *folk* and the *professional*. The Graeco-Roman world saw the significant emergence of *professional* medicine with the compilation of the Hippocratic corpus and the professional training of doctors. It is from this sector that most surviving data is available. As attention is given to this data, it must be continually remembered that it represents perhaps the smallest segment of the world of healing and that participants in this world as writers, practitioners and patients will tend to belong to the more elite strata of society or be connected with them in some way. Through the cracks in this world, however, we may glimpse something of the other two sectors. It will also be likely, given the significance of gender as a defining category culturally,[13] that as males dominate the emerging professional sector and its prestige and power increases, they will seek to control women's participation in it or to shift boundaries so that women can be more easily contained within the folk or popular sectors. Women's healing agency will be the focus of this study rather than male control of the gendered structures of society and this agency will be examined in terms of its shifting or blurring of cultural boundaries and their genderization. Kleinman's categories will provide a framework for these analyses.

The *folk* sector is perhaps the one with the most permeable boundaries. It is comprised of two subsets, the secular and the magico-religious and is described by Kleinman as that of the 'non-beaucratic, non-professional specialist'.[14] Women are presumed to participate significantly as both patients and healers within this sector.[15] Since it has been claimed by many scholars that the boundaries between magic and religion blur in the Graeco-Roman world,[16] this study will examine the way gender functioned around those boundaries and whether women's agency in healing served to maintain or to shift the distinctions they established. Specific attention to this sector will be the focus of the following chapter.

Most of the data considered in these two chapters will be structural and material rather than clinical and hence Kleinman's clinical categories of analysis will be employed less than his structural ones. Where clinical realities are visible, however, his categories may be called into play. With the above frameworks of analysis established, the journey of exploration can begin.

### In the Beginning?... Agamede and Polydama

Healing in ancient Greece was the provenance of goddesses and gods who held this power. Louise Wells surveys the construction of healing within ancient Greek cosmology in the opening section of her study of the language of healing from Homer to the emergence of early Christianity. She notes that in the Homeric epics, Apollo is 'the source of disease and healing' and is associated with Pergamum which was to become one of the greatest healing centres in the Greek world.[17] Other divine figures, male and female, also heal and Wells notes the different language associated with these gendered healings. Paiëon heals by 'scattering medicines that still pain' (ὀδυνήφατα φάρμακα πάσσων)[18] while Dione heals Aphrodite by way of touch: 'with both hands [she] stroked away from her arm the ichor'.[19]

This divine healing power is shared with the human community. Within the Homeric world, the two sons of Asclepius, Podaleirios and Machaon, are named and characterized as 'good healers' (ἰητήρ' ἀγαθώ)[20] and Machaon places healing medicines or herbs (φάρμακα) on the wound of Agamemnon as Paiëon did when healing Hades.[21] Women too have knowledge of *pharmaka* and Agamede knows all the herbs (φάρμακα) that the wide earth nourishes.[22] In *The Odyssey*, Polydama, a woman of Egypt, is the source of knowledge of wisely-chosen healing drugs (φάρμακα μητιόεντα ἐσθλά) and the land of Egypt is honoured as providing many herbs which have healing qualities and as being a place where each one is a healer (ἰητρὸς δὲ ἕκαστος).[23]

Healing is both knowledge and power in the Homeric world. It is in the hands of the divine players and can be used indiscriminately or more generally for restoration, particularly of injured human or divine bodies. This knowledge with its attendant power over life and death is shared by both males and females in the human world. Both have knowledge of *pharmaka* and hence are characterized as healers. In the Homeric texts, only the male is specifically named healer (ἰητήρ).

On the other hand, the failure to name women explicitly as healers within the health care system constructed by this literature, a system which is predominantly folk or non-professional in character at this point, can function to raise certain questions about women's knowledge. They have knowledge of these potent earthly elements but are they excluded from the specialist category of ἰητήρ because of their gender? As Greece constructs its origins by way of these epics, is it also constructing its gender system in which men heal men in the public domain and hence medicine participates in a male-centred gender construction?[24] Women have knowledge of the sources of healing as men do which may offer a glimpse into the ancient origins of women's healing in the secular folk sector but such knowledge is put to a secondary use in *The Odyssey*, the drugging of men's minds for battle so that they are not troubled by the carnage. Healing women are depicted as having a power which they can use over men and hence this must be controlled. Agamede and Polydama, both of whom are introduced to readers by way of relationship with their husbands Thon and Mulius, stand forth from the literature, however, as women with knowledge of herbs and their medicinal powers. Such knowledge is not characterized as extraordinary and hence they may be seen as representative of many more women of ancient Greece and Egypt who shared in this same knowledge and therefore brought healing to others. Healing women may have had agency and power even if the genderizing of the emerging health care system seeks to marginalize it.

In each of the two texts which recognize women healing, Earth is named as the source of the healing herbs or medicines. In the *Iliad*, it is a simple acknowledging of Earth as source. Praise of the earth in *The Odyssey* is more effusive. Homer uses the phrase 'life-giving earth' (ζείδωρος ἄρουρα)[25] which brings forth many herbs, some of which when mixed become healing drugs (φάρμακα, πολλὰ μὲν ἐσθλὰ μεμιγμένα).[26] Praise of Earth and of earth-human interagency in healing are two components of the text so that the materiality of Earth and its resources are not simply for human consumption but are honoured in their own integrity as are the skills of humans as they interact with them. Women together with men are healers who can be read interactively with the gifts of Earth in the task of healing.

### Midwife and Physician: Early Hints of Professional Healing

The focus shifts from ninth-century Ionia to mainland Greece and Athens of the fifth/fourth century BCE although the influence of Homer's classical texts extended far beyond their origins. A passing reference in Plato's *Republic* 454d.2 has teased the minds of scholars of healing in antiquity. In a discussion on who is best suited to be educated for the administration of the affairs of the state, Plato says, '[w]e meant, for example, that a man and a woman who have a physician's mind have the same nature' (οἷον ἰατρικὸν μὲν καὶ ἰατρικὴν τὴν ψυχὴν ὄντας τὴν αὐγτὴν φύσιν ἔχειν ἐλέγομεν).[27] One of the tantalizing features of the longer discussion in which this text is situated is whether it is ridiculing or affirming the position being developed in the argument, namely the wisdom of giving women the same education as men. Plato acknowledges that this is in 'contrast with present custom' (452a) but he presents the present custom, namely 'that there is by nature a great difference between men and women' (453b.7-8), on the lips of his opponents. The text under consideration here is situated in a discussion of what is meant by diversity and identity of nature.

As the text itself states, Plato is giving an example, just as previously he gave the example of a bald and long-haired cobbler (454c.4-6). His audience presumably could imagine bald and long-haired cobblers from their experience and so it could be argued similarly for ἰατρικὸν μὲν καὶ ἰατρικὴν – male and female healer. Women healers (ἰατρική) could be understood to have been part of the world of the implied listeners to the philosophical discussion.[28] By the use of ἰατρικόν and ἰατρικήν, as designating a profession or occupation, the text points to the possibility of healers beginning to be recognized as professional and hence, an emerging professional segment appears within the health care system of classical Greece. It might seem that such a system was genderized towards male and female equality.

It should be pointed out, however, that the entire perspective of Plato is male-centred. The discussion is *about* women and children who are construed as 'other' than the two male disputants. It is they, the disputants, who will decide from their master paradigm if women are or are not of the same nature as the master and hence what education they should receive. And on a number of occasions within the discussion there is a reference to women being weaker than men.[29] As Laquer suggests, this is the way things are, reality is genderized.[30] Within this master paradigm, it is difficult to imagine that Plato is seriously considering that women receive the same opportunities and take up the same positions as men in the State. Women might be healers but this is within the master paradigm Plato is both constructing and affirming.[31]

A second Platonic reference is that in *Theaetetus* 149a in which Phanerete, the mother of Socrates, is introduced as μαῖα or midwife. Socrates, however, then uses the role of midwife as a metaphor for his own task of bringing forth ideas and wisdom from others rather than producing them himself just as a midwife practises her art of bringing forth children after she has given birth to her own children and is too old for further childbearing. Phanarete herself disappears into the background of the text but she stands as representative of women engaged in this role in fourth-century Athens and Greece. In order to set up his metaphor, Socrates explores with Theaetetus characteristics of a midwife with which he would be familiar. We have already noted the first above – beyond childbearing. Theaetetus agrees with Socrates that she also can tell if a woman is pregnant or not (149c); with drugs (φαρμάκια) and with incantations she can time labour and bring on a miscarriage (149d); and she can arrange marriages which will produce the best children (149d-150a). The midwife straddles the boundaries between secular and religio-magic folk medicine, using both herbal drugs and incantations. But having set up his metaphor, Socrates goes on to explain that this work of women falls short in relation to his because her concern is with women and his with men, hers with the body but his with the soul (150a-c). Plato's text either draws upon or constructs the hierarchal dualisms female/male and body/soul. The effect of his text is not just located in fourth-century Athens or even mainland Greece but extends over centuries and over nations as classical Greek thought spreads during the Hellenistic era and shapes not only the worlds of Greece and Rome but Western civilization in its origins and developments. Here, indeed, are the roots or early shoots of the master paradigm that Plumwood has so clearly explicated.

Turning our attention to the world of women healing rather than of male authoring, Phanarete and the midwives who informed Socrates' metaphor begin to people this world. Nancy Demand has examined a number of lekythoi and grave stelae from fourth-century BCE ancient Greece which depict a woman in labour attended by one or two standing female figures and at times a male figure depicted with head in hand, perhaps mourning (Plates 1 and 2).[32] Generally these have been interpreted as memorials of the birthing woman who may have died in labour. Demand, however, draws on two reliefs with epigrams to assist in the interpretation of those without accompanying text. The stele for Malthakê, dated approximately 300 BCE has a woman seated on a couch typical of the other reliefs and a woman stands behind the couch and touches the seated woman's chin. The accompanying inscription reads *Malthakê: Magadidos, Chrêstê*. Demand notes that scholars have demonstrated that *Magadis* means foreign and that *Chrêstê* designates a slave, both of which point to *Malthakê* being the helper or midwife to the birthing woman. Similarly she notes that the fourth-century grave relief for Mnasylla depicted her daughter, Neotima, who died in labour seated on a couch with Mnasylla standing. It is only the epigram which enables observers to know that the tomb is that of Mnasylla and not the seated woman in labour.[33]

Given these indicators and the customizing to some degree of grave reliefs, Demand suggests that the women honoured on the lekythoi and stelae which she examined in detail may, in fact, have been the women standing beside the birthing woman and acting as midwives. She draws on a gendered cultural construct to support this, namely that in Greek society activity was valued more highly than passivity with the male associated with activity and the female with passivity. It is the standing women who are active in the scenes examined and hence the gendered culture may have informed a reading of these scenes in honour of the female assisting birth rather than of the supposedly passive seated woman giving birth.[34] The activity of these midwives, however, need not have disturbed the cultural constructs because if she was midwife and hence beyond child-bearing age, then this allowed her access to certain activities in the public arena in a way that differed from the access of a younger woman.[35]

Demand produces evidence of at least ten memorials of women actively engaged in assisting women in childbirth. Most belong to the second half of the fourth century BCE with one or two a little earlier or a little later. The original provenance of most is uncertain although the grave stele for Plangon and Tolmides (Plate 2) was found on the border of Attica and Boeotia, two belong to Alexandria, and one is from Rhodes. Those now in the Athens or Piraeus museum may have a provenance somewhere on the Greek mainland.[36] They make visible an emerging healing activity (midwifery) being undertaken by women in the Greek world which may, in fact, have been an ancient skill exercised in the popular sector that was now being recognized and acclaimed in the public arena. Perhaps these are indicators of women becoming more visible in the secular folk sector of health care. The activities of these women may not have disturbed the gendered structure of society because of their age and their sphere of activity, namely the household. What we catch a glimpse of in these memorials, however, is the creation of a predominantly women's space which provides the potential for alternate knowledge and power to that valorized in the male public arena. Indicators of this and its challenge to the gendered system will become obvious as the discussion continues.

At the centre of this female space occupied by midwife and pregnant woman are the bodies of women. Bodies touch as the hands of the midwife enable the birthing process in and from the body of the other woman. And such touching creates a particular female space upon which Elizabeth Grosz's exploration of touch can throw light. She notes that 'the toucher is always touched' and that the 'crossing of the subject into the object is more easily recognizable because access to either the inside or the outside is simply a matter of shifting focus rather than literally changing positions'.[37] Later in dialogue with Luce Irigaray, she notes the 'indeterminacy of any distance between them',[38] namely the toucher and the touched. Her work invites imaginative consideration of the possibilities that the female space of childbirth created for women of antiquity. It also alerts us to the power of touch.

Before leaving Theophante (Plate 1), Plangon and Tolmides (Plate 2), Killaron (Plate 3) and Pheidestrate and Mnesagora (Plate 4) who may have given birth or assisted at birth,[39] and Malthakê, *chrêstê* and probably midwife, it is important to draw attention to the materiality of their memorial. It is the clay of Theophante's lekythos and the stone on which is carved the memorial of Nikomeneia and Malthakê that provide us with a glimpse of their life, their story and the stories of many other such women. It is the other-than-human which carries human history and as we re-member these women, so too we re-member the clay and stone of Greece. They come into our present by way of stone and paper[40] carrying the text and analysis of their story. They enliven and texture not only the past but the present, raising questions today about the gendering of women healing and the re-membering of the Earth community. This process of re-membering will continue as stone yields up many more women healers in subsequent centuries.

Plato's reference to Phanarete as μαῖα and his subsequent discussion of midwifery point to a publicly recognized area of skill and knowledge. This designation does not appear on any of the memorials that Demand discusses but a monument from the same time period (around 320 BCE) and from Archarnai in Attica, honours Phanostrate (Plate 5).[41] She is given familial status as the wife of Meliteos and is probably freeborn and not a slave.[42] She is named as μαῖα καὶ ἰατρὸς (midwife and healer/doctor/physician). The inscription goes on to say that she caused pain (λυπη[ρ]ά) to none and that all mourned her death.[43] We know nothing more of Phanostrate, but her inscription suggests that her skill and knowledge were more than just that of midwife.[44] She was also publicly acknowledged as ἰατρός, the male gendered designator of that emerging group of more professional healers who could be called doctors or physicians. She is not the shadowy ἰατρικήν of Plato's dialogue. Here we have an embodied woman (the stele depicts a woman standing) honoured in the public arena and being designated as ἰατρός, the term which was becoming more widespread in both literature and inscriptions as professional medicine developed during this century and beyond.

This raises a number of questions in relation to the activity of Phanostrate. The first is where her healing activity took place. At this point, we could presume that her sphere of activity was the home as this is where most people were cared for in their illnesses. Given the structure of classical Greek houses, it would presumably have been in the *gynaicum* or the women's quarters if she was attending women. Phanostrate's activity would seem, like midwives generally but perhaps even more so, to be putting a certain pressure on the gender construction of active and passive. She is not only active but also recognized and acclaimed as such in the public arena. This raises the question as to whether her activity and her public recognition were shifting or at least challenging existing cultural norms in relation to gender. On the other hand, we could suggest that she was participating actively in the process of gendering space.

Before exploring such a development further, it is important to consider Hyginus' story of Agnodike which is located in third/fourth-century Athens even though probably written in the first or second century CE.

> In ancient times there were no midwives; women and slaves were forbidden by the Athenians to learn medicine. As a result many women died, their modesty preventing them from seeing a male doctor.

> Agnodike, a *puella uirgo*, so wanted to study medicine that she cut off her hair, dressed as a man and became a student of Herophilus.[45]

> Once trained, she heard a woman crying out in labour and went to her assistance. The woman, thinking this was a man, refused help, but Agnodike lifted up her clothes and revealed herself to be a woman...and was thus able to treat her patient(s).

> The male doctors found that they were not wanted and so, in their jealousy, they accused Agnodike of seducing her patients and the women of feigning illness.

> Brought before the Areopagus, Agnodike once again lifted her clothes to reveal her true sex. Proof of innocence on the charge of seducing women patients was, however, an admission of guilt in having broken the law forbidding women to study medicine. At this point the wives of the leading men arrived saying, 'You men are not spouses...but enemies, since you are condemning her who discovered...health for us'.

> At this point the Athenians changed the law, so that freeborn women could study medicine (Hyginus, *Fabula*, 274.10-13).[46]

Helen King has studied this text in much more detail than is possible here, raising the question of the historical or mythic/symbolic nature of the account and concluding that it functions, at least in part, namely the trial, as a 'defence of women's medicine and women's roles' in the social order.[47] This, however, needs further exploration. Hyginus situates Agnodike's story in Athens during the fourth century, a time in which numbers of publicly recognised midwives were emerging and one woman at least was given the title of professional healer. The account of Agnodike highlights the gendered tension between the folk and professional sectors of ancient medicine by completely negating the folk and its association with women and slaves, both 'other' within the Greek public, professional male arena. Given that this represented situation was possibly contradicted by some actual experiences of women attending women (even more so in Hyginus' own time of late-first or early-second century CE), he places the story 'in ancient times'. The consequences of the depicted control of women's labour and the privatization of female health as part of the honour/shame system demonstrate that such a gendered health care system could be fatal for women.

The story of Agnodike is one of agency and of resistance to such a system. She is active in the public arena, dressing as a man, learning medicine at the great school of Heropolis in Alexandria and successfully treating women patients. Also, the female space created by the honour/ shame code becomes a place of resistance where women, healer and healed, worked together to contravene gender structures that were destructive of women's lives.[48] Such resistance empowered, enabling some of these women who had certain political power because they were wives of the 'leading men', probably the members of the city assembly, to challenge their husbands so that the law was changed and freeborn women could study medicine. Lloyd reminds readers that this account may not be descriptive or mimetic since there is no other evidence of women being forbidden to study medicine or of the law being changed.[49] This does not, however, detract from its contribution to the construction of a gendered and layered symbolic universe and its providing a lens for examining women healing as the fourth century BCE gave way to the third.

The shift in accusations against Agnodike may offer some insight into possible gendered readings of this text. In this, Laquer's framework proves helpful. Agnodike had violated the gendered hierarchy and moved into the public arena of male activity, not as an older midwife, but as a *puella uirgo*, a young woman. By putting on male clothing, entering the male arena of education and very successfully practising medicine, Agnodike presented a profound threat to the male gendered hierarchy which needed continually to be maintained so that its 'naturalness' was preserved. That her revealing her true sex simply caused a shift in accusation demonstrates that it was not a violation of her sexed body which was at issue but of gendered hierarchy as it found expression in the world of healing. The conclusion to the story suggests that Agnodike and the women's challenge to this hierarchy were successful. To what degree their challenge as narrated in Hyginus' *Fabula* was facilitated by a more general socio-economic upheaval in fourth-century BCE Greece is difficult to determine but it suggests the possibility that women were able to use a time of unrest to situate themselves differently or at least to claim agency within the gendered system.[50] The time of Hyginus may also have been one of gender contestation. Analysis of this story, therefore, highlights the highly nuanced aspects of women healing, both as patients and as practitioners, within the health care system of ancient Greece and subtle shifts and changes in gendering associated with this.

Before closing this section, it should be noted also that Agnodike is depicted as a woman who could act independently and hence should most probably be read as representative of the more elite class who had the resources to exercise such 'independence'. Also it is only the 'freeborn' women who won the right to study medicine and not slave women or slaves generally who were also mentioned in the initial prohibition. This questions whether the story may not have functioned orally, over a number of centuries and when necessary, as a response to a perceived threat among elite women from a growing medical knowledge among foreign slave women (note Malthakê above).[51] Class and gendered hierarchies may have intersected. With this proviso, we can return to King's conclusion regarding the Agnodike story, namely that it could have functioned to affirm women's role in medicine which was developing a more professional sector. In relation to actual women healing, King recognizes the difficulty of factual claims from the evidence examined above, but she also warns against seeing Phanostrate and Agnodike as the few exceptional women who differed from that whole body of healing women considered marginal rather than integral to the health care system.[52] Boundaries appear to be more porous than has been imagined and healing women may have occupied borderland-type spaces in the interrelated colonizing and genderizing of women's health.

### Through the Eyes of Women Healing in Professional Hippocratic Medicine

Fourth-century Greece saw the emergence of professional medicine, both in theory and in practice as a result of the work of Hippocrates of Cos (c. 460–380 BCE), the multiple contributors to the expanding Hippocratic corpus over subsequent centuries,[53] and the development of places like

Alexandria as significant centres for the teaching of medicine. Owen Temkin summarizes what he sees as an 'essential core' of Hippocratic medical thinking and the significant shift the Hippocratics initiated and developed in medicine:

> They agree in attributing illness to natural rather than supernatural causes and in firmly rejecting the Homeric and Hesiodic idea that gods, *daimons*, or any other sort of supernatural beings cause illness. When they depart from strict empiricism, it is by interpreting illness in terms of the philosophical concepts of the day.[54]

Even though such a change may have been somewhat more nuanced,[55] the shift in the social world of medicine was accompanied by a profound shift in the symbolic reality – language and the system of meaning.[56]

While this study does not wish to give undue attention to the male authored Hippocratic corpus, it did contribute significantly to the genderization of healing through the Hellenistic period and into the Roman world as it was the text which informed subsequent authors such as Soranus and Galen, and through them many subsequent centuries. Its influence must therefore be considered even if briefly. In beginning this task, I acknowledge again my debt in this section to Helen King and Lesley Dean-Jones, both of whom have provided book length studies of different aspects of the genderization of healing in the Hippocratic corpus as well as numerous articles.[57] A number of subtopics will emerge as this section unfolds but given its focus on professional women healing, I turn first to their characterization and representation within the corpus.

This first section will be extraordinarily brief as the Hippocratic corpus genders the professional physician as male. As King notes, there are no names of women healers in the corpus.[58] Women are referred to as healers almost in passing. In *Fleshes* 19, there is passing reference to ἀκεστρίδες or female healers who attend births, and in *Diseases of Women* 1.68 it is the ἰητρεύουσα or the 'female who is doctoring',[59] who is instructed on the removal of a dead foetus. There are other passages which give instructions to a woman presumed present at the consultation to carry out examinations of female patients.[60] The world of professional Hippocratic medicine is, however, constructed male and hierarchical. *In the Surgery* 6.1-4 speaks of those who 'look after the patient' (οἳ δὲ περὶ τον ἀσθενέοντα) who are to keep silence and to obey. Given that most of the care of patients was in the popular sector or in the home, those looking after them would generally have been women. King warns, however, that this was certainly not exclusively so.[61] Whatever of the attendants, women healers are almost invisible in the Hippocratic corpus. They are assistants whose skills are inferior to the professional male and they are to be obedient to his superior knowledge. Women are not represented as having knowledge or power in their own right.

Dean-Jones, however, demonstrates that this is not completely so.[62] She contrasts the Hippocratic doctor's presentation of his own observation, *autopsia*, as generally superior to the account given by patients, *historia*. In considering her discussion, it should be noted that the Hippocratic corpus takes little account of the modesty of women as represented in Hyginus' *Fabula*. Male physicians, according to the *Oath*, are to assist and not harm male and female, slave and free patients (Hippocrates, *Jusj.* 24–28) and Dean-Jones offers evidence of male physicians examining and treating female patients.[63] She goes on to point out, therefore, that on the basis of *autopsia*, the Hippocratic doctor's knowledge of male and female bodies 'was comparable'.[64] It is in the area of *historia* that his attitude to male and female informants differs. He gives authority to women's knowledge of their own bodies because their experience of their body and its illnesses differs from that of men.[65] There is also a recognition here of modesty which may give the male physician pause in his questioning of women in relation to their illnesses. This is best demonstrated in what Dean-Jones calls the 'now famous passage' of *Diseases of Women* 1.62:

> These diseases are dangerous, as has been said, and for the most part they are both acute and serious, and *difficult to understand because of the fact that women are the ones who share these sicknesses.* Sometimes women do not know what sicknesses they have, until they have experienced the diseases which come from menses and they become older. Then both necessity and time teach them the cause of their sicknesses. Sometimes diseases become incurable for women who do not learn why they are sick. For women are ashamed to tell even if they know, and they suppose that it is a disgrace, because of their inexperience and lack of knowledge. At the same time the doctors also make mistakes by not learning the apparent cause through accurate questioning, because they proceed to heal as though they were dealing with men's diseases. I have already seen many women die from just this kind of suffering. But at the outset one must ask accurate questions about the cause. For the healing of the diseases of women differs greatly from the healing of men's diseases.[66]

Given the social construct of honour/shame and its genderization, the Hippocratic recognition of the differences in male and female bodies,[67] and the affirmation of women's knowledge of their own bodies by way of experience, the Hippocratics opened up a space for female authority in relation to bodily knowledge even though making reference from time to time to their preferred affirmation of *autopsia* over *historia*.[68] This is particularly evident in *Diseases of Women* and *On Sterile Women* from which Dean-Jones concludes that 'despite reservations about the reliability of female testimony, the Hippocratics deferred to women's innate knowledge of their own bodies from which they were excluded by being men'.[69] Female knowledge and female sharing of this knowledge were essential to the well-being and health of women within the emerging professional sector, an aspect represented in the story of Agnodike. This process, however, also functioned to enhance the power of the male physician in the health care system and to marginalize not only women healers and their knowledge, but also to valorize the professional sector and to give it centrality as it assumed into itself women's knowledge and women's healing power.[70]

Before leaving these women, healing as a result of their own bodily knowledge which they shared with the growing body of male physicians, we need to ask some further questions of them. First, even though the Hippocratic Oath constructed the physician as available to all whether male or female, bond or free, were these women of knowledge from the elite, the wealthy, the freeborn who could secure the services of physicians more readily than the poor and slaves? Indeed, the house which the Hippocratic physician enters is certainly the citizen's house where he meets 'women, maidens, and possessions very precious indeed' (Hippocrates, *Med.* 1).[71] The testimony of Tenedia/the woman of Tenedos that we encountered earlier suggests, however, that she may have been a slave given that slaves were often named according to their region of origin.[72] To ask of these women, slave, freed, free or elite, as Finkler suggests, what were the life's lesions associated with their illnesses – changes of climate, epidemics, demographics, improvement or deterioration of housing – is to seek the unattainable as their *historia* and the narration of their illnesses ranged over the decades, even the centuries of the compilation of the corpus and over a wide geographic area. The locations, scattered throughout *Epidemics*, extend from Elis and Sparta in the Peloponnese through the Greek mainland, across Macedonia, Thrace, concentrated around the Sea of Marmara and south in western Asia Minor to Halicarnassus and Rhodes off its coastline.

Such data was not, however, just data because, as Howard Clark Kee points out, the Hippocratics took account of these ecological factors in diagnosing or at least narrating the illnesses they encountered: '[d]iagnosis involved not only the specifics of the individual's symptoms, but also information about race and sex, location, climate, water supply, and even social and political conditions'.[73] *Epidemics* 1 opens on Thasos with descriptions of various weather patterns and the diseases and epidemics which resulted. Women healing and healing generally have a context within the physical environment and are part of an ecological system.

Within their contexts, women's symptoms are frequently distinguished from illnesses that affect a population generally.[74] In the fourteen cases narrated at the end of *Epidemics* I, five involve women and four of those five are illness that are associated with childbirth and in the fifth, 'a slight menstrual flow' is one of Melidia's symptoms.[75] Women's most recurrent life's lesions, according to this construction of the Hippocratic health care system, are associated with childbirth and menstruation, the two most distinguishing features of the female body. Although these case studies are involved with clinical realities, they tend to be simply descriptive of symptoms and the progression of the illness with little or no account of medical responses except perhaps the insertion of a pessary. They do not describe the clinical relationship and hence offer little data that would serve analyses using Kleinman's categories.

Reading further in *Epidemics* 3 does, however, offer further insights into the socio-cultural reality of women healing or not healing within the ambit of Hippocratic medicine. Of the twelve cases which open this volume, six are women and only three of the six have illnesses that are gynaecological: two have miscarriages[76] and one suffers after a first-time delivery of a male child.[77] The latter is aged seventeen giving insight into the young age of many of the women whose symptoms are described. Four of these women are not identified by way of familial relationships which may point to their slave status which may nuance the claims above regarding the general social status of female Hippocratic patients. The woman of Case 9 'lodged with Tisamenus' (ἡ παρά Τεισαμενοῦ γυνὴ) and in Case 10, the woman is described as 'of the house of Pantimides' (τῶν περὶ Παντιμίδην). Unnamed women who belonged to the house of a named male, most likely a citizen, would generally be understood as slaves.

From this brief analysis, it emerges that the female patient may not feature as often as the male in the Hippocratic description of illnesses[78] but that female and male patients are located in a wide range of socio-cultural and ecological contexts. The differences in the experience of illness among female patients are not only associated with childbirth and menstruation but the text recognizes different experiences of epidemics and illnesses that are common to women and men.[79] The sexed body of the female rather than social gender constructions seems to be foundational in such recognition of difference. This appears to differ from the Platonic construction of sex and gender where gender is mapped onto the body. It is still, however, the male body which is the norm from which the female body differs in relation to diseases so that *Places in Man* constructs the patient as well as the doctor male and only in the last chapter does the writer turn to 'diseases of women as they are called' (Hippocrates, *Loc. hom.* 47). The single-sexed body on which gender is mapped is, however, reaffirmed in *Nature of Man* 3.6: 'there is no generation unless the copulating partners be of the same kind, and possess the same qualities'. The gender system of antiquity is read onto the sexed body allowing for recognition of differences.

The analysis above suggests that such recognition of difference may have been the result of the contribution of female knowledge of female bodies to the Hippocratic corpus. Female patients' knowledge of their own bodies is represented in the literature as difference and, as such, it has nuanced the constructed system of gender. From their borderland space, they are participating as did women before them, in the construction of a different knowledge from that of men, a knowledge that is shaped in and by their borderland status. The materiality of their own bodies is the source of such knowledge. The possible contribution of this knowledge and experience among female healers to Hippocratic medicine will be examined below.

It has already been demonstrated that female midwives served the health needs of other women not only at the time of childbirth but also for other gynaecological needs such as miscarriage and abortion. Phanostrate's monument suggests that some midwives were gaining healing knowledge and exercising healing power beyond that commonly associated with the midwife. She was perhaps treating other illnesses experienced by women. It seems that at least some of the knowledge which women were thus accumulating within the space of women healing women was co-opted within the Hippocratic corpus for the use of male doctors.

To assist in this exploration, we need to revisit Temkin's claim that the empirical and philosophical nature of Hippocratic medicine does not carry over into the gynaecological material or material explicitly concerned with women's illnesses. This sector, he says 'makes comparatively little use of such philosophical constructs, attributing many difficulties to mechanical causes such as blockages of menstrual or lochial bleeding or displacements of the uterus'.[80] Dean-Jones also notes the 'disproportionate amount of Hippocratic pharmacopoeia' contained in the gynaecological sections by comparison with other segments of the corpus and their 'long lists of alternative remedies',[81] while Temkin records that '[t]he gynaecological treatises in particular contain many recipes and treatments that appear to have originated in midwives' lore'.[82] It is difficult to determine to what extent women's knowledge of healing women has been drawn into the service of a male-centred and professional health care system but the differences in the literature noted above seem to point to at least the operation of such a process. One of the important points made by Dean-Jones, however, is that this co-optation is not definitive in that midwives and female healers are an ongoing source of knowledge for male professionals as evidence in the later writings of Soranus and Galen.[83] What she does not draw out from these observations, however, is that women must have continued their practice of healing in the popular and folk sector as well as within the professional sector where they developed both their knowledge and their skills. Demand also provides another insight into the world of women healing, namely that women as healers and as agents effecting their own healing could have learnt from the collection of women's healing lore within the context of the Hippocratic corpus and from working with doctors who had incorporated this knowledge into a broader Hippocratic framework.[84] Again we can see these healing women as borderland women, being on 'both shores at once, and at once see(ing) through the serpent and the eagle eyes'.[85]

### *Mousa, Antiochis, Secunda, Sotira – Gendering Professional Medicine*

Within the Hellenistic period and into the Roman Imperial era, significant shifts took place in the lives of some women. They became more visible in the public arena, taking up occupations outside the domestic realm and having these honoured by way of public inscriptions and thus shifting to some extent the socio-cultural meaning given to public space.[86] It is not surprising, therefore, given the earlier trend toward women healers emerging in the public professional health care sector, that such societal shifts should take effect in the medical world also. The sources which document this significant social change are predominantly epigraphical and literary and named women become visible in greater numbers from the second century BCE to the first/second century CE.[87] While all those so named will not be able to be studied in great detail, it is envisaged that the questions addressed to the sources and a bringing of them into dialogue will enable these healing women and the contexts in which they healed to emerge with greater clarity.

Mousa is honoured on a small stele just half a metre high. She is the daughter of Agathocles and she is called ἰατρείνη.[88] Below the inscription, in a rectangular relief, stands a woman with a scroll in her hand. On the left, two small dogs look up at her or the scroll[89] and on the right stands a much smaller figure turned toward her.[90] The inscription is dated second or first century BCE and was found at Istanbul. This is the earliest extant inscription which designates a female healer as ἰατρείνη (feminine gender) with no explicit association with midwifery.[91] Robert discusses the two possibilities for understanding this designation in the context of the ancient world. First, it could signify a woman who treats not only gynaecological illnesses but also other illnesses in women. Second, a broader understanding of the term is informed by the data for women physicians who are not just midwives and whose services are not directed solely or explicitly to the healing of women.[92] It is this data which will be studied below. The scroll suggests that Mousa was educated and her companion may point to such an engagement of her time in healing that she required an assistant. Both these indicators would place Mousa within the realm of professional healer and the relief could suggest that she drew other less qualified women into this realm also. Her assistant may have been her apprentice.

Further south in western Asia Minor, the land of the great healing centres of Cos, Cnidos, Ephesus and Pergamum, Antiochis of Tlos carried on her healing role sometime in the first century BCE or CE.[93] She was possibly the daughter of a doctor, Diodotus,[94] and her healing art (τὴν ἰατρικὴν τέχνην ἐνπειρία)[95] was recognized by both the citizens (δῆμος) and the council (βούλη).[96] She set up her own statue which is indicative of her independent access to significant resources. She is acknowledged by Galen for her cures of diseases of the spleen, dropsy, sciatica and arthritis (Gal. 13.250.341)[97] and earlier Heracleides of Tarentum dedicated one of his medical treatises to her.[98]

This accumulation of evidence and recognition points to a reasonable or even significant social status for Antiochis. She was most probably educated in medicine by her father as apprenticeship was common for those unable to attend the great medical schools. It seems clear though that she developed skills proper to herself independently of her father and that these were recognized not only by the city in which she practised but also by medical writers much further afield geographically and temporally. Her healing arts were not confined to women's illnesses but extended to those shared by women and men and hence she may have practised medicine with her father as a city physician.[99] We are not told Antiochis' age but the fact that she is named in relation to her father rather than a husband may suggest that she is not a midwife beyond childbearing age but a younger woman.[100] These factors and the favourable recognition of her active public role must have created some tensions around the genderizing of the honour system and of space in the public realm. Was it that healing took place predominantly in the house that enabled a possible crossing of gender barriers to facilitate a female physician treating male diseases just as women would have been caring for men in the popular sector throughout the entire history already examined? Within this realm, female healing would not threaten the public male status. What we can reconstruct of Antiochis suggests, however, that she had a more public role and her erecting of her own statue may have been her attempt to make public the cultural shift that her work entailed. It may have been an act of resistance.

At Adada, not too far distant from Tlos, another woman, Aurelia Alexandria Zosime, of seemingly elite status given that her statue and that of her daughter were erected in the agora, is publicly honoured by her husband Aurelius (Ponto)ni(a)nos Asclepiades whose name associates him also with medicine.[101] The date of her healing activity and the erection of her statue is uncertain but given the long public life of inscriptions, its effect would have been felt within the time frame being considered. Like Antiochis, it is her medical skill (ἐπιστήμης ἰατρικῆς) which is acknowledged and as Antiochis may have worked with and been educated by her father, Aurelia may have been similarly engaged with her husband. Women patients would have certainly benefited from her skill as they would have from that of Antiochis but we do not have the data to determine if the health care of women improved as women healers entered the professional arena nor do we know what the effect of this may have been on women healing in the popular and folk sectors. Did their status among their patients, particularly among the elite, lessen as the professional sector gained more public recognition and as more elite women entered it? What might the effect of such a possible shift have been on the economic circumstances of poorer women healing in the more private sector/s since there would generally be a fee associated with healing?[102] Such questions alert us to be sensitive to the impact of shifts in gender status on other aspects of life such as class, shifts not always to the advantage of all women. Perhaps the male professional sector accepted the inevitability of a few women joining their ranks because it augmented their own status and gave greater control of women's healing in the other sectors.

One of the questions raised above is that of possible remuneration for the healing services offered by these female physicians.[103] It is interesting that one of the ideals found in the elite medical writers such as Hippocrates and Galen is that of *philanthropie*. In Hippocrates *Precepts* 6, this *philanthropie* is linked with the provision of medical services to those who are unable to provide recompense.

Sometimes give your services for nothing, calling to mind a previous bene-
faction or present good will. And if there be an opportunity of serving one
who is a stranger in financial straits, give full assistance to all such. For
where there is love of man [*philanthropie*], there is also love of the art [i.e.,
the patient will love the medical art].

Galen in his turn sets out the various motives for undertaking healing:

Some practice the medical art for the sake of making money, some because
of the exemption from public services given to them by law, others for the
sake of philanthropy, while others do so because of the glory or reputation
accruing therefrom (Galen, *De Placitis Hippocratis et Platonis* 9.5).

We could assume that some of these women healers from more elite circumstances could, indeed, have been engaged in *philanthropie* with or
apart from husband or father.[104] Like their male counterparts, their
patients could have been quite needy and for them the philanthropy of
these more wealthy women would have made healing possible. Domnina,
whose inscription will be examined in more detail below may well have
been a philanthropic physician like Demiadas, serving her community during a time of disaster or epidemic and hence treating rich and poor alike.[105]
She is praised for having rid her homeland from disease.[106] Given this
more descriptive nature of the honour paid her, perhaps there was a reluc-
tance to praise these women's public service with male public virtues,
indicating another area in which their activity was subtly putting pressure
on the gender system.

What we suspected in relation to the engagement of Antiochis and
Aurelia with father or husband in the healing art, is made explicit in the
epitaph to Pantheia erected by Glycon her husband.[107] The length of the
inscription suggests the freeborn citizen status of this medical family of
Pergamum of the second century CE, Glycon himself being a physician and
his father also who is buried in the same tomb. Did Pantheia learn her art
(τέχνη) within the context of this family? Did she and Glycon conduct
their work separately or did they have a surgery together?[108] Fidelity to
the gender and honour structures would suggest not, but Glycon says of
Pantheia that she raised high their common fame in the art of healing
(ὕψωσας ξυνὸν ἰητορίης). He acknowledges likewise that Pantheia equals
him in skill (τέχνη) but reveals the traditional Greek gender perspective by
way of the rider, even though a woman (οὐδὲ γυνήι).

Lest Pantheia's skill and public service be allowed to threaten the prevailing gender hierarchy, Glycon precedes his high praise of this aspect of
her life with a recitation of her familial and domestic virtues according to
the ideal for the acceptable Roman woman. She is praised for her beauty,

her wisdom and her self-control/chastity/modesty – Glycon insists that she maintained the honour/shame structures perhaps because her activity was threatening them. She gave him children (and one could assume he meant male child/ren) just like himself, she cared for him and their children and she was faithful overseer of their home, the οἶκος. Glycon goes to great lengths to assure those who honour Pantheia's memory that her outstanding healing abilities have not challenged the cultural norms. Given the strength of his affirmation one could suspect that they were doing exactly that and hence the system had to be re-established by way of the public proclamation with the traditional virtues preceding the praise of exceptional skill in the art of healing.

Before leaving Asia Minor, I return to the inscription honouring Domnina of Neoclaudopolis[109] and three others from the region or just beyond. Like the other professional women healers considered in this section, Domnina was a freeborn woman. Her memorial was erected by her husband. None of the terms noted above are used for her service but she is said to have saved her homeland (fatherland) from diseases (πάτρην ῥυομένην νούσων). This seems to suggest a public practice that serviced a broad range of clientele or perhaps responded to an epidemic crisis which was a common occurrence in that world. Apart from this enigmatic statement little else can be gleaned from Domnina's memorial except that she may have died younger than expected as her husband mourns that she has rushed off to join the gods and forgotten her husband.[110] The young age of some of these professional women will be given further consideration below when the exact age of some is inscribed on their tombstones.

There are two inscriptions from central and north-western Asia Minor which cannot be dated exactly and another from Tomis north-west across the Black Sea near the mouth of the Danube which belong to the Imperial era. The first from Ancyra in Galatia honours Treboulia who is called ἰατρινὴ ζῶσα φρονοῦσα (wise and life-giving physician)[111] and a second from Cios in Bythinia is an epitaph to Empeiria who is also named εἰατρείνη, the same title given to the anonymous female physician from Tomis.[112] Parker is right here in recognizing that the most that seems to be able to be gleaned from these inscriptions is the presence of women healing in the professional arena and readily being given the official title of ἰατρείνη or εἰατρείνη. We cannot learn even their status from their short memorials. Empeiria, however, deserves our attention since her name is more a pseudonym since the word *empeiria* designates experience of one's trade or profession. Antiochis was recognized for her *empeiria* (ἐπὶ τῆ...ἐνπειπίᾳ) and Robert provides a well-documented discussion of how this pseudonym developed into a proper name during the Imperial period not only for women.[113] The knowledge, skill and experience of professional women healing were becoming publicly visible during the late Hellenistic and early Imperial periods.

The geographic focus shifts now from Asia Minor to Rome and nearby Osimo where the greatest concentration of epitaphs to women healing either as physicians (*medica*) or as midwives (*obstetrix*) has been found. Professional medicine in Rome had its origins during this period when male and, one might also assume, female healers came from foreign shores like Greece and Asia Minor where professional healing had had a longer history.[114] I will not examine each of the inscriptions in detail but try to determine some aspects of the lives of these women such as the *medicae* like Primilla[115] and Terentia Prima[116] and *obstertrice* like Poblicia Aphe[117] and Claudia Trophima,[118] one of whom was twenty-one years old when she died and the other seventy-five, giving us a glimpse of the varied lives of these women many of whom we know only by their name and their profession and by way of the stone which has preserved their memory.

Among the *obstertrice* or midwives whose memorials have been uncovered in Rome and who carried out their healing art some time during the period between first century BCE and first or second century CE, we find women of varying social status.[119] Secunda[120] and perhaps Hygia[e] Flaviae Sabinae[121] were slaves[122] in elite Roman households. We do not know of any other activities of these slave women but if they served as midwives to the women – freeborn, freed and slave – of the household and tended to their other health needs, this may have been their only assigned task. They may also have been hired out by their masters for profit.[123] These women were clearly valued members of the household given their memorials. One wonders about their housing and their own health given that Hygia Flavia Sabina only lived to thirty years of age.[124] We have no evidence of her life's lesions nor what it was which caused her death. Such information might have given insights into the lives of other midwives whose memorials have not been preserved because they did not belong to imperial households and carried out their activities among poorer women in the popular or folk sector. We do have, however, a glimpse into the hybridity of the lives of the colonized women who were able to exercise their healing arts perhaps much more freely in the houses of their colonizers than the poor midwives of the city. They shared the world of the elite but as freed and/or slave.

Roman inscriptions for midwives of this period also honour four freed-women – Teidia Sex.,[125] Sallustia Athenais,[126] Poblicia Aphe,[127] and Thallusa.[128] Two of these inscriptions mention men who were also freedmen of their patrons, Sex. Teidius and Quintus Sallustius Dioga which suggests that the midwife and her husband may have entered their relationship during slavery and been freed together. It is of interest that in both of these inscriptions the occupation of the man is not named. Korpela says that his occupation would depend on the occupational opportunities available in the particular environment but this does not give any explanation as to why the woman's occupation is named and not his.[129] One wonders whether Teidia Sex. and Sallustia Athenais offered their midwifery skills to their patrons as homage for their liberty and the naming of their healing art was intended to honour their patrons even more than their own art. Even if such an intention were so, the inscription would have had the rhetorical effect of making visible this healing role in the public arena, making the colonized visible in all the complexity of the intersection of the lives of colonizer and colonized.

Poblicia Aphe is the freedwoman of Gaia, a woman patron, as was Artemidorus, the patron of Sallustia Athenais. Poblicia Aphe is named midwife and her age is given as twenty-one years. One wonders where and how she learnt her trade to the point such that it would be the memorial that would accompany her beyond death.[130] Her memorial evokes an older more experienced midwife like Claudia Trophima who is seventy-five years old and whose son and grandson set up her memorial.[131] She is presumably a freeborn woman as is Julia Veneria.[132] Thallasa, on the other hand, is a freedwoman in the imperial household. The relationship between these women of different classes and ranks, patrons, clients, and free/d women carrying out their healing tasks must continue to tantalize us since we have no further data to allow us to prise open the cracks which would give us access to their world. That the slave women would have tended freeborn women during their labour, may perhaps have cared for the medical needs of their children and also their own needs at the vulnerable time of illness, could perhaps have led to significant relationships among these women in a way that would explain their memorials. Female space may have allowed for a crossing of class boundaries that was perhaps frowned upon in the public arena of male honour and shame. It may also have allowed for the control of the labour of the slave women so that their healing art was colonized. The stone which honours these women and carries their memories into our own day is silent in relation to our further questions but the extraordinary aspect is that it is this participant member of Earth community which carries the trace of the other, namely slave and free women who were midwives and physicians in the emerging Roman empire.

The stone of the earth comes to our aid once again to yield a lasting image of Scribonia Attice, a midwife of Ostia in the second century CE. She squats before a birthing woman who is seated on a birthing chair and an assistant stands behind the woman in labour with at least one of her arms supporting the seated woman. It is a female space and bespeaks female relationships around the moment of birth.[133] While there is a danger of maintaining the medicalization of childbirth by the attention given here and above to midwives as healers, the medical treatises make it very clear that in antiquity childbirth was a significant moment in the health of both the woman and child because it was at this point a woman's health was significantly endangered as it still is for many women in the two-thirds world. It was a point of significant life's lesions for many women and the level of skill of a midwife like Scribonia Attice could mean either life or death for the woman and/or her child. Midwives must, therefore, be considered very significant participants in the health care system and the inscriptions which honoured their art are a quiet recognition of what must have been a much more widespread occupation, art or skill that crossed health care boundaries, breaking down distinctions between popular, folk and professional, however these may have been understood in the centuries of antiquity under consideration.[134] And, rather than considering the women who emerged into the professional arena as obscuring other women engaged in healing and being healed, we can consider these women as a lens onto the popular world of healing where older women of the household beyond childbirth would have assisted the younger women who may have married into their households, not only with childbirth but with the care of the family's health needs, generally passing on both knowledge and skill.

It was such knowledge and skill which serviced the male medical writers who make reference to their female sources for gynaecological data and from whom we catch other glimpses of the lives of these midwives not available through the inscriptions. In the extensive writings of Pliny the Elder, which themselves blur the distinction between folk and professional medicine with both coming under his critique, the practice of midwives is taken for granted. It is both honoured and critiqued. Sotira and Salpe are named midwife but they are a source for cures that are not particular to women – mad dog bite, malaria, epilepsy attributed to Sotira (Pliny, *Nat.* 28.23.83), but it is menstrual blood which brings about the cure. Salpe appears in a section on aphrodisiacs and use of products of the sea (*Nat.* 32.44.135), using these to remove the hair from young slave boys being prepared for the market.[135] This may provide further insight into the tasks of midwives in the wealthier households. Like earlier female healers, these women had knowledge of drugs and herbs and the use of natural products for not only medicinal but also cosmetic purposes.

Pliny's disdain of some of his female sources is evident in his dismissal of the varied opinions of Lais and Elephantis regarding the abortifacient power of menstrual blood. His conclusion is that it is better not to believe them (Pliny, *Nat.* 28.23.81) just as he scorns some of the remedies he attributes to 'midwives and harlots', perhaps a literary trope to highlight disapproval (Pliny, *Nat.* 28.20.70). Pliny's disdain, however, uncovers a world of women's knowledge of herbs and drugs developed in the folk and popular sector over generations which was now emerging in a more public way as healing occupied the public domain as well as the popular and folk. While he recognized female sources, they are presented through his own lens and hence are obscured by his perspective. We do not encounter women's own knowledge as they would present it.

Soranus, on the other hand, writing around the time of Scribonia Attice's career, recognizes the professional nature of midwifery and gives instructions regarding the training and conduct of midwives in order to provide a model for those entering the profession and a measuring stick for well-established practitioners. While affirming the professional status, Soranus also seems to co-opt what would have been a significant female arena of activity, namely the training of younger midwives by those of experience. One wonders whether the level of theoretical knowledge that is to be added to professional competence and experience would not have excluded many women who had not benefited from the more accessible availability of education for women in the Roman era.[136] His recognition of the requirement of a breadth of knowledge in all the therapeutic areas (πᾶσι τοῖς μέρεσιν τῆς θεραπείας, Soranus, *Gyn.* 1.3.9-10) – diet, surgery and medication – may be affirmation of the broader knowledge suggested above for those named midwives and the types of services they had to render in imperial households or to wealthy patrons.[137] Such knowledge could then have been shared among women as they gathered outside their professional context in marketplaces, courtyards or at religious celebrations so that it was available to women in all sectors of health care.

According to Soranus, the midwife need not have borne children herself, which could account for the young age of Poblicia Aphe, and he is more concerned that she have the required strong hands than that she be a certain age. The preservation of the male control of fertility is evident in that his ideal midwife will not administer an abortifacient, even though it is clear from Pliny that this is one area of such women's knowledge, indicating the male fear of this area of female knowledge and hence power. Within the female space of women responding to the health needs of other women, however, control of fertility was a significant area of female power and was perhaps most feared by men as it was so difficult for them to control. Soranus also seems to dismiss elements which could be thought of as belonging to the folk sector of health care – dreams, secret remedies and rituals (Soranus, *Gyn.* 1.3.29-31).

Education seems to be an important consideration for the various levels of competence addressed by Soranus in relation to the midwife. Even the apt midwife must have an elementary level of knowledge which includes theory, καὶ διὰ θεωρίας τὴν τέχνην ἰσχύσῃ παραλαβεῖν (Soranus, *Gyn.* 1.3.10-11) and hence more formal education. The perfect one has acquired theoretical knowledge. While Soranus affirms and values the work of the midwife, such expectations bring women healing more under male control because they were the ones who had and distributed theoretical knowledge. Others have already asked whether he saw his treatise as a textbook for such knowledge.[138] but given the small percentage of women who could read, its accessibility to women would be limited. We need to question, therefore, whether educated women passed on such acquired theory to other women who did not have access to it?[139] If the goal was control of this significant area of women's knowledge and activity, did women find ways in which to subvert what may have been increasing control? Answers to all these questions are beyond our grasp at present but one thing that does emerge from Soranus is a positive affirmation of the professional midwife. She may, however, have been only accessible to the elite and hence women's access to quality health care in the popular sector still eludes us both as healing women and women healing.

Another group of healing women likewise become visible in greater numbers in Rome during the early Imperial period and they are those named *medicae* or identified in some other way as engaged in publicly recognized healing. I will begin with Restituta[140] as she may, in fact, provide a link with the earlier women of Asia Minor because her inscription is in Greek which Korpela says may suggest that both Restituta and Claudius Alcimus are foreigners come to Rome.[141] The inscription on which Resituta is named is one dedicated to Claudius Alcimus who is an imperial physician. Restituta names him as her patron and professor or teacher (πάτρωνι καὶ καθηγητῇ) and acclaims him as ἀγάθῳ καὶ ἀξίῳ, a good and worthy teacher. As was assumed for Antiochis, Pantheia, and Domnina, the apprenticeship model of education for women is here made explicit.[142] Restituta is a freedwoman and it is difficult to assume that her naming her

patron as her professor means anything other than that she likewise practised medicine and perhaps in the imperial household.[143] What her skills
were is impossible to determine.

Similarly for Secunda who is actually named *medica* and who is a slave
in the house of Livilla, the sister of Claudius.[144] Her husband is named on
her gravestone, and his occupation is given as guard in the Temple of
Vesta. Given Melissa Barden Dowling's demonstration of the power of the
Vestal virgins during the first century CE,[145] one wonders what power
might have been given to this couple, slave and freed, who carried out significant roles in two centres of power. This yields little, however, about
Secunda's healing art. We know even less of an anonymous *medica* of first-
century Rome and of Melitine[146] who is also named *medica* and who was a
slave of Appuleis whom Korpela has been unable to identify.[147]

As with midwives, these healing women who carry the title *medica*
which identifies them with their male counterparts, the *medicus* or physician, come from across the social spectrum. Of the slave women *medicae*
we have virtually nothing but their names and perhaps their owners. Similarly for the freedwoman, Venuleia Sosis[148] whose patron is even unknown.
Julia Sabina,[149] also a freedwoman, is named *medica* on her tombstone
from Osimo not far from Rome on the Italian peninsula. Her husband is
named on her inscription and as well as being *medica* she is also praised
as a well merited spouse (*bene merenti*), bringing familial and household
virtues alongside those of a more public occupation as we saw earlier in
relation to Glycon's praise of Pantheia.

It is perhaps significant that the freeborn *medica*, Primilla, is praised
more effusively for her familial virtues.[150] She is forty-four years old, daughter of L. Vibius Melito and wife of L. Cocceius Apthorus, neither of whom
can be specifically identified.[151] Throughout her thirty years of marriage to
L. Cocceius Apthorus, she has lived without quarreling (*sine querella fecit*)
and she is highly praised as best and chaste wife (*coniug optima castae*).
Considering Primilla's memorial alongside that of Pantheia raises the question whether it was the activity of these freeborn women in the public
arena which was more challenging to the social structure than that of the
freed or slave women. They could, by their activity, bring shame on their
husbands who seem to be at pains to proclaim their domestic virtues. We
catch a glimpse of their resistance to the gender structures through the
cracks in these texts. On three other memorials naming Roman *medicae*,
however, even these small cracks are closed over. Julia Pye[152] and Minucia
Asste[153] are simply called *medica* and Terentia Prima,[154] who is also *medica*,
is named as the patron of Terentia Nice in whose honour the memorial has

been erected. All we can deduce is that they are freeborn citizen women and hence of reasonable means. How their healing activity contributed to augment the economic status of the family is unknown to us but we can presume that it did that.

Primilla's momument returns us again to the question of the education of these women healers.[155] Primilla married at fourteen years of age and it is reasonable to assume that she, like Pantheia, bore children during the early years of her marriage. How did she become a healer whose skill was such that she would be remembered publicly for it? Some clues have already emerged. As freeborn woman, she may have been educated such that she could read the medical treatises like the Hippocratic or Soranic *Diseases of Women* which seem to have had women like herself as one group within their intended audience.[156] She may have learnt her art from either a slave or freedwoman living in her household who was also *medica* either within that private sphere or in the broader popular sector, pointing to the ways women use female space as a site of resistance. After her childbearing, she may have been apprenticed to a recognized professional healer from whom she learnt her art. This may have given her agency and power to resist male control of female healing. It also could have provided her with knowledge which would have been vital to the health of many women as well as some men.[157]

Another question that has vexed scholars is the scope of these healing women's activity. Gourevitch asks of ancient midwives their field of activity – the home or a more public site like a town or village surgery or clinic?[158] That women healed in homes, their own and that of others, is beyond doubt.[159] There is, however, no specific evidence which would place women in a public place of healing like a surgery,[160] although we have already discussed the possibility of women like Pantheia in particular and perhaps Aurelia Alexandria Zosime working in a public clinic/surgery with their husbands. Such surgeries may have been a room that was part of the physician's house or if he and/or she were slave/s, a room in the household dedicated to healing activities. In such circumstances, women's healing could, therefore, be seen as within the domestic realm and its gendered system. Theirs was, however, active public work rather than purely domestic work and their activity begins to suggest that the public/private dichotomy, the gendering of space, was being shifted in some Roman households, especially in this era of women's increased public activity.[161] Women's agency is, at this time, shifting some of the edges of the gendered system and this new space, this borderland, is a place which enables women's knowledge of and power in healing to find a new expression even though it is not able to deconstruct the entire system.

Scholars are divided, therefore, as to whether women physicians treated only women for a wide range of illnesses beyond the obstetric and gynae-cological or whether they also treated men. Men would have been cared for in illness by women in the familial and popular sector of medicine because of its location within the domestic realm but even Homer seems to place women's use of healing herbs in the public arena. We have seen that public professional medicine was located within a public context, the arena where men predominated but women were also active and becom-ing more so. It is, therefore, much easier to imagine women of the rising professional class treating men as well as women. Lloyd suggests on the basis of '[w]hat we know from other writers, as well as the references we have considered from the Hippocratic treatises'[162] that women's illnesses were generally treated by healing women but certainly not exclusively so as this same evidence also suggests. Similarly, on the basis of Galen's refer-ences to women physicians' treating women's diseases, Jackson deduces that women healers 'probably treated exclusively or predominantly women's disease' but he also wants to add the rider that 'there were doubtless exceptions'[163] thus emphasizing the insecurity of our knowledge in this regard. Parker, on the basis of his careful study not only of the male medi-cal writers but also the inscriptional material examined above, concludes that:

> [i]t is likely, though we cannot know for certain, that the practice of many women doctors was primarily concerned with women's diseases and child-birth. However, the examples of medieval and Renaissance Europe should warn us against too easy an assumption of a limited practice.[164]

### Conclusion

The inscriptions honouring and remembering healing women which have been the particular focus of this chapter, though small in number and with significant temporal and spatial spread,[165] recognize the agency of healing women in the professional sector of Hellenistic and early Imperial medi-cine and their location in the borderlands between health care sectors. Like their male counterparts, these healing women came from different socio-cultural and geographic contexts, no doubt had different educational experiences and hence varied levels of skill.[166] They touched the lives of many women and some men with their healing hands as well as their *pharmaka* and the agency of at least some posed a threat to the prevailing gendered culture in the public arena, a threat which their male kin sought to minimalize or which others sought to ridicule. They often manifest the hybridity of the colonized as women, as slaves and sometimes as both, occupying a borderland space which opens up new social and cultural possibilities for women and men.

While tracing the emergence of healing women healing women and men, this chapter has also provided insights into the materiality of this healing bringing together in co-operative co-agency human bodies and natural and animal remedies. The other-than-human was co-agent with women and men in the healing of bodies and perhaps in a way that is not available to us, healing various aspects of Earth. This other-than-human was enabled to speak and a contemporary ecological reading begins to emerge which not only honours women healing as both practitioners and patients but also the Earth's life giving and life sustaining powers. Onto female bodies, space and the other-than-human, developing and developed gendered and hierarchical dualisms have been mapped. A reading of this interactive reality, of the records which bring to today's readers evidence of the agency of women and the Earth and women's resistance to dualistic cultural constructions, opens up a new story. In it, attention to agency and resistance has enabled some of the subjectivities of healing women/women healing in antiquity to be heard. It has also enabled a remembering of the *pharmaka* which accompanied this healing. This story has not, however, been fully told as this initial reading led along a path into the professional sector of healing in antiquity. Attention must now be directed toward the intersecting sectors of the folk and the popular of which only glimpses have been caught up to this point.

Plate 1: *Lekythos for Theophante*
(National Archaeological Museum, Athens, 1055)

Plate 2: *Grave Stele for Plangon and Tolmides*
(National Archaeological Museum, Athens, 749)

Plate 3: *Lekythos for Killaron*
(Bildarchiv Foto Marburg, 180.569)

Plate 4: *Lekythos for Pheidestrate and Mnesagora*
(National Archaeological Museum, Athens, 1077)

Plate 5: *Grave Stele for Phanostrate*
(National Archaeological Museum, Athens, 993)

Plate 6: *Hygieia mit Sgensgestus/Hygieia with Healing Gesture*
(National Archaeological Museum, Athens, 1338)

Plate 7: *Heilung durch Asklepios/Asklepios Healing, Pireaus Museum*
(Bildarchiv Foto Marburg, 135.065)

Plate 8: *Hygieia Statuette*
(Musei Vaticani inv. 2066 neg. 88 VAT 985)

## Chapter 3

### PHARMAKA, MAGICA, HYGIEIA:
### WHEN REALITY AND STEREOTYPE MEET—WHAT LIES BEYOND?

...the strongest challenge from alternative healers came from practitioners of traditional women's medicine; the *Epid.* (*Epidemics*) contains only half the number of female as male case histories, which suggests women resorted to other forms of healing more often than men.[1]

Yet there still exist among a great number of the common people an established conviction that these phenomena are due to the compelling power of charms and magic herbs, and that the science of them is the one outstanding province of *women*. At any rate tales everywhere are widely current about Medea of Colchis and other sorceresses, especially Circe of Italy, who has even been enrolled as a divinity (Pliny, *Nat.* 25.5.9-10).

Evidently most of this popular-technical writing was composed for men, yet in literature and historical anecdote suspicions are regularly directed to women as food handlers who might add secret ingredients to affect men's eros.[2]

Chronology functioned as the foundation or the scaffolding on which the previous chapter was constructed. As the focus shifts now to consideration of women healing within the popular and folk sectors of ancient health care systems, chronology seems a less useful foundation as the areas of analysis prove much more fluid, the defining of edges is more difficult, and the data is much more scattered. As we seek to observe women healing and the genderization of healing within the popular and folk sectors, the material data, whether textual or artefactual, all but disappears and one is left reading between the cracks in male authored texts. This chapter does not, therefore, seek to be comprehensive but rather to make judicious choices of a limited number of texts which serve to represent the 'literature and historical anecdote'[3] that render more visible to us gendered healing in the folk and popular sectors of the health care system of the Graeco-Roman world.

Brief attention will be given initially to the popular sector in which healing took place within the home or the kinship group and hence rarely attracted the attention of historians, rhetoricians or literary artists. The focus will shift then to secular folk medicine that intersected with popular health care in that the gathering together and publication of remedies serviced those responsible for health care in the popular sector. Here, the lack of information about women's healing arts will be contrasted with the negative portrayal of women's knowledge of herbs, of charms and of magic. This will enable a demonstration of the complex genderization of this field of health care and also its intersection with the magico-religious aspect of healing. Religious healing associated with Hygieia and Asclepius will serve to focus this aspect of healing in the Graeco-Roman world and will be followed by an analysis of healing and its genderization within Hellenistic Judaism.

### Her Home and his Household

The *kyrios* or *paterfamilias* was the head of the Graeco-Roman household and therefore was responsible for all within that household. As with most other aspects of both the Greek and Roman societies, the household was the primary location for and foundational element of the health care system within those societies and it was here that most medical care took place, even that of the professionals as noted in the previous chapter. In the first analysis, therefore, the *paterfamilias* was responsible for the health care of the members of his household.[4] At its foundation, popular health care was gendered male, at least in the arena of official responsibility.

While the *paterfamilias* had responsibility for the health care, a question ought be raised regarding the administration of that care. Given the public functions which the *paterfamilias* had to perform and the construction of gender within the household, it could be assumed that much or at least some of the ongoing care of the sick in a household belonged to the women of the household, both slave and free.[5] The previous chapter demonstrated that some of these slaves may have been trained for the household by professional doctors. The free women of the household may have learned remedies and regimen of care from their own mothers or from folk healers or the trained midwives and/or physicians.

It was such midwives who crossed the sectors of the health care system. While Soranus advocated their professional training and inscriptions recognized and remembered their skills, many would have had little or no formal education but learned their skills from older midwives and developed expertise not only in the delivery of infants but also the care of women's health and health more generally. These women themselves belonged to households, whether poor or rich, and would have used their skills there. Should these skills have been employed solely in familial and kinship households then they could be said to have functioned within the popular sector of health care but where their skills were called upon beyond these areas, there was a more public recognition of their art and they could be categorized as folk healers. Many would have traversed at least these two sectors of the system and some even the three. Writers as diverse as Plato (fourth century BCE, Athens) and Soranus (second century CE, Ephesus) demonstrate the porous nature of contemporary etic categories in this instance. In listing the qualities of the midwife in the dialogue between Socrates and Thaetetus, Plato recognizes her use of drugs (φαρμάκια) and incantations for various aspects of her task – bringing on or allaying labour pains, making a difficult labour easier, and causing a miscarriage (*Theaet.* 149d). While Soranus' perfect midwife is not to be superstitious, nor take account of dreams, omens or other such magico-religious elements, their very mention by him in such a prescriptive text is an indicator that they were common within the midwife's healing arts (*Gyn.* 1.1.30-31).

The intersection between the folk and popular sector was also inhabited by the *paterfamilias* who needed to draw on a knowledge of herbs and other remedies for the care of his family and if necessary, as Stambaugh indicates, 'recite magic charms or offer prayers to such gods as Carna'.[6] Plutarch praises Cato the Elder as an exemplar of such knowledge when he says of him,

> (he) had compiled a book of recipes and used them for the diet or treatment of any members of his household who fell ill. He never made his patients fast, but allowed them to eat herbs and morsels of duck, pigeon, or hare. He maintained that this diet was light and thoroughly suitable for sick people, apart from the fact that it often produced nightmares, and he claimed that by following it he kept both himself and his family in perfect health (Plutarch, *Cat. Maj.* 23).

Cato himself includes some of these recipes in his work *On Agriculture*, and a fine example of his integration of folk and magico-religious medicine is found in paragraphs 156-60 where extensive medicinal uses of cabbage, recipes as Plutarch calls them, are followed by a cure for dislocation which involves a charm and chant. Just prior to this, Cato has advised a sacrifice before harvest accompanied by instructions which included the following:

> Make an offering of cakes to Janus, with these words: 'Father Janus, in offering these cakes, I humbly beg that thou wilt be gracious and merciful to me and my children, my house and my household' (Cato, *Agr.* 134).[7]

Elliott says of this work, couched as it is as instruction for his son, that it is 'a guide to domestic medicine for the use of Roman fathers of the Republic'.[8] Within the socio-cultural realm of healing, empirical knowledge of remedies, the use of magical formula such as chants and incantations and recourse to the gods intersect within the meaning-making system of the Graeco-Roman world. The other-than-human is valued as healing agent within the magico-religious context in a way that renders it valued and significant within the healing process and, like woman, it is healing and being healed.

In terms of genderization as an element of this socio-cultural aspect of healing, not only responsibility but knowledge and skill in relation to medical care in the popular sector of the health care system of Graeco-Roman antiquity is rendered male. This, however, may have been decentered in the popular imagination since much of the actual care, together with knowledge and skill, may have been located among females. There may, in some households, have been a sharing of these roles in a way that was constructing gender. Whether this was sufficient to decentre what we have seen as a developing and developed socio-cultural construct is impossible to determine from this vantage point.

### Pharmaka and Magica

One of the material elements of health care which was common to the three sectors, professional, folk and popular, but particularly the latter two, was *pharmaka* or drugs.[9] These were drawn from a variety of material sources – plant, animal and human substances with the most predominant being plants. The significance of these material elements not only for healing but also as a source of knowledge and understanding of the world is demonstrated by the detailed study of them within antiquity. Theophrastus of Eresus on Lesbos (c. 370-288 BCE) devoted almost sixty years of study to his multiple-volume works *History of Plants* and *Inquiry into Plants*. It is only in Book IX of the latter that he turns to a consideration of the use of roots and plants within folk medicine.[10] His work, therefore, serves as an excellent affirmation of the material, not in its usefulness to humanity but in its own integrity with its own ἱστορίαι or history according to the standards of Aristotle, interconnected with the human. Theophrastus' sources for his final book on herbal lore seem to differ from the empiricism of the rest of his work, demonstrating as Scarborough points out, the movement between folk, empirical/professional and magico-religious approaches to healing.

Book IX of Theophrastus' *Inquiry* from time to time employs 'facts' that come from folk medicine sources, generally labeled the ῥιζοτόμοι; these were a semiprofessional class of 'rootcutters' who had their own standards of knowledge and whose folklore about various roots and herbs mirror the deepest traditions of Greek 'inquiry' on several, simultaneously applied levels from pure 'magic' to utter rationalism.[11]

Two major successors of Theophrastus in Graeco-Roman pharmacy or herbal lore of the first century of the Common Era were Dioscorides of Anazarbus and Pliny the Elder of Rome. Dioscorides was a physician who served at least some time in the Roman legion and his *Materia Medica* records the results of his testing of drugs and herbs to determine effects on patients. His sources, therefore, tended to be his own results. Pliny the Elder, on the other hand, devotes at least ten books of his *Natural History* to the medicinal properties of plant, animal and human substances: '...there is no place where that holy Mother of all things did not distribute remedies for the healing of mankind [sic] so that even the very desert was made a drug store (*medicina*)' (Pliny, *Nat.* 24.1.1). His sources are many and varied. From time to time he acknowledges human sources both verbal and written as well as observation. We have already acknowledged his female sources – Sotira, Salpe, Lais and Elephantis – but these are far overshadowed by the male sources that characterize his text.[12] The same could be said for all the male authored texts of pharmacology in antiquity.[13]

Although the folk sector in which the use of *pharmaka* predominanted is supposedly non-professional and non-bureaucratic according to Kleinman,[14] and hence an area in which one would expect that women's healing could flourish, as it is represented in the literature, it is gendered male. On the other hand, there existed across the Greek and Roman worlds, a dominant literary trope of the woman who deals in herbs and drugs as well as chants and incantations that overpower the male taking away his control. In relation to this trope in particular, it will be shown that the boundaries between scientific knowledge, magic, religion and the world of the divine and the human blur.

In Homer's *Odyssey*, Circe who is called 'the fair-tressed goddess' (Θεᾶς) uses evil drugs (κακὰ φάρμακα) to bewitch the mountain wolves and lions who guard her house and baneful drugs (φάρμακα λύγρα) to cause Odysseus' companions to forget their native land and to turn them into swine. It is only the potent herb (φάρμακον ἐσθλὸν) which the gods call Moly (μῶλυ) and which was given to Odysseus by Hermes that enabled him to rescue his companions from their fate and to eventually depart Circe's realm with all his crew unharmed (*Od.* 10.210-575). Circe, who inhabits a space between the divine and human realms, is represented in relation to *pharmaka*, which are evil or baneful, because of the control they give her over men. Hermes' power, on the other hand, and the drug which he gives to Odysseus are represented favourably because of the power it gives to men in league with the male gods to whom nothing is impossible (Θεοὶ δέ τε πάντα δύνανται).[15]

A much more favourable impression of female knowledge of drugs within Homer's writing was seen in the previous chapter in relation to Agamede, Polydama and Helen who each had knowledge of the use of drugs.[16] It was suggested there, however, that Helen's skill in mixing drugs that could control men's minds and emotions may have been a cause of male fear and it can now be recognized that this tradition belonged to the same literary trope visible in the story of Circe. Women's knowledge of drug lore, a power shared with divine figures, is a source of fear among men and hence these women are portrayed stereotypically. As we explore this literary trope further, however, the question will need to be raised as to women's actual knowledge and skill in the pharmacological arena of folk medicine that might have given rise to the literary trope. I find it of interest, in the face of the virtual silence of the data in respect of women's actual engagement in folk medicine, that Scarborough needs to continue to emphasize that knowledge of herbs and drugs was not the provenance of women only but that men shared this knowledge.[17] Perhaps he is seeking to correct the mythology constructed by the male literary trope. The result, however, is to emphasize even further the male control of pharmacology and folk medicine and augment the invisibility of women in an area in which their practice may have been significant.

Literature abounds which could demonstrate the history of the literary trope of the dangerous sorceress whose knowledge of drugs and other magical powers threatens man's very life and potency, particularly sexual potency. I will illustrate by way of three examples – Seneca's tragedy *Medea*, Petronius' *Satyricon* and Apuleius' *Metamorphoses*.

The male characterization of Medea is typified in the words of Creon:

> Thou, thou contriver of wickedness, who combinest woman's wanton recklessness and man's strength, with no thought of reputation, away! Purge my kingdom and take thy deadly herbs with thee; free the citizens from fear; abiding in some other land, harry the gods (*Med.* 266-71).

This woman's knowledge of 'deadly herbs' is equated with 'woman's wanton recklessness'. Indeed, Medea does use her knowledge of both drugs and magic for death rather than life – death of her two sons and of Creon and his daughter Creusa as a punishment for Jason's infidelity. Her nurse decries Medea's assembling of 'her evil store of baleful herbs' (707), 'all plants that bloom with deadly flower, and all whose juices breed cause of death in their twisted roots – all these she handles' (718–20). The link with magical power is made in the nurse's final words in this part of the tragedy – 'She adds to her poisons words, no less fearsome than they' (737–38). Medea's own incantation and her recitation of the powers she has received from Hecate, whom she says has been 'summoned by my sacred rites' (750), demonstrate the intersection of religious and magical powers (752– 842). In the hands of this 'maenad borne headlong by mad passion', in whom 'anger and love have joined cause' (848, 867–68), the powers of the divine Hecate, the triple-faced goddess who was a source of blessing but also of sorcery, were manifest. Divine and human females could together become the source of man's greatest woes just as Hermes and Odysseus in Homer could join forces to overcome such power. Finally, within the trope, Medea characterizes the very worst of female power – the mother who could even slay her own sons to avenge her husband's infidelity.

In Seneca's tragedy the literary trope was played out to its extreme. One of man's greatest fears was realized, knowledge of herbs and magico-religious rites as a source of female power posed a profound threat to man's sexual freedom and to his male honour. That which could heal and save life could, in the hands of the feared sorceress, also destroy it. The material of the Earth or *pharmaka* was rendered fearful and dangerous as was the woman in whose hands it was made potent.

Petronius' *Satyricon* satirizes such fear more explicitly by characterizing Encolpius impotent toward the end of the literary piece. Chrysis, maid of Circe with whom Encolpius fails in intercourse, explains his condition thus: 'These things often happen, especially in this town, where the women can even draw down the moon from the sky' (*Satyricon* 129). Women with access to magical powers are the cause of such loss of male power. But it is such women who can also restore man's sexual power. Proselenos, a sorceress, uses chant and spell while Oenothea, priestess of Priapus, the god of procreation, prepares a mixture of plant and animal substance. The description of Oenothea's hut characterizes her as wise in folk medicine: 'the wall round was stuffed with light chaff and ready-to-hand clay; on it hung rows of rude nails and slim stalks of green rushes. Besides this, the little cottage roofed with smoky beams preserved their goods, the mellow service-berries hung entwined in fragrant wreaths, and dried savory and bunches of raisins...' (*Satyricon* 135). Oenothea's healing powers are proclaimed in her own words: 'I am the only woman alive who knows how to cure that disease' (134). Both Proselenos and Oenothea are, however, stereotyped through the eyes of Encolpius. Proselonos is described as an 'old woman in ugly black clothes with her hair down' (134) and Oenothea too as 'old woman' and her mixing of drugs as strange (135). The power of these female healers and the power of the materials which work healing at their hands, even their ability to heal one of the most feared male condition, namely impotence, is stereotyped in this work and hence contributes to the development of this literary trope. Although presented negatively in the text, these women are co-agents with the other-than-human, presenting a different paradigm to that of the master when read from the underside. They occupy the boundary space where the cosmic, that which has been separated from the human, can cross over as can the human to provide a new pastiche.

In the story of Aristomenes which opens the first book of Apuleius' *Metamorphoses*, Socrates describes Meroe, the innkeeper, as a witch (*saga*) with supernatural power (*divini potens*) that can lower the sky and suspend the earth, solidify fountains and dissolve mountains, raise up ghosts and bring down gods, darken the stars and light up Tartarus itself' (1.8).[18] She uses such power against any of her lovers whom she deems to have misbehaved, changing them into animal shapes (1.9) and Socrates, in particular, she kills by driving a sword into his neck and drawing out his heart (1.12). As the story progresses, the reader meets a number of such women of power but in particular Pamphile, the wife of Lucius' host, Milo, in Hypata, Thessaly. Lucius' aunt, Byrrhena, calls her 'witch of the first order' (*Maga primi* – 2.5). Like Meroe, she can 'drown all the light of the starry heavens in the depths of hell and plunge it into primeval Chaos' by means of 'sepulchral incantation and by breathing on twigs and pebbles and stuff of that sort' (2.5). Her power too seeks to control men's sexual desires and satisfactions: 'She sows her seductions, attacks his soul, and binds him with the everlasting shackles of passionate love. If any do not respond and become cheap in her eyes by their show of repugnance, she transforms them on the spot into rocks or sheep or any other sort of animal; some, however, she completely annihilates' (2.5). In this trope, woman stands with the cosmic in a paradigmatic way that renders both dangerous. Read against the grain, however, such stories point to the power in the co-agency of the human and the other-than-human, woman and Earth, in undermining the master paradigm at the very point at which it is being intensified.

Lucius' curiosity led him to spy on Pamphile's magic when she was performing a metamorphosis, becoming a bird so that she could fly to her desired lover. Lucius coaxed Photis, Pamphile's maid, to assist him in a similar metamorphosis but either by fault or design, Lucius was changed into an ass rather than the bird he had desired. Much of the rest of the story traces his wanderings as an ass in the hands of cruel Fortune. Stories of women of power, both divine and human, are scattered throughout the account of Lucius' wanderings until he is finally rescued from his fate by Isis into whose rites he becomes initiated. The extravagant stories of women's divine, magical and medicinal powers and their control over men's lives are set over against the religion of Isis who is proclaimed 'holy and eternal saviour of mankind [sic]' and who is praised for her powers which are similar to but exceed those of the women of power above:

> ...you protect men [sic] on sea and land, and you drive away the storm-winds of life and stretch forth your rescuing hand, with which you unwind the threads of the Fates even when they are inextricably twisted, you calm the storms of Fortune, and you repress harmful motions of the stars. The spirits above revered you, the spirits below pay you homage. You rotate the earth, light the sun, rule the universe and tread Tartarus beneath your heel... (11.25).

It would seem that the religion of Isis, a healing deity and 'saviour' of humankind as Lucius called her, and the cosmic and transformative power attributed to her were being contrasted with the magical and medicinal powers of women which gave them control over men's sexuality to their downfall. The women with such powers are stereotyped and rendered larger than life in Lucius' tale. In the religion of Isis, Lucius finds serenity and a healing of all his painful wanderings. This may have well served a world in which magic was periodically outlawed[19] and in which the religion of Isis was attracting new adherents in a way similar to early Christianity.[20] Before exploring further the two paths which Apuleius opens up for us – that of magical healing powers, one of which was the curing of male lovesickness by bewitching the desired one; and that of religious healing in the hands of healing deities – we need to return briefly to the question of women's engagement in folk medicine, particularly the use of herbs and other *pharmaka*.

The difficulty of obtaining data in the area of secular folk medicine belongs not only to women's healing but to both male and female healing in this arena. Richard Gordon says of it:

> But whereas purifiers, exorcists and sorcerers could, if required, provide an account of the healing process because they had explicit, though very diverse, models of the cause of specific disorders acknowledged in their nosology...no such account seems to have existed for many disorders dealt with by root-cutters and diviner-healers. At this level of folk-medical practice, the nature of disorders and of the healing process was almost entirely implicit.[21]

A second factor, particularly pertaining in the later Hellenistic era and into Roman imperial times, was that the ascendency and socio-cultural affirmation of scientific medicine as well as scientific investigation and empiricism[22] tended to devalue, at least in the public arena of record keeping and publication, the art or *technê* of folk practitioners.[23] Pliny the Elder was even aware of this in his own day as he could write:

> ...the reason why more herbs are not familiar is because experience of them is confined to illiterate country-folk, who form the only class living among them; moreover nobody cares to look for them when crowds of medical men are to be met everywhere (*Nat.* 25.6.16).

In relation to women folk practitioners as with their male counterparts, the words of Richard Gordon are most appropriate: '[i]t is a commonplace that the social basis of healing is the establishment of the practitioner's authority to intervene'.[24] Women healing within the secular folk sector would have had to establish their authority by attention to aspects appropriate to the healing event in which they were engaged – the careful collection and preparation of their herbs which contributed to the practical aspect of the healing event and their appeal to knowledge and use of ritual, however simple, as central to the social aspect of healing. The first required careful attention to the material and the second to the socio-cultural and both male and female healers were, therefore, associated with both the material and the social-cultural in a way which contravened what was being established by the philosophical and literary tradition which associated male with culture and female with nature.

Two developments in folk medicine may also have affected female folk practitioners. One has already been indicated above, namely the incorporation of folk medicine into written treatises, especially those of professional healers like Dioscorides, Soranus and Galen.[25] As these became available, therefore, both to the professionals and also to self-help or popular healers within the household, one wonders what became of both the art and trade of the female wise women, herbalists and root-cutters. Did they continue to develop their knowledge and skill and to whom did they offer healing? How, too, was their source of income affected by the much broader availability of their particular knowledge and art with its accompanying healing power and authority? A second trend is noted by Gordon, namely, the tendency of the formula to dominate the healing event, especially among those who were able to write.[26] Since literacy was more available to men than women and was singularly unavailable to poor illiterate women wise in the healing arts, the question arises as to the effect of this development on female folk healers and their very livelihood as more and more professional and popular healers, particularly the male heads of households, had direct access to their art and knowledge.

One of the things noticeably absent from the data available to us in relation to secular folk medicine is the experience of the patient and indicators of the clinical reality. The material focus is on the plants or herbs, their natural environment and the manner in which they should be collected. The positive evaluation of this physical realm of healing and its association with male and female folk healers may have functioned tensively in relation to the master paradigm developing within the Western philosophical tradition and being augmented by the emergence of professional medicine and its world-view or world construction. One learns little of the construction of the body needing healing except that the human body can itself produce healing substances and as participant in the other-than-human world can be both harmed and healed by products from that world.[27] The intersection between the divine and human worlds and the power of human word and action to interact with these worlds, often in conjunction with divine beings and for the sake of healing, is the realm of the magico-religious arena of folk medicine and it is to a consideration of this that we now turn.

The above consideration of *pharmaka* demonstrated the difficulty of separating secular and magico-religious healing since they clearly intersected within both the life-experience as well as world-construction of women and men of antiquity. That attempts were made even within that age to distinguish and even to keep separate the three worlds of empirical or scientific medicine, folk healing by way of *pharmaka* or herbal lore, and magico-religious healing is evidenced in both the Hippocratic Corpus as well as the work of Pliny the Elder to draw on just two examples.

The Hippocratics devote a small treatise to what is called the sacred disease, which begins with the claim in relation to the disease:

> It is not, in my opinion, any more divine or more sacred than other diseases, but has a natural cause, and its supposed divine origin is due to men's inexperience, and to their wonder at its peculiar character (*Morb. sacr.* 1.2-6).

The author goes on to demonstrate that those naming it such disprove its divinity by the 'facile method of healing which they adopt' and citing under these methods 'purifications and incantations' (1.8-10). A little later, the author lists a number of groups of healers whom he disparages, setting their approaches over against his own empirical approach:

> My own view is that those who first attributed a sacred character to this malady were like the magicians, purifiers, charlatans and quacks of our own

day, men who claim great piety and superior knowledge. Being at a loss,
and having no treatment which would help, they concealed and sheltered
themselves behind superstition, and called this illness sacred, in order that
their utter ignorance might not be manifest (*Morb. sacr.* 2.1-10).

The Hippocratic perspective on the disease is that 'it has the same nature
as other diseases, and the cause that gives rise to individual diseases. It is
also curable, no less than other illnesses, unless by long lapse of time it be
so ingrained as to be more powerful than the remedies that are applied'
(*Morb. sacr.* 5.1-7).

Pliny, on the other hand, severely critiqued professional medicine as
well as magic (*Nat.* 29. 5.11; 29.7.14 and *Nat.* 30 1.1-2). On the other hand,
however, he proffers a religious explanation of the very bounteousness of
the earth:

> Without a doubt even the bounteousness of nature herself might seem to
> have been surpassed by them [the men of old] in this way if the discoveries
> had been the result of human endeavour. But as it is, it is clear that this
> bounteousness has been the work of the gods, or at least due to their inspi-
> ration, even when the actual discoverer was a man, and that the same
> Mother of all things both produced the herbs and made them known to us.
> This is the greatest miracle of life [*vitae miraculo maiore*], if we care to
> admit the truth (*Nat.* 27.1.1-3).

Later of a particular remedy he says:

> ...surely nobody doubts that this remedy has been found by Chance [casu]
> and that on every occasion it is even today a new find... This Chance [causus],
> therefore, this is that great deity who has made most of the discoveries that
> enrich our life, this is the name of him by whom is meant she who is at once
> the Mother and the Mistress of all creation (*Nat.* 27.2.8).

Pliny moves both critically and affirmatively between the worlds of secular,
magical and religious folk healing.[28] His affirmation of the divine engagement with healing contrasts with the Hippocratic world of meaning. A
feminist ecological hermeneutic recognizes and seeks to reclaim the interactive worlds of divine, human and other-than-human healing that is
visible in his work as a challenge to the segregation of these worlds in
many contemporary constructions of healing and health care. This perspective will also lead to a renewed critique of his genderizing of divine
bounty in giving the gifts which promote healing and life as female. This
has the danger of divinizing the master paradigm's association of the
female with nature or the other-than-human, the male with human culture
and its ongoing transformation. On the other hand, however, gendering
the divine world of healing as female as well as linking it to the other-than-

human points to the possibility of strands of resistance to the gender construction of healing in antiquity but this is a complex issue which will require further consideration in the latter part of this chapter.

Contemporary scholarship also recognizes the difficulty of clearly defining the boundaries between magic, religion and empirical science in the world of antiquity. This is a complex discussion beyond the scope of this work but suffice it to acknowledge here that there has been a very significant shift in this area of research across the past century as detailed in the work of David Aune.[29] The consensus at present seems to be the heterogeneous nature of the relationships as demonstrated in these words of Peter Schäfer and Hans Kippenberg in the introduction to their work *Envisioning Magic.*

> Magic essentially belongs to religion (and, indeed, language), and any attempt to separate one from the other turns religion into bloodless spirituality and magic into an uncontrollable and destructive force (and language into lifeless convention). There is no evolution from one direction towards the other, not within one particular religion and even less so from the higher point of view of the history of humankind, but a constant and dynamic struggle of different forces within religion.[30]

Major sources for the study of magical healing in antiquity are the Greek Magical Papyri. The number of texts in which healing is sought are quite miniscule in relation to the corpus as a whole and those in relation to women healing are even fewer with the unarticulated assumption in the texts that the practitioner is male. The patient constructed in the papyri, on the other hand, seems to be both male and female. While a study of these papyri in search of women healing gives a fascinating insight into this world of magic, it does not contribute new insights into the gendered construction of healing and so I turn now to the religious world of healing characterized in Hygieia and Asclepius.

### Religious Healing

#### Hygieia and Asclepius

> I swear by Apollo Physician, and Asclepius, Hygieia and Panacae and by all the Gods and Goddesses...[31]

A central element of the health care systems of Hellenistic Greece and Rome was the Asclepieion which functioned as a symbol of the union of religion and health in the Greek health care system.[32] This temple complex honouring Asclepius, the emerging god of healing, developed as a place of pilgrimage for supplicants who travelled to sleep in the *abaton* attached to the temple in the hope that they would be visited by Asclepius and be healed. This aspect of ancient healing has received vast scholarly attention that I will not try to repeat in this section; nor will I summarize the wealth of that scholarship as that, in itself, would be a major task. Rather, I will focus on women healing and the accounts of their healing in the Asclepieia and the gendering of divine healing as glimpsed in the short excerpt of the Hippocratic Oath quoted above. In this section and the next in which healing in ancient Israel is explored, the factor which will receive much more specific study is the widespread understanding in antiquity that human healing was effected by relationship with divine figures whose power could be sought and obtained by way of certain rituals as is the case in the magical papyri. Such beliefs had developed prior to the rise of professional medicine as seen in Chapter Two and continued to develop alongside of it through the centuries being studied in this work. This is reflected in these words of Robert Garland:

> The growth in the cult of Asklepios at the beginning of the fifth century exactly parallels the growth of a tradition of systematic medical inquiry in the Greek world. Now for the first time investigations were being conducted into the causes and treatments of disease. Now, too, attempts were being made to elevate medicine from mere *magganeia* or magic to the status of a *technê* or rational discipline. The reason why Asklepios and medical science make a simultaneous appearance is due wholly to their complementarity. Sickness and its cure were now being identified for the first time as legitimate and self-contained areas of professional and divine concern.[33]

Not surprisingly, this aspect of the health care system like those already examined earlier in this work bears the mark of the construction of gender operative in the worlds of Greece and Rome. It is also characterized by the intersection of the divine, the human and the other-than-human since Asclepieia were often constructed in locations where spring water, clear air and other natural conditions favourable to health were operative. Healing in such a context will be studied for its nuanced qualities rather than simply another instance of hierarchal dualism.

There is general agreement that one of the earliest Asclepieia was that of Epidauros with some of its foundational structures dating to the fifth century BCE.[34] An extensive rebuilding project in the middle of the fourth century left the city with a Temple, a Tholos or *Thymele*, and an *Abaton*. At this site, toward the end of the nineteenth century, archaeologist Panayotis Kavvadias found fragments of a number of stelae containing Iamata-inscriptions or narrative accounts of healing. It seems that these stelae may have stood on a base along the walls of the *abaton*, the place where supplicants slept during the night to be visited by Asclepius.[35] These stelae were of stone approximately 170 cm high, 76 cm wide and around 14 cm thick and once again the durability of the stone over twenty-five centuries has enabled us to encounter the stories of healing it preserves.

The stelae discovered at the Epidaurian Asclepieion differ from the dedicatory inventories of the Athenian Asclepieion[36] in that they contain tales or accounts of healing as do the gospels.[37] I will interrupt the consideration of the Iamata-inscriptions briefly to note the gendering of the Athenian inventories. Sara Aleshire provides the following data:

> Considering only those dedications where the sex of the dedicant can be determined, the proportion of women to men for all inventories is 51.39 per cent to 45.82 per cent, with dedications made by couples, by two men or two women, and by the Athenian demos making up the remaining 2.79 per cent. Outside Inventory V the discrepancy is more striking, with women responsible for 54.96 per cent of the dedications, while men were responsible for no more than 42.55 per cent (2.48 per cent others). In Inventory V the numbers are more nearly equal, with 49.41 per cent women, 47.64 per cent men, 2.95 per cent others.[38]

She further nuances these findings by noting the differences during certain priesthoods but finds it more difficult to give explanations for this. A more significant nuance, however, is in relation to the dedications with women offering more anatomical ex votos and men more coins, an outcome, no doubt, of women having less access to coinage than men. From the point of view of this study, however, it is significant that only men dedicate medical instruments, which would be in keeping with the small number of professional medical women and also the public/private differentiation of this professional healing which has been hinted at earlier while being difficult to substantiate.

What is significant in relation to this data is that women were participants in the cult of Asclepius and the healings in the Athenian temple equally with men. This was a religious activity in the public arena and not one particular to women only.[39] The Athenian Asclepieion may have been used predominantly by Athenians and hence the women supplicants would not have had to travel long distances in public which may be one explanation for their numbers being equivalent to the men.[40] We have seen also that some of the earliest evidence of women healing emerges around the time of the development of the Athenian Asclepieion (mid-fourth to the end of the third century BCE). Neither of these possibilities seems, however, to adequately explain the equal access of women to the new temple and healing cult. The dedications, nevertheless, are to honour the divine healer and to seek the continuance of healing, a concern for women as well as men in a time when wellbeing was precarious.

Returning to a consideration of the Epidaurian inscriptions, we find that in considering Stele A and Stele B at Epidauros, the two of the four stelae of Iamata-inscriptions which escaped severe damage, we can determine that Stele A recounts three healings of women out of twenty (15%); and Stele B contains eight of twenty-three (34.4%). These percentages are quite different to those of the Athenian Asclepieion. LiDonnici discusses the tradition history of the tales whose earliest sources may have been votives, some without names and then with the name of the one healed. The Athenian inventories represent an intermediate stage before the redactional stages of the explanatory tales by the priests of the temples and they did not develop to this next stage according to the evidence available to us. The redactional activity at Epidauros points to a process in which the biblical scholar recognizes similarities with the tradition history of the gospels even before LiDonnici draws attention to this.[41]

One aspect of the process that is readily visible in a gender analysis is the drop in the percentage of women between the Athenian inventories and the Epidaurian tales. One questions whether women's greater exclusion from literary resources and the control of the narratives in their final composition phase predominantly by the priests of the temple, who seem to have been all male, account for the smaller percentage in literary tales of women healed. The votive offerings may reflect more realistically women's actual participation. It should also be noted that in this process women's perspectives that may have been more visible on their dedicatory votives become obscured within the confines of male storytelling.

Another factor accounting for the fall in the representation of women in the Iamata-inscriptions may have been that supplicants at the Epidaurian Asclepieion came from towns throughout Greece. Of the eleven stories of women healing on Stelae A and B, ten come from towns and cities other than Epidauros, one, Ambrosia, coming from Athens. This phenomena of journeying to Epidauros, which applies to men as well as women, is most probably explained by the centrality of the Epidaurian sanctuary but it may also give rise to fewer women making arduous journeys over long periods of times away from the care of house and family, a role that tended to control women's lives in Greece in this late Classical, early Hellenistic period.

Examining the eleven Epidaurian women's healing represented in the narratives contained on the Stelae and using Kleinman's Criteria of Analysis,[42] some of the following conclusions can be drawn. First, the setting is institutional, in the *abaton*, connected to the sacred area of the temple by ritual and location. Even though seven of the eleven healings of women are associated with pregnancy and birth, none of the births takes place in the temple, a sacred space not to be polluted by birth or death. This is made explicit in A1 (1) and A2 (2), the stories of Kleo and Ithmonika of Pellene.[43] In A1 the inscription says of Kleo that '[a]s soon as she left it [the abaton] and was outside the sacred area, she gave birth to a son...' The account given of Ithmonika's healing concludes with the statement that she 'rushed out of the Abaton, and as soon as she was outside the sacred area, gave birth to a daughter'. Such accounts not only highlight the healing that takes place but also the sanctity of the abaton as a place of healing. They reveal also attitudes to the potency of life and death that may have been feared. There is a tension here between different healing powers, some of which seem to be able to be controlled in the religious context but others not so. It points to the multi-dimensional nature of healing in antiquity as today.

The *characteristics of the interpersonal interaction* are varied in these accounts. In all but one account (B5 [25], that of Sostrata, a woman of Pherae who suffered from a false pregnancy), the woman supplicant enters into the healing process alone. Only Sostrata, 'borne entirely on a litter', was carried into the temple by others.[44] All of the supplicants are identified in relation to their location and not in terms of their relationship with male family members, which is quite extraordinary at this time.[45] We noted earlier that most of the professional women healers are identified in keeping with the gender constructions, 'wife of' or 'daughter of'. It seems, however, that it is not human gender constructions that are important in these narratives but rather the individual supplicant in relation to the god Asclepius and the healing which takes place in the encounter. In a similar manner, there is no indication of class or ethnic distinctions either. The woman comes, identified by her illness.

The accounts are all episodic and the relationship is formal according to the etiquette of the temple for both women and men. There are variations in wording but the pattern is that of sleeping in the Abaton, dreaming or seeing a vision, and the phrase 'it seems to her that' (ἐδόκει), followed by the experience of encounter with Asclepius or some other process of healing. In this way, the healing seems to be divorced from the rest of the woman's life and belongs to this sacred space. The pattern is similar for women and men and so there is no gender distinction in this process of healing. The attitude of the supplicant is not made explicit but it is assumed in the action of coming to the Temple. There is a fascinating exception to this in A4 (4), the account of Ambrosia of Athens. She comes as a supplicant, blind in one eye according to the narrative, but as she walks around the sanctuary, 'she ridiculed some of the cures as being unlikely and impossible, the lame and the blind becoming well from only seeing a dream'. Her scepticism is not punished by a refusal of healing; but rather, when she encounters the god in a dream or vision,[46] she is in-structed to 'pay a fee by dedicating a silver pig in the sanctuary as a memorial of her ignorance'. Her healing is then effected.

The *idiom of communication* of healing in these narratives takes place in a borderland space between the somatic and the spiritual. The accounts make clear that it is the power of the god, Asclepius, which effects healing of women and men but there are also dreams or visions of processes which are reminiscent of emerging professional medicine. In Ambrosia's vision, for instance, the god cuts out her sick eye and pours φαρμ[ακόν], a medicine or drug, over it. This is the same φάρμακόν used by a wide range of health care workers in the professional and the secular folk areas as well as in popular healing in homes away from the public scrutiny.[47]

The *clinical reality* structured into the Iamata-inscriptions draws on the sacred nature of the supplicant-deity relationship. It is the implicit faith in the power of Asclepius to heal that initiates the process and this intersects with the desire of the deity to heal. This serves the ideological purpose of the narratives on the walls of the Abaton, namely to encourage faith that enables healing. That the reputation of the deity is at stake in these accounts is evident in B3 (23) in which Aristagora of Troesen is treated by the 'sons of the god' in her dream in the temple in Troezen. They are unable to put back her head after they cut it off for treatment and it is only the next evening that Aristagora sees in a vision Asclepius come from Epidauros to effect her cure which includes the restoration of her head to her neck. It is not only the reputation of Asclepius but also of Epidauros which is at stake in these accounts.

In terms of the culturally legitimated illness label given to the eleven women in the Imata-inscriptions, seven are in relation to pregnancy or offspring which is very gender specific.[48] The remaining four labels are blindness (A4 [4]), dropsy (B1 [21]), worm in the belly (B3 [23]); and pain in the stomach and burning with fever (B 21 [41]). Women are not labelled ill with paralysis (A15 [15]; B17 [37] and B18 [38]) or lameness (B15 [35]; A16 [16]), both of which affect male movement in the public arena but they, like men, are blind. The manipulated new cultural label given the supplicant following healing generally relates to wellness (ὑγιής) and applies equally to women or men. Kleo is made well (ἔθηκε ὑγιῆ); Ambro-sia leaves well (ὑγιὴς ἐγένετο) and Aristagora became well as did Erasippa from Kaphyiai (ὑγ[ι][ὴ]ς ἐγένετο). In some instances the new label is a reversal of the illness or a granting of the offspring desired in the case of the women (B14 [34]; B19 [39]).

Within the health care system of Hellenistic Greece and emerging imperial Rome, there developed a strong tradition of divine healing associated with the male deity, Asclepius. It was not, however, completely distinct or separate from the developing professional tradition nor the magical which likewise combined technique with divine supplication. In this context, however, women are supplicants only in a world of a prevailing male divine healer and male priests of the temples. The only subversion of this world construction and its genderization is that rendered by Hygieia in particular and Isis more generally in that healing is but one of her many attributes.[49] It is to an exploration of Hygieia that we now turn.

Hygieia, daughter of Asclepius,[50] is the most widely attested family member in inscriptions, literature, coins and statuary apart from Asclepius himself.[51] Pausanius records that at Epidauros, the Roman senator Antonius built a temple (ναόν) to Hygieia (*Descr.* 2.27.6) and that at Boeae there was a 'not insignificant sanctuary' (ἱερόν) of Asclepius and Hygieia (*Descr.* 3.22.13). Stone again has come to our aid and statues of Hygieia abound, some noted by Pausanius (at Athens in *Descr.* 1.23.4; ἀγάλματα from Aegium in *Descr.* 7.23.7-8; and an ἄγαλμα at Gortys in *Descr* 7.28.1, at Tegea, *Descr.* 7.47.1, at Corinth *Descr.* 2.4.5, and at Olympia, *Descr.* 5.20.3). While the literature tends to connect Hygieia with Asclepius as does the statuary noted by Pausanius,[52] her statues may also have stood alone throughout the Graeco-Roman world but unfortunately a lack of inscriptional material prevents us from access to whatever religious practices in relation to healing were associated directly with Hygieia.[53] We have no evidence of any women physicians, whose presence we know from the inscriptions examined in Chapter Two, being associated with the temples or cult of Hygieia as the male physicians were associated with Asclepius.

Hygieia appears independently of Asclepius in the early-fifth century BCE in Athens where she is associated with Athena as Athena Hygieia on the acropolis. Plutarch records the story of Perikles' healing of an injured workman at the instructions of Athena Hygieia and his dedicating an altar to her on the south-east corner of the Propylaia.[54] Aleshire notes, however, that after the arrival of Asclepius in Athens in 420 BCE, Hygieia does not appear independent of him until the third century BCE.[55] There is very little inscriptional evidence that can give us clues into the function performed by Hygieia in the health care system of Hellenistic Greece and the Roman empire but on one of two agalmata found in Epidauros, she is claimed as

ΣΩΤΕΙΡΗ or Saviour as was Asclepius.[56] She stands with Asclepius (see Plate 6 where she extends her hand in a healing gesture) or at times behind him (Plate 7) and is represented, as he is, with a snake and often too with a platter from which she seems to feed the snake (Plate 8).[57]

In this study on gender and healing, one of the significant aspects for consideration is the gendering of the representation of divine healing in the context of the world of human healing which we have outlined above. This is a complex area of consideration as many scholars have indicated.[58] Goodison and Morris make clear an area of contention when they say that '(t)he relationship between divinity and society…emerges as an important but complex theme'.[59] Tikva Frymer-Kensky in her careful study of the gradual demise of the goddess in ancient Sumeria nuances the function of representations of the divine in relation to human culture. She notes that '(w)hen modelling is done by the divine, the modelling does not simply illustrate; it authorizes and approves what it models'.[60] The subtle shifts, she suggests, happened over a long period of time and almost imperceptibly as the male divine figures replaced the female or took precedence over them so that the female divinities in pairs like Asclepius and Hygieia were the less dominant in the religious imagination and tradition than the males.

This is evident in the fact that while the votive-offerings depicting Hygieia are numerous,[61] there are no narratives of healing found in the vicinity of the temples or sanctuaries dedicated to her. She is greeted in prayer together with Asclepius in Terentius, *Hecyra*, 3.2.337-38,[62] as well as having the sixty-eighth Orphic Hymn dedicated to her as is the sixty-seventh to Asclepius. In this hymn, she is greeted as 'Blessed Hygieia, mother of all, bringer of prosperity'.[63] The hymnist prays that Hygieia will 'vanish the diseases that afflict men' and 'keep away the accursed distress of harsh disease'.[64] In the Hellenistic period into the early Roman Empire, Hygieia stands with Asclepius as religion and medicine intersect. There seems to be no specific relationship between the representation of divine healing as female and the emergence of a significant number of women for whom inscriptions are preserved and who function as healing professionals. These women healing are not associated with the sanctuaries of Hygieia nor specifically with prayer to her. Whether women healing in the folk sector used some of the small reliefs of Hygieia or offered prayers or incantations to her is equally unknown.

The presence of Hygieia may, however, have both modeled and authorized female healing in very subtle ways. Her presence provides a distinct modeling of women healing in the divine realm at the same time that professional women emerged in the public arena even though it does not seem to be directly connected with these women. There were numerous social and cultural factors that enabled women to become more active in a range of public professions in the late Hellenistic and early Roman period. The presence of Hygieia in the increasingly popular realm of religious healing along with other sanctioning processes may have authorized, in subtle ways, healing women's cultural participation. Perhaps the constant presence of Hygieia with Asclepius is one way in which we might account for the equal number of women dedicants as men at the Athenian Asclepieion as well as the significant number of women who frequented Epidauros at least and, even though narrative records are not available to us, other shrines such as Cos, Pergamum, Olympia, and Corinth. Compton says in this regard that 'like other male-female deity pairings', the presence of Hygieia with Asclepius may have made the sanctuaries 'more approachable for women seeking divine aid'.[65] That the first known supplicant of Hygieia was male, Perikles, and that women dedicants and women healed acknowledge Asclepius' healing power warns us, though, to avoid too static a gender distinction within the divine-human nexus of healing.

Hygieia, like Asclepius, pointed the religious imagination to the healing power represented in the material world as she was repeatedly accompanied by the snake as symbol of regenerated or restored life as was Asclepius. Her representations have also been found in thermal pools and nymphaeum, especially during the Roman period,[66] pointing to the significance of hygiene that is a product of the material world as the Hippocratics demonstrated in their regimen which included right foods, water, and air. Both Sobel[67] and Compton[68] highlight what they think might have been a particular role which Hygieia played in the health care system along with that of healer, namely, the preserver of health, the one who causes diseases to vanish and keeps them away. She may have been the particular patron of those who were healthy who participated in the healing cult. The religion of Asclepius and the presence of Hygieia, the gendered pair of divine healers, emerged at a time when female and male healers were becoming more numerous in the human realm. The temples and shrines of this divine pair became centres of healing and preservation of health. Religion and health intersected in the Graeco-Roman world in new ways so that Compton can conclude that 'healthcare in the Asklepieion was undoubtedly a numinous, highly ritualistic, and spiritual phenomenon, superimposed upon the constructs of healing and health'.[69]

This was paralleled in that same world by the presence and function of another divine pair, Serapis and Isis. Their temples were places of incubation and healing[70] and Isis, in particular, was designated a restorer of life. Neither, however, were associated only with healing but with many other divine functions.[71] Since, therefore, more detailed and specific study of Isis and healing does not promise to yield more than we have claimed in relation to Hygieia, I turn now to women healing within the biblical tradition.[72]

### Women Healing in Biblical Judaism

There is a paucity of material on which to draw any conclusions in relation to women's participation in the health care system in Israel.[73] It is generally agreed that healing was depicted as the exclusive work of Israel's God or what Seybold and Mueller call 'Yahweh's healing monopoly',[74] with the key illustrative text being Exod. 15.26: He [God] said, 'If you will listen carefully to the voice of the Lord your God, and do what is right in his sight, and give heed to his commandments and keep all his statutes, I will not bring upon you any of the diseases that I brought upon the Egyptians; for *I am the Lord who heals you* (ὁ ἰώμενός σε)'.[75] As with Apollo, as seen in the early Greek tradition, so too the claim is made for Israel's God, 'I kill and I make alive; I wound and I heal/κἀγὼ ἰάσομαι' (Deut. 32.39; see also Gen. 20.17; Num. 12.13; Job 5.18; Isa. 19.22, 57.18; Jer. 30.17, 33.6).[76] Life and death, health and illness are all in the hands of the divine with religion providing the explanation for the causes of illnesses and the options available to patients. Israel, however, does not seem to have developed the complex health care system that we have seen in Hellenistic Greece and the early Roman Empire.

Hector Avalos critiques Seybold's analysis, claiming that 'medical anthropology…has helped us to become aware of the variety of consultation options that were available in ancient health care systems', claiming that Israel 'had a variety of consultation options'.[77] This section will briefly explore these claims and counter-claims in a search for healing women in biblical Judaism, recognizing, as Thomas C. Römer claims, that '(t)he Hebrew Bible is to a large extent a literary product composed by intellectual elites from the Persian period in order to reorganize or even create Judaism out of the crisis of the exile'.[78]

Israel's foundational story, the Exodus, provides a brief glimpse of women in the health care system of biblical Judaism, namely the midwife/*maia* (Exod. 1.8-21), suggesting that midwives may have been as natural in Israel's health care system as was divine healing power, though rarely mentioned in the biblical texts whose authors are predominantly if not exclusively male and whose concerns were not women's care of women (See Gen. 35.17, 38.28 and 1 Sam. 4.20 outside of Exod. 1.8-21). Hector Avalos says in this regard that '(a)lthough precise statistics are not available, the midwife may have been one of the most ubiquitous health care consultants in the ancient Near East'.[79] We have seen earlier in Chapter Two their significant presence throughout the Hellenistic period into the early Roman era.

Tal Ilan includes the profession of midwife among the occupations available to the women of Palestine in the Graeco-Roman period, noting that this profession must have been limited to women since only feminine forms of related words are used in rabbinic literature.[80] She conjectures from this and also Josephus' reference to Joseph, son of an ἰατρίνη (*Vita* 185), which she translates as 'midwife', that women may have supplemented the knowledge gained in midwifery to enable them to work as physicians also. The inscriptional material from this period has, however, demonstrated that those designated ἰατρίνη were not simply midwives but were, indeed, physicians. Data in this regard in Graeco-Roman Palestine is so scarce though that one is left with the image of women's healing functioning almost invisibly in the socio-cultural construction of healing and especially within its semantic and symbolic universes despite Ilan's suggestion that women would have been familiar with plants and herbs and hence could have learnt 'which had medicinal uses'.[81] Given the impact of social and cultural influences from the broader Graeco-Roman world on Palestine at this time, though, it should not be surprising that the emergence of women in the public arena of healing would have begun there also but the absence of data makes conclusions elusive.

Avalos has noted that in Israel as in the Graeco-Roman world explored earlier in this chapter, that the home was the primary locus of health care.[82] This is seen in the story of the Shunammite woman and her son who becomes grievously ill and is returned to the house by his father (2 Kgs 4.8-37) and in the story of Amnon and Tamar (2 Samuel 13). Women's care of those ill in the home seems to be assumed to be a natural occurrence to Tamar's detriment when she is raped by her brother Amnon who feigns illness. Adrien Janis Bledstein, on the basis of an extensive examination of healing or divination rituals known from ancient Near Eastern texts, offers a further dimension to healing in the home and women's role in it. He suggests that Tamar may have been performing a healing ritual in a way which was entirely acceptable and hence she had no cause for alarm until Amnon's intentions became clear.[83] The popular arena was, therefore, an arena in which women's healing skills could be wrought. These were skills with the medicinal use of herbs as noted above, skills gained through midwifery that may have approached those skills and arts exercised by the ιατρίνη of professional medicine (although the evidence for this is not available to us), and skills in religious healing rituals which were in place but were condemned by Israel's official theologians.

That women were engaged in the area of folk healing involving religious or magical arts and rituals in biblical Judaism is evident to us by way of prohibition which may parallel the stereotyping of these arts among women in the literature of Greece and Rome. The prohibition of Deut. 18.10 (cf. 18.9-14), 'No one shall be found among you who makes a son or daughter pass through fire, or who practices divination, or is a soothsayer, or an augur, or a sorcerer' is made more explicitly gendered in Exod. 22.18, 'You shall not permit a female sorcerer to live'. Saul expels all the mediums and the wizards from the land (1 Sam. 28.3) but then goes to consult the 'woman who is a medium' at Endor (1 Sam. 28.7). Ezekiel (13.17-23; cf also Jer. 44.15-30) speaks out against women who seem to be engaged in some form of magical activity involving wrist bands and veils (and for Jeremiah, cakes offered to the queen of heaven), proclaiming that God will save God's people from their hands. The construction of the health care system allows for God alone as healer and fidelity to God's covenant as grounds for health, while the presence and activity of those who might have been also engaged in healing rituals is prohibited by prescription or by stereotype, especially those who are female.

Within Israel generally, the only ones who seem to be the legitimate agents of divine healing are the prophets or the 'man of God' as the prophet is sometimes called (1 Kgs 17.24 and passim).[84] Elijah and Elisha both carry out healing functions on God's behalf. Elijah restores life to the son of the widow of Zarephath in her home (1 Kgs 17.17-24) and restores the withered hand of Jeroboam in the sanctuary of Bethel, a place of prophetic contestation not a healing sanctuary (1 Kgs 13.1-6). Elisha likewise restores life to the young son of the Shunammite woman in her home (2 Kgs 4.8-37) and heals the leprosy of Naaman (2 Kgs 5.1-19). Of this latter healing Avalos says, in relation to its meaning-making function within Israel's health care system, that 'obedience to Yahweh and his authentic prophet, not a routine prescription, is the determinant of therapeutic efficacy'.[85] He contrasts this with the 'theology of Asclepius which placed a high value on the temple locus because the god could not be everywhere within a large geographic area'.[86] Women seem to be excluded from this role of prophet as healing intermediary. Miriam is named prophet in Exod. 15.20 with her role being proclamation of God's deeds while Deborah is called 'prophetess' in Judg. 4.4 with the accompanying role of judge. Huldah too (2 Kgs 22.14-20) is named prophet but she has no healing role, only a short proclamation.

We have seen earlier that during the period of the formation of Israel's biblical traditions into coherent narratives during the Persian and Hellenistic periods, professional medicine was developing in Hellenistic Greece alongside the rise of the religion of Hygieia and Asclepius. Given the central theology of God as healer with itinerant prophets acting on God's behalf in relation to a small collection of healings, however, there is little evidence of professional medical personnel presented positively in Israel, male or female. Jeremiah, for instance, reiterates the claim that healing belongs to God (Jer. 17.14: Heal me, O God, and I shall be healed; Jer. 30.17: 'I shall restore your health and I shall heal your wounds'). And he asks the somewhat sarcastic rhetorical question, 'Is there no balm in Gilead? Is there no physician (ἰατρός) there? Why then has the health of my poor people not been restored?' (Jer. 8.22). Here the prophet seems to decry both physicians and healing materials such as balsam as equally ineffective in the face of God's healing power. Only the leaves of the trees that grow by the river flowing out of the restored temple (Ezek. 47.12) escape the condemnation of Israel's theologians and these because they are connected to the cultus through which God's healing powers function.[87] There is little room here for an ecological reading of the *materia medica* unless one reads against the grain of the biblical text in order that the rich material resources for healing hidden within the biblical text can be uncovered together with those who worked with them, some of whom may have been women as suggested earlier.[88]

Another text which contributes further to Israel's construction of the physician as a danger to its theology of healing is 2 Chron. 16.12: 'Asa was diseased in his feet, and his disease became severe; yet even in his disease he did not seek God, but sought help from physicians (ἰατρούς)'. Tobit too consults with physicians (Tob. 2.10) but even though they treat his eyes with ointments (φάρμακα), they are unable to heal him and he becomes totally blind. There is a strong tradition, therefore, within Israel's health care system which negates the role of the physician in a way which differs from medicine in the Hellenistic world in which divine healing and the work of the physician co-existed both within Hippocratic professional medicine and the folk tradition of religious healing of the Hygieia/Asclepius and other traditions of divine healing. This does not mean, however, that there were not physicians and a rich tradition of *pharmaka* or *materia medica*. Rather the constant biblical theme of proclaiming their illegitimacy points to their function in biblical Judaism.[89] A change occurs, however, with the decline of the prophet in the Second Temple period.[90]

By the mid-Hellenistic period, the Testament of Job 38.7-8 and Sir. 38.1-15 recognize physicians and their healing power as well as their *pharmaka*. There is no explicit indication of the gender of the physicians in either of these texts but the symbolic universe of Israel's healing in general and that of the Book of Sirach in particular,[91] seems to leave little official space for female healers. Sirach 38.1-5 opens with the call to honour the physician who has been appointed or assigned by God; but the domination of the health care system by a single male divinity seems to conspire with Ben Sira's portrayal of women according to the degree of honour or shame they bring to the male (see for instance Sir. 23.22-26, 25.16-26.18, 36.26-31 on wives; and 7.24-25, 22.3-5, 26.10-12 and 42.9-14 on daughters),[92] to continue the tradition in Israel of giving no official public space to those female healers who, no doubt were functioning as midwives, ritual healers and folk healers using *pharmaka*. Sirach 38.4-8 and its praise of *pharmaka*, although late in Israel's tradition and not explicitly associated with women healing in Judaism, can be drawn into the construction of Judaism's health care system and its close association with female healers may make a symbolic space for them.

The divine and human worlds of Israel's health care system, especially as manifest in biblical Judaism, are, however, gendered almost exclusively male. Women healing appear only in the cracks, the spaces, the stereotypes and, heeding Joshel and Murnaghan's warning about not creating 'more noise', we glimpse them obscurely only, their subjectivities unavailable to us. A similar situation exists in relation to the female divine healer. Even though recent feminist scholarship has provided glimpses of the silenced female divine in Israel's symbolic universe, especially as Sophia,[93] she does not function as one of a pair with Israel's God as Healer as does Hygieia, nor is healing a sole or even a significant quality associated with her or other female deity condemned in Israel's scriptures.[94] Divine and human healing in biblical Judaism is gendered male in the texts available to us. This is the context and the world-view which shaped early Christianity and its health care system. This shaping, however, took place not only in Palestine during the *basileia* movement but also in the towns and cities of Syria, Asia Minor and the Roman Empire as far as Rome where healing women were active and where a religious tradition of healing that would rival emerging Christianity imaged divine healing female as well as male.

## Conclusion

This chapter has been broad ranging and has drawn together a number of threads. Through some of the cracks and spaces in literature, marked as it is by the use of earth's products on parchment or papyri, we have caught glimpses of women healing in the folk sector of the health care system of the Graeco-Roman world and of the *pharmaka* that characterized their place in the folk sector of the health care system. Often, healing women and women healing were stereotyped negatively not only by the ancients but also by tactics of contemporary scholars who further obscured and colonized them. Women practitioners seemed to be completely absent from the Hygieia/Asclepius tradition but women healed took us into the world which mirrored the increasing emphasis on divine intercession as an alternative source of health care. A turn to Biblical Judaism likewise gave brief glimpses of the colonizing and stereotyping of women healing together with construction of divine healing as the monopoly of Israel's God who is gendered male. The late legitimization of physicians and their *pharmaka* in this health care system may have further contributed to the exclusion of women healing from Israel's health care system.

With the knowledge of the various traditions of women healing and the gendering of health care in the Graeco-Roman world, including Palestine, that has emerged from this study, we turn now to the gospel narratives whose tradition history and final provenances are located in this world in which these traditions intersect in complex ways depending on location, time and other social, cultural, political and religious factors. This will inform our continuing search for women healing in the synoptic gospel narratives of early and emerging Christianity.

Chapter 4

## TELLING STORIES OF WOMEN HEALING/HEALING WOMEN:
## THE GOSPEL OF MARK

> When cross-cultural studies focus on disease, patients, practitioners, or healing without locating them in particular health care systems, they seriously distort social reality.[1]

> ...bodies and illnesses can never be studied independently from their cultural context. Corporeality – including that of the diseased body – is not merely a given; it is a cultural symbol, and it is produced and generated as such.[2]

Healing stands at the heart of the gospel story developed and told within the Markan community. Stories of healing, exorcisms and summary references to these activities occur in all the chapters recounting Jesus' Galilean ministry, that is, from chapters 1–10, except for chapter 4 in which Jesus is presented as a teacher of parables.[3] Later in the gospel, this healing activity is taken up by others when a woman pours healing ointment over the head of Jesus as he faces into the rigors of condemnation and death (14.3-9) and Mary Magdalene and Mary the mother of James and Salome go to the tomb to anoint the body of Jesus (16.1). There is reference also in Mark 6.13 to the Twelve who are sent out two by two casting out demons and anointing with oil those who were sick and healing them (6.13) but the gospel's recipients (hearers and/or readers) are not given any explicit stories of their healing activity.

The *basileia* of God which characterizes the gospel proclaimed by the Markan Jesus (1.15) is identified, therefore, with healing, an activity that is associated with human bodies, the materiality of human lives, as well as the socio-cultural world of meaning. The Markan audience hears little explicit teaching from Jesus in his ministry save for the parables of chapter 4 (4.1-34) even though Jesus is identified as teacher in a positive way throughout the gospel by way of the title Διδάσκαλος.[4] Also the language of teaching and healing intertwine within or between stories throughout the gospel (1.21, 22; 2.13; 5.35; 6.2, 6; 8.3; 9.38; 10.35). Indeed, in the opening story of Jesus' ministry following his first steps to establish a new fictive kinship group who will be engaged with him in the task of identifying and bringing about the *basileia* of God, a reference to Jesus' teaching (1.21-22) and a proclamation of his healing action as 'a new teaching' (1.27) frames his casting out of an unclean spirit. Teaching in the Markan gospel is concerned with the materiality and the spirituality of healing. It is significant that the term ἐξουσία is associated with this teaching in action that characterizes this story. At the outset, Jesus the teacher-healer or healer-teacher[5] is claimed to be authorized to cast out demons and to heal.[6] This was important in a world in which healers had to establish their authority by the effectiveness of their art, their *technê*.[7] The Markan narrator seems to be at pains to establish the *technê* of Jesus the healer since, as Louise Wells notes, 'seventeen of the nineteen cases of healing reported by Mark occur in the first eight chapters of his gospel prior to Peter's recognition and declaration of Jesus as the Messiah'. She claims` that 'Jesus himself is proof of his own identity'.[8]

The gospel of Mark creates, therefore, a world of healing, a glimpse of understandings of some aspects of the health care system of an early Christian community. It is a narrative world encoding elements of the physical, social, political, economic and cultural worlds that are shared by author and audience.[9] We do not have direct access to the explanatory models of health care practitioner, of supplicant seeking healing, or of family and friends nor to the clinical reality of the first-century health care systems as these functioned in the various emerging Jewish-Christian communities whose narratives have been preserved. These have been 'abstracted and interpreted', to use the language of Garrett,[10] into a narrative but traces of them may still be visible. The process I will undertake here, therefore, is to reconstruct the narrative world of healing in the Markan gospel. Examination of the narrative's rhetoric in dialogue with or through the lens of Kleinman's modeling of health care systems within a broad ecological context will enable some tentative conclusions to be drawn about the Markan health care system. This process will also be informed by cultural and socio-religious aspects of the Graeco-Roman world of healing established in the previous chapters some of whose characteristics would have been shared by the Markan and other early Christian communities.[11] Closer analyses of narratives of women healing will then enable an informed reading of the gendering of the Markan text and context to become more visible.

## The Markan World of Healing

The Markan narrative, in which healing is a key characteristic, seems to distinguish two types of healing both in summary statements and in healing narratives, namely the healing of named and or described physical illnesses and the casting out of demons or unclean spirits.[12] The line of demarcation seems, however, to blur as the two are continually brought together in summary passages so that the reader might recognize them as two aspects of the *basileia* ministry of Jesus. Within the Markan text, there are nine healings of illness (1.29-31; 1.40-45; 2.1-12; 3.1-6; 5.21-24a, 35-43; 5.24b-34; 7.31-37; 8.22-26; 10.46-52) and four exorcisms (1.21-28; 5.1-20; 7.24-30; 9.14-29) and of these, three healings and one exorcism are of female patients or supplicants. This is approximately one third.[13]

The verb most generally used to indicate healing in the Markan gospel, apart from the descriptions of healings, is Θεραπεύω. It occurs in the first major summary statement of Jesus ministry surrounded on two sides by the phrase κακῶς ἔχοντας and is integrally linked with the casting out of demons (1.32-34). Similarly in 3.10-12, the verb is used with a similar phrase εἶχον μάστιγας followed by a reference to unclean spirits. Again, in summary form in 6.5, it describes the minimal healing that Jesus was able to undertake in Nazareth because of the unbelief of the townsfolk. The disciples, whom Jesus commissions to go out two by two with authority over unclean spirits (6.7), are described in a subsequent verse as casting out many demons and healing those who are sick by anointing with oil (6.13). They are participants in the work of healing restoration with Jesus. Mary Rose D'Angelo suggests that we re-member Jesus 'as prophet *within a prophetic movement*'.[14] I want to extend her claim on the basis of evidence emerging in the Markan narrative to suggest that we re-member Jesus as healer *within* a movement that has healing as a core characteristic, a healing movement. She suggests that the community of women and men who constituted the movement with and around Jesus shared a common spirit of prophecy. I am suggesting that this can be amplified by a recognition of their sharing of a common spirit of healing. The exploration I am undertaking seeks to determine how this community of healing is gendered.

The Markan use of δύναμις and its plural δυνάμεις is associated with the language of healing. The first occurrence is in Mk 5.30 where the touch of the woman with the haemorrhage draws forth power (δύναμιν) from Jesus. At the scene in Nazareth, Jesus' townsfolk question the source of Jesus' deeds of power (6.2) and at the end of this scene, the narrator states that Jesus could not do any deeds of power (δύναμιν) except the healing of a few people. In these texts, δύναμις is associated with healing and it is these deeds of healing and those of Jesus' commissioned Twelve (6.13) that attract the attention of Herod in 6.14. The only other occurrence of δύναμις referring to a deed or deeds of power rather than simply power is in 9.39 and there too it is in conjunction with the art or the act of casting out demons which we have already seen is intimately linked to the healing work of Jesus and the Jesus movement. Mark 9.1 links power or δύναμις with the *basileia* of God which is at the heart of Jesus' ministry (1.15). Within the Markan world or from an emic perspective, the healing works of Jesus are named deeds of power. To use the language of wonder and miracle which is so prevalent in scholarly interpretations is to bring an etic perspective that colors the reading of the text and any attempt to understand and reconstruct the Markan world of healing. I will, therefore, use the language of healing and of power throughout this analysis to draw attention back to the first century and the worlds its language constructs.

Louise Wells notes the burgeoning of meaning of the verb Θεραπεύω in late Hellenistic and early Roman times. Earlier, it had been used to designate the loving service of caring for a patient when a cure may not have been in sight.[15] Ἰάομαι, on the other hand, was often associated with divine intervention and immediate cure.[16] The latter is the most commonly used in the dedicatory narratives on the walls of the Asclepieia.[17] It would seem that Θεραπεύω has been used in the Markan narrative to replace ἰάομαι which occurs only at 5.29 in which the power of Jesus is able to heal the woman with the haemorrhage when many physicians (πολλῶν ἰατρῶν) fail to do so. Θεραπεύω is found, however, only in summary passages describing the activity of the healer/s rather than being descriptive of the transformed state of the one healed, the use one finds for ἰάομαι in the Asclepian inscriptions. The narrative indication, however, is that the healing is generally immediate as in the Asclepieia and undertaken by one who enjoys divine favor as Mk 1.11 would indicate. Both Jesus and his disciples are, therefore, described as healing – all male healers – and those healed are both male and female. Jesus heals with authority/ἐξουσία and he passes this authority to his male disciples (6.7) who likewise heal. The healer as constructed in the Markan health care system is gendered male in contrast to the male-female gendering in both the professional, folk and popular sectors of the broader Graeco-Roman world of healing. This is the dominant construction but a voice from the borderland, a counter voice, may be heard later when we turn our attention to Mk 14.3-9.

Another verb associated with the healing activity of Jesus in the Markan narrative is σῴζω.[18] In contrast to Θεραπεύω, when it is used in relation to physical healing, it describes the transformation or transformed state of the one seeking healing. The first use is indirect in that Jairus begs Jesus to come and heal his daughter by laying hands on her so that she might be saved/freed from disease[19] and live (ἵνα σωθῇ καὶ ζήσῃ – 5.23). While the verb does not occur in the description of the daughter healed, it is there in the aspirations of her father. It is used as descriptor of the healed woman in the intercalated story of the woman with the haemorrhage and on the lips of Jesus himself ἡ πίστις σου σέσωκέν σε – your faith has saved you/has freed you from your disease – 5.34). It is, though, also descriptive of the woman's healing aspiration as it was for Jairus when she says (seemingly to herself although Mark does not specifically stipulate this): '[i]f I touch even his garments, I shall be made well/saved – Ἐὰν ἅψωμαι κἂν τῶν ἱματίων αὐτοῦ σωθήσομαι' (5.28). Like Θεραπεύω, σῴζω also characterizes the healing of many who, as does the woman with the haemorrhage, touch even the fringe of Jesus' garment (6.56). It may not be accidental that in the concluding verse of the final healing narrative in the Galilean ministry of Jesus, the phrase ἡ πίστις σου σέσωκέν σε is once again on the lips of Jesus, this time prior to the actual description of the transformation of the blind Bartimaeus to sight (10.52). There is an ironic twist constructed around this verb in the passion narrative when the chief priests and scribes mock Jesus the healer who is being mercilessly crucified because of his fidelity to the *basileia* of God which is characterized with healing at its core: '[h]e saved others; he cannot save himself – ἄλλους ἔσωσεν, ἑαυτὸν οὐ δύναται σῶσαι' (15.30-31).

Given the development noted above, as ἰάομαι was replaced by Θεραπεύω, it would not have been surprising for many in the Markan audience to find Θεραπεύω and σῴζω associated with healing, particularly of physical illness. Louise Wells has pointed out that '[i]t is clear that where divine intervention is required or expected the verbs ἰάομαι and σῴζω are preferred. Both can provide a permanent quick-fix'.[20] In the Markan narrative world of healing, however, the 'quick-fix' which does indeed characterize the healing stories, is not ethereal but very material. Healing is concerned with human bodies, both of the healer (divinely authorized) and the healed, and is effected most consistently in this gospel by touch, by the meeting of bodies: male-male and male-female bodies. The verb ἅπτωμαι is found in ten verses all of which are in contexts of healing except the last which is a blessing (1.41; 3.10; 5.27, 28, 30, 31; 6.56; 7.33; 8.22 [10.13]). Three times Jesus takes a supplicant's hand to raise them up healed (κρατήσας τῆς χειρός): Simon's mother-in-law; Jairus' daughter; and the epileptic boy (1.31; 5.41; 9.27). And four times, he stretches out his hand to heal (ἐπιθεὶς τὰς χεῖρας): 6.5; 7.32; 8.23, 25. Also, Jairus invites him to do so in his request to heal his daughter (5.23). There does not appear to be a gendering of touch in this narrative. The language, however, highlights the materiality of bodies as a significant element in the world of healing as recounted in Mark. Healing power is associated with the sacred, the divine, but it is communicated between material bodies that touch, a touch which is, therefore, corporeal.

Through careful use of language, the Markan text constructs a narrative world of healing in which the transformation described takes place instantaneously as in many of the healing accounts recorded in the Asclepieia and in the few healing accounts in the Hebrew Bible (1 Kings 17; 2 Kings 4–5). Jesus is authorized by the divine voice at his baptism (1.11) and he takes up his mandate as proclaiming the good news of God, the imminence of God's *basileia*. Healing is the most consistent manifestation of that *basileia*, of that good news in the Markan narrative. Women and men are healed although not in the same numbers but only men are explicitly called into the new fictive kinship whose members are commissioned to share in the healing work of Jesus.

Focusing the lens of medical anthropology on this narrative world that carries the kernel of the symbolic reality of the Markan health care system will enable us to extend our understanding of this system in social and cultural terms. Kleinman's models of the internal structure and clinical reality of a local health care system, together with the categories for analyzing the therapeutic relationship as described in Chapter 1, will further expand our understanding of the Markan text. Awareness of the constructive nature of social and cultural reality will, however, ensure that the dialogue between the models and the text will remain tensive, especially in relation to gender but also space and the body.

There are two references within the Markan gospel to professional healers or physicians, a category of healers that emerged within the Greek and Roman worlds. The first reference is in the context of Jesus reclining at table with a number of tax collectors and sinners and being challenged about this by the scribes of the Pharisees (2.15-16). His reply (2.17) is that those in possession of their power, those in good health (οἱ ἰσχύοντες)[21] have no need of a physician (ἰατρόν) but those who are sick (τοὺς κακῶς ἔχοντες), the phrase used in the first summary passage in the gospel (1.32, 34). There is a seeming contradiction here, however, in that Jesus who is described as healing those with all kinds of diseases is never given the title ἰατρόν, he has never received the training that a professional physician or healer would receive from one skilled in the art, and nor is he described as working with symptoms and cures as is characteristic of the professional healer. Indeed, Jesus is contrasted with professional healers when the woman with the haemorrhage is described as suffering much under many physicians and not being cured but, in fact, becoming worse (5.26), and yet on touching Jesus garment, her haemorrhage ceases (5.29). On the other hand, however, Jesus sets his ministry to sinners, those out of right relationship with God and/or the human community, within the frame of the physician who heals the sick, those whose bodies are out of right order.[22] Jesus the healer will, in fact, both heal the sick and establish right order for the sinner and the outcast. It can be assumed that the Markan audience knows of the professional sector of the health care system and that such professionals functioned in their context.[23] The Markan storyteller does not, however, characterize Jesus within this sector but does place the healing ministry of Jesus within the metaphoric frame of the healer/physician.

One of the extraordinary characteristics that one notes from a careful examination of the healing stories in the Markan narrative[24] is that they are episodic. They occur as Jesus is on the way or passing through a region (see 1.40; 5.1, 21, 24b-27; 6.5, 53; 8.22; 9.14; 10.46). He is not established in a sanctuary or shrine to which supplicants come as to the Asclepieia and other healing shrines. And even those healings that occur within a house or a synagogue are episodic in that Jesus is in that place as part of his itinerant ministry.[25] As Jesus becomes known as healer, however, people do bring the sick or the demon-possessed to him for healing (1.32; 2.3; 7.32; 8.22; 9.17, 19, 20). Healing is, however, not Jesus' full-time activity even though we have noted its centrality. Jesus' itinerant ministry is for the purpose of preaching the gospel of God (1.15) and his healing belongs to that task. He could be said, therefore, to be a folk healer or participant in the magico-religious arena of folk healing according to the Kleinman categories.

In seeking to understand Jesus as healer, many scholars point to the healing done by the prophets Elijah and Elisha (1 Kings 17; 2 Kings 4–5); or the expulsion of demons in the Book of Tobit (6.7, 16; 8.1-3; 11.8-14) and Josephus' *Antiquities* (8.46-47)[26] as evidence of a symbolic world of healing shared by at least some members of the Markan audience. Geza Vermes suggests that the 'man of God' or Jewish charismatic healer or holy one like Honi and Hanina ben Dosa might also have informed the Markan health care system's construction of healer.[27] These references, however, are fragmentary and scattered both chronologically and across different genre of literary texts.[28] It would seem, therefore, that the collection of story upon story of healing and exorcism and summaries of these activities attributed to Jesus in the Markan gospel had no real parallel in the first-century world of antiquity although elements from that world would have informed interpretation.[29] If Green is correct in his claim that during first-century Judaism, there was a shift of religious authority from that of the priests and cult to the rabbis and study, this might explain the other aspect of the Markan story of Jesus the healer, namely that Jesus could not save himself from those whose move toward power was threatened by his healing activity.

> ...any Jew who claimed access to God outside the new rabbinic structure would have seemed to them suspect. Charismatic figures who professed supernatural powers – magicians, miracle workers, or 'prophets' – naturally would have presented a challenge to the emerging rabbinic piety and claims to authority.[30]

The challenge that Jesus is possessed by Beelzebul and casts out demons by the power of this prince of demons (Mk 3.22); or the watching of Jesus the healer by the Pharisees to see if he would put healing before the cult of Sabbath observance may well point beyond the gospel narrative to a health care system in which there was conflict and contestation around the authority of the magico-religious folk healer, an instance perhaps of indigenous healing being colonized not from the outside but by an emerging system of rabbinic power within Judaism.[31]

Consideration of the physical reality in which healing takes place allows further amplification of the analysis above. Only two healings occur in designated sacred space, namely the synagogue, and during designated sacred time, on the Sabbath (1.21-28; 3.1-6). As noted above, Jesus' presence there participates in the episodic or itinerant nature of his healings. The synagogue is not, therefore, designated a place of healing within the health care system of the Markan community which is perhaps further manifestation of the religio-political contestation in first-century Judaism noted above. Rather it is a site of contest. Jesus the magico-religious healer is caught in a struggle with politically and culturally authorized religious leaders within Judaism and with a spirit or power named 'unclean', a particular naming or construction from within the religio-cultural system. The story in 1.21-28 focuses on such a contest rather than on the person with the unclean spirit. It is the spirit that cries out, naming Jesus, and it is the spirit that is described as leaving the man (1.26). There is no description of the man being transformed in his body which is characteristic of healing stories and which will characterize another dramatic struggle between Jesus and demonic power (5.15). In this second story, the Gerasene demoniac is 'sitting, clothed and in his right mind' as a result of Jesus' casting out of the demons. His body is transformed.[32]

With this general introduction to the Markan health care system and to Jesus, the Markan healer within that system, I turn now to the stories of women healed. I will read these stories through my socio-rhetorical lens and using Kleinman's categories of analysis: institutional setting; characteristics of the interpersonal interaction; idiom of communication; clinical reality; and therapeutic stages and mechanisms.[33] This will enable me to draw conclusions about the gendering of healing in Mark. In this way not only cultural but also theological meaning will become more visible.

### A Fevered Woman Is Raised Up to Diakonia
### (Mark 1.29-31)

This very brief narrative opens with a clear demarcation between the setting or material space for the first and this second healing narrative marking the opening of Jesus' Galilean preaching. Jesus leaves the synagogue (ἐξελθόντες) and comes or goes into (ἦλθον εἰς) the house of Simon and Andrew, the first two brothers called away from their fishing nets (1.16-17). The public religious space of the narrative of confrontation between Jesus and an unclean spirit in which the spirit is overpowered by Jesus and hence leaves the man's body gives way to the more private space of a household.

It is difficult to reconstruct the household of early-first-century Galilee or of later-first-century Rome, southern Syria or whatever city of the Empire was the location for the Markan community's storytelling.[34] While some social scientific critics would see the cultural code of the public/private and its close link to gender to be an established element in first-century Mediterranean culture,[35] a feminist constructivist approach considers gender and the related category of public and private to be under negotiation through the very act of storytelling and the subsequent shaping of lives and spaces in light of such storytelling.[36] Jorunn Økland makes this clear by distinguishing gender as a category and the active infinitive 'to gender'. Økland defines the infinitive as 'a way of thinking about it [gender], conferring meaning and values on it, and of legitimizing its structures'. This leads to the conclusion that 'the gendering of spaces has little to do with the presence of male and female bodies in a place'.[37] Eric Meyers has concluded his study of the gendering of space in Syro-Palestinian architecture with the claim that 'Jewish households cannot be considered areas of confinement or concealment for women'. He demonstrates that archaeological evidence supports the notion that the impact of the 'open-market economy' of the Roman empire meant 'a much higher degree of participation of women in the full range of social and professional activities'.[38] The house links the material, the economic and the gendered realities of the first century of the Common Era in quite complex ways and these are evoked for readers in the naming of the space.[39] Meyers makes clear for Galilee, therefore, what has been established for Asia Minor and other sectors of the Graeco-Roman world, namely that women through a variety of professions were participating in public activities whether these were in the public or private space.[40] Healing was one such activity as the inscription honoring Pantheia attests. The space of the house is not, therefore, significantly gendered in relation to Markan healing as both women and men are healed in the house as well as outside the house, just as both groups carried on significant activities inside the first-century house as well as outside it.

When considering the function of gender in this story, it is important to speculate how this domestic space of Mk 1.29 might have been 'read' in the Markan community. The house of a family engaged in the fishing industry on the Sea of Galilee might be imagined as a courtyard-style house given the economic stability suggested for those engaged in that industry.[41] That the house was able to expand to include Simon's mother-in-law might indicate to the reader that it was not one of the *insulae* of the larger cities, for as Marianne Sawicki suggests, 'traditional kinship connections in many cases simply could not be housed there' because of the inability for expansion.[42] Guijarro, however, demonstrates that the 'insula sacra' of Capernaum consisted of a courtyard with the dwellings of three or four related families surrounding the courtyard.[43] Markan readers might have imagined a number of these and other possibilities depending on their context.

It is in this material and socio-cultural space of the house that the healing of Simon's mother-in-law takes place. It is the first healing of a physical illness as distinct from an exorcism and the recipient is female. The description of this healing invites readers into the popular sector of the Markan health care system, that sector which Kleinman says is the 'lay, non-professional, non-specialist, popular cultural arena in which illness is first defined and healthcare activities initiated'.[44] This is even more evident when the narrator says that they (presumably the four) tell Jesus about her (v. 30). This is typical of the attitudes of the participants in a number of Markan healing stories when a person in need of healing or someone on that person's behalf requests healing in a variety of ways (1.40; 2.3-4; 5.22-23; 7.26, 32; 8.22; 9.22; 10.47-48, 51).[45] In this popular sector where the sick or those acting on their behalf initiate the healing activity, a belief in the power of the healer is manifest. There does not appear to be any significant gender differentiation in relation to this attitude toward the healer. Others approach Jesus on behalf of men as well as women, sons as well as daugh-

ters, the Syro-Phoenician woman being one of these. The woman with the
haemorrhage (5.27-28) could be understood to approach Jesus indirectly
believing that even the touch of his garment would heal her while the leper
approached Jesus directly asking to be made clean (1.40). Such a difference
is, however, too slight to allow us to draw any conclusions about the function of gender within the popular sector of the Markan health care system
where both women and men participate in the activating of health care. I
think, therefore, that Pilch has overstated his claim in relation to the woman
with the haemorrhage that 'it is out of the ordinary for a women (*sic*) to
plead her own case (and hence she) only intends to touch Jesus' garment,
but is then forced by circumstances to face him directly'.[46] Indeed, her
initiative activates healing that is then effected as 5.29 indicates: immediately the haemorrhage ceased. This will be explored more fully when considering this story in detail.

The narrator introduces Simon's mother-in-law[47] as lying in bed with a
fever (κατέκειτο πυρέσσουσα). Fever is the 'culturally legitimated name'
written on the body of this woman with such naming being the first stage
in the therapeutic process.[48] It is the name given by the narrator. Readers/
listeners, therefore, do not know if this is how the woman named her
sickness or how the four with Jesus or Jesus himself understood it.[49] The
exact understanding the gospel recipients would have had of 'fever' is
ambiguous as John Granger Cook suggests. He offers four possible first-
century cultural meanings evoked by the above description 'with a fever':
an illness with somatic or physical causes; a result of demon possession; an
outcome of astrological features; or a divine punishment.[50] He provides
data from the Greek and Roman worlds to underpin his claims, although
some of his sources are much later than the Markan narrative. David
Garland notes in a more nuanced way that 'fever was considered to be an
illness in and of itself and was not viewed as a symptom of a disease'.[51] The
Hippocratic corpus seems to suggest that this claim is not always the case
in that different types of pleurisy manifest in fever and pneumonia.[52] Fever
seems a characteristic of many different illnesses in Hippocrates' *Epidemics*.

At one level, the narrative description of Simon's mother-in-law evokes
the physical body of the woman and its location. There is a 'reading' and a
'writing' of space and of body to use the language of Marianne Sawicki.
The house is male public space, not the domain of the private only, as is
indicated by Jesus being invited into this space that belongs to Peter and
Andrew.[53] In this space that is gendered both male and female, a woman
lies sick with a fever (κατέκειτο πυρέσσουσα). The focus shifts to the body
of a woman. She is prostrate as the verb κατάκειμαι indicates, unable to

participate in the activities of the household that may well have been a complex of male and female activities as noted above. The description of the woman is given by the narrator and at the level of characterization presumes shared meaning.

Regarding gendering at this point, the description participates in the multiple designations of both male and female illnesses characteristic of professional health care that populate Hippocrates *Epidemics*. Fevers are described in their complexity in *Epidemics* 1.18-21. In the fourteen cases that follow, nine are male and five are female. The only significant difference is that four of the women contract fevers in relation to childbirth and Melidia, the final case, is said to have a slight menstrual flow. There are, however, many other instances of men and women with fevers scattered throughout the *Epidemics* and not all female fevers are associated with gynaecological symptoms.[54] We do not have access to the understanding of fever in the folk and popular sectors but even the brief description of the wife of Delearces provided by the Hippocratics (*Epid.* 3.320), that from the beginning of her fever she would wrap herself up, points to the possibility of female patients recognizing symptoms and possibly taking steps to activate healing.[55] Helen King, on the other hand, points out that while '[s]elf-knowledge is permitted; self-help is not',[56] an indication of the Markan system being gendered in a way similar to health care in the Graeco-Roman world generally. Within the popular sector of the Markan health-care system, therefore, the four activate healing by telling Jesus about the woman's condition. They do not ask for healing in language which might indicate their attitude to Jesus as healer and so it is difficult in this story, the first of the stories of the healing of physical illness, to determine attitudes to Jesus by the supplicants or the attitude of Jesus to the task of healing that might generally be present in the idiom of communication in a healing seeking episode.[57]

Subsequent to Jesus being given information about the fever of Simon's mother-in-law, the narrative indicates action on the part of Jesus (καὶ προσελθὼν). He comes or goes toward where Simon's mother-in-law is lying. In terms of the domestic space, this might mean moving from the courtyard into one of the rooms of the house in which sleeping mats would be laid for the evening or when someone in the house was ill. This is private space and would generally be so if it were a male or female member of the family who was lying ill on a bed or sleeping pallet. It would seem less likely that Jesus would have initially been invited into the private space of the house where a woman was ill. If this was so, then the narrative presents the four conversing with Jesus about the woman and her illness in a way that renders her and her sick body invisible save in the words of the male characters and subsequently the narrator. In either case, healing enters the private or domestic arena but is carried out by the folk healer and so the readers are invited to enter the borderland space where popular and folk healing cross.

The mode of healing or the type of clinical intervention is named: Jesus takes her hand (κρατήσας τῆς χειρός). The very placement of this phrase after the verb ἤγειρεν demonstrates the instrumentality of the action. The taking of her hand is all that is needed. There is no elaborate listing of interventions as in professional medicine, nor even the sometimes simple, sometimes elaborate, actions of Asclepius in the Asclepian narratives. Only rarely does the touch of Asclepius suffice to cure: he draws open the eyes of Alketas of Halieis; he touches Andromache with his hand.[58] Jesus drove out the unclean spirit with a command/word (1.25) but the fever leaves at the touch of Jesus on the hand of the woman with the fever – he takes her hand and lifts her up. This mode of healing, that of taking the hand of the sick, describes Jesus' action in relation to Jairus' daughter (5.41) and the boy with the dumb spirit whose father begs Jesus for healing (9.27).[59] It is not gendered in that the male healer takes the hand of both female and male patient. The materiality of flesh meeting flesh raises up the woman who is lying sick, and the fever leaves her. Her body is described as transformed by touch in this the first healing narrative in Mark. The human body as participant in the Earth community is narrated as agent of mediation of cosmic powers of healing, reminding readers/hearers of the location of human healing within an ecology of healing.

Using Kleinman's final category, therapeutic stages and mechanisms, as a lens, the cultural label, namely 'having a fever' is 'manipulated' by the touch of Jesus and the woman is described in a new way: she is raised up and the fever has left.[60] The mechanism of change is somatic. The Markan account, however, doesn't end there. It goes on to describe the woman's ongoing healed state: she was serving them (διηκόνει). Such an addition is rare in the Markan healing narratives.[61] The only other post-healing description which parallels that of Simon's mother-in-law is that of Bartimaeus: he follows Jesus along the way (to Jerusalem) – ἠκολούθει αὐτῷ ἐν τῇ ὁδῷ (10.52). In both cases, the imperfect form of the verb is used indicating not a single completed action but an ongoing one. Indeed, the final phrase in these two stories, the first and last of the healings of physical conditions, may suggest that they in some way frame the healing narratives in the Markan story. Healing is about transformation, a transformation that opens into participation in the *basileia* which Jesus is preaching and enabling.

In recent years, feminist scholars have given significant attention to this final phrase in the Markan account of the healing of Simon's mother-in-law. Deborah Krause brings much of it into dialogue in her article in which she highlights some of the points of contention around whether one should understand διακονέιν in terms of domestic service or discipleship.[62] In the context of Markan healing, it is possible that this text would have been heard and interpreted on two levels within the Markan community. The first may well have been at the level of the household as Krause[63] and van Eck and van Aarde[64] argue. But I want to return to the earlier discussion of house and to suggest that the restoration at the level of the social, the house, is not an affirmation of fixed gender and spatial categories but that the restored household can encompass male and female activities of both a public and private nature as discussed earlier. Initially, the reader may understand the text to refer to the woman's role of offering hospitality to guests as a domestic service that would be an expression of her transformed state. This, may, however, have been but one of many activities which this first-century Galilean woman would have undertaken both within the house and outside, activities of a private and public nature. The imperfect form of the verb and the fact that listeners did not hear this story only once but many times over would mean that on a second and subsequent reading/hearing, they could understand the woman's service, like Bartimaeus' following, in light of the closing of the gospel when the faithful female disciples follow Jesus to the foot of the cross, ministering to him (15.41). For these second and subsequent readers who include present-day readers/interpreters, the healed mother-in-law of Simon went on to be a disciple, as did the restored Bartimaeus. What the gospel does not tell us is whether she could be considered among those women disciples who stood beneath the cross or among subsequent disciples commissioned by Mk 6.12-13 to cast out demons, anoint with oil and to heal in the re-telling of the story. Healing could open into discipleship in the Markan world of healing for women as well as men,[65] and that discipleship meant participation in the community of healers that was the *basileia* movement. Healing touches and transforms not only human bodies but the socio-cultural reality of the household and the material space in which household and gender function and take shape.

This initial socio-rhetorical analysis of healing of a woman in the context of the Markan world does not suggest marked gender distinctions. It reveals possible lack of voice for women in relation to their own healing. On the other hand, however, a counter voice is heard if the healed woman is read as becoming participant in the *basileia* healing movement. Such a reading would be in keeping with the shaping of gender categories around healing that was happening elsewhere in first-century Graeco-Roman society. It opens up new spaces for the reading of gender and healing in sacred/symbolic realms of the religious imagination as well as socio-cultural and material realms of space and human bodies touching.

### A Young Girl and a Woman with a Blood Flow Are Healed
### (Mark 5.21-43)

The brevity and simplicity of characterization in the narrative of the heal-ing of Simon's mother-in-law gives way to a pair of intercalated stories rich in not only narrative details but also dialogue as we trace Markan women healing. On encountering these stories, the reader/listener has just read or heard the account of the exorcism of the unclean spirit from the man of Gerasa that exhibits similar narrative and rhetorical characteristics (Mk 5.1-20). It is clear, therefore, that healing narratives in Mark do not nec-essarily follow a clear formula or pattern even though there are certain characteristics common to them. Narrative differences, however, are not, it would seem, shaped by gender.

The locations or settings for the two healings change through the narrative, making movement a characteristic of this piece of the Markan story-telling. Jesus arrives at the edge of the lake and is surrounded by a large crowd (ὄχλος πολὺς) and Jairus, a leader of the synagogue, approaches Jesus requesting healing for his daughter (5.21-23). As Jesus goes with Jairus toward his house, a large crowd (ὄχλος πολὺς) follows him, including a woman with a flow of blood who is healed (5.24-37). On entering the courtyard of Jairus' house, Jesus encounters another crowd (κλαίοντας καὶ ἀλαλάζοντας πολλά - 5.38-39). When Jesus finally enters the room where the girl is, he has with him only the mother and father and the four disci-ples, Peter, Andrew, James and John, who were also present at the previous healing of a woman. The episodic nature of healing is even more obvious here, captured by the verbs of movement attributed to Jesus. The attention to space, both outside in the public arena by the edge of the lake and along the way and then within the two stages of movement into the house and encounter with the sick one, recognizes the ecology of healing, the inter-connected system in which human and other-than-human elements and factors function for healing.[66] And this ecology involves communities of peoples not just the individual healed. The open air is the setting for the healing of the woman with the haemorrhage in a way that can suggest a symbolic interpretation of space and healing.

The Markan narrator has very skillfully intercalated the healing of a young girl and of an older woman in an extraordinary variety of ways. We have already seen how the crowds and the outdoor setting link the two at least initially (5.21, 24). Each story is initiated by an approach to Jesus, the folk healer, but they differ in that the leader of the synagogue approaches and makes a request to Jesus directly, the woman with the haemorrhage comes up behind Jesus and makes her request by touching Jesus' garment and speaking seemingly to herself (5.22-23, 27-28).[67] The quality of the relationship, taking up Kleinman's categories, is informal in both cases,[68] integrated into the ongoing activity of Jesus. There is also a formal quality to the therapeutic relationship in that each recognizes the authority of the healer: Jairus falls at the feet of Jesus to make his request and the woman with the haemorrhage does the same when her healing has been discovered (5.22, 33). The attitude to the healer evidenced in the request or desire of each supplicant draws on the same expectation that the mode of healing would be somatic (laying hands on/touching: 5.13, 28) and each uses the same language of desire – to be saved (σωθῇ - 5.23; σωθήσομαι – 5.28).

The links from the intercalated story to the second half of the frame are fewer but significant. We have already seen that the expected mode of healing would be somatic although the language differs. In the first half of the framing story, Jairus begs Jesus to lay his hands on his daughter (ἐπιθῇς τὰς χεῖρας αὐτῇ). Four times the language of touch (ἅπτομαι) occurs in the healing of the woman with the haemorrhage (5.27, 28, 30, 31 – on the lips of the narrator, the woman, Jesus and the disciples – all the key actors in the narrative together with the narrator). Then in the second half of the frame, the healing action of Jesus is similar to that which we saw in the healing of Simon's mother-in-law – Jesus takes her hand (κρατήσας τῆς χειρὸς τοῦ παιδίου). Touch or the meeting of bodies is a significant thread in the narrative and will require further exploration below. The closest link between the intercalated story and the conclusion of the framing story is the very clear articulation of the new label for the healed woman (5.29) and the young girl (5.42) and the related narrator's comment as to her age (twelve years) which links the reader back to the twelve years of the woman's flow of blood (5.25). Regardless of whether Mark received the stories intercalated or constructed them so, the level of both verbal and rhetorical intercalation in the Markan version suggests careful redaction and hence provides a significant glimpse into the Markan world of healing.

Gender and disease link these two stories. In order to explore this link, I will use the lens of the tripartite organization of the therapeutic stages and mechanisms according to Kleinman's model.[69] This will be linked to a rhetorical analysis of this text, exploring two different types of intertext, enabling me to reconstruct and understand more deeply the Markan world of healing and its construction of gender.

The Markan text labels the young girl in three ways through the story. First, she is at the point of death (ἐσχάτως ἔχει – v. 23). Immediately following the healing of the woman with the haemorrhage, messengers from Jairus' house inform him and the reader that the young girl has died (ἀπέθανεν – v. 35). The reader is unclear about this status as Jesus the healer announces to the mourners that she is not dead but sleeping (οὐκ ἀπέθανεν ἀλλὰ καθεύδει – v. 39). For the first time, we glimpse Jesus' perspective on an illness rather than that of the narrator or supplicant/s. At the very end of the story, the reader is informed, almost in an aside from the narrator, that the daughter is twelve years old (5.42).

The most common interpretation of the labelling of the young girl is that she has died. This, however, is manipulated in Jesus' contest with those weeping and wailing. His label for the young girl is that she is sleeping, a point generally ignored by scholars. For those who so ignore Jesus' label, the intertext presumed to give meaning to the narrative is the Jewish legal text of corpse uncleanness (Num. 19.11-13, 14-21).[70] If we take the labelling in the text seriously in its entirety, another intertext suggests itself from the medical literature. Even if the text itself was not known to all Markan listeners, their knowledge of the world of professional medicine may have meant that at least some were familiar with diseases as they were described by the profession.

The statement of the girl's age as twelve together with the intercalation of the story of the woman with the excessive flow of blood may have evoked for readers the possibility that the girl was at the transitional stage between girlhood and womanhood perhaps awaiting her menstrual flow. Annette Weissenrieder draws on later rabbinic texts (*b. Ketub.* 39a; *b. Sanh.* 66b and *b. Ketub.* 98a) to suggest that 'Jairus's daughter could be seen as either a virgin or a marriageable virgin'.[71] Tal Ilan examines rabbinic texts and historical data and more cautiously suggests that 'there is no firm indication that 12 was the customary age of marriage for girls'.[72] It is generally agreed that in both Graeco-Roman and Jewish society of the first-century, early marriage for young women was common practice even though we do not know the exact age. It seems, however, that twelve may have evoked that possible transition stage for young women.[73] For some young women, especially around twelve or the early teen years, the prospect of the transition from her family home to marriage and a new home would have been quite frightening. It was also the time at which menstruation might begin. With the threat of transition could come illness.

Transition periods are dangerous periods or crisis periods and stories developed in Greek and Roman as well as Rabbinic literature to demonstrate, as Antoinette Wire indicates that '[s]urvival, health, beauty, dowry and the right man all have to come together at one time to carry her through the narrow part of the hourglass if her life is to open out into a future'.[74] Male authors were writing women's lives and constructing socio-cultural codes that were gendered and were evoked in the Markan healing narrative. A young woman's treacherous transition was, however, not only constructed in literature but also in medical texts in a way which may point to other possible intertexts for the story of Jairus' daughter.

The Hippocratic texts, *Diseases of Young Girls* and *Diseases of Women*, address a phenomenon that the writer suggests is common among young girls who have not married, namely the retention of monthly bleeding. This build-up of blood is caused because of the narrowness of the cervical opening of the young woman and her intake of food accompanying her growth. This causes symptoms that the author likens to the sacred disease (which some suggest is epilepsy): the seeing of threatening demons, the impetus to throw herself into a well or to hang herself. *Diseases of Women* 1.2 and 1.7 in particular, gives further symptoms of this retention of blood, linking it to the movement of the womb and noting that it is less common in women who have married and are having intercourse than in young girls. One of its manifestations significant for our interpretation is loss of appetite. In *Diseases of Women* 1.32, insufficient food can cause the womb to move preventing menstruation and bringing on the variety of symptoms articulated in the various texts already cited.[75] The young woman might even appear as dead as certain stories in antiquity indicate. Helen King closes her discussion of the disease associated with the closed womb or the moving womb in women and young girls (and its historical development) with the words 'women are sick and men write their bodies'.[76] The body of Jairus' daughter has been so written in the text of Mk 5.21-23, 35-43. She has been constructed in the text by way of socio-cultural codes that include gender.[77]

These codes are manipulated and a new label is given to the healed young woman which seems to have little gender connotation: She gets up and walks (ἀνέστη... καί περιεπάτει) and she is to be given something to eat (δοθῆναι αὐτῇ φαγεῖν). She is lead through the time of transition by the healer and she takes up ordinary life again. With the medical texts still functioning as intertexts, readers/hearers could recognize her symptoms being reversed. Both *Diseases of Young Girls* and *Diseases of Women* describe the woman who suffers from the retention of blood as swelling in the legs and feet causing immobility and her breathing being affected when near death. The young girl is raised up by Jesus (ἀνέστη), following his command: ἔγειρε (5.41). These two verbs in various forms are used extensively in Mark.[78] Ἐγείρω is used most often in relation to healing (1.31; 2.9, 11, 12; 3.3; 5.41; 9.27 and 10.49) but it also describes Jesus having been raised from death (16.6 cf. also 14.28) and is used in reference to resurrection from death (6.14; 12.26). Ἀνίστημι, on the other hand, is only used in two healing stories: to describe the young girl's restoration to life or full life freed from the disease which afflicts young women culturally as well as physically (5.42) and Jesus' restoration of the boy with the spirit which caused symptoms similar to those associated with the sacred disease (9.27). On the other hand, while not used to describe Jesus' resurrection, ἀνίστημι is the verb used most often in the resurrection predictions in the Markan text and other references to resurrection (8.31; 9.9, 10, 31; 10.34; 12.23, 25). It is difficult to draw conclusions from this use of language except to say that the new label and the command which functioned as the mechanism for change within the Markan narrative designate the young woman as healed and with life restored.[79]

As with the story of the healing of Simon's mother-in-law, this healing is somatic, it touches on the materiality of bodies. Jesus takes the hand of the young girl (5.41) as he took the hand of Simon's mother-in-law (1.31) and as he does for the young boy with the spirit that convulses him (9.27). And that touch together with the word of healing heals her. Word and flesh on flesh together bring wholeness. The materiality of flesh is restorative. The material and the social intersect in 5.43 when Jesus commands that the young woman be given something to eat. Healing has been completed in her body but it has also been completed in the socio-cultural context of the household. The two intersect and are gendered so that in the semantic realm of the community's ongoing storytelling, transformed social and cultural possibilities for young women within a community of *basileia* vision can be imagined. For contemporary communities, restoration and transformation which honour the materiality of flesh, the sociality of gender and the politics of transformative power can be envisaged through the power of this narrative of transformation.

I turn back now to the intercalated story of the woman with the irregular flow of blood who mirror images the young woman of the framing story, her blood flowing too profusely rather than failing to flow. She is, therefore, older, at least in her twenties or more depending on when her illness commenced. Even though, as Tal Ilan suggests, 'women older than 20 were still desirable brides',[80] it could be assumed that this woman is a married woman. She, however, enters and leaves the narrative alone, a woman without familial connections that is quite extraordinary in the world of Jew, Roman or Greek of the first century. This raises the question as to whether her affliction has left her alone. Marie-Eloise Rosenblatt has drawn attention to the fact that we also do not know the woman's ethnicity from the narrative even though she is generally presumed to be Jewish.[81] All that distinguishes her is her gender and her gender-related illness.

The woman is described or introduced into the narrative (labelled in the language of medical anthropology) in somatic language. She carries in her body a debilitating disease. It is almost as if she is her disease. She is γυνὴ οὖσα ἐν ῥύσει αἵματος δώδεκα ἔτη. She has had a flow or discharge of blood for twelve years. Amy-Jill Levine, in seeking to intervene in what she calls the obsession of 'students of Christian origins' with Levitical purity legislation, suggests, at least in relation to the Matthean text, that there is no indication that the flow of blood is menstrual.[82] The Markan label, however, suggests two sources of intertext, at least one of which points to the illness as being gender constructed and therefore menstrual.

The phrase ῥύσει αἵματος evokes very clearly the language of Lev. 15.19-30, particularly 15.25-28 regarding the woman with a discharge of blood for many days, not at the time of her regular menstrual flow: γυνή, ἐὰν ῥέῃ ῥύσει αἵματι ἡμέρας πλείους. Careful analysis of the text indicates that the uncleanness associated with such a blood flow is confined to the woman's bed and what she sits on and this is transmitted to the one who touches these things and remains until the evening. Also, if the restrictions of the normal menstrual period apply, as v. 25 indicates, a man who has sexual intercourse with a woman during a regular or irregular flow of blood will be rendered unclean for seven days (15.24). There is no restriction in this text in relation to the woman's touching a person or object during the time of an irregular discharge of blood, no indication that such an object or person would be rendered unclean.[83]

In recent years, two Jewish scholars, Shaye Cohen and Charlotte Fonrobert have undertaken very careful studies to try to determine how the Levitical laws in relation to menstruation, both regular and irregular, were being interpreted and practised in the first century of the Common Era in Galilee and/or Judea. Cohen notes that 'there is no clear evidence that any Jewish group in the second temple period isolated the menstruant from society'.[84] Concern with impurity was particularly in relation to the Temple as it had to be kept free from impurity. For residents of Galilee, short term periods of uncleanness, especially just until the evening, would have been a normal part of daily life. Cohen concludes that 'the Gospel story about the woman with the twelve-year discharge, clearly a case of *zābâ*, does not give any indication that the woman was impure or suffered any degree of isolation as a result of her affliction'.[85] Fonrobert notes the extension of the biblical text in the rabbinic ruling of *m. Zab.* 5.1 that is often evoked in relation to this story. The one who touches a woman with an irregular discharge of blood or anyone she touches becomes unclean and transfers that to food, drink and vessels.[86] What she makes clear, however, is that to transfer uncleanness is not a transgression. The person is simply made unclean until the evening. She concludes that '[t]he woman in the Gospel story, therefore, never commits a transgression when she touches Jesus' garment' and that as far as she knows, 'there is not a single *case story* in talmudic literature of someone in the status of impurity touching somebody else'.[87] She recognizes that 'concern about touch remains at the very most subdued in rabbinic literature'[88] and yet there is an extraordinary emphasis on touch in the Markan story. This suggests that Jewish legal texts do not provide the most appropriate intertext for understanding the Markan labelling of the woman.

In turning to the ancient medical texts as intertext, a more complex world emerges. Annette Weissenrieder has undertaken extensive research that indicates that there is a variety of terms for both regular and irregular female blood-flows in the medical literature.[89] She also locates four different referents in the possible medical intertexts for the terminology ῥύσις αἵματος: the issue of blood is the result of ruptured arteries; of injury, decay and tearing of tissues; strenuous movement during pregnancy; and regular female bleeding. Only two of these are gender specific.[90] Beyond the exact terminology, however, the medical texts, especially given their construction of the female body as 'soft and spongy flesh and excess blood' according to Helen King,[91] give particular attention to irregular blood-flows in women, especially uterine flows, while their concern for the balance of bodily fluids suggests other orifices as places of escape for excess blood as well as the uterus.[92] *Diseases of Women* 2.110 addresses some of the symptoms that can accompany irregular blood-flows.

The Markan label does not specify accompanying symptoms indicating that the concern of this text is not the professional biological reality that is the focus of the medical texts although it evokes this. The specification of the length of time of the illness, the reference to the woman having suffered much at the hands of many physicians and being worse rather than better, turns the readers' attention to this world of professional medicine and to the severity of the woman's condition that professional medicine was unable to heal. Given the intercalation of this story, it could even be deduced that the Markan storyteller is suggesting that like the young girl, the woman is close to death.[93] On the other hand, the narrator's words that extend her label (that she suffered much – πολλὰ παθοῦσα) evoke intratextually the sufferings of Jesus. Twice Jesus refers to his fate as suffering much: πολλὰ παθεῖν (8.31) and πολλὰ πάθη (9.12). The woman carries in her female body the same symbolic reality that is associated with Jesus, the healer, who will suffer because of his healing work in the bringing near of the *basileia* of God. No other character in the Markan text is thus designated.

The woman's label, within the semantic or symbolic reality of the health care system, is manipulated, first and foremost by herself. She takes the initiative in this healing encounter, reaching out and touching Jesus' garment (ἥψατο τοῦ ἱματίου αὐτοῦ). This is accompanied by her words (to herself it seems) that reveal her perspective, her desire for healing: ἐὰν ἅψωμαι κἂν τῶν ἱματίων αὐτοῦ σωθήσομαι (5.28). She touches and she speaks and healing is effected, just as we saw earlier that Jesus touched and spoke and the young girl was healed (5.41). Again, no other character is presented as effecting healing for themselves in the way that is so for this woman with the flow of blood. And her desire is that she be saved.

In the Markan narrative's construction of its health care system, the verb σῴζω contributes to the symbolic world of meaning. In 3.4, the context of a man with a withered hand appearing in the synagogue, Jesus challenges those who might accuse him regarding his Sabbath observance with the question whether it is lawful to save life on the Sabbath. Saving life in this instance is almost the equivalent of healing or restoring the man's withered hand but the context in the synagogue suggests another level of meaning also – not just the restoration of the material body but restoration or transformation to full and right relationship with God, with others of the human community and with the material world, the righteousness which characterizes the *basileia* of God.[94] Similarly in the summary passage of 6.56, the sick in the market place seek to touch the fringe of Jesus' garment and the narrator says that those who did touch it were saved, made well, healed (ὅσοι ἂν ἥψαντο αὐτοῦ ἐσῴζοντο). The manipulated label given to the healed Bartimaeus is the same as that given the woman with the flow of blood (10.52; 5.34), again associating the verb with healing and perhaps with more than just bodily restoration as seen above and as suggested by Bartimaeus' following along the way with those of the Jesus movement (10.52b).

There are more general usages (8.35; 10.26; 13.13, 20) but the term is ironically reversed in relation to Jesus as he hangs on the cross, his predicted suffering effected. Jesus' antagonists taunt him to save himself just as he saved others (15.30, 31). We can, therefore, rightfully claim that language associated with Jesus the healer is written on the body of this woman and it is repeated three times in this short account of her healing (5.23, 28, 34) in a way that doesn't happen in any other healing story. She carries suffering in her body as Jesus did and she both desires and effects healing in her body symbolizing in a quite extraordinary way the healing power of Jesus, power which he was not prepared to use on his own account.

Verse 29, with its new labelling of the woman, her body knowing that she had been healed of her illness (ἔγνω τῷ σώματι ὅτι ἴαται ἀπὸ τῆς μάστιγος), could constitute the end of a healing encounter. The woman was labelled with a culturally legitimate name. That cultural label was manipulated in a quite extraordinary way by the woman herself, and a new label was given. The new label draws on a seemingly different semantic field. Rather than ῥύσις for the flow of blood, the narrator uses πηγή. In the phrase πηγὴ τοῦ αἵματος of Lev. 12.7, it is associated with the flow of blood following childbirth rather than the irregular flow of Leviticus 15. It is difficult to determine what this change of language might mean unless it is meant to function symbolically for the new life made possible for the woman, including the possibility of child-bearing. Similarly, there is the quite unusual use of the verb ἰάομαι that occurs only in this verse in Mark's gospel and normally characterizes the healing performed by physicians (the ἰατρῶν of 5.25). Is this to indicate that the woman has been healed as she had hoped to have been healed by her pouring out of her resources on physicians? This same verb also characterizes the healings by Asclepius, as already indicated, and perhaps turns attention to a clinical reality here beyond the power of doctors. It points to the sacred and the power of the sacred to heal. This story is about healing, the healing of a woman. She is made whole in her female body, a body that has symbolically borne the language of Jesus' suffering and Jesus' healing/saving power. The change is not only physical but also socio-cultural in that it is the body of a woman which in both Jewish and Graeco-Roman constructions, biblical or medical, was inferior. There is also a hint, however, that this unnamed woman who stands alone in the text, is cross-characterized to be like the healer, Jesus. Healed of her disease, healed as a result of her own initiative, does this woman point to female healing power that seems to be obscured in the Markan text but available in the Markan world?

Her story does not conclude here but continues and further exploration may assist in answering the above question. As the woman is healed, Jesus recognizes that power has gone out from him and he searches in the crowd for whoever has touched his garment (5.30). In this verse we find the first use of δύναμις in the Markan text. We have already seen above that in the plural it refers to Jesus' deeds of power, in particular his healings and casting out of demons. This power to which Jesus alerts the reader is not the power of the physician as the earlier part of the narrative made clear. Rather it is the power that Jesus has as the authorized one of God. The extraordinary thing in this story is that the woman also has power to draw forth Jesus' power from him without his prior consent. The woman has power as Jesus has power, and she gives testimony to what has taken place even though we do not hear her words (5.33). They are, however, characterized as truth (πᾶσαν τὴν ἀλήθειαν).

The account closes with Jesus, the healer, offering his perspective on the mechanism of change in language that is religious rather than somatic. It is the πίστις of the woman that has brought her not just healing but wholeness and restoration to the right relationships which characterize the *basileia* of God which Jesus brings near. It is difficult to determine just exactly what πίστις or faith means in this context. As a noun it is generally used in contexts of healing (2.5; 5.34; 10.52) except for 11.22, an imperative to have faith in God who has power to do what is beyond human imagining; and 4.40 in reference to the disciples' lack of confidence or faith when they are in the boat with Jesus, tossed by the wind and sea. Belief in these instances affirms that Jesus has power to heal in the face of the desperation, of paralysis, long-term blood loss and blindness. It is accompanied by the sustained hope and courage to reach out beyond obstacles to grasp and gain healing. For the woman of this story, it must be all of these, together with the courage that enabled her to take an initiative, contrary to cultural codes of healing, and to reach out and touch the garment of the healer.

Jesus terminates the therapeutic relationship by sending the woman out in peace: ὕπαγε εἰς εἰρήνην. The command to go is not unusual in the termination of healing stories with this same verb of commission appearing in a number of stories. The leper was sent to the priest to be pronounced clean (1.44); the paralytic was sent home (2.11); the Gerasene man possessed by demons was sent home likewise but to make known to his kin the healing power of Jesus. The 'go in peace' phrase of 5.34 seems to be unique. The Syro-Phoenician woman is sent home with the assurance that the demon has left her daughter (7.29) and Bartimaeus is simply told to go (10.52). What is unique is the phrase εἰς εἰρήνην occurring only here in Mark's gospel. Craig Evans suggests what has already emerged elsewhere, namely that the woman may go 'in a state of wholeness and restoration'.[95] Interestingly, the woman is not directed to go home as is the Gerasene man and the paralytic. Rather she stands healed of her disease (ἴσθι ὑγιὴς ἀπὸ τῆς μάστιγός σου) in the public arena. Is she sent as an emissary of εἰρήνην, of wholeness and restoration? Bartimaeus' faith restored him and made him whole allowing him to follow Jesus on the road to discipleship, becoming a member of this itinerant *basileia* of God movement that included teachers and healers. The second time readers/hearers of this woman's story can recognize in this healed woman's going, not just a leaving of the healer but a going, a commissioning to make whole and restore, to heal. This story yearns toward a healing or negotiating of gender in the Markan healing system. The woman carries the marks of the healer on her body. Her word and touching and its power to draw forth the power of Jesus foreshadows his word and touch and power to heal in the conclusion of the intercalated story. Her story is not only a physiological and symbolic transformation but also a socio-cultural transformation of the community shaping and being shaped by this Markan story. She is named 'daughter', one who belongs in this community of transformation.[96]

Before leaving this story, I want to return to the mode of communication of healing, namely touch. The verb ἅπτομαι occurs four times in the ten short verses of this story. The other two phrases associated with healing touch, laying on of hands in 5.23 and taking the hand in 5.41, are included in the framing story. Touch is certainly the mode of communication of healing power in these two stories. I have already drawn attention to the materiality of touch whereby bodies are healed and made whole but also new social and cultural possibilities are established, especially when that touch crosses gender boundaries. From an historical point of view, David Flusser has noted through comparison with the *Genesis Apocryphon* 20.21-22 and 29, that the practice of laying on of hands was already current in some strands of Judaism at the time of Jesus ministry although he recognizes that it is not found in the Hebrew Bible or Rabbinic literature.[97] Jean-Louis Chrétien explores touch in his recent work *The Call and the Response*. He begins with the call, the word or the words and later looks to the inner voice, the inner call. The woman with the flow of blood issues an inner call to herself but this follows on her touch, a touch which is both a touching of the other and of herself, a 'self-experiencing'.[98] She calls herself to healing and wholeness before the touch of another, of Jesus, does the same. But Jesus too is touched and touches, his tactile experience also being a 'self-experiencing'.[99] Healing by way of touch creates a community of those touching and those being touched in all its reciprocity. It is material, but it is also psychological, social and symbolic. It points to a healing that truly does make for wholeness. This is the Markan ideal, an ideal that the gospel holds out to contemporary readers, both women and men.

The materiality of touch, of bodies, of skin with its attendant crossing-over reminds us that touching in this story takes place on the margins. It invites readers to cross over into another space also, that space in which the human and other-than-human can touch and be touched in a way that makes for wholeness and transformation in these relationships also. It is to this that the story of the woman with the haemorrhage invites contemporary readers seeking feminist, ecological and postcolonial transformation.

### A Daughter Is Healed of an Unclean Spirit
### (Mark 7.24-31)

This story of the daughter of the Syro-Phoenician woman would seem to be the only account of the casting out of a demon from a female. A number of scholars have rightly noted, however, that the focus of the story does not seem to be on the exorcism. Gerald Downing claims that 'even as a healing, this exorcism is so under-played...that the healer is almost a secondary character'.[100] In Twelftree's concluding paragraph of the section in which he analyses this story, he states that 'Mark's interest in this pericope as an exorcism story seems slight'.[101] Sharon Ringe also notes that 'the act of healing itself fades into the background'.[102] A brief glance at the three major Markan narratives recounting Jesus' encounter with unclean spirits (the man with the unclean spirit in the synagogue: 1.21-28; a second man with an unclean spirit in the country of the Gerasenes: 5.1-20; and the young boy who has a dumb spirit: 9.14-29) reveals that each of these stories is characterized by a vivid description of the effect on the person of the contest between Jesus and the spirit who calls out a challenge and of the departure of the spirit. All of these characteristics are absent from the story of the Syro-Phoenician woman and her daughter.

Rather, in this story, the focus is on the encounter between the woman and Jesus with the woman's reply being the turning point in the story. The healing of her daughter is, however, key to the story as is indicated by the twice repeated culturally descriptive label: εἶχεν τὸ θυγάτριον αὐτῆς πνεῦα ἀκάθαρτον (7.25) and ἵνα τὸ δαιμόνιον ἐκβάλῃ ἐκ τῆς θυγατρὸς αὐτῆς (7.26). This is further emphasized by the similarly repeated reverse labels: ἐξελήλυθεν ἐκ τῆς θυγατρός σου τὸ δαιμόνιον (7.29) and τὸ δαιμόνιον ἐξεληλυθός (7.30). A careful analysis of the rhetoric of the story through the lens of the Kleinman categories will enable us to determine how this story contributes to the construction of the Markan health care system and its gendering.

The setting for this healing is the region around Tyre. It is one of the regions in the summary passage of 3.7-12 from which great crowds come having heard what Jesus was doing (healing and casting out demons). It is borderland space between the open space of Galilee through which Jesus has just traveled and the city of Tyre itself with the city likely to be more strongly Syro-Phoenician and the hinterland probably a mixture of Galileans and Syrians. That it is borderland territory, a place where language and power is constantly being negotiated between Jewish and Syro-Phoenician inhabitants, is hinted at even by the veiled language around the Markan description of setting: Jesus came εἰς τὰ ὅρια Τύρου, into the region of Tyre.[103] Gerd Theissen has explored in detail the cultural, social, economic, political and socio-psychological conditions of the Tyrian-Galilean borderland.[104] He indicates that the designation of the woman as Greek (7.26) suggests that she is a member of the upper class and this designation separates her further from the Jewish population of the hinterland than the simple designation Syro-Phoenician would do.[105]

Within this borderland context, Jesus goes into a house where he wishes to remain anonymously. This suggests that he does not go to the area to extend the task he was undertaking in Galilee of 'preaching the gospel of God' by healing and casting out of demons. He has been shown in the narrative as religious folk healer, as prophet of God within the Jewish health care system, whose prophetic power heals and casts out demons to restore people to health, to right relationships within the *basileia* of God which he is preaching (1.15). In this context of desired anonymity from this task, a woman hears about him (ἀκούσασα γύνη) as did the woman with the haemorrhage (5.27) and as will blind Bartimaeus (10.47). The woman draws forth healing power from him even though he did not go into the area as part of his healing ministry. The language of the Markan text places her with two other very needy supplicants: a woman with a haemorrhage who was almost dead, locked in an illness which seems to have left her isolated and alone in a world of dyadic relationships; and a blind man likewise isolated in the public arena, begging by the roadside rather than being cared for within his family. This woman is introduced into the narrative, therefore, in a way that parallels that of the woman with the haemorrhage before we learn anything of her possible social and economic status. She also stands among the others from about Tyre and Sidon (3.8) who, hearing all that he was doing (ἀκούοντες ὅσα ἐποίει), came to him.

The number of participants in this healing encounter is difficult to state explicitly. The daughter who has the unclean spirit is not a full participant in the therapeutic encounter but her mother comes to the one whom she has heard of as healer to seek release for her daughter. Like the woman with the haemorrhage, this woman is not embedded in dyadic family relationships as far as the narrative makes known to us and she must take the initiative for the healing of her household, of her daughter, just as Jairus sought healing for his daughter (5.22-23) and as the father of the boy with the dumb spirit will do (9.14-29). Gender in the Markan construction of healing does not preclude a woman taking the initiative in approaching the healer when she or her family is in need of healing.

The quality of her interaction with Jesus the healer is formal: she falls down at his feet. This too was the action of Jairus when he sought Jesus' healing for his daughter (5.22, with the only difference being in the verb πίπτω and προσπίπτω) and of the woman with the haemorrhage when she approached Jesus following her healing. This action by the supplicant seems to constitute recognition of the power of the healer, especially the religious or spiritual power that one authorized by God has within the Jewish health care system. It is this power which the unclean spirits recognize in 3.11 causing them to fall down before Jesus and cry out that he is son of God, one vested with the power of God because of intimate relationship with God. It is this power that the foreign woman seems to recognize, thus indicating her attitude to the healer and her belief that he has the power to heal. It is only after her acknowledgement of healing power that the narrator tells the reader that she is Greek, a Syro-Phoenician by birth, evoking her status, her wealth and her ethnic origins as noted above.

We do not hear the woman's explanation of her daughter's illness in contrast to the father whose son has a dumb spirit (9.17-18). The narrator communicates to readers the illness label that the culture has provided: she has an unclean spirit (εἶχεν...πνεῦμα ἀκάθαρτον). The woman's desire for healing is likewise communicated in the language of the narrator (in contrast to the woman with the haemorrhage whose aspirations we hear in her own words, 5.28). She desires that the demon be cast out of her daughter, and she communicates her belief that the folk healer, Jesus, can do this by her approach to him. She is an outsider according to the description of her in the narrative and she occupies, with Jesus, the borderland of the region of Tyre. The idiom of communication of her daughter's illness is recognizable in both the Greek and the Jewish culture.

The language world evoked by the explanatory model provided by the narrator is not that of Hippocratic medicine and the medical texts. Indeed, the text *On the Sacred Disease*, which addresses many symptoms similar to those attributed to the one possessed of an unclean spirit – becoming mad and demented, doing many things out of place, foaming and sputtering – claims this so-called sacred disease has natural causes like all other diseases and it does not belong to a divine or sacred realm.[106] Rather the world that the Markan language evokes is that of sacred folk medicine which constructs a world of conflicting spirits. Wendy Cotter indicates that the work of Plutarch in the latter half of the first century reveals this world construction in his work *De Defectu Oraculorum* (415a-418d).[107] For the Greeks, whose language and culture names the woman of Mark's story, there are 'four classes of rational beings': gods, demigods, heroes...and men (*De Defectu Oraculorum* 415b). Later he recognizes that some of the *daimonas* or demigods can be evil – *daimonon* (*De Defectu Oraculorum* 417e) and we see the effects of possession by such demons in his *Lives* (*Marcellus*, 20, 5f) when Nicias throws himself on the ground, speaks in a strange voice, leaps up half naked, acting as one 'possessed and crazed'. We have already noted, however, that such symptoms belong to male spirit possession in the Markan narrative. We are given no indication of the effects of the unclean spirit on the woman's daughter.

It is late within Biblical Judaism, except for the references to the evil spirit which came upon Saul (1 Sam. 16.14, 15, 16, 23; 18.10; 19.9), that we find a world of demons or unclean spirits emerging. It is particularly evident in the book of Tobit (3.8, 17; 6.8, 14, 16, 17; 8.3) in which Sarah is possessed by an evil spirit and it is only when Tobias carries out the ritual proposed to him by Raphael who is sent by God to heal her in answer to her prayer (Tob. 3.17) that Sarah is healed, freed from the demon.[108] Josephus too knows this world of demon spirits and in *Ant.* 8.45-49, he speaks of the τέχνη, the art used against such spirits (κατὰ τῶν δαιμόνων) and he too links this art with healing: θεραπείαν τοῖς ἀνθρώποις. Josephus goes on to describe Eleazar's use of the τέχνη that he, Josephus, links to Solomon. At the conclusion of the description of Eleazar's freeing of a man possessed, Josephus praises Solomon whom God had favoured. The one who has the power to drive out demonic, unclean or evil spirits (demons) receives this power from God in the Jewish health care system as is clear from both the Book of Tobit and Josephus' *Antiquities*.

The Syro-Phoenician woman's daughter is thus labelled in language that is cultural, both Greek and Jewish, evoking the sacred realm of conflicting powers played out in the body of a young girl. A cultural anthropological approach to this label would also ask if she bears in her body the social, economic and political conflict that Theissen associates with her region:

> Aggressive prejudices, supported by economic dependency and legitimated by religious traditions, strained the relationships between the more thoroughly Hellenized Tyrians and the Jewish minority population living either in Tyre or in its vicinity, partly in the city and partly in the countryside. The economically stronger Tyrians probably often took bread out of the mouths of the Jewish rural population, when they used their superior financial means to buy up the grain supply in the countryside.[109]

A woman who might well have had the wealth not only to consult physicians but also to access Asclepieia or other healing shrines in the folk sector of the health care system comes seeking healing for her daughter who suffers the effects of what was known as demon possession from a Jewish charismatic healer who has entered the borderland region between the city of Tyre and upper Galilee.

The one aspect of the socio-cultural, political and economic context of first-century Tyre and its hinterland that Theissen did not consider was gender. In the Markan unfolding story of healing, this is the first narrative in which a woman approaches Jesus, the healer, directly. If Theissen is correct in his analysis, this woman would have been a member of the colonizing Tyrian upper class whose continued expansion into Jewish territory impacted on the life and wellbeing of the Jewish peasants in the hinterland. She could well have considered herself superior to Jesus, free to approach him as women of her class and wealth could have traveled to the Asclepieia. The needs of her child, however, lead her to cross status boundaries and to kneel before the Jewish healer asking for release for her daughter. Women's presence in the Asclepian narratives of healing as well as in the Hippocratic *Epidemics* suggest that it is status rather than gender being negotiated in this narrative.

It is at this point that the readers/hearers are drawn into the communication between healer and supplicant. The narrator tells of the woman's desire that the demon be cast out of her daughter that is the final aspect of an explanatory model, the results hoped for. We learn nothing, however, of her belief system in relation to healing or what motivates her crossing cultural, status and presumably religious boundaries save her desire for healing for her daughter. The words of Jesus cut across this desire suggesting 'conflicts in beliefs and values'.[110] Jesus becomes an obstacle in the healing process.

The words of Jesus regarding bread for children and dogs (7.27) have proven highly problematic for all commentators on this passage. It is the not the task of this project to revisit those problems.[111] Rather, I want to continue to read this narrative through the lens of medical anthropological categories and a focus on healing. We have already seen that the clinical reality evoked by the labelling of the daughter is sacred: possession by powers that are in conflict with divine power with resultant bodily disorder. In this verbal interaction between Jesus the healer and the supplicant Syro-Phoenician woman, a counter interpretation of disorder is posited. Perhaps using a saying that was well-known among the Jewish population of the Tyrian hinterland,[112] Jesus the healer shifts the clinical engagement from the personal grief and need of the Syro-Phoenician mother to the socio-cultural and economic disorder in the region which, as I've already suggested, may have been carried in the young girl's body and which the woman's presence before Jesus may have evoked. Jesus, from his cultural association with the Jewish hinterland and his therapeutic association with those who are sick (including those whose lives are disordered by economic and political oppressions), confronts the woman: it is not good to take the food from the children of the land and to throw it to the gentile city dwellers.

The initial phrase that the children be fed first (Ἄφες πρῶτον χορτασθῆναι τὰ τέκνα) is not used in the Matthean redaction which may suggest that it is Markan and that the traditional saying is the second half of the verse which Matthew retains. The verb χορτάζω has very specific use in Mark. It carries the meaning of eating to satisfaction and its only other occurrences, than in this passage, is in the two accounts of the feeding of the multitudes (6.42; 8.4, 8). This gives further weight to the healer, Jesus, shifting the import of the clinical interaction. For Jesus, the plight of the one daughter of the Syro-Phoenician woman evokes the plight of the many children of Israel in the Jewish hinterland.[113] Jesus' words challenge what might be simply a somatic understanding of the girl's illness and give it socio-cultural, economic and political layers of meaning. Disorder at these levels will be borne in the bodies of citizens.

The woman replies formally using the title of respect: Κύριε. She continues the metaphorical language of the saying but turns it around so that both the children and the dogs are to be fed. Also, the language shifts from the public arena of satisfying multitudes to that of the private arena: the little dogs under the table eating the crumbs of the children (7.28). From a postcolonial perspective, caution might be needed here as the woman, representing the colonizers, appropriates the imagery of the colonized that challenges the infrastructure of colonization. What she does, however, is to take the language of separation and division and change it to the language of inclusion. It is possible that the children (the Jewish people) can be fed as well as outsiders, sharing in what may seem like crumbs (including the healing of a daughter). And it is this language, this word (τοῦτον τὸν λόγον) which effects healing according to the assessment of the healer (7.29). Because of the absence of the daughter, there is no touch involved in this healing. But nor is it the word of the healer which brings about transformation but the word of the woman who not only recognizes the healer's perspective on a demonic situation but also proposes a more inclusive therapeutic intervention.

This woman is sent, as was the woman with the haemorrhage: ὕπαγε (7.29; cf. 5.34b). She, however, is to take up responsibility for the health of her daughter. Then Jesus pronounces the new label: the demon has come out of her daughter. This is the reversal of the cultural naming of the problem in 7.26. The meaning of this was contested within the narrative and so now the healing takes on another level of meaning. If the demon has left the young girl, then it is possible for economic, social/ethnic and political disorder to be cast out. The narrator re-iterates Jesus' assessment that healing has taken place: the woman returns home to find the child lying on a bed, the demon having left her. The telling of the story shapes the religious imagination to hope not only in the transformation of individuals but also of ethnic, cultural, economic and political structures which create disorder, causing many to suffer.

I am aware that this interpretation has focused on the symbolic level of this therapeutic relationship in a way that might obscure the materiality of bread and of children and dogs in need of the nourishment of food/bread even though the economic layer of reading was evoked by this very materiality. There may be another layer of meaning that can be given to this materiality when one turns to other narratives of healing or more particularly of healers, those written in the stone of first-century CE funerary stelae. Mousa, whom we encountered earlier, and who is called ἰατρείνη, is depicted with two dogs at her feet looking up toward the object she has in her hand. In a second-century stele, Mokazoire is accompanied by a small dog that looks up toward her. She, however, is not named as healer. Another woman, whose name is missing but whose father's name is Moukaporis, is depicted with a dog leaning up toward the object in her hand but she too is given no professional designation.[114] It is difficult to determine the significance of the dogs on these stelae and whether there is any particular significance to the world of healing and for the meaning of the saying of Jesus. It was noted when discussing Mousa earlier that the dog was associated with divine healers: accompanying Asclepius but even more significantly linked to the ancient Mesopotamian deity Gula. Avalos suggests that Gula was almost indistinguishable from her dog.[115] This may indicate that there were multiple layers of meaning for the image of the dog in this Markan healing story, some of which were more explicitly linked to healing and perhaps contestation around healing power. This points us to the multiple meanings possible for us as we interpret this healing story today in a world of contestation in relation to healing. It draws attention to the other-than-human which we have seen associated with healing and the way the other-than-human, can be constructed in opposition to the human. In this female genealogy, however, we have seen more and more hints toward a strong association of healing with the other-than-human.

### Healing Women/Women Healing in the Markan Health Care System: A Summary

In examining the explicit presence of women in the Markan health care system, especially as patients/supplicants, we have noted gender patterning that is characteristic of the Greek and Roman worlds, but we have also become aware of gender being negotiated within this system. It seems appropriate, therefore, to review this process before turning to examine women's presence around the death of Jesus that participates in the construction of healing within the Markan world.

First, the number of healings of females narrated in the Markan story would lead readers to think that fewer women were healed than men but comparison with both the Athenian dedicatory inventories and the Epidaurian stelae reveals that the number of women supplicants decreases when the medium is male storytelling. This suggests that the Markan narrative shares this gendering characteristic. Where the narrative differs, however, is in relation to its gendering of healers. The key character in the narrative is Jesus, the healer, who establishes a new kinship of healers. The male members of this group are explicitly commissioned to heal although the reader does not hear stories of their healing, simply the narrator's telling of it. There are hints, however, in the narration of two female healings (Simon's mother-in-law and the woman with the haemorrhage), that these healed women become participants in the new kinship of healers. These are voices from the borderland where dominant and subverted narratives cross over and a new but shared voice is heard. Women healing/healing women can characterize the Markan health care system as they do in the socio-cultural world in which the Markan community is situated, especially the world of folk healing. As has been seen in that wider world, however, women engaged in healing in the folk sector are often hidden within literary tropes or male narratives and at times male invectives.

There is also a tension in the Markan narrative around two of the female healings that are drawn forth from Jesus without or beyond his intention (the woman with the haemorrhage and the Syro-Phoenician woman). In the first, a woman's initiative in touching Jesus draws out his power and he knows this only after the event. In the second, Jesus is in retreat from his ministry when a woman crosses borders to challenge him to heal across ethnic, socio-economic and political boundaries. Both stories take Jesus and the reader into borderland spaces between healer and healed where the word of the supplicant effects healing, and this healing is acknowledged by the healer. Again gender is negotiated in these places of hybridity so that the spaces themselves become transformed with potential for healing the other-than-human but not only that, also the cultural, the socio-economic and the political.

The crossing over that characterizes these spaces of negotiation was particularly evident in the story of the woman with the haemorrhage who carries the marks of the suffering and the saving one on her textualized body. Her touch and her word that heals foreshadow the healing touch, the healing word of Jesus who restores health and life to a young girl. Her story teases the imagination of the gospel recipients especially those who know the healing power of women in their world. Can women be healers as Jesus is healer?

I will suggest that this question is answered, again with hints and nuance from the borderland, but with a stronger counter voice than previously, in the story of the woman who pours ointment over the head of Jesus as he faces suffering and death. We will turn now to an analysis of this story.

### A Woman Pours Out Healing Ointment
### (Mark 14.3-9)[116]

Characterization is central to this Markan narrative. The early introduction of a γυνή (v. 3) and the four-times repeated αὐτῇ (vv. 5, 6 [x 2]; 9) draw attention to gender. This could be read over as the story opens and closes with focus on Jesus; the social space is that of Simon; and the reader would undoubtedly assume, in terms of the genderization of the entire Markan narrative, that the certain ones who disapprove of the woman's action are likewise male. Male naming and male voice characterize the story but they cannot silence the agency of this woman and her healing ointment that have been given voice by the telling of this story.

Location focuses attention on Bethany, a place or space which is near to Jerusalem (11.1) but is not Jerusalem. Jerusalem is where one finds the 'chief priests and scribes' of the opening verses of this chapter (14.1-2; cf. 10.33; 11.15-18, 27), those who are characterized as desiring the death of Jesus, indeed actively plotting to bring it about (8.31; 10.33; 11.18; 14.1). Jerusalem is, therefore, a place of death threats, of fatal bodily harm, while Bethany is the place of retreat from these. Yet it is not complete retreat. It is a borderland space in which, as we have seen, transformative healing can take place.

The more explicit setting for this healing narrative is a house, that of Simon the Leper. Such a setting recalls for readers that the house has been a place of healing from the beginning of the Markan narrative (1.29; 2.1; 2.15). In the first story, bodily boundaries were transgressed as Jesus stretched out his hand and raised Simon's mother-in-law who went on to do *diakonia*. A paralytic is healed and religious boundaries crossed in the second story and controversy erupts over the reclining body of Jesus and over the transgression of socio-cultural boundaries – eating with tax-collectors and sinners at 2.15. Both healing and new kinship play, therefore, in the rhetorical space which the reference to *oikos* in 14.3 creates. The naming of the householder as Simon the Leper adds to this evocation of healing early in this story. The reference to Jesus' reclining as at a supper or *deipnon* would evoke differing understandings of the gendering of this particular space depending on the Markan audience's experience of the shifting nature of women's and men's participation in more formal meals in Greek, Roman and Jewish societies.[117] By the first century, wives of upper class men could be found reclining or sitting at meals with them, especially at the *deipnon* but this was a transition since as Corley notes '(d)uring Hellenistic times those women present for dinner parties with men were stereotypically considered to be prostitutes of some kind, or at least promiscuous, whatever their social status or occupation'.[118] The *deipnon* was, therefore, a borderland space where gender was being negotiated.

The woman who enters this space is unnamed which may suggest that she is a respectable woman.[119] While her status is obscure, the description provided in the text is not. She is a γυνή having an alabaster jar (ἔχουσα ἀλαβάστρον) of very costly oinment of pure nard (μύρου νάρδου πιστικῆς πολυτελοῦς). She breaks the alabaster jar (συντρίψασα τὴν ἀλάβαστρον) whose contents she pours out (κατέχεεν) over the head of Jesus. Reading within the dominant narrative, not only has this unknown and unnamed woman transgressed the predominantly male space but she has countervened the honour code by acting decisively in this public space in relation to the male body of Jesus. No wonder certain ones present were indignant!

Reading beyond any male colonization of space, however, the *oikos* in the gospel narrative, as we have seen, can be reclaimed as male and female space within a new fictive kinship. It is a space where male and female bodies can be transformed by healing action, and where a place has been created for the possibility of a woman's action in relation to the male body of Jesus to be healing.[120]

This description of the woman and her action does not seem to contain any of the healing language encountered in healing narratives, on inscriptions or generally used in the Graeco-Roman world as explored earlier. Nor is the woman described as anointing with oil for healing as were the twelve male disciples commissioned by Jesus (6.13). The use of ἀλείφω, ἔλαοιν, χρῖσμα, χρίω, or χριστός in their various forms would have served intertextually to evoke the priestly or prophetic task of anointing which would point to the traditional interpretation of this text (see Exod. 29.7; 2 Kgs 9.3, 6; Ps. 23.5). A different intertextuality seems, therefore, to be suggested.[121]

One of the most significant concentrations of the language of Mk 14.3 is in Athenaeus' *Deipnosophistae*, especially Book 15. Athenaeus wrote his *Deipnosophistae (The Sophists at Dinner)* around the year 200 CE but it clearly represents the language and practices not only of Imperial Rome but also classical Greece as myriads of texts from earlier writers and thinkers are drawn explicitly into his text.[122] The language and practices of *Deipnosophistae*, therefore, reflect those of classical and Hellenistic Greece taken into the Roman world. They could readily have been evoked by the description of the woman of Mk 14.3 who pours perfumed ointment over the head of Jesus even though Athenaeus' writing is later than that of the Markan gospel.

Perfume or μύρον is discussed at length at the symposium which follows the *deipnon* described in *Deipnosophistae*. It is stated in Book 15 that 'when the slaves passed round perfumes (μύρα) in alabaster bottles (ἀλάβαστροις)' (*Deip.* 15.686c), the discussion could commence. Cynulcus began by quoting Socrates from Xenophon's *Symposium* who deduced that there was one kind of smell appropriate to women and another to men, gendering these wonderful mixtures of materials of the earth whose aromas were a feast for the senses and whose effects on the human body were recreative.[123] Ἔλαιον he associated with the gymnasium, the world of men, and μύρον with women in the contrasted phrase μύρου γυναιξὶ (*Deip.* 15.686e). Despite this distinction, however, the discussion among the male diners, reclining at table, after their meal, is of the μύρα passed around among them and not of ἔλαιον.

Masurius responds to Cynulcus' opening remarks on the gendering of perfumes with the challenge that 'sensations of *our* brain' (the ἐγκεφάλον of the males at the *symposium*) are soothed as well as healed (θεραπεύονται) by the 'sweet odours' of perfumes; and he goes on to quote Alexis: '[a] highly important element of health (ὑγιείας) is to put good odours to the brain' (*Deip*. 15.687d; cf. 2.46b). Later in his speech, Masurius notes the different perfumes which are appropriate for the symposium, *nard* (νάρδος) being included among them (15.689d).[124] One is efficacious for those suffering from lethargic fever. Another 'is wholesome and keeps the brain clear' and another is helpful to the digestion (15.689c-d). Reclining at table for the symposium following the *deipnon* and participating in the passing around of various μύρα, men can be healed of various bodily ailments but most particularly those associated with the head or brain,[125] the bodily zone which together with the heart and eyes, Malina and Pilch associate with 'emotion-fused' thought.[126]

The woman of Mk 14.3 enters the space of male reclining, evoking the *deipnon/symposium*. She has the alabaster flask of very costly ointment of pure nard that one would expect at such a meal and rather than passing it among the guests, she breaks presumably the long thin stem of the container and pours the entire contents over the head of Jesus as he reclines at the table. The story has not labelled Jesus with a culturally appropriate label for one in need of healing as has been the case in the other healing stories already explored. The text does not present Jesus and Simon discussing the healing capacities of such fine ointment/oil of pure nard for their male bodies as does Masurius' dialogue with his fellow diners. The narrator has, however, re-invoked for listeners, the death threats facing Jesus of which he is acutely aware as the earlier indicators of impending death signify. Only the participial description of Jesus (v. 3) separates the action of the woman from the death threat hanging over Jesus. There is, however, no direct description of illness in this narrative.

That the woman knows Jesus' condition suggests her membership in the discipleship/fictive kinship group who have heard Jesus' own awareness of the death threats directed toward him. She reaches out across the space in which healing can happen; and takes into her hand the rich earthly resources of healing ointments, associated with women but appropriated by men for their healing and enjoyment. Her action is a borderland one which links the male and female world by pouring out her resource over the head of the male Jesus enveloping him in the earth's healing resource and women's healing power.

The response to this healing in the liminal space where gender is being negotiated, a space which we have seen characterizes aspects of the Markan healing system, is indignation. Those at table with Jesus name the woman's action as *waste* of the μύρον, clearly failing to recognize the pain in the body of Jesus and contrasting their response to that of the woman healer who is perhaps a member with them in the healing *basileia* movement accompanying Jesus.[127] They seek to take back the space that has been transgressed. And, into the healing space her action has created, they introduce another language – that of waste which has not been heard in the gospel story to this point. The woman's action has been questioned as Jesus' healing actions were questioned by his opponents. The force of the response to the woman's action highlights the challenge that the crossing or negotiating of marked and gendered space might have meant, especially if, as I am suggesting here, the woman's action was recognized as healing since women have not been explicitly included in the Markan health care system as healers.

Elsewhere, I explored Jesus' interpretation of the woman's action in greater detail.[128] Here, I will simply highlight his claiming of the healing in the very materiality of his body, to his very heart, the place of deep anxiety and pain (ἐν ἐμοί). Although the initial dis-ease of Jesus was not named explicitly, but implied, Jesus indicates that the woman's action has manipulated the implicit naming so that the pouring out of healing ointment like the reaching out of his own healing hands across spaces between bodies has wrought a change. The new label Jesus gives to the healing action is a 'good work' that has been done 'in me' (καλὸν ἔργον ἐν ἐμοί). The borderland space created by the woman's action, which certain ones sought to take back, has been re-claimed by the words of Jesus. Female healing action which has been silenced in the dominant narrative except for the faint hint in the *diakonia* of the mother-in-law of Simon and the cross characterization of the woman with the haemorrhage has been named as an appropriate and fitting action for women in not only this *kairos* time of Jesus but the in-between time before the accomplishment of all things proclaimed in the reign-of-God ministry of Jesus (1.14-15; 13.4-37).

Jesus' final interpretation of the woman's action retains the language of healing ointment but now in the aorist active infinitive form (μυρίσαι). Her healing has been claimed, not only in relation to its effects on the head, eyes and heart, the emotion-fused region of the one suffering the anguish of death threats, but for the body of Jesus in preparation for burial. Into this healing space of male and female interaction in which cultural boundaries around gender, space and the materiality of bodies and resources have been renegotiated, Jesus commits the textualizing or naming of his body. The healing action of an unnamed woman, perhaps one of the healing community he has established by his ministry, has prepared Jesus' body for burial. A second new label is given by Jesus to his healed body – it has been prepared for burial. There is an ambivalence here, however, as death and burial would seem to be the enemies of the health care system. People sought healing from Jesus against the threat of death. The healing action undertaken by this Markan female healer prepares Jesus' body for death itself.

Here I will briefly explore this second re-labelling in relation to Mk 16.1 where women go, after the burial of Jesus, with spices (ἀρώματα) to anoint him (ἀλείψωσιν), the verb here being the same as that used to describe the healing work of the commissioned male disciples (6.13). What is the relationship between the μυρίσαι...εἰς τὸν ἐνταφιασμόν (the ointmenting of Jesus' body for burial) of Mark 14.8 and the anointing with spices after burial of 16.1 and how do they contribute to an understanding of the gendering of healing in the Markan narrative and world?

It seems that it is difficult to distinguish these two phrases linguistically. In the *Deipnosophistae* where one finds a concentration of the language of ointmenting and of anointing, the verbs μυρίζω and ἀλείφω seem to be used almost interchangeably. At 15.691, the text states that 'the act of anointing with such unguents as these is expressed by the verb *myrizo* (Τὸ δὲ χρίσασθαι τῷ τοιούτῳ ἀλείμματι μυρίσασθαι)'. On the other hand, one finds the phrase 'then you must anoint my body (ἀλείφεσθαι πρίω τὸ σῶμά μοι μύρον ἴρινον)' at 15.689. Anointing or ointmenting have many functions, one of which has been discussed above, namely for healing, for health. The addition of the phrase τὸν ἐνταφιασμόν in Mk 14.8 focuses the ointmenting, it is the anointing that accompanies burial or in other words, embalming. The only time any form of ἐνταφιάζω appears in the LXX is in Gen. 50.2 where Joseph engages the embalmists to embalm the body of his father for burial. BAGD identifies only one instance where μυρίζω is carried out on the dead.[129] The phrase used in Mk 14.8 seems intended, therefore, to maintain a clear verbal link with μύρον as used in 14.3 to describe the action of the woman and to claim its effect. It will indeed strengthen Jesus through to his anointing for burial. In this sense, it may not be claiming that the woman's action is the burial anointing but, as in previous healing narratives, the new label which points to the effectiveness of the healing.

In this reading, there is no tension between 14.8 and 16.1. The women's visiting of the tomb on the third day and their association with spices for anointing and embalming of the dead seems to link two traditions which associate women with the rituals around death even though it would be unusual to anoint a body that has been two to three days in the tomb.[130] They do what the woman of Mark 14 was unable to do, they honour the body of Jesus in the death for which her ointmenting strengthened and prepared him.

Women were not commissioned to heal within the dominant narrative of the Markan gospel story that explicitly associated commissioned healing with a select group of twelve males. In this borderland story, a woman healer takes the initiative in reaching out beyond socio-cultural boundaries to offer healing to Jesus. It is not the narrator who describes the changed or manipulated state as in most of the healing stories but Jesus himself. Also, the healing action of this woman does not simply become one story among many within the unfolding narrative but it is affirmed with the highest possible honour at a climax point in the gospel as Jesus enters into his final hours. Indeed, it strengthens him for that time to the point where he is able to name his body as prepared for the embalming associated with burial. The woman herself has carried out the work which was hers. It is this that is to be told to her memory whenever the gospel story is proclaimed. Women healing is made a constitutive element of the proclamation of the gospel at this climactic point.

## Conclusion

A reading of the gendering of the Markan world of healing reveals the ambivalence that often surrounds gender, especially when it is being negotiated very explicitly. A number of the stories of healing women occur in borderland spaces, places of such negotiating, where both the colonizer and the colonized can cross over to different places, to shared places and where a pastiche is created. Or, viewed differently, the borderland can be a place where some of the dualisms of the master paradigm can be shifted if not overturned.

Like the Markan readers/hearers who may have read/heard the narratives of healing women differently on their second and subsequent readings, so too for the contemporary reader, the final story of a healing woman sends the reader back to Galilee, back to the ministry of Jesus, with new eyes for reading, with a shift in the gendering of the Markan world of healing.

Not only can gender and women be read anew, so too can the body, space and the other-than-human elements like perfumed ointment. Bodies that reach out and touch are bodies which can heal whether they be male or female. Spaces need not be gendered discriminately but can be honoured as places pregnant with possibility for health and wholeness and right ordering not just of the human community but the Earth community also. The materiality of life-enhancing perfumed ointment can likewise permeate this gospel story and shape its reading as does the woman whose memory is to accompany it. Healing and stories of healing in the Markan gospel of Jesus are not only in memory of him but are also to be in memory of her. Healing women and women healing shape this memory.

# Chapter 5

## RE-TELLING STORIES OF WOMEN HEALING/HEALING WOMEN: THE GOSPEL OF MATTHEW

> Bultmann held that as the oral tradition developed, names and details would be inserted, reflecting a 'novelistic' concern with the 'characters' in the tradition. This implies that, other conditions being equal, the simpler tales will be closer to the original tradition; details are also added to provide links between originally discrete groups of material.[1]

> The ability of counterstories to reconfigure dominant stories permits those who have been excluded or oppressed by a 'found' community to gain fuller access to the goods offered there.[2]

In turning to the gospel of Matthew and its characterization of women healing in the context of the Matthean construction of a health care system, one notes that the same stories of healing women are recounted as in the gospel of Mark. This could lead to the assumption that there is mere repetition of stories. One finds, however, a re-telling of stories and a reshaping of the Jesus narrative so that the emphases are quite distinct.

An Infancy Narrative and a much more extensive John the Baptist/Jesus story (Matthew 3–4), means that the ministry of Jesus in Matthew's gospel does not begin until 4.17. The narrator tells us that Jesus begins to preach repentance for the *basileia* of the heavens is at hand, a message similar to Mk 1.15.[3] Following the call of four fishermen from beside the Sea of Galilee into a new fictive kinship, the Matthean reader encounters the narrator's voice again in the first of ten summary passages which characterize Jesus' teaching, preaching and healing (4.23-25).[4] From *telling* of this two or three-fold activity, the narrator then *shows* Jesus doing just as he has been characterized. He preaches and teaches (the Sermon on the Mount, Matthew 5–7) and heals (Matthew 8–9 in which ten stories of healing[5] are clustered, interspersed by two short buffer pericopes breaking them into groups of three, three and four healing narratives).[6] The narrator then returns to telling mode repeating the initial summary of 4.23 almost verbatim in 9.35: Jesus goes about preaching, teaching and healing.[7]

The Matthean gospel places the healing activity of Jesus alongside, indeed intersecting with, his teaching and preaching and each as different modes of the proclamation of the *basileia* of the heavens, in a way which differs from the Markan emphasis on healing with much less explicit teaching. The Matthean health care system is intimately connected to the religious system characterized by preaching and teaching in this narrative.

This three-fold depiction of Jesus' ministry, framed by the parallel summaries, is itself further framed by stories of discipleship. As noted above, immediately following the announcement of the beginning of Jesus' ministry (4.17), four fishermen are drawn into a new fictive kinship group around Jesus (4.18-22), leaving their family and their occupations and following Jesus. The first use of the verb ἀκολουθέω, to follow, occurs in 4.20 and then again in 4.22 to describe the actions of the four brothers who leave to become part of the itinerant group around Jesus, a grouping which the social science critics call *fictive kinship*.[8] Immediately subsequent to the last of the healing stories in Matthew 8–9, Jesus calls to himself 'his twelve disciples'.[9] To these he gives the authority to cast out unclean spirits and to heal every disease and every infirmity (ἔδωκεν αὐτοῖς ἐξουσίαν πνευμάτων ἀκαθάρτων ὥστε ἐκβάλλειν αὐτὰ καὶ θεραπεύειν πᾶσαν νόσον καὶ πᾶσαν μαλακίαν), repeating the phrases which described Jesus' ministry in 4.23 and 9.35 as seen above. In 10.7, the preaching of the same message that Jesus preaches (the *basileia* of the heavens is at hand) is added to the commission, and healing is reiterated: heal the sick, raise the dead, cleanse lepers, cast out demons (10.8). Between the two parts of the commission, the names of the Twelve are listed and they are all male. No woman is explicitly included among those commissioned to continue this ministry of Jesus, this religio-health care ministry. Given the roles of women in the professional and the folk sectors of the health care system in the broader Roman world, this seems to be a significant omission. It should be noted here also that within the nine healing stories of Matthew 8–9, three are of women, approximately one-third, which corresponds with the percentage in the Markan gospel as well as in the Epidaurian iamata.

Given the very ordered and patterned depiction of Jesus' healing and his commissioning of those among the fictive kinship group to do likewise in the first ten chapters of the gospel, the development of this theme in the remainder of the gospel seems more haphazard. There are only five additional healing narratives (12.9-14, 22-32; 15.21-28; 17.14-20 and 20.29-34), only one of which involves a female recipient (15.21-28). A number of summaries intersperse the latter part of the gospel (11.2-6; 12.15-21; 14.14, 34-36; 15.29-32; 19.2; 21.14-15), two of which explicate clearly the types of illnesses that are healed (11.5; 15.30-31). Even though Jesus has commissioned the Twelve to be healers shaping communities of healers as he is doing, the reader/hearer does not learn of this happening. Rather Jesus continues as healer right into the temple precincts when the blind and the lame come to him and he heals them (21.14).

This concluding text, unique to Matthew's gospel, may provide a lens through which to look back at the way Jesus is characterized as healer in the Matthean gospel in order to situate him within the first-century health care systems. The presence of the blind and the lame in the temple acts as an intertextual reversal of the proclamation that 'the blind and the lame shall not come into the house' cited in 2 Sam. 5.6-10. In that text, these two groups defended Jerusalem against David's taking of the city for his capital and drew down on themselves exclusion from the temple and perhaps even the city. Jesus, as a new descendant of David, named in the opening verse of the gospel as 'son of David' (1.1), reverses this situation when he not only welcomes but heals the blind and the lame in the house or the temple (21.14).

What is implicit in Mt. 21.14, namely the intertextuality that gives meaning to Jesus the healer in the Matthean gospel, is made explicit both in its immediate context and in other summary passages. In 21.9, the crowds have welcomed Jesus to Jerusalem with the cry: 'Hosanna to the Son of David' and in 21.11, these same crowds proclaim: 'This is the prophet Jesus from Nazareth of Galilee'. In Mt. 21.15, immediately following the reference to the blind and lame being healed in the temple precincts, the narrator repeats for readers/hearers the welcome cry proclaiming Jesus as 'Son of David'. The healing one is prophet in the line of David, a holy one of God. This is further demonstrated by the fact that all the other occurrences of the designation 'Son of David' outside the Infancy Narrative and up to this point in the gospel occur in stories of healing (9.27; 20.30, 31 – blind men cry out for mercy; 15.22 – a Canaanite woman likewise cries out for healing mercy; and 12.23 following the healing of the blind and dumb demoniac, the people ask if this healer could be the Son of David). Jesus is characterized as a therapeutic Son of David, healing not only human bodies but also social and cultural divisions and exclusions.[10]

In 8.16-17, the text of Isa. 53.4a (the carrying of our weaknesses and bearing our diseases) is cited as being fulfilled in Jesus' healing of all who were sick (πάντας τοὺς κακῶς ἔχοντας) and his casting out of demons from many who were possessed. The servant of God, the holy man of God of Deutero-Isaiah, provides a model for understanding the healing activity of Jesus in the Matthean community who turn to their sacred story to provide a way of making meaning of the life and work of Jesus. Likewise in the summary passage of 11.5, in which Jesus responds to John's question whether he is the coming one, the prophet Isaiah is evoked although not explicitly cited (Isa. 26.19 – the dead shall live; 29.18 – the deaf shall hear and the blind shall see; 35.5-6 – the blind shall see; the deaf shall hear, the lame shall leap like a deer and the dumb shall sing for joy). One hears echoes of these same passages in the listing of transformations in the last verse of the Matthean summary, 15.29-31. This text ends with the crowd glorifying the God of Israel. The Jesus who heals in the Matthean gospel story is the holy one of God through whom God, the healer in Israel, heals.[11] From an etic perspective, we can say that Jesus stands within the religio-folk sector of the health care system.

A brief glance at the language of healing developed in the Matthean story will further confirm this positioning. The verb θεραπεύω dominates the Matthean description of Jesus' healing activity (sixteen occurrences in Matthew compared to five in Mark). It is used predominantly by the narrator to describe the healing activity of Jesus – twelve times (4.23, 24; 8.16; 9.35; 10.1; 12.15, 22; 14.14; 15.30; 17.18; 19.2; 21.14). It is heard on the lips of Jesus twice: once when he says that he will come and heal the centurion's servant (8.7) and again when he commissions the Twelve to heal (10.18). And twice, other characters use the verb: the opponents who question Jesus' healing (12.10)[12] and the father of the epileptic boy describing the disciples' inability to heal (17.16). The verb is used generally on only two occasions without an object (12.15; 19.2). Elsewhere it describes those healed in various ways: as having all kinds of illnesses and weaknesses (πᾶσαν νόσον καὶ πᾶσαν μαλακίαν – 4.23; 9.35; 10.1);[13] as being ill (πάντας τοὺς κακῶς ἔχοντας – 4.24; 8.16; 9.12; 14.35); and with the various diseases named (4.24; 10.8; 12.22; 15.30 and 21.14). The verb ἰάομαι which characterizes healing in the Asclepieion is used only four times in Matthew (8.8, 13; 13.15; 15.28). Three of these usages are in relation to the healing of a foreign servant and child and will be considered in more detail below. The fourth (13.15) is in a quotation from the Septuagint (Isa. 6.10). The healing language seems, therefore, to reflect the emic perspective of the Matthean storyteller and community and distinguishes Jesus as healer in Matthew's gospel from the professional healer of the Hippocratic corpus[14] and from the healing of Asclepius. In the Matthean context, healing is intimately linked to preaching and teaching and is the work of the holy one of God. The general and the explicit descriptions of illness, however, counter Louise Wells' claim that θεραπεύω 'refers to spiritual, rather than physical healing'.[15]

Just as the general descriptions of Jesus as healer are episodic within the itinerant ministry of Jesus, so too are the explicit stories of Jesus healing.[16] Each one of the nine healings in Matthew 8–9 occurs as Jesus moves from place to place. The locations, therefore, are also occasional, depending on the point along the journey. None take place in an institutional setting. This is, therefore, a further indication of Jesus being characterized as a folk healer.

The Matthean healing narratives originated in oral storytelling contexts within early first-century Galilee. They were developed within the broader provenance of Matthean traditioning across the arc of cities linking upper Galilee with Antioch through to the latter half of that century, combining independently developed traditions with the received Markan stories.[17] An analysis of the rhetorical or symbolic function of the narratives of women healing as they were told in the Matthean community, together with the use of Kleinman's medical anthropological categories of analysis, will provide further insights into women healing in early Christianity. Since the Matthean storyteller and community re-tells the Markan stories and since our search is for women's agency within the health care systems of early Christianity, I will be attentive to the possibility of the Matthean community's development of possible 'counterstories'. Heilde Lindemann Nelson describes each such counter story as contributing to 'the moral self-definition of its teller by undermining a dominant story, undoing it and retelling it in such a way as to invite new interpretations and conclusions'.[18] My earlier study of the characterization of women in the Matthean gospel story suggests such a trend[19] and the following study of the stories of women healing will further exemplify this claim.

### Re-telling the Raising Up of Peter's Mother-in-law to Diakonia (Matthew 8.14-15)

To the casual observer, it may appear that these two short verses simply repeat the Markan account of a fevered woman, Simon's mother-in-law, being raised up to *diakonia*. Careful analysis of the text, however, reveals quite a different scenario.

The account is episodic as it is in the Markan gospel but there is no explicit link to the previous story in the Matthean account as there is in Mark. The setting is similar, namely a house, but in the Matthean re-telling, it is the house of Peter rather than of Simon and Andrew and there is no reference to the latter two being present with James and John.[20] Jesus enters the house of Peter alone in the Matthean story. Given our discussion earlier of the types of house construction in Capernaum, and the possible stages of entry into the house of the group of males in the Markan story, the entry of Jesus alone into the very presence of a woman lying sick with a fever seems a breach of even the most carefully nuanced construction of public and private space in first-century imaginations. The story is, therefore, a borderland story, located on the boundaries of both gender and space constructions. House may also carry additional symbolic import by the end of the first century when houses rather than the synagogue were becoming the religious meeting place for the Matthean Christian-Jewish community. The setting is non-institutional but evokes different borderland scenarios for understanding this story of healing.

In seeking to uncover the quality of relationship between healer and healed and the attitudes of both to a possible therapeutic interaction, the reader has little available data except the clarity and brevity of the narrative. Given the absence of other characters, the account states that Jesus *sees* Peter's mother-in-law (εἶδεν) whose condition is described and he then touches her hand (ἥψατο τῆς χειρὸς αὐτῆς). Jesus the healer, who has been approached by the two previous suppliants for healing (the leper and the centurion on behalf of his servant – 8.2-13), is here described as taking the initiative to heal, a characteristic which is not common in the gospel accounts of healing nor in the Asclepian narratives. Jesus is presented as a borderland character, reaching out across the culturally legitimated boundaries. This is a task that the one who stands in the space of the colonizer, the position of power, must undertake for the healing of those boundaries to begin, but the colonizer does not stand alone in this task. There is the woman, the πενθερὰν Πέτρου.[21]

The writing of the body of this woman with a 'culturally legitimated name' can be considered similar to the Markan naming and writing. The woman is πυρέσσουσαν (Mt. 8.14; cf. πυρέσσουσα – Mk 1.30). This description places her among many, both male and female, who were named and described as ill in this way in the health care systems of Greece and Rome as we saw earlier when considering the Markan account. The second descriptor of the woman lying ill (βεβλημένην rather than the Markan κατέκειτο) reflects the Matthean community perspective. Three times such a description occurs in Matthew 8–9 to name legitimately, using the explanatory models of the community,[22] those needing healing: the centurion's servant is lying sick in his house, paralysed and in great distress (8.6); Peter's mother-in-law in the next story is lying sick with a fever (8.14); and in 9.2, the paralytic is described as lying on his bed. The perfect passive form of the verb βάλλω in each of these descriptions and the explicit linking of 8.6 and 9.2 with paralysis may give further insight into the Matthean re-telling of this healing story. The woman in this borderland story is characterized as paralyzed: by the demands of the household; by the cultural construction of gender, of space or indeed of an entire system of dualistic hierarchies that were discussed in Chapters One and Two as being under construction in the worlds of Greece and Rome; or by social and cultural as well as physical determinants?[23] The interpreting community is left to provide the most appropriate meaning.

Jesus, having seen the woman's condition which is described for the reader/hearer by the narrator, is characterized as traversing the borderland space, intervening instrumentally by touching the woman's hand (ἥψατο τῆς χειρὸς αὐτῆς). This description of Jesus' healing action differs from the Markan account. There Jesus raised the woman by taking hold of her hand (ἤγειρεν αὐτὴν κρατήσας τῆς χειρός). In the Matthean account, the touching of her hand is the instrument of healing and it is this action rather than the Markan raising up which causes the fever to leave (ἀφῆκεν αὐτὴν ὁ πυρετός). This is the first phrase in the two accounts which is an exact parallel and it is the climactic phrase, that of the sanctioning of a new label, the reversal of the original description – having a fever (πυρέσσουσα/ν).

It was noted in the Markan account that the healing story does not finish with this description of transformation. Unlike most other Markan accounts of healing, except the story of Bartimaeus receiving his sight, the Markan story describes ongoing activity in the healed state (Simon's mother-in-law does ongoing *diakonia*). Given the Matthean retelling, the therapeutic change, the fever leaving her, is followed by two verbs which write the body of the healed woman. She is raised up and she is serving him (ἠγέρθη καὶ διηκόνει αὐτῷ).

The verb ἐγείρω carries a variety of meanings and is used in several contexts throughout the Matthean gospel. I will focus here only on those which seem most relevant to an understanding of this story of a woman healing. Its usage in 8.15 to describe the woman healed is the first time it occurs in a context of healing. This is followed by its usage three times in the healing of the paralytic (9.5, 6, 7) and in the final description of the young girl raised to life (9.25). In 10.8 and 11.5 it is used explicitly in relation to the dead being raised as characteristic of Jesus' healing ministry. The other cluster of usage is in the passion predictions of Jesus being raised on the third day (16.21; 17.23; 20.19; and 27.63, 64) and the description of the raised Jesus (28.6, 7). In the stories of healing, the narrator writes the bodies of the healed ones with the language of Jesus raised. These are not distinguished by gender as it is the bodies of two women and one male which are so written. But when one considers these texts more closely, in the case of the paralytic, the description is not of ongoing transformation but rather it is instrumental to the paralytic returning to his home, the transformation complete (9.7). In the healing of Peter's mother-in-law, the description, ἠγέρθη, is accompanied by the imperfect of the verb διακονέω. In the ongoing activity of *diakonia*, Peter's mother-in-law continues, beyond the healing transformation, to carry in her body the having-been-raised-ness of Jesus as well as the *diakonia* which, in 20.28, characterizes Jesus' own ministry. Given that I have argued elsewhere that this healing story shares the key elements of a vocation or call story, an invitation into the new fictive kinship, more than those of a healing account (see parallel with Mt. 9.9),[24] the telling or re-telling of this Matthean story draws a woman healed into the new fictive kinship, writing her body with language characteristic of Jesus, the raised one whose *basileia* ministry can be characterized as *diakonia*. There is a hint that this story may be re-writing or re-configuring traditions in a way which could give women healing greater access to healing roles through the shaping of a different religious imagination, a reconfigured health care system. It is indeed a borderland story in borderland space which enables the healing woman to cross over between the spaces of healed and potential healer. As such, it could also be named a counterstory, reconfiguring the developing and the received traditions to provide healing women with greater access to the ongoing *basileia* ministry. It is, however, only a hint and our attention must turn now to the two intercalated stories of women healing in Matthew 8–9.

### Re-telling the Young Girl Raised and the Woman Saved (Matthew 9.18-26)

If LiDonnici's claim cited at the head of this chapter, namely that 'simpler tales will be closer to the original tradition',[25] can be challenged, the Matthean re-telling of the intercalated stories of the woman with the haemorrhage and the ruler's daughter surely provides such a challenge. The twenty-three verses of the Markan account (Mk 5.21-43) are reduced to eight, or nine if one includes the general statement of the report of the incidents going out at the end of the Matthean account (Mt. 9.18-26), providing readers/hearers with a concise and focused story of women healing. Attention to the socio-rhetorical effect of the Matthean re-telling in dialogue with Kleinman's medical anthropological categories of analysis mapped onto the accounts will enable us to further the reading of healing women in the Matthean health care system.

While the Markan account begins with movement (Jesus crossing to the other side) and is characterized by movement, the Matthean account is linked to a series of stories set in a house (9.10) in Jesus' own city, Capernaum (9.1). These stories demonstrate characteristics of the borderland – a discussion of who can forgive sin on earth (9.3-6); an invitation to a tax collector into the new fictive kinship (9.9); and a dining with tax collectors and sinners (9.10-13). A woman has been healed in a house (8.14) and the ruler enters the house in Capernaum where Jesus is, inviting him to his home where his daughter has just died.[26] The space of the house is emerging symbolically as a borderland space, a place where culturally legitimated boundaries might be crossed and a negotiated newness emerge.[27]

In the highly abbreviated Matthean account of the healing of the young woman, one important Markan element is missing, namely the reference to her being twelve years old. This was a key to the consideration of her illness as that of the transitional stage from girlhood to young womanhood with all the physical and socio-cultural changes that this entailed. Another element which suggested such a reading, however, was Jesus' claim that the young woman was not dead but sleeping. Given that this is included in the Matthean storytelling (Mt. 9.23), it is possible to consider the daughter as young since she is still in the home of her father and her life has been threatened by an illness which is given two explanations in the story. Her father describes her as having just died (ἄρτι ἐτελεύτησεν) while the explanatory model given to Jesus is that she is sleeping (καθεύδει). Such ambivalence of explanatory model between supplicant and healer in relation to this young girl could have evoked for the first-century hearers the social, familial and personal precariousness of the time of transition from young girl to nubile maiden and the diseases accompanying this.[28] It may also suggest, however, that the Matthean focus is on the young girl being considered dead.

We get a brief glimpse of the attitude of the ruler to the healing relationship. He requests Jesus to lay his hands on his dead daughter, to reach out across the borderland of purity regulations,[29] so that she would live (ζήσεται). Rather than enter the death rituals that seek to 'repair fissures, heal wounds, and (temporarily at least) conquer the awful threat of death',[30] the ruler calls on the healer to undertake the repairing and healing by restoring the young woman to life. This would seem to be indicative of the Jewish belief that God has the power to heal even death and that Jesus as a holy one of this God has received such power (cf. the request of the Shunamite woman to Elisha – 2 Kgs 4.18-37). The semantic world of healing is extended to include the restoration of life. Within the Matthean narrative, the verb ζάω of 9.18 is predominantly used as descriptive of God who is called the 'Living God' or 'God of the Living' (16.16; 22.32) and therefore intimately associates restoration to life with divine power. This first-century Christian Jewish community was constructing healing as a transformative and restorative encounter with divine power, mediated through the one commissioned with this healing or restoration.

This story shifts the boundaries between life and death in the human arena and the symbol of that is the ruler's request that Jesus stretch out his hand over the young girl (ἐπίθες τὴν χεῖρά σου ἐπ' αὐτήν). The instrument of healing is Jesus' taking of the young girl's hand (9.25). The final culturally manipulated label is not, however, a simple reversal of the ruler's description of his daughter having just died using his reversal request, that she live. Rather the single label is that she is raised up (ἠγέρθη). In the Matthean account, this label stands alone without any instruction to give her something to eat (Mk 5.43) which would, like the reference to the paralytic's return to his house (9.7), have indicated a concluded healing, a restoration to one's house and family, rather than pointing to an ongoing state. Like Peter's mother-in-law, her healed body is written with the language descriptive of Jesus the healer who, having been crucified because of his commitment to his *basileia* ministry of which healing is a central element, is also described as being raised.

Despite the borderland nature of the two stories of healing women already encountered, in the Matthean narrative to this point, healing accounts in the dominant layer of narrative are constructing women as passive and in need of male healing power, as in the dominant narratives of the Hippocratic treatises as well as the Epidaurian inscriptions. The symbolic universe of women healers is all but obscured so that, like the Epidaurian texts, these Gospel narratives participate in and hence maintain the ideology of healing and its genderization current in first-century CE Palestine and in Jewish communities beyond its borders.[31] Intercalated into the story of the healing of the ruler's daughter, however, is the very abbreviated Matthean account of the haemorrhaging woman who takes initiative to secure her own healing.

One of the indicators of this in the Matthean storytelling could be the narrative paralleling of the ruler and the woman more so than that of the young girl and the woman which is stronger in the Markan account. Both ruler and woman are introduced with the Matthean demonstrative participle ἰδού, a common feature used to draw attention to what follows the demonstrative.[32] In this instance, both are supplicants, taking the initiative in approaching Jesus the healer for healing. The major difference is that the woman approaches from behind (ὄπισθεν). But prior to alerting the recipients to this difference, the narrator provides the initial setting for each of the two healing accounts. Matthew 9.18 opens with the phrase 'while he was saying these things to them', situating the ruler's approach to Jesus within the borderland space of the house of Mt. 9.9-17 as noted earlier. The setting for the woman's approach is along the way described in the transitional verse 9.19: '[a]nd Jesus got up and followed him, with his disciples'. This is the only time in the gospel that Jesus is said to follow. Elsewhere, it is the language used of those who become engaged in some way with Jesus' *basileia* ministry. Here in this situation of reversal, Jesus is following but toward a context where he will be challenged to restore life to one already dead.

It is into this context, this challenge to Jesus the healer, that the Matthean καὶ ἰδοὺ bursts, drawing attention to a woman haemorrhaging for twelve years (γυνὴ αἱμορροοῦσα δώδεκα ἔτη). The explanatory model seems similar to that of the Markan community though the words differ slightly. The Markan description of the woman seems to evoke the phrase ῥύσει αἵματι of Lev. 15.25-28 while the participle αἱμορροοῦσα in the Matthean narrative may call to mind its single use in the summary verse of Lev. 15.33 where it is followed by the qualifier ἐν τῇ ἀφέδρῳ αὐτῆς (in the infirmity of her period). This woman referred to in these final verses of Leviticus 15 may cause impurity in limited circumstances, but she is not ill. In Matthew, however, the time indicator is twelve years – the woman is labeled by way of the explanatory model αἱμορροοῦσα δώδεκα ἔτη. In exploring the Markan narrative and the intertextuality with both Levitical and medical texts, it was suggested that the longer description of the woman's suffering, especially at the hands of many physicians without success, may have been intended to suggest that the woman was close to death like Jairus' daughter. In Matthew, however, this cannot be so for the young girl is described by her father as dead. The opening phrase γυνὴ αἱμορροοῦσα may simply have evoked the Hippocratic understanding of the mature γυνή as one who bleeds.[33] It is the δώδεκα ἔτη which indicates the extraordinary nature of the woman's condition.

The narrator, however, does not dwell on this description but continues the parallel with the narrator describing her approach to the healer, contrasting it with that of the ruler in a way which may point to a gendering of the health care system. The ruler approaches and kneels before the healer making a direct request on behalf of his daughter. The woman comes up behind him (ὄπισθεν) in a way that I have not found paralleled in other healing accounts. We noted above, however, that the ruler by his action in approaching Jesus reaches out across the boundaries of life and death to gain healing for a daughter who is already dead. The woman too reaches out across the boundaries which caused her to come up behind the healer: perhaps boundaries of gender or of space which the text does not explicate but which first-century audiences may have been able to supply from their knowledge of the health care system. She touches the hem of Jesus' garment (ἥψατο τοῦ κρασπέδου τοῦ ἱματίου αὐτοῦ). She reaches out across boundaries and touches, not flesh on flesh as when Jesus touched the hand of Peter's mother-in-law for healing (ἥψατο τῆς χειρὸς) but flesh on garment. Her action parallels that of the healer, her action is the instrument of healing, and the words she says to herself provide the readers or audience with her attitude toward healer and healing. She says: If I only touch his cloak, I will be made well (ἐὰν μόνον ἅψωμαι τοῦ ἱματίου αὐτοῦ σωθήσομαι).[34] Two extraordinary challenges confront the healing being predicated of the religious/prophetic folk healer Jesus at this point in the Matthean narrative. Can he raise to life a young girl who has died and will the initiative of a woman of reaching out across boundaries with a touch seeking healing cause healing to flow as it does when Jesus initiates the touch?

At this point, I wish to diverge a little to consider the woman with the haemorrhage and her action in light of Helen King's study of women patients in the Hippocratic system in an article focused on women's self-help and self-knowledge.[35] She draws the following conclusion mid-way through the article:

> ...the ancient medical writers accept women's knowledge with the important proviso that it may be a knowledge they have constructed for women but they reserve to themselves the right to judge whose knowledge they will accept... Within this finely balanced situation, women's knowledge must be constructed within the parameters of the male theory which states that the male is the appropriate provider of health care. Self-knowledge is permitted; self-help is not.[36]

She goes on to demonstrate, however, that even within these parameters, women had ways of being active agents in the therapeutic encounter, making choices based on women's knowledge within the parameters of the therapy. The woman with the haemorrhage is described in language which suggests self-knowledge, leaving open the question of whether or not she demonstrates self-help subtly crossing therapeutic boundaries as did many of the Hippocratic women healed.

The answer to the question of the woman's initiative, her self-help and its efficacy, is immediately forthcoming in the abbreviated narrative. Jesus turns and sees the woman, and his words indicate that he has recognized healing has happened: your faith has saved you (ἡ πίστις σου σέσωκέν σε). The verb σῴζω is used in the perfect, indicating that the action began prior to Jesus' speaking. The woman's belief in the power of healing which could be drawn forth from Jesus, the healer, by her touch has been acknowledged. The narrator too acknowledges the healing with the use for the third time within two short verses of the verb σῴζω, this time in the aorist passive: and she was saved or made well from that hour. The new culturally legitimate label recognizing the transformation is not simply a reversal of the original condition. Rather, once again, the healed body of a woman is written with language associated with Jesus.

An angel writes the newly conceived child in Mary's womb with this language: he will save his people (1.21), designating Jesus' future role that will unfold as his *basileia* ministry. It is the cry for help on the lips of the disciples during the storm on the lake (8.25) expressing a profound desire for transformative or restorative intervention similar to that claimed by the haemorrhaging woman. At a number of other points in the narrative, it carries stronger connotations of final transformation or restoration (10.22; 16.25; 19.25; 24.13, 22). Toward the end of the gospel, those around the cross mockingly write the body of Jesus, the one being crucified, with this same language (27.40, 42, 49). The only other occasion when it is associated explicitly with healing is in the summary passage of 14.36 which describes many begging Jesus that they might touch the fringe of his garment (as the haemorrhaging woman sought to do and in fact did) in order that they might be healed, the verb being διεσώθησαν. The verb σῴζω constructs the semantic world of healing in terms of freedom from disease but also situates that healing within a broader religious framework given that the verb carries with it connotations of divine salvation or preservation from eternal death.[37] It is this language used to characterize the ministry of Jesus which writes the transformed body of the woman with the haemorrhage. The woman crossed into the borderland space of initiating her healing, reaching out and touching the hem of Jesus' garment. Transformation results in her carrying on her healed body the mark of Jesus, the one who is to save others but who cannot save himself from death.

In each of the three narratives of healing women in Matthew 8–9, a cultural label from the Matthean health care system is manipulated by way of the instrument of touch. As a result, a new label is sanctioned. It is these that are of interest in terms of both the semantic and symbolic nature of healing and gender in this gospel account. The woman of Mt. 9.20-22 can no longer be described in terms of her illness but she has been made well or saved (ἐσώθη), participating therefore in the fullness of what that word entails within the symbolic universe of the Matthean narrative as described above. Both Peter's mother-in-law and the young girl are labelled anew as having been lifted or raised up (ἠγέρθη) reversing paralysis and death. While this new description of the two women can be understood simply on a clinical level, it must be remembered that it also evokes the new interpretive lens through which the emerging Christian community understood the most destructive of forces, namely death (see in particular 28.6 in relation to Jesus). Peter's mother-in-law is not only raised but she also ministers to Jesus (διηκόνει αὐτῷ). Pilch understands this as restoration to a 'desirable state of being' but he considers that for women in Mediterranean culture the state more proper to women rather than men is that of 'doing' rather than 'being' and the sphere for that is the home.[38] Examination of the semantic value of διακονέω within the narrative world of the Matthean text and the call or vocation element in the story type,[39] leads to a recognition that the healing accounts function not only to construct healing as transformative of somatic aspects of women's lives but also of their socio-cultural and religious lives as well. Each woman is named as participant in the transformative universe associated with Jesus – that of service (20.28), of saving (1.21) and of being raised to new life (28.6).[40]

Women are not the healers in these transformative encounters but the healed with the slight blurring of these boundaries in the healing of the woman with the haemorrhage. Women's bodies, however, configure the divine healing power, mediated through Jesus. There is a reciprocity within these narratives, especially as analyzed by way of the medical anthropological model, which suggests that the healer and the healed cannot be isolated from one another nor constructed completely hierarchically within the symbolic universe of early Christianity. They cross over into a borderland space where some of the socio-cultural and religious inequities can be healed. Even as mediator of divine healing, Jesus cannot be isolated from those healed. Women healed carry in their restored bodies the signification of those aspects of transformation that Jesus himself both represents and enacts. To re-tell stories of the healing of women in this way in the Matthean community is to construct counter stories which may have been able to function to provide women with at least some access to participation in the healing activity characterizing the *basileia* ministry, not only of Jesus, but of the ongoing community.

As these stories are appropriated beyond the constructions of healing and gender of the Graeco-Roman world, the transformative healing of

Jesus may be configured more explicitly by the bodies of women: their bleeding, their dying and their rising, contributing to a more multivalent metaphoric construction of Jesus among contemporary communities of believers. Women too can be configured anew as initiators of the transformative powers inscribed on the bodies of their foresisters as well as recipients of divinely mediated healing. This is to read the gospel narrative symbolically and rhetorically for today's world. Women as active participants in their own healing, in the healing of human relationships and human brokenness, and in the healing of the universe may be transformed by their faith to be healers as well as healed in the interplay of movement toward transformation. Such a reading points us forward to consider a very different story, that of the Canaanite woman's daughter.

### A Demon-Possessed Daughter Is Healed
### (Matthew 15.21-28)

I have in the past read this story from a number of perspectives[41] and the earlier exploration of the Markan parallel text in this study highlighted the often forgotten aspect of this story, namely the daughter and her demon possession.[42] In the context of this study, I wish to turn attention to what distinguishes this story from those already considered in this chapter, namely the interconnection of gender and ethnicity. Since I have already studied this in detail elsewhere,[43] here I will simply highlight the insights that will advance an understanding of gender and healing in the gospel of Matthew.

What characterizes this narrative is the challenge/riposte style debate between the woman and Jesus which shifts the narrative focus from the woman's explanatory model for the daughter's illness (15.22c) to the woman's outsider status, shifts the story-type from healing narrative to debate.[44] Demon possession, in this instance, seems to be linked with the ethnic outsider debate.[45] Story-types cross over in this borderland narrative. Both the woman and her daughter are designated 'out of place' and Jesus who is likewise 'out of place' in this story must confront and struggle with both on the margins or at the border.[46] His retreat to traditions associated with the centre (15.24) is not accepted by the woman within the therapeutic expectations of the healing relationship. Her kneeling in front of Jesus and her turning of Jesus' words about the children's food back on him point to her responsibility for her daughter and her challenge to Jesus as healer (15.25, 27). She refuses to leave without her daughter being healed.

The therapeutic stages and mechanisms in this story are significant. The daughter is labelled as demon possessed, a label rich in cultural meaning in the Graeco-Roman world of the first century as discussed earlier. This cultural label is manipulated by Jesus, in this instance, in a way that is not made visible to the reader. As a result, however, a new cultural label is sanctioned – the daughter who was demon possessed (v. 22) is now healed (v. 28). It is not a simple reversal, claiming that the demon had left the young girl.[47] The verb used in this new cultural designation is ἰάομαι – the daughter is healed (ἰάθη ἡ θυγάτηρ) rather than demon possessed (ἡ θυγάτηρ μου κακῶς δαιμονίζεται). This verb ἰάομαι occurs much more rarely in Matthew than θεραπεύειν to designate healing (8.8, 13; 13.15; 15.28). It is, however, the same new cultural label that is given to the centurion's servant who is healed:

> καὶ ἰάθη ὁ παῖς αὐτοῦ ἐν τῇ ὥρᾳ ἐκείνῃ (Mt. 8.13)
> καὶ ἰάθη ἡ θυγάτηρ αὐτῆς ἀπὸ τῆς ὥρας ἐκείνης (Mt. 15.28).

The only Matthean use of the verb and its root is in relation to the new cultural labelling of two gentiles – the centurion's servant whom we assume to be gentile and the Canaanite woman's daughter.[48] We have seen that the verb ἰάομαι was in common usage in the Graeco Roman world to describe healing. Θεραπεύειν, in that same world, had a more general meaning, 'to serve', but it was taken up as a key designation of healing in the Christian Jewish communities of the *basileia* movement. The Matthean text seems to reflect those origins in its predication of these two verbs to recipients of healing, one more predominantly to those associated with the Graeco-Roman world, and the other the Jewish or Christian Jewish world.

Healing and the language of healing are shaped, therefore, by ethnicity rather than gender in these narratives. A particular cultural label is considered more appropriate for gentile recipients of healing and another for Jewish recipients.[49] Both male and female among the ethnic outsiders can be healed. The Matthean story of healing women would not be told fully, therefore, without the inclusion of the demon-possessed daughter of a woman called 'Canaanite'. The interweaving of healing and ethnicity points to the function of telling stories of healing that point not only to the healing of physical illness but also of all other break-downs in the social, cultural, religious and even inter-national aspects of a community's life.[50]

We turn, finally in this section, to a consideration of how the story of the healing of the Canaanite woman's daughter participates in the Matthean re-telling of healing women in the overall Matthean narrative. We have seen above that new cultural labels are given to the three women healed in

Matthew 8–9 (serving/διηκόνει, being saved/ἐσώθη and being raised/ ἠγέρθη – 8.15, 9.22 and 9.25).[51] These share in the semantic universe which characterized the transformative activity associated with the Jesus of that gospel narrative, opening up possibilities for recipients of the gospel story to hear a counter-story to the dominant narrative which authorizes a crossing over of women from healed to healer. In the dominant narrative, gender seemed to categorize healing in that males only were commissioned to share in the healing ministry of the male healer Jesus (Mt. 10.8). Women were not so commissioned but women's healed bodies configure the divine healing power mediated through Jesus. This study has provided hints that the gospel constructs ethnicity in a way which intersects with and shifts the gender construction in the borderland space which the story both creates and inhabits. The transformative re-labelling of the Canaanite woman's daughter does not share in the symbolic universe associated with Jesus as does that of the other females healed in the Matthean narrative of healing to this point – Peter's mother-in-law, the woman with the haemorrhage and the ruler's daughter – all of whom are culturally Jewish. Rather the story, by way of a shift in story-type from healing narrative to debate, and careful use of language, tells that healing undertaken in the borderland spaces in which healer and healed cross gender and ethnic boundaries, constructs the Matthean health-care system in relation to ethnicity as well as gender. The lack of specificity in relation to physical space enables the story to speak access to the excluded not only in relation to ethnicity but any other boundary markers that deny such access to the fruits of Jesus' *basileia* ministry.

### Re-telling the Pouring Out of Healing Ointment
### (Matthew 26.6-13)

The opening verse of this story situates this story of a woman healing in a number of ways. As in the Markan account, it takes place in a house. For the Matthean reader, however, the house is an expected location for teaching (both as place of teaching and content of teaching: 5.15; 7.24, 25, 26, 27; 10.12, 13, 14; 12.25, 29; 13.1, 36, 57; 17.25; 19.29; 24.17, 43) and for healing (8.6, 14; 9.10, 23, 28). The explicit use of Jesus' name links the story just beginning to the literary context. Jesus' name appears already in 26.1 and 4. In v. 1, the name 'Jesus' stands as a linchpin between the extensive teaching in the Temple precincts which began in 21.23 and Jesus' warning his disciples that he will be delivered up to be crucified, a frightening awareness for this healer, this holy one of God, to bear. In v. 4, Jesus is again named explicitly as the object of the plotting of the chief priests and elders of the people to arrest and kill him. It is this Jesus who is located in the house of Simon the leper.

The setting for this story is, therefore, a house but more than that, a house associated with one named leper, a place that evokes healing. It is located in Bethany, a name heard only once previously in the Matthean story, namely 21.17. Bethany is the place Jesus retreats to following the indignation and challenge of the chief priests and scribes in response to his healing of the blind and the lame in the temple, his final act of healing in the gospel. The explanatory model, one might say, that the Matthean narrator uses in relation to Jesus in this opening verse of the story is that he is facing sure death because the plot is already being enacted (v. 4) and Jesus knows this, as v. 2 indicates.

It is in such a setting that a woman takes action. This unnamed woman (simply γυνή in the text), is the subject of the first main verb in the story when she enters this house which calls for healing. She is described, as is the woman in the Markan story, as having an alabaster jar of *muron* or perfumed ointment (ἔχουσα ἀλάβαστρον μύρου), which she pours over the head of Jesus. This Matthean description likewise evokes healing intertextually as was claimed in much greater detail in relation to the Markan story. Her action is an action of healing, healing not only the body but the distressed spirit of Jesus who is reclining at table (ἀνακειμένου), an action reminiscent of the description of Jesus in 9.11 where he was reclining at table in a house in Capernaum. What took place in that context we described as borderland activity, as is the action in the context of this house in Bethany. There is a crossing over that takes place on the border when the healer becomes the healed and the one who is traditionally in the role of healed becomes healer. It is a climactic moment in the world of healing being constructed in the Matthean gospel story.

This woman, with her beautiful jar of expensive perfumed *muron*, may have recalled for first-century readers those women healers who were absent from or hidden in their story. These were the women encountered in Chapter Three whose stories were not told except as caricature, whose work with herbs and ointments was feared because of the power it placed in women's hands in a world where power, including healing power, was gendered. They were also the women subsumed under the collective ῥιζοτόμοι about whom we know so little. The woman of Mt. 26.7 uses as her instrument of healing μύρον rather than ἔλαιον which carried stronger ritual connotations in Judaism.[52] She stands, therefore, among her sister-healers but her healing power is not narrated as destructive but as restorative and strengthening to Jesus who faces death.

The twice repeated μύρον (26.7 and 26.12) locates this healing and re-newing substance at the heart of this healing story. It, rather than human touch, is the instrument of healing as such ointments and other substances were in the Graeco-Roman world. The story brings the other-than-human into its centre along with the human action of a healing woman. The Matthean story-telling does not embellish the description of the ointment except to indicate that it was expensive (βαρυτίμου). This, however, seems to be the Matthean community's way of capturing the μύρου νάδρου πιστικῆς πολυτελοῦς of the Markan account. William Houghton suggests that this 'pistic nard' as he calls it was imported into the Middle East from India. It was the root of the Indian plant *Nardostachys jatamansi* which made the ointment costly but it was also, he suggests 'aromatic...used as an ingredient in ointment and as a stimulant medicine'.[53]

The gift exchange element of this story is the focus of an ecological reading. Anne Primavesi draws attention to this when she says that 'the huge, interdependent, self-regulating global environment is a gift to all earth's inhabitants: it gives the necessities of life to all members of the earth community: human and non-human'.[54] The *muron* is symbol of this gift exchange. It is graciously given by the earth to the woman who, in turn, pours it out generously to give healing compassion to Jesus as he faces into his death. In Jesus' interpretation of this gift in 26.12, he recog-nizes that this gift of the earth poured out over his body, not just his head, will be taken with him back to the earth as it prepares him for burial. The transformation which the *muron* has wrought has brought the one plotted against and facing crucifixion to the point of being prepared for burial. There is, in this, a manipulation of the culturally legitimated label of the healed one that we have seen in other healing stories. The action of the woman subverts the plotting of the opponents, reaching out across and through the pain of crucifixion to ointmenting the human body of Jesus to return to the earth.

Another aspect of gift exchange that is evident in this Matthean story is in the first of Jesus' interpretations of the woman's healing action. Jesus names it a good work, ἔργον καλὸν...εἰς ἐμέ. I pointed out in an earlier study of this text that the ultimate in good work in this gospel is parabled in the last great parable of the gospel narrative (25.31-46) in which the righteous are praised for having done to Jesus what they do for the least – when they feed the hungry, give drink to the thirsty, welcome the stranger, clothe the naked and visit the sick and the imprisoned.[55] In 25.40 and its negative counterpart of 25.45, the dative ἐμοὶ is used but it carries the same connotation of the εἰς ἐμέ of 26.10. The giving in full of the gift

received by this unnamed woman to effect healing is, in the Matthean
narrative, the ultimate good work. And for this woman at this time (26.11),
it is not the needy who stand in the place of Jesus but it is he himself who
is the most needy. There is a crossing over in this borderland story – the
parabling healer becomes the one in need of healing. Over the head and
the body of the healer she pours out the gift that she has received from the
earth, the ointment from the alabaster jar. And, as the story indicates,
Jesus is healed and strengthened to go into what lies ahead. It is this that
will be told to her memory.

That the woman's healing action has been effective and that her ointment has strengthened Jesus into death itself is made more evident in the
Matthean story when in 28.1, readers are told that the women go to see or
witness the tomb. They do not go to the tomb with spices to anoint the
body of Jesus. This has already been completed according to Jesus words in
26.12 by way of the *muron* poured out. The final healing action of the
gospel is that of a woman whose outpoured ointment permeates the body
of Jesus and this body is written by the narrator as prepared for burial. It
simply remains for us now to read back into the earlier stories through the
lens of this final healing, as would be done by both first-century and contemporary second-time and subsequent readers.

## Conclusion

Writing bodies by way of exchange of gift, touching and the pouring out of
healing ointment characterizes the Matthean storying of women healing.
In a narrative from which women healers seem to be excluded, the writing
of the healed bodies of women with language characterizing Jesus' ministry seemed to suggest early in the narrative that these healed women were
transformed for participation in the *basileia* ministry of Jesus. This is not
as surprising to second-time and subsequent readers who know the
extraordinary healing exchange in which Jesus is healed and strengthened
to face death by the outpoured ointment. The story of the woman healer
and its literary context render her gift exchange with Jesus climactic in the
unfolding Matthean narrative. It receives the highest of praise, rendering it
constitutive of the preaching of the gospel, the *basileia* ministry of Jesus
and the community of teachers and healers commissioned by him and his
story. The more inclusive character of the health care system constructed
by this gospel is portrayed in the language which writes the demon-free
body of the Canaanite woman's daughter and the centurion's servant.

In stories of women healing/healing women in the Matthean gospel,
aspects of the Markan narrative are reconfigured in ways which construct

the Matthean health care system and its gendering so that a little more access to participation in the *basileia* ministry of healing may have been available to women in a world in which women did function as healers as well as healed in the professional sector of its health care system. Their stories also point beyond the healing of bodies to the healing of all brokenness, all broken relationships in the ecological, cultural, political and social aspects of the life of the Matthean story-telling households. Such a reconfiguring can shape the religious imagination of not only the first-century gospel communities but also those of the twenty-first century authorizing healing that crosses whatever boundaries are constructed around healer and healed that prevent full access to the healing which is at the heart of God's *basileia* dream for the human community. The Matthean reconfigured story of women healing/healing women also invites contemporary readers into the borderland spaces in today's church and world where healing may be able to be enacted as it is in this gospel story.

## Chapter 6

## WOMEN CURED OF EVIL SPIRITS AND INFIRMITIES: THE GOSPEL OF LUKE

As in the other gospels, so also in Luke, Jesus' healing is of the social body as well as of individual bodies. In Luke, however, such social healing figures much more prominently.[1]

The role of women healers has been inexorably married to shifts in the ecology, the economy, and the politics of the area in which they lived.[2]

The stories of healing women in the Lukan gospel may have originated from similar traditions to those shared by the Markan and Matthean communities but they are shaped quite differently by this gospel community and take on different nuances in the literary context of this particular story of Jesus. As a result, I propose, in this chapter, to focus on what seems to be a unique characteristic of women healing in this gospel, namely their close association with demon possession. After considering the health care system in the Lukan gospel through the lens of Jesus the healer, I will begin the study of women healing with the short summary passage of 8.1-3 that is unique to the Lukan gospel and let this key story intersect with other stories of healing women in the narrative to form the Lukan perspective. The socio-rhetorical approach which has been the methodology for this study will enable the rhetoric of the Lukan text to be examined in dialogue with an analysis of socio-cultural and religio-political codes embedded in the text. From this, some conclusions will be drawn about the healing of the social as well as the individual body that the Lukan gospel seems to address, and about the gendering of such healing.

One of the key characteristics of the world constructed by the Lukan narrative is the active presence of spirits of various kinds and demons.[3] The word πνεῦμα or spirit, whether good or evil/unclean, occurs thirty-six times in this gospel compared with nineteen in Matthew, twenty-three in Mark and twenty-four in John. The more explicit term διαμόνιον or demon appears twenty-three times in Luke compared with Matthew, eleven; Mark, thirteen; and John, six times. Power, whether benevolently transformative

or destructive, characterizes the health care system of the Lukan community. Kleinman, drawing insight from Glick, claims, in relation to such
power, that

> knowing a culture's chief sources of power (social, political, mythological,
> religious, technological, etc) allows one to predict its beliefs about the
> causes of illness and how it treats illness. In a metaphorical sense, we can
> speak of socially legitimated power as the active principle fueling health
> care systems and of social reality determining what that power is...and how
> it is to be applied...while symbolic reality lays down the pathways by which
> the application of that power may be effective.[4]

Religious power in the Lukan world has its source in God and is therefore
considered holy. The very conception of Jesus resulted from a spirit that
was holy coming upon Mary and the power of the Most High overshadow-
ing her (1.35). The same spirit descended on Jesus at his baptism (3.22),
and led him to and through the time of transition in the wilderness (4.1)
which prepared him for taking up his ministry, which is overshadowed by
the spirit of God, Jesus claims, as he reads from the prophet Isaiah in the
synagogue in Nazareth (4.18). Jesus takes on the mantle of the prophet of
restoration, restoration of socio-economic and cultural relationships as
well as restoration of the body to health and wholeness, symbolized in the
blind receiving sight in the Isaian intertext (4.18).

There is another power, however, which is in conflict with the power of
God in Jesus in the Lukan world-view. Although Jesus is full of a spirit that
is holy as he returns from the Jordan and is led into the wilderness by this
same spirit, he there encounters the devil (ὁ διαβόλος) who tempts him to
use power or choose authority contrary to that of the spirit that is with
him (4.1-13). As Jesus moves on from his claiming the prophetic spirit in
the synagogue at Nazareth, he encounters this other power in a synagogue
in Capernaum ('What have you to do with us, Jesus of Nazareth? Have you
come to destroy us? – 4.34). In this instance, the other spirit is said to be of
an unclean demon (πνεῦμα δαιμόνιου ἀκαθάρτου). It is manifest in human
bodies, in human lives and is the cause of illness in those bodies or disrup-
tion in those lives. Jesus has the power to exorcize or cast out the demon
simply with a command ('Be silent and come out of him!' – 4.35). This
conflict between powers evident at the beginning of the gospel can be
traced throughout.[5] Jesus is prophet healer and exorcist within the Lukan
health care system, healing and casting out demons by the power of the
spirit of God.[6] He belongs, therefore, in the folk sector of the health care
system according to the etic perspective established by Kleinman, in
particular, within the magico-religious rather than the secular sphere of

that sector. He is prophetic healer with power from God over the demonic power associated with the *diabolos*/devil (4.2, 3, 6, 13; 8.12) or Satan (10.18; 11.18; 13.16; 22.3, 31) within a Hellenistic Jewish health care perspective.

There are a number of models which assist in understanding this Lukan health care perspective which in turn will better facilitate our exploration of its gendering.[7] Susan Garrett interprets it through the lens of magic as it functioned in the Hellenistic world and impacted on Judaism[8] and Graham Twelftree through exorcism as we have already noted.[9] Bruce Malina and Jerome Neyrey, on the other hand, have turned the lens of Mary Douglas' cultural anthropological model of witchcraft societies on the Matthean gospel and community and have demonstrated that it is rife for the accusation of witchcraft brought against Jesus in Mt. 12.24 – it is only by Beelzebul, the prince of demons, that this man casts out demons.[10] That this text in its context (Mt. 12.22-30) is virtually paralleled in Lk. 11.14-23 invites a brief exploration of the Lukan narrative in light of the Neyrey and Malina study.

In the Jewish-Christian communities from which the gospels of Matthew and Luke emerged, three of Douglas' characteristics of a witchcraft society seem to be present.[11] Their internal relations were still in process of being stabilized, their authority structures were weak and they were in intense competition with their Jewish parent body and, in the Lukan Hellenistic world, perhaps also with other healers and other models of healing. In such contexts, accusations of 'witchcraft' as label could be expected. In a rare glimpse of the accuser's perspective, we find in Luke as in Matthew the charge: He casts out demons by Beelzebul, the prince of demons (Lk. 11.15). This is a typical witchcraft accusation, to be in league with evil spirits, to have power from the spirit world, however these are named and understood culturally. This accusation is followed in Luke (but not so in Matthew) by the statement – others to test him, sought from him a sign from heaven (Lk. 11.16), testing being a typical response to fear or accusations of witchcraft. Interestingly, one of the key characteristics that Malina and Neyrey highlight in relation to Jesus' deviance (i.e. his acting outside of his inherited social roles and ranks) which led to the witchcraft accusations, is his geographical mobility.[12] It is not the necessary mobility required for religious or economic purposes but it is a mobility that is deviant in relation to the stability of family and group in a first-century Mediterranean context. A typical context in which such accusations of deviance occur in the gospels, according to Malina and Neyrey, is that of 'sick care, hence of healing and sickening, of demon possession and demon expulsion'. The Lukan healing narratives are also characterized by their episodic nature as are those of Mark and Matthew: Jesus and his group are itinerant healers. Malina and Neyrey go on to note that 'witchcraft accusations in a health-care context seem typical of the Mediterranean region'.[13]

Whether the model is that of magician, exorcist or witch, the Lukan Jesus, the healer prophet, is labelled by certain ones among the crowd (11.15 cf. the Matthean reference to the Pharisees as accusers in 12.24) as healing by the power of the Beelzebul, the prince of all demonic powers, and of being possessed by the same power. Naomi Janowitz throws light on such narratives as 'social discourse'[14] when she says in the introduction to her study of magic in the first three centuries of the Common Era:

> Charges of magic reveal social tensions, internecine battles, competition for power, and fear that other people have special powers. Charges of witch-craft represented socially-acceptable modes of attack against political enemies when other modes of asserting rivalry were not an option.[15]

The above suggests struggle or conflict over authority, especially authority within the health care system in the Lukan community.[16] This struggle may have been magnified at the stage of the Lukan re-telling of eye-witness memories of Jesus' healing so that for the Lukan community this healing involved not just individual bodies but the social body of the community as well.

Before turning to the stories of women healing, it must be noted that the verb ἰάομαι (5.17; 6.18, 19; 7.7; 8.47; 9.2, 11, 42; 14.4; 17.15; 22.51) is used almost interchangeably with θεραπεύω (4.23, 40; 5.15; 6.7, 18; 7.21; 8.2, 43; 9.1, 6; 10.9; 13.14; 14.3) and θεραπεία (9.11; and 12.42) in Luke's gospel. Linguistically, the Lukan gospel constructs the symbolic reality of the health care system in its own unique way. Of particular interest are the texts in which ἰάομαι and θεραπεύω are used together or in close proximity. We first see this phenomenon in Jesus' proverbial saying to the Nazareth synagogue community – Physician heal yourself: ἰατρέ, θεράπ-ευσον σεαυτόν.[17] The term that is a typical referent to the professional healers of the Hellenistic world is used with the verb which has connota-tions in that world of long-term treatment rather than cure, the latter of which seems to be the sense presumed in the proverb.[18] In the summary passage 6.17-19, the two-fold ministry of Jesus of teaching and healing is presented from the perspective of the great multitudes who come to hear and to be healed (ἀκοῦσαι αὐτοῦ καὶ ἰαθῆναι ἀπὸ τῶν νόσων αὐτῶν). We noted in the previous chapter the repeated Matthean summary (θεραπεύων πᾶσαν νόσον – Mt. 4.23; 9.35; 10.1) and the minimal use of ἰάομαι which suggests that the Lukan use has a particular purpose. In the same verse of the Lukan summary (6.18), the verb θεραπεύω is used in relation to those with unclean spirits, which is atypical as the unclean spirits are generally commanded to come out or are described as having come out or been cast out, often after having been rebuked by Jesus (note that the same verb is used in 8.2 in relation to the woman with evil spirits and infirmities). This Lukan interchange of the two verbs within three verses is, therefore, unique, as is the concluding ἰᾶτο πάντας in relation to those seeking to touch him. Louise Wells does a more elaborate analysis of verb tenses and moods than is possible here,[19] but her conclusion seems to be similar to what is emerging in this study, namely that Luke uses θεραπεύω which has characterized the synoptic tradition in relation to healing, almost interchangeably with ἰάομαι, which is more typical of various types of healing in the Graeco-Roman world generally, to speak to an ethnically diverse community.[20] Perhaps the meaning of this becomes clearest in 9.11 when the curing of those in need of healing (τοὺς χρείαν ἔχοντας θεραπείας ἰᾶτο in which the two words occur side by side) is paralleled to Jesus' speaking to the crowds about the *basileia* of God. Healing understood in terms of Jesus' ministry of restoration of human as well as social corporeality is at the heart of God's transformative dream for the human community symbolized in the *basileia* and that healing is inclusive of all. A reading of women healing will test how this construction of the Lukan health care system intersects with the community's construction of gender.

### Women Healed of Evil Spirits and Infirmities
### (Luke 8.1-3)

8.1 Καὶ ἐγένετο ἐν τῷ καθεξῆς
   καὶ αὐτὸς διώδευεν κατὰ πόλιν καὶ κώμην κηρύσσων
      καὶ εὐαγγελιζόμενος τὴν βασιλείαν τοῦ θεοῦ
   καὶ οἱ δώδεκα σὺν αὐτῷ,
8.2 καὶ γυναῖκές τινες αἳ ἦσαν τεθεραπευμέναι ἀπὸ πνευμάτων πονηρῶν
καὶ ἀσθενειῶν,
   Μαρία ἡ καλουμένη Μαγδαληνή, ἀφ' ἧς δαιμόνια ἑπτὰ ἐξεληλύθει,
   8.3 καὶ Ἰωάννα γυνὴ Χουζᾶ ἐπιτρόπου Ἡρῴδου καὶ Σουσάννα καὶ
   ἕτεραι πολλαί,
αἵτινες διηκόνουν αὐτοῖς ἐκ τῶν ὑπαρχόντων αὐταῖς.

I indicated above that I would begin with an analysis of Lk. 8.1-3 because it seems to function as an interpretive lens for the examination of women healing in the Lukan narrative. The opening phrase is what Annette Weissenrieder calls 'the formula that the author frequently uses to begin a sentence...which signals a new beginning'.[21] It is difficult in this instance, however, to determine just what is new as Jesus has been going about town and village preaching and enacting his prophetic task of restoration as he proclaimed programmatically in the synagogue of Nazareth (4.18) and as the narrator indicated (4.43-44) and reiterated (7.22).[22] The opening verse seems to function to remind the reader/listener of the heart of the gospel – the preaching of the good news of the *basileia* of God.[23] There is a second reminder in this opening verse, namely, that the Twelve whom Jesus singled out in 6.13 are still with Jesus, listening to his preaching, being drawn into the circle of healing.

What is new is the introduction of a group of women (γυναῖκές τινες). The reader/listener has become familiar with the group of men around Jesus as noted above but this is the first time that a group of women has been introduced. Following the reference to the Twelve who have been introduced earlier by name as all male (Lk. 6.13-16), a reference to 'certain women' introduces gender very specifically into this text. Attention will be directed, therefore, to who these women are and how they function in the unfolding gospel story. They are introduced we might say, borrowing the words of Malina and Neyrey cited above, in a context of 'healing and sickening, of demon possession and demon expulsion'.[24] The literary type is not, however, a healing narrative but a summary pointing to an unknown number of women healed as the τινες of v. 2 and the ἕτεραι πολλαί later in v. 3 indicate.[25] It is difficult, therefore, to apply the Kleinman categories of analysis as we have with narratives of healing but there will be some categories that can be noted. At the outset, for instance, one observes that the context is itinerant and episodic as in all other healing narratives encountered in the gospels to this point. Indeed, the opening verse seems to emphasize the itinerancy of a group among whom were certain women.

This group of unnamed and unnumbered women has been healed and continues to be healed as the periphrastic tense of θεαπεύω indicates, the only time this form of the verb is used in the Lukan narrative.[26] In this short summary, the culturally manipulated label ἦσαν τεθεραπευμέναι, referring to the group of women, occurs at the beginning of the summary followed by the description of the illness. This differs from the usual pattern in healing narratives.[27] The women have been healed from evil spirits and infirmities (8.2). The description of the women's affliction seems to be in hyperbolic terms. They are not healed of unclean spirits as are other individuals: the man with the spirit of an unclean demon (4.33) or the Geresene demoniac (8.29) or the young boy with the demon (9.42). Rather, they are described in a way similar to those whom Jesus is said to heal before the eyes of John the Baptist's disciples. In a verse unique to Luke, after the disciples' question 'Are you the coming one or shall we look for another?', the Lukan narrator recounts that Jesus heals not only from diseases (ἀπὸ νόσων) but also from severe affliction (μαστίγων)[28] and evil spirits (πνευμάτων πονηρῶν), the first time this last phrase has occurred in Luke's gospel (7.21). The other time that this same phrase is encountered outside 8.2 is in 11.26, the illustrative story of the return of seven spirits more evil than the one driven out, a story integrally connected to the Beelzebul controversy discussed earlier. We will return to it below in seeking to understand the description of the women from a medical anthropological point of view, noting that it is how the narrator, the outsider, describes the women, not how they describe themselves.

The women are also described as having been healed from either a spirit of infirmity or from infirmities or weaknesses,[29] a term that seems to be predicated of women more than men, but the data is too limited to draw any conclusions. Following the healing of the leper, crowds gather to hear Jesus and to be healed of their infirmities (5.15). The word is used twice in the healing of the bent-over woman; initially to describe her condition where it is linked with πνεῦμα as it is in 8.2 (13.11) and alone in Jesus' subsequent proclamation of her having been freed from this infirmity (13.12). If ἀσθένεια is another descriptor of the spirit which possessed the women and of which they have been healed, then we have one of the first signs of these verses acting as a focal point with links to other stories of women healing so that each impacts on the rhetorical effect and interpretation of the other.

From this group of women, certain ones are singled out to be named and further described. The first is Mary called Magdalene from whom it is said seven demons had gone out. It is generally agreed, especially when read in conjunction with Lk. 11.26 and the shared understanding within first century Judaism and other neighbouring cultures, that seven is the optimum number, that Mary Magdalene's demon possession is described as the extreme of demon possession.[30] It should be noted, on the one hand, that such a tradition is absent from elsewhere within the gospels and early Christianity generally. On the other hand, however, there is a strongly attested alternate tradition within the gospels and other early Christian literature which represents Mary Magdalene as first named among groups of women[31] and a leader even among the male disciples.[32] It can be argued, therefore, that rendering her demon possessed to the most extreme degree is clearly a Lukan construction either shaped earlier in the community and incorporated into the gospel storytelling or shaped within the gospel storytelling itself.

Following this extreme description of Mary Magdalene, writing onto her body the ultimate of demon possession, labelling her with the culturally acceptable 'possessed of seven demons', the narrator explicitly names two more women healed and then adds many others to the group of certain women as noted above. I will not explore membership of the group further except to draw attention to Marianne Sawicki's reconstruction. She suggests a possible engagement of Mary Magdalene and Joanna in businesses associated with the lake and with villages like Magdala and towns such as Tiberias where Chuza, Herod's steward, may well have been located.[33] Such Galilean women may have had access to independent resources (ὑπαρχόντων of v. 3).

I want to turn now to examine more closely the cultural label given to this group of women (possessed of evil spirits and spirits of infirmity as well as by seven spirits in the case of Mary Magdalene), drawing on the insights of cultural anthropology.[34] Before turning to cross-cultural and cross-disciplinary analyses of this text, a simple explanation of the label would be that unexplained behaviour exhibited by a group of women was understood to be the result of outside power, namely an evil spirit or demon. Jesus as prophet healer in conflict with such spirits drives them out of the women and they are healed. One of the extraordinary aspects of such an explanation, however, is that except for the healing of a young girl who is possessed by a demon (Mk 7.24-30; Mt. 15.21-28), there are no other women recipients of Jesus' power to cast out demons in the entire canonical gospel tradition except those in this unique Lukan verse. Recent New Testament studies have, however, also alerted us to the possibility that what is named as 'demon possession' might have been a protest against social roles and cultural norms that manifested in physical symptoms which were socially suspect.[35] It is in this category that the medical explanation of *hysteria* among women belongs.[36] The women manifest symptoms which their society labels as demon possession but which the professional sector of the health care system would more probably have named *hysteria*.[37] The narrative, however, does not portray Jesus as professional healer dealing with such symptoms. Rather, it is faithful to its representation of Jesus as prophet-healer and although there is no indication of the instrument of healing in 8.2-3, namely by touch or by word, readers/listeners assume that it is by Jesus' command as they have come to expect from other accounts where demons come out of those possessed (4.35, 41).

Earlier, we considered the accusations of demon possession directed against Jesus the prophet healer in the Lukan gospel (Lk. 11.14-23) as indicative of conflict and contestation *between* the emerging Jewish-

Christian community and other communities in whose midst they dwelt
or amongst whom their traditions were developing. Given the somewhat
vicious or at least extreme labelling of the women healed in Lk. 8.2-3, it
may expand our understanding of these verses if we examine them also
through the lens of labelling, deviance or witch accusation. Because of the
single attestation of these verses, it is difficult to locate their origin.[38] Also,
the accusations are not attributed to a particular opponent but are found
on the lips of the narrator. This might suggest that they represent a perspective of at least some within the Lukan community and that there was
contestation around some activity of a group of women in that community
('certain women'). As Guijarro suggests:

> ...public accusations are negative labels used to control behavior which
> some individual(s) have interpreted as negative or dangerous to society at
> large, or to a group within it.[39]

In relation to Jesus, the public accusations were used to try to control his
healing or perhaps in particular his exorcisms, his engagement with the
spirits in a way that evoked fear, especially fear of his power. If the demon-
possession attributed to the group of women in Lk. 8.2-3 is, in fact, a label
or accusation, we are faced with the question as to what power these
women had which certain opponents might be seeking to control. The
explorations of Chapter Three and the negative labelling of those women
healers who worked with herbs, drugs and other powers provide us with a
possible explanation and this text from Pliny's *Natural History* demonstrates the literary trope that encoded the cultural process of labelling or
deviance, a process, in this instance, which is gendered:

> Yet there still exist among a great number of the common people an
> established conviction that these phenomena are due to the compelling
> power of charms and magic herbs, and that the science of them is the one
> outstanding province of women. At any rate tales everywhere are widely
> current about Medea of Colchis and other sorceresses, especially Circe of
> Italy, who has even been enrolled as a divinity (*Nat.* 25.5.9-10).

Pliny has invited readers into a genealogy of texts, especially Homer's
*Odyssey* and Seneca's *Medea*, which we explored earlier and which demonstrate gender labelling and gender construction in relation to healing to be
powerfully at work. In such a cultural climate and context, it is possible
that the women of Lk. 8.2 have been singled out and labelled as demon-
possessed because they were female healers who worked with *pharmaka*
or drugs as did Circe and many other women as Pliny suggests. They are
also characterized as sharing in the itinerancy of Jesus that Malina and

Neyrey indicate is one cause of his being accused of witchcraft. For women, however, such itinerancy would have been much more of a social threat since they were predominantly associated with the household not the open road.[40] In a world in which health and healing were precarious, their work and their *pharmaka* or herbs could very readily have been labelled evil had healing not occurred or had it occurred in a way which threatened rival powers of healing. In either instance, these women's power could easily have lead to their being singled out for witch-accusation or being labelled demon-possessed as was Jesus. It may have been that their power was considered in the community to be threatening to the power of Jesus or to the gendering of the health care system in which Jesus and the male disciples were central. This emerging Christian movement may have been labelled and demonized because of its association with women's healing power and hence wished to distance itself from such power. Or did the Lukan community, or at least sectors of that community, seek to demonize women's healing powers over against those of Jesus and the Twelve who are commissioned to heal in 9.1, just as the healing power of Odysseus was pitted against the supposedly harmful power of Circe? Was it a function of the construction of gender? In these questions, text and context permeate one another.

If Guijarro is correct when he claims that such '[a]ccusations of madness, witchcraft and possession were frequently used by the dominant classes as a means of social control, especially in times of social unrest',[41] then it seems that the Lukan community is participating in the same type of control that has already been examined in Chapter Three in relation to women healing in the folk sector of the Graeco-Roman world. Many recent studies have also explored the variety of ways in which women's more open access to the public arena and to occupations including healing during the late Hellenistic into the Roman era were being brought back under male control.[42] Indeed, many studies of women in Luke's gospel suggest that this community was, in fact, participating in such gender construction and its attendant social control of women's lives.[43]

If the cultural labelling suggested above is being effected in the Lukan storytelling and women healers are labelled very negatively, then we need to explore what the narrating of their healing might symbolize.[44] We noted above that the healing is described very simply by the periphrastic ἦσαν τεθαραπευμέναι that includes the pluperfect of θεραπεύω. Of the latter, Zerwick says 'it indicates a *past* state of affairs constituted by an action still further in the past',[45] and we have noted earlier how rare is its use. It is significant to note also that the verb is in the passive and that, although it is generally assumed that Jesus was the healer, the narrative does not explicitly state this. Rather, it seems to suggest that these 'certain women' who accompany the itinerant Jesus group are no longer considered a threat to the community. They have been constituted a part of the community by the new cultural label ἦσαν τεθαραπευμέναι (having been healed). If my reading is valid, then women's healing has been colonized and the Lukan health care system is being gendered. Rather than being called into the Jesus movement with their skills in healing and invited to contribute as healers within the Lukan health care system that is gendered male, the women and their healing arts are demonized and colonized.[46]

In the light of the above reading, how might we then understand the concluding description of these women – they were serving them (διηκόνουν αὐτοῖς) out of their resources (8.3).[47] In the Lukan context, the verb διακονέω is three times associated with women (8.3; 4.39 and 10.40). In two parables (12.37 and 17.8), it clearly refers to table service.[48] Subsequently, its final use in 22.26 and 27 as characteristic of anyone who would lead in this new Jesus community as it is of Jesus himself provides little context to give precise meaning to the terminology. John Collins has amassed data on the various aspects of mediation or going-between that was associated with διακον- terminology in the Graeco-Roman world, especially its use by Josephus to refer to the mediator between the people and God, the one who acts and speaks in the name of God. Given the overarching characterization of Jesus within the Lukan narrative as prophet-healer, it would seem that the Lukan use of the verb διακονέω as predicative of Jesus could carry similar connotations to those of Josephus.[49] Jesus mediates both word of God and the healing action of God as ὁ διακονῶν. As commissioned leaders with Jesus in the mission of restoration of the *basileia* of God, the Twelve, who are on the itinerant mission with Jesus and the women, are given the task by Jesus in 9.1-6 to have authority over demons, to preach the *basileia* or transformative dream of God, and to heal.

These women healers, on the other hand, are not given such a commission as the narrative unfolds. Characterized as wealthy, or at least with resources, they seem to finance and service the itinerant band of preachers and healers out of what must have been independent means. They are women of power but their most significant power or resource, namely their healing art, has been both demonized and colonized as demonstrated above. As colonized women whose healing has been brought under control by the storytelling community, their service cannot, therefore, be meant, in the Lukan narrative, to refer to the mediating of word and healing action that is constitutive of Jesus and which will be passed on to his twelve male apostles in the next stage of the story. Rather, it seems, in the dominant strand of the narrative, that the women's valuable resources, which could include their healing art as well as any physical resources they might have,[50] will be directed toward supporting the *basileia* ministry of Jesus and the Twelve.[51] Women healing have been obscured and subordinated and the Lukan health care system has been gendered in the violent mode of demonization and colonization.[52]

To leave this story at this point would be to abandon these healing women to their colonization and also to ignore the subversive function of narrative that allows another reading.[53] The labels given to these women healers point to their demonization but within the Lukan story they have been healed, freed from the power of demonization so that their healing activity can be embraced by the community and incorporated into the itinerant ministry of the group around Jesus as they travel with Jesus and the Twelve on the open roads of Galilee and up to Jerusalem (23.55; 24.1, 10). The service of these women can likewise be read in light of the mediatory function of the service of Jesus and the ideal leadership in the community, mediating God's word and God's healing. In this way, women's healing function is restored to the heart of the gospel and we can read the remainder of the gospel conscious of women as well as men in the circle of preaching and healing around Jesus, shaping communities of healers and teachers, indeed shaping prophetic communities. As noted earlier, Mary Rose D'Angelo suggests that we 're-member' Jesus 'as prophet *within* a prophetic movement'.[54] I suggested earlier that we also re-member Jesus as healer *within* a movement which has healing at its core, a healing movement. The reading of healing women in Mark and Matthew pointed to the possibility of including healing women in that movement. Similarly the above reading of Lk. 8.1-3 directs us to include women in such a healing movement. Women healers who were practised in this art would have made a significant contribution to such a movement so that their 'service' mirrors that of Jesus. To read in this way, it will also be necessary to read against the grain of the legitimation of the masculization of the Lukan health care system noted above in a way that will be in keeping with the ministry of restoration envisaged in the text of Isaiah that Jesus reads in the Nazareth synagogue. Healing of the social body and its construction of gender is possible for today's readers also in a way in which we might hope that it was also possible for the Lukan women for whom the symbolic and social reality of their healing was being colonized.

Luke 8.1-3 has been treated at length because it is pivotal to the Lukan portrayal of healing women. It sends us back to the first woman healed in the ministry of Jesus and forward to another woman possessed by a spirit of infirmity, The first of these, the healing of Simon's mother-in-law, will now be given attention.

### Another Woman Healed for Diakonia
### (Luke 4.38-39)

When we turn back from reading Lk. 8.1-3 to 4.38-39, the very short story of the healing of Simon's mother-in-law with which we are familiar from both Mark and Matthew's gospel, we notice two significant features, one of which is unique to the Lukan account. First, as in Matthew and Mark, the healed woman is described in the ongoing activity of rendering service, the description being given in the same imperfect form of the verb διακονέω descriptive of the women healers of Lk. 8.2-3. The major difference in the Lukan account is that Jesus rebukes the fever as he does the demons (4.41; 9.42) and the Leviathan force that stirs up the sea (8.24). The narrative constructs the woman as possessed by a demonic type spirit manifesting in a fever. With this description, she is linked to the women of Lk. 8.2-3. I will not examine this text in the same detail as the previous two accounts but give attention to the differences in the text in the context of the Lukan narrative.

Luke follows the Markan order at this point in their narratives with the healing of Simon's mother-in-law following, and linked in the opening verse to, the healing of the man with the unclean spirit in the synagogue. Both accounts mention the move from the synagogue to the house, a setting that has already been explored earlier. As in Mark, the house is named as Simon's but in the Lukan account, this is the first mention of Simon. The readers/hearers, however, are not told that Simon is present and the Lukan account does not name Andrew, James and John.[55] Immediately following the description of Jesus' exit from the synagogue and entry into the house, the Lukan spotlight focuses on the woman who is named as 'mother-in-law of Simon' but without the explicit mention of Jesus seeing her as in Matthew's account.

The explanatory model or approved cultural label given to the woman is that she is afflicted with a severe fever (ἦν συνεχομένη πυρετῷ μεγάλῳ), but the language of this description differs significantly from the Markan and Matthean accounts. The periphrastic form of the verb συνέχω which carries connotations of 'seize, attack, distress, torment'[56] is followed by the agent which is attacking and seizing her body, namely a πυρετῷ μεγάλῳ or great fever.[57] It is as if she is possessed by the fever. It is only at this point that the reader learns that there are others in the house when the narrator describes their appealing on behalf of this fever-possessed woman (ἐρωτάω περί). Just as the description of the woman is in much stronger language so too is the appeal compared to Mark's simple use of λέγω: they simply speak to Jesus about the woman. In the Lukan appeal we learn something of the attitudes of those who make the appeal. They believe that Jesus is able to heal the woman and simply on the basis of their appeal. We do not, however, learn anything of the woman's attitude to Jesus or her own condition nor any therapeutic expectations she might have. She is rendered almost invisible in this account with the fever being the active agent on the scene. The clinical reality described is not sickness and desired healing but the religious world of the demon fever being confronted with the holy one of God who has been anointed with divine power or a spirit that is holy.

As a result of the opening description of the woman's condition in v. 38, it is not surprising that the mode of healing is likewise very different from that in the Markan and Matthean accounts where human touch characterized the therapeutic intervention. In the Lukan account, however, Jesus stands over the fever-possessed woman and commands (ἐπετίμησεν) the fever and it leaves her. This is the same verb used to describe Jesus' commanding of the unclean spirit in the previous story (4.35) and it will be used later with this same connotation in 4.41 and 9.42. The initial re-labelling of the woman is the simple reversal to which we have become accustomed in healing stories and which we encountered in Mark and Matthew's account: the fever left her (ἀφῆκκεν αὐτήν). In the Lukan storytelling, however, the verb ἀφίημι, has a particular quality given the twofold use of the noun ἀφεσίς in the programmatic Isaian text of Lk. 4.18-19. Both the woman and the household have been restored.

As in the other two accounts of this story, the woman gets up or is raised up. Luke adds immediately. The woman or her healed state is then described; not momentarily but as a continuous state: she was rendering service to them (διηκόνει αὐτοῖς), as were the women of Lk. 8.3. Given that this story has been shaped significantly in the Lukan storytelling, and in order to better understand the final labelling of the woman healed, we will be assisted by the cultural anthropological approach used above which questions the initial labelling of this woman. She is located in the house of her son-in-law and is not, therefore, categorized with the itinerancy of the women of Lk. 8.2-3. Intratextually, however, the only other occurrence of a mother-in-law in the text is in 12.53 and it is in the house divided.

Given the earlier suggestion that women's participation in folk healing was the cause of their being labelled with demon possession in Lk. 8.2, we need to ask a similar question here. Has the Lukan community written the body of this woman as possessed by a spirit of fever and needing, therefore, to be healed by Jesus in order that the household, seen to be disturbed by her presence with her healing arts, might be restored? Is she and her healing likewise being demonized and colonized? And what of the restored household? Is it restored, as Pilch suggests, to the proper patriarchal or gender constructed order in which women, whom he argues, are culturally valued for 'doing' rather than 'being' which is the desired state of the male, are restored to their culturally approved role of rendering table or domestic service to men?[58] Pilch's study does not allow any room for contestation over or construction of gender in a first-century context, two processes which we now know were in fact taking place and, at times, quite actively. He takes no account of gender boundaries becoming blurred as we saw earlier in relation to the complex gender relations in first-century Galilean households as suggested by Eric Meyers or being more systematically reconfigured as is becoming evident in this study.

Because we have no other traditions about Simon's mother-in-law as we have for Mary Magdalene, it is more difficult to draw the above conclusions than it was in the study of Lk. 8.2-3. We do, however, have the Matthean development of this tradition in which the story of Peter's mother-in-law is, I have argued, a call story whose response in service can be interpreted as discipleship within the *diakonia* ministry with Jesus. The tradition around this woman has developed very differently in the Lukan community in which Mary Magdalene and other women were being labelled in order that their power might be controlled, harnessed in a way that would not disturb the community's gender construction, especially around healing. From a cultural anthropological perspective, therefore, which recognizes that healing of the social body is a significant aspect of the telling of stories of healing, the recipient of the story of Simon's mother-in-law is left to fill in his or her understanding of what the demon fever might be which is possessing not only the body of the woman but the household. They would know the accusations that were being levelled against certain women of the community of whom Simon's mother-in-law, like the women of Lk. 8.2-3, seems to be a representative.

The charge against Jesus by his opponents as witch or possessing the power of Beelzebul because of his casting out of demons from those like Simon's mother-in-law may give us further clues toward an understanding of this story. It is possible to imagine, within the frame of Malina and Neyrey's construction of prominents to counter the charge of deviance, that Jesus is characterized by his adherents as one who frees insiders to the

Jesus movement from charges of witchcraft against them in a context of charge and counter-charge. To conclude a story of a woman's healing with the woman offering domestic service to Jesus and the unnamed others in the restored house would seem to have colonized this woman and her healing or whatever power it was that caused her to be labelled as possessed by the spirit fever.[59] Her healing power which could have crossed the boundaries between popular, house-based healing into the public arena of the folk sector is not liberated or liberating but confined by what is argued as a restoration to domestic service.

But just as it was possible to read the underside of Lk. 8.2-3, so too is it possible for the second and subsequent-times reader/hearer of Lk. 4.38-39 to read with this woman healer whose healing art is demonized or labelled and who represents others who are likewise so labelled.[60] Jesus, the one who was himself labelled because of the power he was seen to possess, but whose power was recognized and whose honour was restored by his adherents, now restores the power and authority of this woman within the community. He becomes her adherent and she, in turn, becomes a participant with Jesus and others in the circle of healing and teaching characterized by serving or *diakonia*. She is indeed, go-between as the διακον- vocabulary indicates, as she stands with the women who are healers but she also stands free of the labelling. One wonders whether there were not women healers in the Lukan community who were likewise reading from the underside of the dominant narrative as they saw their power and authority to heal being demonized and colonized in the name of the gospel but also saw this being contested as their community struggled to enact the gospel of the ὁ διακονῶν (the one serving of Lk. 22.28). Such a reading invites contemporary readers, as it did first-century recipients, to enter the transitional space where being demonized and being healer cross over enabling a more active, a more finely-tuned participation in the *diakonia* of the gospel, constructing gender in ways which allow the power and the authority of gift to cross boundaries. At this point, however, our pivotal text turns us in another direction, namely to the story of the bent-over woman.

### A Woman Bent Over
### (Luke 13.10-17)

In our examination of the women of Lk. 8.2-3, attention was drawn to the woman of Lk. 13.10-17 who has been bent over by a spirit of infirmity (πνεῦμα ἀσθενείας), and whose story further develops the emerging Lukan narrative thread of women possessed by spirits or demons which are of evil or of infirmity. This story is unique to the Lukan gospel as was 8.2-3 and again a woman is presented as possessed by a spirit of infirmity that has held her captive, bent over and unable to stand at all for eighteen years. It differs from the stories already considered, however, because its setting is a synagogue on the Sabbath and it is followed by open contestation around her healing between Jesus and the ruler of the synagogue.

The setting in the synagogue on the Sabbath is one of four such occasions in Luke's gospel (4.15-16, 31-33; 6.6 and 13.10), apart from a general reference to preaching in the synagogues of the Jews in 4.44. Three of these are contexts for contestation in relation to Jesus and his healing: the first with the people of Nazareth, the second (6.6) with the scribes and Pharisees, and this story with the ruler of the synagogue. They belong then with the accusations against Jesus in 11.14-23, as in each Jesus' healing activity is challenged or labelled in the context of a first-century agonistic society.

The explanatory model or label given to the woman is that she has a spirit of infirmity (πνεῦμα ἀσθενείας). She is labelled first, therefore, in a way which Lukan readers have come to expect in relation to women, namely she is spirit-possessed. As in the previous two stories already considered, the Lukan text magnifies the severity of this possession, in this case by providing the number of years of the woman's affliction: eighteen in fact (which is repeated in the dialogue following the story at 13.16). Annette Weissenrieder examines the Lukan emphasis on the duration of an illness against the backdrop of Hippocratic medicine indicating that 'an illness lasting twelve or eighteen years could signal an incurable disease or impending death'.[61] She concludes this section of her study by noting that 'illness signifies an entry into the sphere of the dead (and) is accompanied by a loss of function in society'.[62] One could argue that a large part of this woman's life had been spent in the sphere of the dead rather than the living.

This initial labelling is then followed by the description of the impact of this spirit of infirmity possessing the woman's body in language that is closer to the description of a physical illness than spirit possession. She is bent double and not able to stand up at all (13.11), with severity again being emphasized. Noting that this is the last of the explicit stories of women healing in Luke's gospel, one wonders whether the severity emphasized in this woman's illness is intended to point to the severity of the struggle that seems to characterize the Lukan narratives of the healing of women, at least those already studied above. Jesus is faced with the severest of spirit-possessions and severest of bodily deformation written on the body of a woman who is located among those other possessed and ill women who threaten the Lukan construction of healing and gender.

The instrument of healing in this story, however, is not a standing over and rebuking the spirit as in the healing of Simon's mother-in-law but rather the action we have come to expect in the other two gospels already examined, namely touch. The narrator does not, however, use the much more familiar ἅπτομαι (5.13; 6.19; 7.14, 39; 8.44, 45, 46, 47; 18.15; 22.51) which we have explored earlier with its imagery of flesh on flesh. Rather the description of Jesus' action, namely laying his hand on the woman (ἐπέθηκεν αὐτῇ τὰς χεῖρας), used only here and in the summary of healing in 4.40, carries more of a ritual connotation or a similar effect to the formal command of the demon.[63] It is, therefore, closer to the rebuke of the demon than the touch of healing. In almost every aspect this story seems to hover between spirit-possession and illness.[64]

The new cultural label manipulated by Jesus for this woman by his stretching out of his hand is that she immediately stood upright (παραχρῆμα ἀνωρθώθη), the only time the verb ἀνορθόω is used in the gospel of Luke. It carries the connotation of restoration.[65] And like Simon's mother-in-law and the women of 8.2-3, this woman also is restored to ongoing activity: she is glorifying God (with the verb in the imperfect form). There is no explicit reference to the spirit of infirmity leaving her and in the subsequent verse, v. 14, the verb θεραπεύω is used twice to refer to her healing.

This story is unique to Luke and unique to the gospels in that it is the only story of a woman with a paralysis.[66] In seeking to understand its significance to this study of women healing in the Lukan gospel, I will consider it together with the previous two stories because of the designation of spirit-possession of women which links them and the gendered world of healing being constructed by them in combination. I will also raise questions as to the symbolic significance of the woman's being bent over double for eighteen years.

Warren Carter enumerates the variety of ways in which disease and illness was understood in the first century of the Roman Empire, summarizing many of the constructions that have been demonstrated in this study.[67] He isolates a particular feature which has been emerging in this study of Luke's gospel, namely that '[s]ocial scientists have argued that in the harsh contexts of social tensions, economic exploitation, and political control, sickness can be psychosomatic'.[68] If we consider the social healing that this story may be narrating within the context of the Lukan community, the paralysis predicated of the woman may symbolize the burden women carried in the Lukan community as their healing powers were demonized and colonized as noted above. The full import of this control, this marginalizing, on all the women healers of the Lukan community is written on the bent over body of this woman. The eighteen years may simply indicate that this process went on over a long period of time, bringing women's healing almost to a point of annihilation. The supplement to the healing story reminds readers that contestation accompanied the healing of this bent woman within the Lukan community and indeed, within the Lukan storytelling.

In this final healing story in which a woman is healed, the contest seems to be resolved and restoration is symbolized, at least as fully as seems possible in the Lukan context. Jesus heals the woman who stands up straight.[69] A brief study of the final description of the woman's ongoing activity in the gospel context affirms this. She is praising God (ἐδόξαζεν τὸν θεόν). This is the action of the shepherds at the birth of Jesus (2.20); the people of Galilee during his first tour of that region's synagogues (4.15); and the paralytic who is healed (5.25), whose story is thereby linked with that of the bent-over woman. The description of the paralytic, however, is in the present only,[70] while that of the woman is ongoing, in the imperfect. The crowds also glorify God following the healing of the paralytic (5.26) as those witnessing the healing of the bent-over woman rejoice (13.17). Within the frame of these two healings, the large crowd who witness the raising of the son of the widow of Nain glorify God but they are given voice. They proclaim that 'A great prophet has arisen amongst us' and 'God has visited his (God's) people'. (7.16) This is a recognition of the anointed prophet of Lk. 4.16-21, the prophet proclaimed by Zechariah (1.76) in whom God has visited God's people (1.68). Both male and female paralysis as well as death and whatever is symbolized in the social body by the paralysis or death, can be healed and reversed by the prophet-healer, Jesus.

As the gospel further unfolds beyond 13.10-17, a healed leper glorifies God (17.15) as does the blind beggar of Jericho (18.43). Not only does this beggar whose sight is restored follow, as in Mark and Matthew (Mk 10.52; Mt. 20.34), he also praises God. This final healing narrative in the Lukan gospel can function, therefore, to throw light back on earlier narratives. To be healed and to praise God can be represented as discipleship if the response is ongoing. It may be possible, therefore, to read the restoration of the bent-over woman, this 'daughter of Abraham' (13.16) whom the Satan of negative labelling bound for eighteen years,[71] as being restored to her full height of discipleship within the teaching and healing movement around Jesus.[72] The social body in which women's healing activity was labelled, demonized, and colonized is restored as far as is possible in the Lukan healing narrative. The narrative still, however, does not show the restored healers undertaking the healing work of the prophetic/healing community that is going about with Jesus.

It is only through reading from the underside of the story that women healers can be fully restored to the Lukan narrative.[73] Women healers are not simply restored by Jesus and the powerful effects of the labelling reversed. This story can be read through the lens of ongoing discipleship to point beyond to women healers' glorifying of God through their full functioning in the Jesus movement as healers around the prophet-healer and with other healers who carry on the restorative work of Jesus. Such a reading points us to consider briefly another Lukan story that, like this story, is linked linguistically with 8.2-3 and 4.38-39, namely the story of Martha and Mary (10.38-42).

### *Martha and Mary*
### *(Luke 10.38-42)*

It is the διακον-terminology which links this story with that of the women of 8.3 and Simon's mother-in-law (4.39). Martha is described in Luke as 'distracted with much serving' (περιεσπᾶτο περὶ πολλὴν διακονίαν) in Lk. 10.40. This active role of serving has layers of meaning depending on context and here it is pitted against Mary's listening role. Many studies, and in particular many feminist studies, have explored this text.[74] Here, I wish simply to focus on the description of Martha in the light of what has already emerged from this current study.

In each of the other two contexts in which this διακον-terminology is employed in relation to women, there has been an account of women being healed. It has been suggested as a result of exploring the language of labelling or contestation in each of the texts, that women's healing roles were at the heart of the contestation as they were for Jesus in a similar context of contestation. Elisabeth Schüssler Fiorenza has demonstrated quite convincingly, in a way that is in keeping with what has been argued above, that this Martha/Mary text 'was generated by and addressed to a situation in the life of the early church – rather than an episode in the life of Jesus'.[75] She suggests that the reference to Martha's *diakonia* points to her hosting of itinerant missionaries. This study has developed a possible reading scenario in which such an understanding could be extended, not to counter Schüssler Fiorenza's suggestion but to include within this description Martha's possible participation in healing which has been suggested for the women of the interconnected stories.

If this is so, then the community storytelling is seeking to subordinate women's active engagement in the healing ministry that is included in and parallels Jesus *diakonia* to a silent listening role that is taken up by Mary. The contrast with the close of the previous story in which the inquiring lawyer is sent to 'go and do likewise' (10.37) and the role given to Mary who is said to have chosen the better part is striking and inconsistent. It enables Schüssler Fiorenza to claim that 'the rhetorical construction of Lk. 10.38-40 pits the apostolic women of the Jesus movement against each other...in order to restrict women's ministry and authority'.[76] This study enables us to make a more specific claim, namely that the ministry and authority that was being restricted in Luke's gospel was very explicitly healing. Such a claim, however, need not restrict the contested ministry and authority of women to healing but at least it should include it.[77]

In reading Lk. 10.38-42 from the underside, I have undertaken a creative reconstruction of the community's memory which, free of contestation, could have shaped a different story. In this, I am informed by Elisabeth Schüssler Fiorenza's *hermeneutics of creative articulation*[78] that she entitles *imaginative interpretive methods* in later works.[79] She likens this activity to 'feminist midrash' which she says 'puts wo/men's voice back into the text and retells the biblical story in a spirit of "tikkun olam", of mending or healing the world'.[80] This is to take the story beyond what was possible in the Lukan context because of the genderization of healing in the restrictive way that has emerged above, seeking to exclude women from the healing which they may already have been undertaking. It imagines what might have been the story told if women's healing could have been embraced in the Lukan telling of the Jesus story as the fullness of *diakonia*.

> *Jesus together with the men and women walking with him came into a village and they went to the house of Martha, one of the leaders of the movement in that village. Now Martha had just returned from a busy day of diakonia in the village and beyond. She had been called out this morning early because Suzanna, one of the women out on the edge of the village was in labour and it seemed that the birth was not proceeding as it should. Martha went off with her bag of instruments and herbs. She and Hannah, Suzanna's sister had sat with her, supporting and encouraging her. As the morning wore on Martha took out a small flask of oil and began massaging Suzanna's body to help her to relax and she also prepared for her a herbal mixture. As Suzanna relaxed the birth process became easier and in no time Martha was able to give her a healthy newborn daughter. As Suzanna lay exhausted, Hannah and Martha*

*rejoiced in the wonderful miracle of life and they gave thanks to Rahamim, the Womb Compassionate Divine One whom they had come to know in their sacred story and their women's gatherings for prayer.*

*As Martha hurried home, she was waylaid by young Samuel who was running toward her. Breathlessly he told Martha that his father was at home very ill and all that they had done for him seemed to be of no avail. She hurried off after Samuel. Matthias was indeed very ill and Martha could not determine readily what was the cause. Again she drew on her supply of herbs preparing a drink for Matthias and washing him with herb-infused water. Then Martha sat with him talking with him:*

> *Matthias, do you remember when Jesus was last with us in the village, how they took Jeremiah to him on his pallet because he was doubled up with that terrible pain that neither I nor any other healer amongst us could heal? Remember how Jesus stretched out his hand over Jeremiah and we watched in astonishment as the writhing pain seemed to leave Jeremiah's body and that in the coming days he regained his strength and returned to his fields. I want to stretch out my hands now over your pained body and together we will call the healing power of God into our midst as Jesus does.*

*Martha stood with hands outstretched over Matthias for a long time and the room was in utter stillness as not only Matthias but all the family seemed to be drawn into the movement of power through Martha's outstretched hands. As time went on she lowered her hands with a deep sigh and all turned to Matthias. It was clear that his body was no longer wracked by the same terrible pain and he was sleeping. Martha left exhausted promising to return early the next day.*

*Despite her exhaustion, Martha was delighted to welcome Jesus and the women and men in his company into her house and she gladly performed all the rituals of welcome until they were all comfortably settled. Just at that point Mary, Martha's sister arrived. Mary was a wise woman of the village and since she had met Jesus and heard his preaching she had been studying the scriptures each day trying to understand the way that Jesus was teaching them using their sacred story. She too welcomed their guests and she sat down among them as they began to share stories and Martha went off to prepare a meal for them.*

*There was great excitement as the group shared stories and remembered the scriptures. This evening they were talking a great deal about some of the healings which had astounded them all recently. Jesus recalled how the prophet Isaiah had reflected on his own prophetic ministry claiming that the spirit of God had been poured out on him and that God had anointed him to bring good news to the poor, freedom to those held captive by oppression like that of the Romans and also by diseases of all kinds. The gathering was discussing how that same thing seemed to be happening in their ministry. From time to time Martha would come to the door to listen to a story or a discussion of a piece from one of the prophets, share elements of her healing ministry from the day which would provoke more reflection, and then she would hurry back to her task. Mary like all the others was remembering texts that she had studied that seemed appropriate to the stories of Martha, Jesus and his company. At one point she drew attention to the servant songs of Isaiah and how the prophet had imagined the Suffering One taking on all their diseases and curing all their ills. Jesus and his little band of prophetic healers found this an insight that they could well use in their teaching. Suddenly, they became aware of Martha having to come and go and suggested that they keep their storytelling until they were all assembled and in the meantime sing some of the songs they had constructed as a way of teaching and of linking their experiences to their sacred story. In this way Martha could participate too.*

*After they had broken bread and drunk wine together the group continued their storytelling. As the night drew to a close, Jesus thanked Martha and Mary for their hospitality and prayed a blessing over these two women who were participating deeply in the teaching and healing ministry that they had learned from Jesus and within the company of healers and teachers around him.*

### Women Healing: A Remainder

At the outset, I indicated that the focus of this chapter would be the Lukan depiction of healing women as demon-possessed. Before closing, however, and in light of what has been developed above, I shall cast a rather cursory glance over the remaining stories of women healing in this gospel.

A significant place to begin is to note ways in which the Lukan storytelling differs from that of Mark and Matthew. The first observation is that the Lukan gospel does not include the story of the Syro-Phoenician/Canaanite woman's daughter who is healed of demon-possession. Given the Lukan emphasis on female demon-possession this seems strange. On the other hand, two Lukan tendencies provide a possible explanation of the omission. First, the daughter, as a young girl, cannot represent women healers who are being vilified as do the women of 8.2-3, Simon's mother-in-law and the bent-over woman, all of whom are characterized as demon-possessed. Second, the focus of the omitted story is the mother who enters into contestation with Jesus about the status of herself and her daughter in relation to the receiving of healing. Such confrontational speech on the lips of a woman in the public arena would be contrary to the Lukan silencing of women's voice in public.[81]

A second notable difference is in relation to the woman who pours out healing ointment over the head of Jesus in Mark and Matthew. If the Lukan storytelling community has used a similar tradition,[82] it has been changed so that the woman anoints Jesus' *feet* with ointment. The location also differs in that it is the house of Simon the Pharisee and during Jesus' Galilean ministry. I have argued in relation to the Markan and Matthean stories, placed as they are as Jesus enters his passion (Mk 14.3-9; Mt. 26.6-13), that the woman is a healer whose healing art is directed toward Jesus as he enters into the suffering involved in facing imminent death as his healing art was directed toward others during his life-time. The Lukan story, however, is placed much earlier in the gospel and the woman does not enter the story as healer with an alabaster jar of ointment as symbol of her art but rather as 'woman of the city, who was a sinner' (Lk. 7.37), another example perhaps of the Lukan demonization of women of power. The focus of the story is the conversation between Simon and Jesus – a male conversation over the body of the woman located at Jesus' feet (7.38). When Jesus finally turns the conversation toward the woman, he remains the active agent.[83] The focus of his words is her having been forgiven rather than her as active healing agent as in the Markan and Matthean texts. It should be noted that in Athenaeus' *Deipnosophistae* 15.689, the only reference to anointing the feet with a type of *muron* carries strong sexual connotations which fit with the Lukan depiction of the woman as a sinner in the city.[84] The Lukan text at 7.38 and 46 also employs the verb ἀλείφω as does Athenaeus. This verb is not used in the Markan or Matthean accounts and it is used only in this story in the entire Lukan gospel and hence it does not give us further insight into the Lukan emphasis. It seems, therefore, that the most explicit story of women healing in the entire gospel tradition, that of a woman who pours out healing ointment over the head of Jesus as he faces the suffering of imminent death, has been radically changed in the Lukan community to that of a sinner recognizing that she has been forgiven and the prophet Jesus likewise demonstrating the same recognition.[85] All vestiges of women healing have disappeared in a way that would be in keeping with the Lukan construction of women healing through a process of demonizing and colonizing, especially evident in 8.1-3 which immediately follows this story of the woman who is portrayed as sinner.

The only remaining stories which I will make reference to in this chapter are the intercalated story of the woman with the haemorrhage and Jairus' daughter.[86] The Lukan storytelling of these two accounts is much more diffuse when compared with the gospel of Matthew and less so than

the gospel of Mark. It lacks, therefore, the explicit re-writing of the body of
the woman with the haemorrhage as saved and the young girl as raised
that we find in Matthew. This is not surprising given the Lukan colonizing
of women's healing which has been demonstrated earlier in this chapter,
a tendency which runs contrary to that of the Matthean text.[87] There
is contrast or conflict in Luke between the woman not being able to be
healed presumably by physicians,[88] and her telling the story of how she was
healed immediately by Jesus (8.47) that places the focus on contestation in
the Lukan health care system. Such contestation seems, however, to shift
the focus away from the woman's claiming of her own healing and it places
her very explicitly as the healed one trembling at Jesus' feet when her
action was realized by Jesus the healer from whom power had gone out.
She is healed woman, restored to the community. The social body has
been restored. Similarly the Lukan story of the young girl does not conclude with the re-written body of the young girl raised as in the Matthean
storytelling but she is to be given something to eat, pointing to the restoration of the familial body. These stories have been able to be included in
the Lukan narrative in a way which augments the Lukan presentation of
Jesus as prophet of healing and in no way undermines the construction of
gender in the Lukan health care system especially the genderization of its
practitioners.

## Conclusion

What has emerged from this study of women healing in the Lukan narrative is an indication of what seems to be fierce contestation. Women
healed are labelled demon-possessed in a way which suggests a deviance
from a Lukan community norm which was in existence or which was being
constructed by the community. I have suggested in light of both social
processes and intertexts explored earlier in Chapter Three and present in
the Lukan context, that the deviance predicated of the woman labelled
demon-possessed is, in fact, their healing arts. In the dominant narrative,
these demonized women are healed by Jesus to a service which is within
the male-dominant paradigm of the gendered health care system. Reading
from the underside of the narrative, as it has been suggested that some
sectors of the Lukan community may well have done, women's healing
can be restored fully within the healing ministry that characterizes Jesus
and the circle of prophets and healers. Ironically, it would seem, women
healers emerge more strongly from the underside of the Lukan narrative
than in the other two synoptic gospels. To read beyond the colonization

process present in the dominant narrative, however, readers of the first and twenty-first centuries need to be like those whom Gloria Anzaldúa characterizes as on their way to a new consciousness, seeing through 'serpent and eagle eyes'.[89]

## Conclusion

This project began with the discovery of a lacuna in the gospel narratives, namely that no women were commissioned to heal. This was accompanied by an awareness of the popular claim that women had always been healers. The task undertaken, therefore, was to test the popular claim and to determine, by way of a careful examination of the evidence available from a variety of sources, whether women were healers in the Graeco-Roman world of the Hellenistic and early Roman eras, the period most influential of early Christianity. The pastiche woven from the glimpses gained of healing women in such a context informed a new reading of women healing in the gospel narratives.

The careful development of a multidimensional hermeneutic fusing postcolonial and eco-feminist perspectives provided the categories and the questions that guided the reading of a wide variety of sources. Women healing emerged from the stone, the papyrus and the parchment as midwives and physicians shaping, even in small ways, the construction of gender, offering resistance in the face of a process of genderization informed by the master paradigm. The multidimensional hermeneutic allowed new questions to be asked of these women in order that they might be encountered with as much subjectivity and particularity as possible. Our separation from them in time, however, and the paucity of data preserved meant that many of the questions asked of them and their context were not able to be answered. What became clear, however, is that in the Graeco-Roman world, women of many different classes and ethnicities participated in the rise of professional medicine. They provide a significant genealogy for contemporary women healing.

Less visible, but rendered in more vivid colour, were women healing in the folk sector of the health care system. They were stereotyped or constructed as deviant in the male literature, presented as traversing the world of *pharmaka* and magic in ways that gave them transformative powers to heal but also to destroy or harm. The emphasis in the literature fell on the harm they could bring upon men but the multidimensional hermeneutic which provided for a reading of what is silenced by texts enabled another group of healing women to become more visible. These were women in the borderland spaces, women marked by hybridity as they moved between the different sectors of the health care system and as they worked as co-agents of healing with the other-than-human, the rich resources of Earth. Together with the women healing in the professional sector, they developed healing knowledge of such co-agency that was incorporated into the medical treatises being written by professional physicians, herbalists and other ancient writers. Sometimes they were acknowledged but often their voices are lost in a way that supported the development of the master paradigm. The voice of the other-than-human, however, was not lost. The interactive engagement of these healing women with the other-than-human for healing, their crossing of boundaries, their working and their walking on the margins, may have resisted and challenged a number of the dualities being embedded in the emerging master paradigm.

Women patients within the Hippocratic health care system and supplicants of Hygieia and Asclepius demonstrated women's participation in their own health care and their taking of the initiative in that care. The gendering of the system, shaped as it was by honour/shame, contributed to women's self-knowledge and self-help in relation to their bodies. Women healing in this way were not just passive objects of a health care system dominated by men. They were able to function as active agents who, together with the healing women of the professional and folk sector, claimed different female spaces as places of power.

The presence of Hygieia with and beside Asclepius in the religious sector of the health care system of the Graeco-Roman world and the visibility of women supplicants, probably in numbers that equalled those of male participants, provided further glimpses of the gendering of healing in antiquity. Hygieia's presence and activity prevents the divine realm of healing being completely male dominated as it is in Israel and early Christianity. The relationship between her activity in the divine realm and that of women healers in the professional and folk arenas is, however, obscure. An ecology of healing emerges though in which the other-than-human, the air, water, space and diet, accompany the work of the divine healers toward transformation and healing. This is an area that warrants a specific study in its own right so that more extensive exploration of the co-agency of the forces for healing across the religious sector of the health-care system in antiquity could be undertaken.

What emerged from the first part of this study was what I would call a transformation of the historical imagination as new questions enabled fresh insights to become visible. It has become clear that the development of the master paradigm and its constitutive dualisms was not a triumphant march forward. Rather gender was being negotiated in the health care system in a wide variety of ways that continually nuanced this paradigm and its processes. This new historical imagination provided a lens through which to read women healing in the synoptic gospel narratives shaping and transforming the religio-theological imagination of readers. From a world that appeared to exclude women from healing except as recipients, there emerged borderland narratives in which women being healed were characterized in ways that countered the dominant story-line. Against the backdrop of women healing in Hippocratic and folk medicine and the Asclepian tradition, the healing women of the gospels of Mark and Matthew can be read in all their hybridity. They heal in their bodies, touched and called forth by Jesus the healer, and they carry in/on their bodies the language that characterizes the healer in ways that differ from the description of men healed. Their narratives, however, point to the possible engagement, beyond bodily transformation, of at least some of them in the *basileia* movement as a community of healers. The hints in the early narratives in these two gospels crystallize in the story of the woman who pours out healing ointment. She emerges as healer in a way which interrupts the dominant gendering of healing in these gospel stories. She is co-agent with perfumed *muron*, the healing resource that the Earth provides, rendering not only the human but the other-than-human as healer in an ecology of healing. A new reading, a re-reading, a re-visioning has been made possible. It is historical and religio-theological.

A very different story of healing women is found in the Lukan narrative where the process of stereotyping or deviance-construction seems to be active. Drawing on the tools provided by cultural anthropology for the interpretation of such processes enables the demon-possessed women of the Lukan narrative to emerge as healers whose activity in the professional or folk sectors of the health care system was challenging gender constructions, both religious and social. Hints gleaned from the underside or between the crevices of the Matthean and Markan stories seem to be confirmed much more explicitly in the Lukan gospel. Women were healers and healed in the health care system of emerging Christianity and their presence and their healing power enhanced the *basileia* movement as well as challenged its construction of gender, power and the other-than-human.

The new religio-theological imagination that has been shaped by this study can guide contemporary re-readings of the gospel in ways which will challenge and heal contemporary gendering processes, constructions of the human 'other', and the other-than-human. It is my hope that what has been begun in this project will stand with the many studies with which I have dialogued and also encourage other readings of healing which may be able to develop and strengthen the postcolonial and ecological aspects which I have begun to uncover but which are not as strong in this work as the gendered reading. Together such studies will continue to shape new historical and religio-theological imaginations that will contribute to the transformation of gender, race, class and nature oppressions so that the other-than-human together with women, men and all members of the Earth community might live in right-relationship toward not only the survival but the enhancement of Earth.

NOTES

## Introduction

1. J.E. Blum, *Woman Heal Thyself: An Ancient Healing System for Contemporary Women* (Shaftesbury: Element, 1996).

2. This study will seek to be attentive to the multiplicity of subjectivities between, among and within women and so it needs to be made clear at the outset that the term 'woman' is not used as essentializing but is simply re-invoking the call of the title.

3. R. Pringle, *Making Some Difference: Women in Medicine* (Griffith University: Uniprint, 1996), in which she notes that some aspects of medicine, especially surgery, are still almost impenetrable by women.

4. G. Lerner, *Why History Matters: Life and Thought* (New York: Oxford University Press, 1997), p. 117, says that '[m]aking history means form-giving and meaning-giving...[it] is a creative enterprise, by means of which we fashion out of fragments of human memory and selected evidence of the past a mental construct of a coherent past world that makes sense to the present'.

5. See the excellent article of A.E. Clarke and V.L. Olesen, 'Revising, Diffracting, Acting', in A.E. Clarke and V.L. Olesen (eds.), *Revisioning Women, Health, and Healing* (New York: Routledge, 1999), pp. 3-48.

6. See R. Pringle, *Sex and Medicine: Gender, Power and Authority in the Medical Profession* (Cambridge: Cambridge University Press, 1998).

7. During the course of my writing of this book, I took up a position in Aotearoa New Zealand where I have found that similar conditions prevail.

8. While this history may be much longer than detailed here, I point to what began toward the end of the nineteenth century and continued during the first half of the twentieth in a similar way.

9. M. Albert, *Les médicins grecs à Rome* (Paris: Hachette, 1894).

10. T.C. Allbutt, *Greek Medicine in Rome: The Fitzpatrick Lectures on the History of Medicine Delivered at the Royal College of Physicians of London in 1909–1910* (London: Macmillan, 1921).

11. L. Cohn-Haft, *The Public Physicians of Ancient Greece* (Northampton, MA: Department of History of Smith College, 1956). This is not to exhaust the list but to indicate the broad general nature of the research.

12. S. Jex-Blake, *Medical Women: A Thesis and a History* (Edinburgh: Oliphant, Anderson and Ferrier, 1886).

13. M. Lipinska, *Histoire des femmes médicins depuis l'Antiquité jusqu'à nos jours* (Paris: G. Jacques, 1900).

14. K.C. Hurd-Mead, *A History of Women in Medicine: From the Earliest Times to the Beginning of the Nineteenth Century* (Haddam: Haddam Press, 1938).

15. W. Schönfeld, *Frauen in der abendländischen Heilkunde: Vom klassischen Altertum bis zum Ausgang des 19. Jahrhunderts* (Stuttgart: Enke, 1947).

16. E. Brooke, *Women Healers through History* (London: Women's Press, 1993), D. Gourevitch, *Le mal d'être femme: La femme et la médicine dans la Rome antique* (Réalia; Paris: Société d'Edition 'Les Belles Lettres', 1984), and J. André, *Être médecin à Rome* (Paris: Société d'Édition 'Les Belles Lettres', 1987).

17. V. Nutton, 'Healers in the Medical Market Place: Towards a Social History of Graeco-Roman Medicine', in A. Wear (ed.), *Medicine in Society: Historical Essays* (Cambridge: Cambridge University Press, 1992), pp. 15-58 (57).

18. H. King, 'Beyond the Medical Market-Place: New Directions in Ancient Medicine', *Early Science and Medicine* 2.1 (1997), pp. 88-97 (95).

19. P.J. van der Eijk, H.F.J. Horstmanshoff and P.H. Schrijvers (eds.), *Ancient Medicine in its Socio-Cultural Context: Papers Read at the Congress on Ancient Medicine Held at Leiden University 13-15 April 1992* (Atlanta: Rodopi, 1995).

20. L.I. Conrad *et al.*, *The Western Medical Tradition: 800 B.C. to 1800 A.D* (Cambridge: Cambridge University Press, 1995).

21. King, 'Beyond the Medical Market-Place', p. 95.

22. King, 'Beyond the Medical Market-Place', p. 96.

23. King, 'Beyond the Medical Market-Place', p. 97.

24. One of the most recent studies of women healers in antiquity is the excellent work of H.T. Parker, 'Women Doctors in Greece, Rome, and the Byzantine Empire', in L.R. Furst (ed.), *Women Healers and Physicians: Climbing the Long Hill* (Lexington: University Press of Kentucky, 1997), pp. 131-50.

25. I use this term very specifically here to include both classical and Hellenistic Greek as well as imperial Roman societies because, in both, Asclepius dominated the world of divine healing.

26. In this, he stands within two streams of tradition – one that analyzes the medical aspects of biblical references to disease or illness and a second that interprets biblical healing solely from a theological point of view. These are not the specific approaches of this study and hence I will not be in dialogue with the body of literature representative of these two approaches. There is a wide range of studies of biblical healing in the context of contemporary Christianity and spirituality that are not informed by biblical or theological methodologies. These too will not function as dialogue partners in this study but are representative of the contemporary interest in healing within Christianity.

27. H. Avalos, *Illness and Health Care in the Ancient Near East: The Role of the Temple in Greece, Mesopotamia, and Israel* (Atlanta: Scholars Press, 1995) and *idem*, *Health Care and the Rise of Christianity* (Peabody, MA: Hendrickson, 1999).

28. J.J. Pilch, *Healing in the New Testament: Insights from Medical and Mediterranean Anthropology* (Minneapolis: Fortress Press, 2000).

29. B. Ehrenreich and D. English, *Witches, Midwives and Nurses: A History of Women Healers* (London: Writers and Readers Publishing Cooperative, 1973).

30. It will be claimed that the woman who pours healing ointment over the head of Jesus is, indeed, a healer and that this aspect is obscured in the Lukan gospel when the woman pours the ointment over Jesus' feet. One could argue that there is a similar obscuring of the healing aspect in the Johannine text as women healing is not a focus of the story as a whole. This could warrant further exploration beyond this study.

*Chapter 1*

1.   V. Plumwood, *Feminism and the Mastery of Nature* (London: Routledge, 1993), p. 1.

2.   A. Kleinman, *Writing at the Margin: Discourse between Anthropology and Medicine* (Berkeley: University of California Press, 1995), p. 5.

3.   B. Skeggs, *Formations of Class and Gender: Becoming Respectable* (London: Sage, 1997), p. 17.

4.   M.E. John, *Discrepant Dislocations: Feminism, Theory and Postcolonial Histories* (Berkeley: University of California Press, 1996), p. 2, makes clear the limitations even of the theories which inform any one reading position when she says that '[p]ostcolonial and feminist theorists need to become more aware of the partial and composite characteristics of the theories they depend on'.

5.   'Heal', http://dictionary.reference.com/search?q=heal [Accessed 23 June, 2005]

6.   'Heal', http://encarta.msn.com/dictionary_/heal.html [Accessed 30 March, 2001].

7.   C. Sargent and C.B. Brettell, *Gender and Health: An International Perspective* (Upper Saddle River: Prentice Hall, 1996), p. 21.

8.   J. Elias and K. Ketcham, *In the House of the Moon: Reclaiming the Feminine Spirit of Healing* (London: Hodder & Stoughton, 1995), p. 6.

9.   J.K. Coyle and S.C. Muir, *Healing in Religion and Society, from Hippocrates to the Puritans: Selected Studies* (Lewiston, NY: Edwin Mellen Press, 1999), p. i.

10.   This is the terminology used by K. Finkler, *Women in Pain: Gender and Morbidity in Mexico* (Philadelphia: University of Pennsylvania Press, 1994), p. 12.

11.   Coyle and Muir, *Healing in Religion and Society*, 'Introduction', p. ii, make this point: '[s]ickness and healing also often have a *religious* dimension, for healing and religion were frequently related in the ancient world. Religious groups of antiquity sought to provide health issues with a religious significance, or at least avoided separating issues of sickness and health from the overarching religious dimension perceived in all aspects of living.'

12.   Elias and Ketchman, *In the House of the Moon*, p. 53.

13.   Z. Daysh, 'Foreword: Human Ecology and Health in a Global System', in M. Honari and T. Boleyn (eds.), *Health Ecology: Health, Culture and Human-Environment Interaction* (London: Routledge, 1999), pp. xv-xviii (xvi).

14.   M. Honari, 'Health Ecology: An Introduction', in Honari and Boleyn, *Health Ecology*, pp. 1-34 (2).

15.   Sargent and Brettell, 'Introduction', p. 1, and T.M. Pollard and S.B. Hyatt, 'Sex, Gender and Health: Integrating Biological and Social Perspective', in T.M. Pollard and S.B. Hyatt (eds.), *Sex, Gender and Health* (Cambridge: Cambridge University Press, 1999), pp. (1-17) (1).

16.   Finkler, *Women in Pain*, p. 5, draws attention to the differences that women's actual life situations make to their experience of sickness and healing, while L. Doyal, *What Makes Women Sick: Gender and the Political Economy of Health* (New Brunswick: Rutgers University Press, 1995), pp. 1-2, speaks of 'patterns' of sickness and health which differ between women and men.

17.   Plumwood, *Feminism and Mastery*, p. 33. Kleinman, *Writing at the Margin*, p. 5, notes that '[p]erhaps it is only at the margin that we can find the space of critical

engagement to scrutinize how certain of the cultural processes *that work behind our backs* [emphasis is mine] come to injure us all, constraining our possibilities, limiting our humanity'. Within the field of biblical studies, which will be a central focus of this project, E. Schüssler Fiorenza, *But She Said: Feminist Practices of Biblical Interpretation* (Boston: Beacon Press, 1992), pp. 102-32, uses the term 'kyriarchy' to describe this paradigm of Western consciousness that for her is grounded in Aristotelian democarcy.

18. A. Kleinman, *Patients and Healers in the Context of Culture: An Exploration of the Borderland between Anthropology, Medicine, and Psychiatry* (Berkeley: University of California Press, 1980), pp. 44-45.

19. B. Ehrenreich and D. English, *Complaints and Disorders: The Sexual Politics of Sickness* (London: Writers and Readers Publishing Cooperative, 1976), p. 9, focusing particularly on the area of reproduction and contemporary reproductive technology, say: '[i]t holds the promise of freedom for hundreds of unspoken fears and complaints that have handicapped women throughout history. When we demand control over our own bodies, we are making that demand above all to the medical system. It is the keeper of the keys.' It is important to note here that this technology is available much more freely to white, middle-class Western women while an unnecessarily high percentage of women of the two-thirds world still die in childbirth. Care needs to be taken, therefore, that white Western perspectives on the liberating possibilities of medicine do not obscure the very different ways that liberation of women's reproductive health may take place in different locations among a wide variety of groups of women globally.

20. C. Feldman, *The Quest of the Warrior Woman: A Path of Healing, Empowerment and Transformation* (San Francisco: Aquarian, 1994), p. ix.

21. See Plumwood, *Feminism and Mastery*, and M. Mellor, *Feminism and Ecology* (Cambridge: Polity Press, 1997) who warn against idealizing or essentializing women as healers because of a presupposed affinity with nature and the material. Such a perspective is reflective of the 'master' paradigm.

22. L. Lamphere, H. Ragoné and P. Zavella, *Situated Lives: Gender and Culture in Everyday Life* (New York: Routledge, 1997), p. 16.

23. The reference here is to D.J. Haraway's now famous article, 'Situated Knowledges', in her, *Simians, Cyborgs, and Women: The Reinvention of Nature* (London: Free Association, 1990), pp. 183-202.

24. John, *Discrepant Dislocations*, p. 21.

25. A number of feminist biblical scholars have studied the paradoxical nature of the biblical tradition for feminist Christian women and men. Two of the earliest examples of this are P. Trible, *God and the Rhetoric of Sexuality* (OBT; Philadelphia: Fortress Press, 1978); and E. Schüssler Fiorenza, *In Memory of Her: A Feminist Theological Reconstruction of Christian Origins* (New York: Crossroad, rev. edn, 1992).

26. It is around these issues that feminist scholars of biblical and early Christian traditions have differed. E. Schüssler Fiorenza, *Sharing her Word: Feminist Biblical Interpretation in Context* (Boston: Beacon Press, 1998), p. 26, advocates that '[j]ust as other religious feminists want to transform their own religious "home bases", so Christian feminists attempt to do so by introducing wo/men into theological discourse as new thinking and speaking subjects. By critically reflecting on their own location within

institutionalized biblical religions, feminist theologians are able to claim their own religious voice, heritage, and community in the struggle for liberation.' Lone Fatum, on the other hand, seriously questions whether early Christian women were 'thinking and speaking subjects' in the patriarchal contexts of early Christian communities such as that of Thessalonica and Galatia. See L. Fatum, '1 Thessalonians', in E. Schüssler Fiorenza (ed.), *Searching the Scriptures.* II. *A Feminist Commentary* (New York: Cross-road, 1994), pp. 250-62; and *idem*, 'Women, Symbolic Universe and Structures of Silence: Challenges and Possibilities in Androcentric Texts', *ST* 43 (1989): 61-80.

27.  A. Elvey, 'Leaf Litter: Thinking the Divine from the Perspective of Earth', in K. McPhillips (ed.), *What's God Got to Do with It? Essays from a One Day Conference Exploring the Challenges Facing Feminism, Theology, and the Conceptions of Women and the Divine in the New Millennium, August 2nd 1999, Sydney University* (Hawkes-bury: Humanities Transdisciplinary Research Unit, University of Western Sydney, 2001), pp. 59-68.

28.  D.J. Haraway, *Modest_Witness@Second_Millenium. FemaleMan©_Meets_ Oncomouse™: Feminist and Technoscience* (New York: Routledge, 1997), quoted in Clarke and Olesen, 'Revising', p. 5.

29.  Clarke and Olesen, 'Revising', p. 10, go on to talk about the significance of 'maps' because of their multi-sidedness, their multidimensionality.

30.  S.R. Joshel and S. Murnaghan, 'Introduction: Differential Equations', in S.R. Joshel and S. Murnaghan (eds.), *Women and Slaves in Greco-Roman Culture: Differ-ential Equations* (London: Routledge, 1998), pp. 1-21 (20-21).

31.  M.W. Conkey and J.M. Gero, 'Tensions, Pluralities, and Engendering Archae-ology: An Introduction to Women and Prehistory', in J.M. Gero and M.W. Conkey (eds.), *Engendering Archaeology: Women and Prehistory* (Oxford: Basil Blackwell, 1991), pp. 3-30 (8).

32.  Such a consideration of gender as fixed object or category characterizes many cultural anthropological studies of early Christianity. See B.J. Malina, *The New Testa-ment World: Insights from Cultural Anthropology* (Louisville, KY: Westminster/John Knox Press, rev. edn, 1993), pp. 28-62, 117-48.

33.  In this regard, Lamphere, Ragoné and Zavella, *Situated Lives*, p. 4, point out that gendered studies cannot simply focus on women, stating that '[a]ny formulation about women has to include men, since gender is socially constructed and produced rela-tionally... These relations are now understood to be constituted within a cultural, economic, and political system that is also historically situated. Such systems involve race, ethnicity, class, and other forms of inequality that must be integrally incorporated into any gender analysis.'

34.  H. King, 'Self-Help, Self-Knowledge: In Search of the Patient in Hippocratic Gynaecology', in R. Hawley and B. Levick (eds.), *Women in Antiquity: New Assessments* (London: Routledge, 1995), pp. 135-48 (141).

35.  King, 'Self-Help, Self-Knowledge', p. 145.

36.  Skeggs, *Formations*, p. 38.

37.  S.B. Ortner, *Making Gender: The Politics and Erotics of Culture* (Boston: Beacon Press, 1996), p. 18.

38.  J. Okely, *Own or Other Culture* (London: Routledge, 1996), p. 212.

39.  R.S. Rajan and Y. Park, 'Postcolonial Feminism/Postcolonialism and Feminism',

in H. Schwarz and S. Ray (eds.), *A Companion to Postcolonial Studies* (Oxford: Basil Blackwell, 2000), pp. 53-71 (53).

40. Plumwood, *Feminism and Mastery*, p. 43. See also V. Plumwood, *Environmental Culture: The Ecological Crisis of Reason* (Environmental Philosophies; London: Routledge, 2002), pp. 13-37.

41. With regard to this last category, public/private, C.S. McClain, 'Reinterpreting Women in Healing Roles', in C.S. McClain (ed.), *Women as Healers: Cross-Cultural Perspectives* (New Brunswick: Rutgers University Press, 1989), pp. 1-19 (5-8), points out that only recently has it begun to feature in studies of women's healing roles.

42. G.C. Spivak, 'Can the Subaltern Speak?' in P. Williams and L. Chrisman (eds.), *Colonial Discourse and Post-Colonial Theory: A Reader* (New York: Harvester Wheatsheaf, 1993), pp. 66-111 (93).

43. There has been some severe criticism of this article of Spivak's but she has responded that she was not denying the subaltern her voice but rather acknowledging that sometimes we don't have the evidence in which to hear such a voice in its authenticity.

44. P.T. Ebron and A. Lowenhaupt, 'In Dialogue? Reading across Minority Discourses', in R. Behar and D.A. Gordon (eds.), *Women Writing Culture* (Berkeley: University of California Press, 1995), pp. 390-411 (390).

45. Lamphere, Ragoné and Zavella, *Situated Lives*, p. 14.

46. Ortner, *Making Gender*, p. 181

47. F. Lionnet, *Postcolonial Representations: Women, Literature, Identity* (Ithaca, NY: Cornell University Press, 1995), p. 6.

48. G. Anzaldúa, *Borderlands/La Frontera: The New Mestiza* (San Francisco: Aunt Lute Books, 1987), p. 78.

49. Clarke and Olesen, 'Revising', p. 9.

50. Clarke and Olesen, 'Revising', p. 9, where Clarke and Olesen say that this shift of attention is indeed 'fundamental to retheorizing women, health, and healing'.

51. Honari, 'Health Ecology', p. 19. H. Avalos, *Health Care and the Rise of Christianity* (Peabody, MA: Hendrickson, 1999), p. 20, suggests that from a medical anthropological perspective, aspects such as 'ecology, demography, and paleopathology' be considered in a study of the health care system of early Christianity.

52. One of the principles of the Earth Bible project initiated by Norman Habel is that of connectedness: 'Earth is a community of inter-connected living things that are mutually dependent on each other for life and survival'. N.C. Habel, 'The Challenge of Ecojustice Readings for Christian Theology', *Pacifica* 13 (2000), pp. 125-41 (126). For more extensive discussions of the six principles which inform the project, see N. Habel (ed.), *Readings from the Perspective of the Earth* (The Earth Bible, 1; Sheffield: Sheffield Academic Press, 2000), pp. 38-53.

53. Finkler, *Women in Pain*, p. xii.

54. Finkler, *Women in Pain*, p. 17, where she notes that 'to be human is to simultaneously perceive, evaluate, and embody the physical and social environments and to impose order on them'.

55. By way of example among the rich resources, S.B. Pomeroy, *Goddesses, Whores, Wives, and Slaves: Women in Classical Antiquity* (New York: Schocken Books, 1975); L.J. Archer, S. Fischler and M. Wyke, *Women in Ancient Societies: An Illusion of the*

*Night* (New York: Routledge, 1994); J.F. Gardner and T. Wiedemann, *The Roman Household: A Sourcebook* (London: Routledge, 1991); M.R. Lefkowitz and M.B. Fant, *Women's Life in Greece and Rome*: A Sourcebook in Translation (Baltimore: The Johns Hopkins University Press, 2nd edn, 1992); and T. Ilan, *Jewish Women in Greco-Roman Palestine* (Peabody, MA: Hendrickson, 1996).

56. Plumwood, *Feminism and Mastery*, p. 191. Note too Mellor's claim, *Feminism and Ecology*, p. 7, that '[f]or ecofeminism, the natural world of which humanity is a part has its own dynamic beyond human 'construction' or control'. A. Primavesi provides an excellent study of the way in which the construction and function of 'Christian hierarchy' underpins a particular understanding of these dualisms in 'Ecology and Christian Hierarchy', in A. Low and S. Tremayne (eds.), *Women as Sacred Custodians of the Earth? Women, Spirituality and the Environment* (New York: Berghahn Books, 2001), pp. 121-39.

57. Plumwood, *Feminism and Mastery*, p. 5.

58. For an excellent summary of her work and its significant call on contemporary thought see her conclusion, Plumwood, *Feminism and Mastery*, pp. 190-96.

59. It is this which Schüssler Fiorenza warns against in relation to biblical interpretation which focuses only on the sex-gender system and not on women's agency and resistance. See, E. Schüssler Fiorenza, *Jesus – Miriam's Child, Sophia's Prophet: Critical Issues in Feminist Christology* (New York: Continuum, 1994), pp. 34-43.

60. Plumwood, *Feminism and Mastery*, pp. 61-65.

61. Plumwood, *Feminism and Mastery*, p. 64.

62. Plumwood, *Feminism and Mastery*, pp. 36-40.

63. Plumwood, *Feminism and Mastery*, p. 40. Plumwood concludes *Environmental Culture*, pp. 218-35, with another very nuanced proposal for addressing the ecological crisis, namely a materialist spirituality of place.

64. Note Plumwood's recognition, *Feminism and Mastery*, p. 21, of 'denied dependency on the whole sphere of reproduction and subsistence...[which] is a major factor in the perpetuation of the non-sustainable models of using nature which loom as such a threat to the future of western society'.

65. For example, E. Grosz, *Volatile Bodies: Toward a Corporeal Feminism* (St. Leonards: Allen and Unwin, 1994); M. Wyke (ed.), *Gender and the Body in the Ancient Mediterranean* (Oxford: Basil Blackwell, 1998); M. Gaetens, *Imaginary Bodies: Ethics, Power and Corporeality* (New York: Routledge, 1995); and R. Diprose, *The Bodies of Women: Ethics, Embodiment, and Sexual Difference* (London: Routledge, 1994).

66. Mellor, *Feminism and Ecology*, p. 68

67. Ortner, *Making Gender*, p. 179.

68. A. Low and S. Tremayne, 'Introduction', in Low and Tremayne, *Sacred Custodians of the Earth*, pp. 1-20 (2), who note in relation to their collection of essays that '[m]ost of the ethnographic material...suggests that no transcendental links exist between women and nature, and in the case of those societies where women appear "closer" to nature than men, this is considered to be as much a cultural construct as a natural one'.

69. Mellor, *Feminism and Ecology*, pp. 101-109.

70. These phrases are taken from the last paragraph of Plumwood, *Feminism and Mastery*, p. 196.

71. N. Demand makes a similar claim in *Birth, Death, and Motherhood in Classical Greece* (Baltimore: The Johns Hopkins University Press, 1994), p. xix.

72. H. King, 'The Daughter of Leonides: Reading the Hippocratic Corpus', in A. Cameron (ed.), *History as Text: The Writing of Ancient History* (London: Gerald Duckworth, 1989), pp. 11-32 (13). She goes on to warn of the 'power of medicine...to make the social appear natural' and so contribute to the master paradigm.

73. P. duBois, *Sowing the Body: Psychoanalysis and Ancient Representations of Women* (Chicago: University of Chicago Press, 1988), p. 4.

74. duBois, *Sowing the Body*, p. 188.

75. S. Johnstone, 'Cracking the Code of Silence: Athenial Legal Oratory and the Histories of Slaves and Women', in S.R. Joshel and Sheila Murnaghan (eds.), *Women and Slaves in Greco-Roman Culture: Differential Equations* (London: Routledge, 1998), pp. 221-35 (222).

76. Schüssler Fiorenza, *In Memory of Her*, pp. 41-60.

77. In E.M. Wainwright, *Shall We Look for Another? A Feminist Rereading of the Matthean Jesus* (Maryknoll, NY: Orbis Books, 1998), I constructed a socio-rhetorical approach particular to that project. Others such as V. Robbins, *Exploring the Texture of Texts: A Guide to Socio-Rhetorical Interpretation* (Harrisburgh, PA: Trinity Press International, 1996) and E. Schüssler Fiorenza, *Rhetoric and Ethic: The Politics of Biblical Studies* (Minneapolis: Fortress Press, 1999) have also used the term to describe differing approaches. It can be understood, therefore, in a broad and general way. Particular aspects will be used in particular configurations to shape the construction of the approach most suitable to the project in hand.

78. See L. Alexander, 'Luke's Preface in the Context of Greek Preface-Writing', *NovT* 28 (1986), pp. 48-74; and *idem, The Preface to Luke's Gospel: Literary Convention and Social Context in Luke 1.1-4 and Acts 1* (SNTSMS, 78; Cambridge: Cambridge University Press, 1993).

79. For a more extensive exploration of intertextuality within a socio-rhetorical approach, especially its narrative/rhetorical aspect, see Robbins, *Exploring the Texture*, pp. 40-58.

80. J.J. Pilch, 'Understanding Biblical Healing: Selecting the Appropriate Mode', *BTB* 18 (1988), pp. 60-66.

81. Kleinman, *Patients and Healers*, p. 42.

82. Kleinman, *Patients and Healers*, p. 24. Avalos, *Health Care*, p. 19, draws attention to this relatively recent understanding of health and healing as functioning within an interrelationship of all the factors contributing to a society's health needs. Avalos himself defines such a system as 'a set of interacting resources, institutions, and strategies that are intended to maintain or restore health in a particular community'.

83. Kleinman, *Patients and Healers*, pp. 25-26. See also the work of A. Weissenrieder, *Images of Illness in the Gospel of Luke: Insights of Ancient Medical Texts* (WUNT, 2.164; Tübingen: Mohr Siebeck, 2003), pp. 20-42, for a different perspective on theories of constructivism within contemporary German scholarship. She critiques, however, a purely cultural approach to the construction of illness that does not take account of the historical, claiming, p. 38, that 'the sick body is historically constructed and culturally influenced'.

84. Kleinman, *Patients and Healers*, p. 27.

85. Kleinman, *Writing at the Margin*, p. 6.

86. Kleinman, *Patients and Healers*, p. 41.

87. Kleinman, *Patients and Healers*, p. 45.

88. See the Introduction for my critique of their lack of attention to gender as a social construct always in process.

89. Pilch, 'Understanding Biblical Healing', p. 63.

90. Avalos, *Health Care*, does give attention to geographical location, to economics, to space and to time in the context of a medical anthropological model.

91. It is here that the feminist anthropology of S.B. Ortner and H. Whitehead, *Sexual Meanings: The Cultural Construction of Gender and Sexuality* (Cambridge: Cambridge University Press, 1981), p. ix, becomes significant. They acknowledge the importance of the 'symbolic' or 'hermeneutical' approach to anthropology generally but warn that 'where symbolic anthropology often tends toward a somewhat uncritical relativism, the systematic asymmetry of gender relations in all known cultures forces the analyst toward a more critical analytic stance. Similarly, although symbolic anthropology, like anthropology in general, tends to ignore the individual, the fact that gender symbols always pertain simultaneously to individual and social processes forces the analyst to maintain the vital analytic link between the individual and society, between "the personal and the political".'

92. Kleinman, *Patients and Healers*, pp. 28-45.

93. Kleinman, *Writing at the Margin*, p. 7.

94. Kleinman, *Writing at the Margin*, p. 8.

95. Kleinman, *Patients and Healers*, pp. 50-60. Demand emphasizes in *Birth, Death, Motherhood*, p. xix, that 'folk' is not a pejorative but a descriptive term within the medical anthropological model.

96. The work of S.A. Sharp, 'Folk Medicine Practices: Women as Keepers and Carriers of Knowledge', *Women's Studies International Forum* 9 (1986), pp. 247-48, points out some of the barriers to knowledge of women healing especially in the folk sector:

1. Women's roles as healers have been widely assumed to be a mere extension of wives' duties, one facet of women's roles. Consequently, female practitioners have often been taken for granted.

2. Female healers have been much more likely than male healers to practice as non-professionals; i.e., to define themselves as informal practitioners,...

3. Operating within the sphere of home and community, female healers are more likely to be underreported in folklorists' studies...

4. The history of medical practices, like many other areas of history, 'has been written as if it were the history of Western man...'

5. Studies of women's contributions to folk medicine are doubly handicapped by the fact that it is poor, uneducated, rural females who are more likely to be involved as practitioners.

97. For a much more extensive discussion of these categories, see Kleinman, *Patients and Healers*, pp. 207-208, 240-43, 303-10.

98. J. Pitt-Rivers, *The Fate of Shechem or the Politics of Sex: Essays in the Anthropology of the Mediterranean* (Cambridge: Cambridge University Press, 1977), p. 1. The language is intentionally gendered in this paragraph to demonstrate this aspect of the scholarly construction of the honour/shame system.

99. Pitt-Rivers, *Fate of Shechem* p. 28.

100. Pitt-Rivers, *Fate of Shechem* p. 29. It should be noted here that this is the understanding of honour/shame which has been taken over by scholars working in Second Testament studies under the influence of Bruce Malina. See M. Sawicki's critique of not only the static construct of the Mediterranean world at issue in these studies but also their static construction of gender. M. Sawicki, 'Spatial Management of Gender and Labor in Greco-Roman Galilee', in D.R. Edwards and T. McCollough (eds.), *Archaeology and the Galilee: Texts and Contexts in the Graeco-Roman and Byzantine Periods* (Atlanta: Scholars Press, 1997), pp. 7-28.

101. Pitt-Rivers, *Fate of Shechem*, p. 76.

102. Ortner and Whitehead, *Sexual Meanings*, p. 16.

103. Ortner, *Making Gender*, p. 18.

104. See Lerner, *Why History Matters*, p. 117, in the context of her essay, 'The Necessity of History'.

105. W. Dilthey, *Pattern and Meaning in History: Thoughts on History and Society* (ed. H.P. Rickman; New York, 1962), pp. 86-87, quoted in Lerner, *Why History Matters*, p. 118.

106. See K. Schaffer, 'Colonizing Gender in Colonial Australia: The Eliza Fraser Story', in A. Blunt and G. Rose (eds.), *Writing Women and Space: Colonial and Postcolonial Geographies* (New York: Guilford Press, 1994), pp. 101-20.

107. H.A. Veeser, 'Introduction', in H.A. Veeser (ed.), *The New Historicism* (New York: Routledge, 1989), pp. x-xvi (ix), the list being Vesser's own.

108. E. Fox-Genovese, 'Literary Criticism and the Politics of the New Historicism', in Veeser, *The New Historicism*, pp. 213-24 (222).

## Chapter 2

1. John, *Discrepant Dislocations*, p. 95.

2. Parker, 'Women Doctors', pp. 131.

3. Nutton, 'Healers', p. 57, recognizes the danger of 'wide generalizations' but also that 'the precise relationship between ancient society and its medicine is impossible to determine'.

4. Parker, 'Women Doctors', p. 131.

5. Jukka Korpela, *Das Medizinalpersonal im antiken Rom: Eine sozialgeschichtliche Untersuchung* (Helsinki: Suomalainen Tiedeakatemia, 1987).

6. N. Demand, 'Monuments, Midwives and Gynaecology', in P.J. van der Eijk, H.F.J. Horstmanshoff and P.H. Schrijvers (eds.), *Ancient Medicine in its Socio-Cultural Context: Papers Read at the Congress Held at Leiden University, 13-15 April, 1992* (Atlanta: Rodopi, 1995), pp. 275-90.

7. L. Dean-Jones, *Women's Bodies in Classical Greek Science* (Oxford: Clarendon Press, 1996), and *idem*, '*Autopsia, Historia* and What Women Know: The Authority of Women in Hippocratic Gynaecology', in D. Bates (ed.), *Knowledge and the Scholarly Medical Traditions* (Cambridge: Cambridge University Press, 1995), pp. 41-59, by way of example.

8. H. King, 'Daughter of Leonides', pp. 11-22; *idem*, 'Self-Help, Self-Knowledge', pp. 135-48; and *idem*, *Hippocrates' Woman: Reading the Female Body in Ancient Greece* (Cambridge: Cambridge University Press, 1999).

9. Nutton, 'Healers', p. 58.

10. Nutton, 'Healers', p. 58.

11. Kleinman, *Patients and Healers*, pp. 50-53.

12. Kleinman, *Patients and Healers*, p. 50.

13. T. Laquer, *Making Sex: Body and Gender from the Greeks to Freud* (Cambridge: Harvard University Press, 1990), p. 8, proposes that until the Enlightenment, within the sex-gender system, a one-sex model predominated within which gender was not considered a cultural construction but was real, the natural construction of the universe. Gender, he says 'mattered a great deal and was part of the order of things'. It was not, however, fixed but was continually being negotiated as social, cultural and religious changes impacted on this ordered universe. This study will draw upon but continue to test Laquer's thesis in relation to the data being analyzed.

14. Kleinman, *Patients and Healers*, 59. Sharp, 'Folk Medicine Practices', p. 244, also makes a similar distinction using the designations 'natural' and 'magico-religious', the one treating illness by using herbal and other natural remedies and the second drawing on charms, spells or religious rituals.

15. Kleinman, *Patients and Healers*, p. 206, suggests that in contemporary contexts the majority of clients in folk medicine are female. Whether such was the case in antiquity will need to be tested from the available data.

16. D.E. Aune, 'Magic in Early Christianity', in *ANRW* 23.2, pp. 1507-557, and H.C. Kee, *Medicine, Miracle and Magic in New Testament Times* (SNTSMS, 55; Cambridge: Cambridge University Press, 1986).

17. L. Wells, *The Greek Language of Healing from Homer to New Testament Times* (BZNW, 83; Berlin: W. de Gruyter, 1998), pp. 7-8. I am indebted to Wells for some of the textual references informing the following discussion.

18. Homer, *Il.* 5.401-402. Note that Wyatt [LCL] renders the phrase 'spread on it herbs that slay pain'.

19. Homer, *Il.* 5.416-17.

20. Homer, *Il.* 2.731-32. See Wells, *Language of Healing*, p. 9, for this translation which Wyatt [LCL] renders 'skilled healers'.

21. Homer, *Il.* 4.218.

22. Homer, *Il.* 11.740-41.

23. Homer, *Od.* 4.228-32.

24. This scenario is in keeping with the centrality of gender construction in the ancient world as it is described in the opening chapters of Laquer, *Making Sex*.

25. Homer, *Od.* 4.228-32.

26. Homer, *Od.* 4.228-32.

27. Plato, *Resp.* 454d.2 (Shorey, LCL). For a discussion of the manuscript tradition as well as possible interpretations, see S.B. Pomeroy, 'Plato and the Female Physician (Republic 454d2)', *AJP* 99 (1978), pp. 496-500.

28. G.E.R. Lloyd, *Science, Folklore and Ideology: Studies in the Life Sciences in Ancient Greece* (Cambridge: Cambridge University Press, 1983), p. 70 n. 47, gives, however, a reminder of the precariousness of this text: '(t)here is...no firm indication in this passage either that this happened *regularly* or that it *never* happened'.

29. Plato, *Resp.* 451e.1-2; 455e.1; 456a.7-9.

30. Laquer, *Making Sex*, p. 8. Plato's material also supports Laquer's thesis of a one-sex paradigm – women and men are of the same nature but that reality is significantly gendered.

31. G.M. Jantsen, *Power Gender and Christian Mysticism* (Cambridge: Cambridge University Press, 1995), pp. 32-39, especially pp. 37-39 in relation to the *Republic*. She draws attention to his 'radically dualistic ontology'.

32. Demand, 'Monuments, Midwives', in which she examines four lekythoi and six grave stelae. Of these only two contain a male figure (another, however, has had a female figure changed at a later date to a male figure). Five contain two female figures accompanying the woman in labour, two contain three and one has two figures but one is child-sized.

33. Demand, 'Monuments, Midwives', pp. 283-84.

34. Indeed, women who give birth would question profoundly this perspective of childbirth being passive.

35. Demand, 'Monuments, Midwives', p. 284.

36. Demand, 'Monuments, Midwives', pp. 276, 279, 283,

37. Grosz, *Volatile Bodies*, p. 101.

38. Grosz, *Volatile Bodies*, p. 107.

39. Demand, 'Monuments, Midwives', p. 276 for Theophante, p. 279 for Nikomeneia, and p. 284 for a discussion of the difficulty regarding the labelling of these memorials.

40. See A. Elvey, 'Earthing the Text? On the Status of the Biblical Text in Ecological Perspective', *ABR* 52 (2004), pp. 64-79, for a more extensive discussion of paper carrying text.

41. W. Pleket, *Epigraphica*. II. *Texts on the Social History of the Greek World* (Leiden: E.J. Brill, 1969), pp. 26, 1.1; and M.R. Lefkowitz and M.B. Fant, *Women's Life in Greece and Rome: A Source Book in Translation* (Baltimore: The Johns Hopkins University Press, 2nd edn, 1992), pp. 266-67, §376.

42. L. Robert, 'Index Commenté', in Firatli and Robert (eds.), *Les stèles funéraires de Byzance Gréco-Romaine, avec l'édition et l'index commenté des épitaphes par Louis Robert* (trans. A.N. Rollas; Paris: Librairie Adrien Maisonneuve, 1964), pp. 131-89 (176).

43. H.G. Liddell and R. Scott, *A Greek-English Lexicon* (New York: American Book Company, 1897), p. 907, give two meanings for λύπη, namely bodily pain and grief. K.P. Rushton, 'The Parable of John 16:21: A Feminist Socio-Rhetorical Reading of the (Pro)creative Metaphor for the Death-Glory of Jesus' (PhD dissertation, Griffith University, 2000), pp. 117-21, demonstrates that this word cannot be confined to the pain of childbirth and, in this context, we could add, women's pain.

44. See the long discussion of terminology in Robert, 'Index Commenté', pp. 175-78, and in relation to Phanostrate see p. 176, and his affirmation 'c'est une bonne attestation de ἰατρός au féminin dans l'Attique' (a clear attestation of ἰατρός to the female in Attica).

45. Herophilus was a famous physician and teacher of medicine in Alexandria in the late-fourth and early-third centuries BCE.

46. This is the translation of H. King, 'Agnodike and the Profession of Medicine', *Proceedings of the Cambridge Philological Society* 32 (1986), pp. 53-54.

47. King, 'Agnodike', p. 68.

48. M. Alic, *Hypatia's Heritage: A History of Women in Science from Antiquity to the Late Nineteenth Century* (London: Women's Press, 1986), pp. 28-29, likewise recognizes the potential for power in such a healing space that belongs to women, noting that midwives were here able to control fertility (which is what Socrates confirms in *Theaetetus*) and that such control was a supreme threat to male power because it could strike at a foundation of the master paradigm, the production of a male hier. King, 'Agnodike', pp. 60-61, suggests that the story of Agnodike moves between medicine as an 'exclusively male sphere' and childbirth which she describes as 'what women, by refusing male assistance, chose to make an exclusively female sphere'.

49. Lloyd, *Science, Folklore, and Ideology*, p. 70 n. 47.

50. King, 'Agnodike', p. 68, by way of a thorough study of the function of *anasyrmos*, or the lifting of the garments to reveal the lower part of the body, suggests that the male laws which endangered women's reproductive health represented their failure to uphold the goals of a gendered society, namely the production of future men of the city. She suggests that the story is intended to 'shame the men into restoring correct roles', one of which is women's facilitating of other women's health, especially in childbearing.

51. N. Demand, 'Women and Slaves as Hippocratic Patients', in S.R. Joshel and S. Murnaghan (eds.), *Women and Slaves in Greco-Roman Culture: Differential Equations* (London: Routledge, 1998), pp.69-84, draws attention to Plato, *Leg.* 720a-e, in which he uses the example of physicians who are slaves treating slaves and free practitioners treating citizens. Demand, in line with F. Kudlien, *Der griechische Arzt im Zeitalter des Hellenismus: Seine Stellung in Staat und Gesellschaft* (Abhandlungen der Geistes- und Sozialwissenschaftlichen Klasse, 6; Mainz: Akademie der Wissenschaften und der Literatur, 1979), and Cohn-Haft, *Public Physicians*, questions whether this is an actual historical reference or a metaphorical one on the basis of the Hippocratic evidence. Its use, however, by both Plato and Hyginus in their literary works, even if metaphorically, and later evidence of slaves functioning as doctors means that we should perhaps leave open the possibility that this was an issue in classical Athens which, like gender changes, was making its impact on cultural boundaries. The elite perspective of the Hippocratic treatises may have functioned or even been intended to function to obscure the contribution of slave physicians to the developing field of medicine. Cohn-Haft, *Public Physicians*, pp. 14-15, 17, suggests that while the Greek physician was generally a free man, there is evidence for slaves practising healing, perhaps as assistants rather than independently.

52. King, 'Agnodike', p. 60.

53. Demand, 'Women and Slaves', p. 72, dates the Hippocratic corpus from approximately 410 BCE to the second century but suggests that most falls within the classical period of 410–350 BCE and so provides a literary backdrop to the material examined in the previous section.

54. O. Temkin, *Hippocrates in a World of Pagans and Christians* (Baltimore: The Johns Hopkins University Press, 1991), p. 73. See also Demand, 'Women and Slaves', p. 73.

55. Kee, *Medicine, Miracle and Magic*, p. 28.

56. At the same time, however, the Asclepieia and the religion of Asclepius took on a prominence. This will be examined in the subsequent chapter.

57. See King, *Hippocrates' Woman*, and Dean-Jones, *Women's Bodies* for their most recent book-length explorations of this subject.

58. King, 'Self-Help, Self-Knowledge', p. 137.

59. For the text of the gynaecological treatises, see E. Littré, *Oeuvres complètes d'Hippocrates*, VIII (10 vols.; Paris: A.M. Hakkert, 1961).

60. Lloyd, *Science, Folklore and Ideology*, pp. 70-73. See also Hippocrates, *Epid.* 5.25, which describes the woman who inserts her hand into another woman's womb and draws out an obstruction. Demand, *Birth, Death, and Motherhood*, pp. 66 and 204 n. 85, points to those references which instruct the doctor to have another woman who may be the midwife present to carry out certain examinations.

61. King, *Hippocrates' Woman*, pp. 166-67.

62. Dean-Jones, '*Autopsia, Historia*'.

63. Dean-Jones, '*Autopsia, Historia*', pp. 42-43.

64. Dean-Jones, '*Autopsia, Historia*', p. 43.

65. This raises an interesting question in relation to women's attitude to their own bodies. Did they see them as different from those of men with the male body being considered the norm, shaped as they would have been by the gendered system, or did their experience of their own body shape understanding?

66. Dean-Jones, '*Autopsia, Historia*', p. 48. The emphasis is hers and the translation is that of A.E. Hanson, 'Hippocrates: *Diseases of Women 1*', *Signs* 1 (1975), pp. 581-82, as contained in Dean-Jones' article.

67. It seems that the Hippocratic construction of male and female bodies does not so easily fit Laquer's construction of the one-sex body of antiquity.

68. The testimony of the wife of Achelous is reported but followed by the comment 'I do not know whether that was true' (Hippocrates, *Epid.* 4.6). Similarly Tenedia's testimony (*Hippocrates, Epid.* 4.20g), is followed by 'so she said'. Dean-Jones translates ἡ Τενεδίη as Tenedia while Wesley Smith, LCL translator, calls her 'the woman of Tenedos'.

69. Dean-Jones, '*Autopsia, Historia*', p. 55.

70. Demand, *Birth, Death and Motherhood*, p. 65, says in this regard that '(a) more accurate picture of the relationship between the Hippocratic author/compiler of a gynaecological treatise and his material would be one that portrayed him as making use of the rich resources of women's lore, but as perceiving this raw material through the value-laden conceptual screen of traditional Greek male assumptions about female physiology. This 'male slant' turned female lore into the male-filtered female (but hardly common) tradition of the male-authored treatises.'

71. On the extent of the physician's service, G. Clark, *Women in Late Antiquity: Pagan and Christian Life-Styles* (Oxford: Clarendon Press, 1993), p. 64, says of a later period, that medical writers were at the top of their professional class and hence their patients would have been from the wealthy class who could afford to hire a doctor.

72. Hippocrates, *Epid.* 1.17.11, identifies the patient Cratis as the one who 'lodged with Xenophanes, the slave of Areto' and hence who was presumably either slave or freed. Demand, 'Women and Slaves', p. 81, discusses the difficulty in determining the status of many of the patients named in the *Epidemics*. Her study, however, gives specific attention to the Hippocratic construction of the slave as patient.

73. Kee, *Medicine, Miracle and Magic*, p. 29.

74. In the opening chapters, Hippocrates, *Epid.* 1.1.22, we find the statement: 'no women were attacked'. In *Epid.* 1.12.13-14, women's specific symptoms are narrated as are those of children and older people with both age and sex as distinguishing features. For a much more thorough study of the treatment of female patients in the *Epidemics* and in particular the gynaecological cases, see Demand, *Birth, Death and Motherhood*, pp. 48-55.

75. Hippocrates, *Epid.* 1, Case 4 (wife of Philinus), Case 5 (wife of Epicrates), Case 11 (wife of Dromeades), Case 13 who is described as 'a woman lying sick by the shore', and Case 14 (Melidia, who lay sick by the temple of Hera). One wonders whether this temple may have been a centre of healing and if so, it demonstrates the intersection of the professional and the religious folk sectors and possible movements between them of perhaps both healer and the one needing healing.

76. Case 10 (a woman who was one of the house of Pantimides) and Case 11 (the wife of Hicetas).

77. Case 12 (a woman who lay sick by the Liars' Market).

78. Lloyd, *Science, Folklore and Ideology*, p. 67, provides statistics: '[i]n not one of the seven books of the *Epidemics* taken as a whole are female patients in a majority... In *Epidemics* I and III, eleven of the thirty-eight patients mentioned in Book I were female (29 per cent), as were twelve of the twenty-eight cases in Book III (43 per cent).'

79. See Hippocrates, *Morb.* 1.22, 'a man differs from a woman in the ease or difficulty with which he recovers, a younger man differs from an older man, and a younger woman differs from an older woman; additional factors are the season in which they have fallen ill, and whether or not their disease has followed from another disease'.

80. Temkin, *Hippocrates*, p. 73.

81. Dean-Jones, '*Autopsia, Historia*', p. 47.

82. Temkin, *Hippocrates*, p. 73.

83. Dean-Jones, '*Autopsia, Historia*', p. 47.

84. Demand, *Birth, Death, and Motherhood*, pp. 53 and 67.

85. Anzaldúa, *Borderlands/La Frontera*, p. 78.

86. See generally, Lefkowitz and Fant, *Women's Life*.

87. The difficulty of dating many inscriptions with precision means that the most concentration of inscriptions is in this broad period and many of the individual inscriptions can only be located approximately and hence may be given a date C1 BCE-C1 CE or C1/2 BCE or C1/2 CE.

88. See Robert, 'Catalogue', in Firatli and Robert, *Les stèles*, pp. 96-97.

89. Avalos, *Illness and Health Care*, pp. 60-61, discusses the association of dogs with Asclepius and temple healings. He also notes, pp. 112-13, the association of dogs with the Mesopotamian healing deity, Gula. Just how these associations may have influenced the memorial to the physician, Mousa, is difficult to determine but it may indicate that she is associated with a tradition of religious healing in some way.

90. Firatli and Robert, *Les stèles*, Plate 139, Planche 35.

91. Robert, 'Index Commenté', pp. 175-78, uses his discussion of Mousa's inscription as a context for a much broader consideration of the meaning of this and related language that is associated with women honoured by inscriptions.

92. Robert, 'Index Commenté', p. 175.

93. Pleket, *Epigraphica* II, 27-28, 1.12. For a much more extensive listing of the references to these inscriptions and discussions of them, see Parker, 'Women Doctors', pp. 140-44.

94. Dioscorides makes reference to a Diodotos in his *Materia Medica* in the first century. See citation in Korpela, *Medizinalpersonal*, p. 160, §28.

95. The word τέχνην is used by the Hippocratic writers to refer to their art (Hippocrates, *Epid.* 1.11.12-15). It is important to note too that an almost identical phrase repeated twice (τὰν τέχναν τὰν ἰατρικὰν and τὰν ἰατρικὰν τέχναν) is used of Xenotimos, the Hippocatic physician from third-century BCE Cos, for his services during an epidemic and on whom a gold crown was conferred. The text is given in Appendix 4.2 in Wells, *Language of Healing*, 308. She has taken the text from W.R. Paton and E.L. Hicks, *The Inscriptions of Cos* (Oxford: Clarendon Press, 1891), pp. 4-5. This parallel phraseology may strongly suggest that Antiochis was a physician in the Hippocratic tradition as was Xenotimos.

96. An earlier inscription, *IG* II2 .772 from around the middle of the third century BCE demonstrates that at least in Athens, there are physicians who are in the service of the state. The recognition of Antiochis' service by the *demos* together with the public standing of her family could indicate that she with her father were physicians in the service of the state presuming that this type of position had extended beyond Athens into the Empire. Cohn-Haft, *Public Physicians*, p. 8, however, warns that the public physicians of the Hellenistic period of which there is ample documentation, cannot be assumed to be the same institution as during the later Roman Empire.

97. References to Galen are taken from C.G. Kühn, *Caludii Galeni Opera Omnia* (Hildersheim: Georg Olms, 1965).

98. Both Parker, 'Women Doctors', p. 141, and Korpela, *Medizinalpersonal*, p. 160, §28, make reference to this attestation, Korpela suggesting that she was probably a foreign physician in Rome in the early part of the first century BCE.

99. For more detailed study of city physicians, see A.R. Hands, *Charities and Social Aid in Greece and Rome* (London: Thames and Hudson, 1968), pp. 133-39, and Cohn-Haft, *Public Physicians*.

100. It should be recognized, however, that her being linked to her father may be because of their association in the realm of healing which is what she is honoured for in the inscription.

101. *IGRR* 3.376.

102. Avalos, *Health Care*, pp. 91-93, discusses the different aspects of economics in the Graeco-Roman health care system.

103. Cohn-Haft, *Public Physicians*, p. 20, says of the male physician 'we do not know the annual earnings... No more do we know what fees were charged'. The same applies to women.

104. Unfortunately these second- and first-century BCE inscriptions of female physicians do not yield up information such as that of Demiadas who showed 'unlimited energy and devotion...in serving fairly all alike, whether poor or rich, slaves or free or foreigners' as quoted in Hands, *Charities and Social Aid*, pp. 35-36. See also Temkin, *Hippocrates*, p. 10.

105. R. Stark, *The Rise of Christianity: A Sociologist Reconsiders History* (Princeton, NJ:

Princeton University Press, 1996), argues in relation to the first century of the Common Era that epidemics were a contributing feature in the rise of early Christianity.

106. Pleket, *Epigraphica* II, 38, 1.26.

107. Pleket, *Epigraphica* II, 32-33, 1.20.

108. The Hippocratic corpus refers to the physician's surgery (ἰητήριον) in the treatise entitled, *In the Surgery*. Avalos, *Health Care*, p. 99, refers to the Roman *tabernae medicae* as does R. Jackson, *Doctors and Diseases in the Roman Empire* (London: British Museum Publications, 1988), pp. 65-66.

109. Pleket, *Epigraphica* II, 38, 1.26.

110. Domnina's association with her *patria* rather than a particular town may raise the very difficult question whether women physicians were ever itinerant as was quite typical for their male counterparts. See Cohn-Haft, *Public Physicians*, p. 21, and the Hippocratic evidence in *Epidemics*.

111. Robert, 'Index Commenté', p. 177.

112. Robert, 'Index Commenté', pp. 177-78.

113. Robert, 'Index Commenté', p. 178.

114. Hence Korpela's deduction that Antiochis was a healer of foreign origin in Rome. For a more general account of medicine in Rome, see Korpela, *Medizinalpersonal*, Jackson, *Doctors and Diseases*, and Nutton, 'Healers'.

115. *CIL* 6.7581, and Lefkowitz and Fant, *Women's Life*, p. 264, §370.

116. *CIL*, 6.9616, and Lefkowitz and Fant, *Women's Life*, p. 264, §371.

117. *CIL*, 6.9720, and Lefkowitz and Fant, *Women's Life*, p. 267, §377.

118. *CIL*, 6.9723, and Lefkowitz and Fant, *Women's Life*, p. 267, §377.

119. V. French, 'Midwives and Maternity Care in the Greco-Roman World', in M. Skinner (ed.), *Rescuing Creusa: New Methodological Approaches to Women in Antiquity* (Lubbock: Texas Tech University Press, 1987), p. 72, notes the small number of inscriptions in the Roman west which identify women as midwives among the thousands of funeral epitaphs preserved. Gourevitch, *Le mal d'être femme*, p. 222, gives a greater number but it is difficult to know what distinguishing factors were used by the two scholars to determine numbers.

120. *CIL* 6.6325, Korpela, *Medizinalpersonal*, p. 179, §141, and Lefkowitz and Fant, *Women's Life*, p. 267 §377.

121. *CIL* 6.6647, Korpela, *Medizinalpersonal*, p. 190, §202, and Lefkowitz, and Fant, *Women's Life*, p. 267 §377.

122. Lefkowitz and Fant consider Hygia to be a greeting of Hygieia, the goddess of healing while Kopela, *Medizinalpersonal*, p. 190, §202, posits the name of the midwife as 'Hygia' and 'Flaviae Sabinae' a genitive, the one to whom Hygia belonged as slave. Lefkowitz and Fant make 'Flaviae Sabinae' the one honoured in the monument.

123. Avalos, *Health Care*, p. 92, points out that medical training was often given to slaves so that they could profit their masters and he draws attention to the restriction of such a practice by Domitian or Trajan. If this practice was happening with male salves there is no reason to think that it would not also be happening with female slaves, especially in the area of midwifery.

124. Her monument is erected by her husband Apollonius and also Marius Orthrus whose relationship with her is unknown.

125. *CIL* 6.37810, and Korpela, *Medizinalpersonal*, p. 163, §45.

126. *CIL* 6.8192, and Lefkowitz and Fant, *Women's Life*, p. 267, §377.

127. *CIL* 6.9723, Korpela, *Medizinalpersonal*, p. 163, §44, and Lefkowitz and Fant, *Women's Life*, p. 267, §377.

128. *CIL* 6.8947, and Korpela, *Medizinalpersonal*, p. 179, §142.

129. Korpela, *Medizinalpersonal*, p. 163, §45, notes possible patrons and places the date somewhere between 50 BCE and 30 CE.

130. A similar question concerns Scantia Redempta, the twenty-two years and ten months old mistress of the art of medicine who is honoured in a fourth-century Roman inscription (*CIL* 10.3980).

131. *CIL* 6.9720, and Lefkowitz and Fant, *Women's Life*, p. 267, §377.

132. *CIL* 6.9722, and Lefkowitz and Fant, *Women's Life*, p. 267, §377.

133. See Jackson, *Doctors and Diseases*, p. 99, for an illustration of the relief.

134. Such categories are *etic* rather than *emic*, belonging to twenty-first-century theory rather than first-century practice and understanding. It would not necessarily be the way participants in Graeco-Roman health care would have described their perspective of the system and the boundaries they crossed.

135. For further references to Salpe, see Pliny, *Nat.* 28.23.82; 28.7.38; 28.18.66; 28.80.262; and 32.51.140.

136. S.G. Cole, 'Could Greek Women Read and Write?', in H.P. Foley (ed.), *Reflections of Women in Antiquity* (New York: Gordon and Breach, 1981), pp. 230-45.

137. Soranus, *Gyn.* 1.2-3, addresses the subject who is qualified to become a midwife and the qualities of the perfect midwife.

138. As one example, see O. Temkin, 'Introduction', *Soranus' Gynecology* (trans. O. Temkin; Baltimore: The Johns Hopkins University Press, 1956), p. 37, who says, '[t]his raises the question as to what readers Soranus addressed in his *Gynecology*. Was it addressed to midwives, physicians, or a more general lay public? The domain of the ancient midwife extended beyond the field of obstetrics; it certainly included gynaecology. Soranus' first requirement of a midwife is literacy. It would, therefore, be reasonable to assume that in his *Gynecology* he wished to present a comprehensive textbook from which prospective as well as practicing midwives could learn everything concerning their profession.'

139. Demand, *Birth, Death, and Motherhood*, p. 66, suggests that even earlier the Hippocratic *Diseases of Women* was intended for women healers: '[a]s noted, the author of *Diseases of Women* was addressing an audience that included midwives, and instructing them in the handling of problems both before and after deliveries. This presupposes that women were either auditors in a medical course in which he presented this material (these treatises are not rhetorical show pieces directed at a lay audience), or were expected to read it themselves. Is it then possible that midwives were literate?' She goes on to say that there is no need to imagine that midwives were illiterate and that the very existence of these treatises with instructions for them presumed at least that some could read.

140. *IGRR* 1.283.

141. Korpela, *Medizinalpersonal*, p. 166, §65. She goes on to demonstrate that this is not likely to be so since both names are typically Latin or Roman in origin.

142. Evidence is emerging for Clark's claim, *Women in Late Antiquity*, p. 68, that

'women could have learnt medicine from textbooks, practice, and association with experts whether professionally trained male doctors or experienced women healers'.

143. Parker, 'Women Doctors', p. 142, §18, critiques Korpela's suggestion that it might be otherwise.

144. *CIL* 6.8711.

145. M.B. Dowling, 'Vestal Virgins: Chaste Keepers of the Flame', *Arch* 4.1 (2001): 42-51.

146. *CIL* 6.6851.

147. Korpela, *Medizinalpersonal*, p. 163, §42.

148. *CIL* 6.9617.

149. *CIL* 9.5861.

150. *CIL* 6.7581, and Lefkowitz and Fant, *Women's Life*, p. 264, §370.

151. Parker, 'Women Doctors', p. 143, §25.

152. *CIL* 6.9614, and Lefkowitz and Fant, *Women's Life*, p. 265, §372.

153. *CIL* 6.9615, and Lefkowitz and Fant, *Women's Life*, p. 265, §372.

154. *CIL* 6.9616, and Lefkowitz and Fant, *Women's Life*, p. 265, §371.

155. Gourevitch, *Mal d'être femme*, p. 226, raises this same question about Scantia Redempta, a fourth-century Roman healer who died at twenty-two years and ten months old, who is praised for having reached the highest level of the art of medicine – *CIL* 10.3980.

156. This, itself, is an indicator of the education of women.

157. Nutton, 'Healers', p. 54, confines their education to training by a father, husband or patron but goes on to note that their knowledge was drawn upon by famous physicians such as Galen.

158. Gourevitch, *Mal d'être femme*, p. 222.

159. Clark, *Women in Late Antiquity*, p. 63, begins the opening of her chapter on 'health' with the words: 'medicine was part of the lives of ordinary women. They were agents as well as patients, the first line of defence against illness…sick people who had homes were usually nursed there.'

160. Pliny, *Nat.* 29.5.12, claims of Archagathus, who he says is the first physician to come to Rome from the Peloponese, that 'citizen rights were given him, and a surgery at the cross-way of Acilius was bought with public money for his own use'.

161. Nutton, 'Healers', p. 49, argues that the Hippocratic physician would have had a room in his own home for treating patients who could not be treated in their own home and would often be assisted by the patient's servants or slaves. In terms of this study, it also raises the question as to whether many of these assistants may have been women who learned many healing skills in such attendance and could use them independently in other situations.

162. Lloyd, *Science, Folklore, and Ideology*, p. 79.

163. Jackson, *Doctors and Diseases*, p. 86.

164. Parker, 'Women Doctors', p. 136. Similarly Robert, 'Index Commenté', p. 175, argues that there is not the evidence to confine women healers to the role of midwife or to gynaecological medicine.

165. I have chosen not to examine the inscriptions from the Western part of the Empire beyond Rome which honour Julia Saturnina, Flavia Hedone, Metilia Donata, Julia Pieris, Sarmanna and Sentiai Es nor those of later centuries beyond the second CE

honouring Scantia Redempta, Valeria Beracunda, Valia and others of the Byzantine era. My goal was to develop an understanding of the context for emerging Christianity and its foundational literature.

166. S.P. Mattern, 'Physicians and the Roman Imperial Aristocracy: The Patronage of Therapeutics', *Bulletin of the History of Medicine* 73.1 (1999), pp. 1-18, says in this regard that 'physicians can be found at every level of ancient society and in a great variety of status situations. There were itinerant rural physicians and semi-professional village physicians, quacks working street-corners, public physicians in cities, slave-physicians in aristocratic or imperial households.'

## Chapter 3

1. Dean-Jones, '*Autopsia, Historia*', p. 45.

2. J.J. Winkler, 'The Constraints of Eros', in C.A. Faraone and D. Obbink (eds.), *Magica Hiera: Ancient Greek Magic and Religion* (New York: Oxford University Press, 1991), pp. 214-43 (221).

3. Winkler, 'The Constraints of Eros', p. 221.

4. J. Stambaugh, *The Ancient Roman City* (Baltimore: The Johns Hopkins University Press, 1988), p. 135.

5. Stambaugh, *Ancient Roman City*, p. 349 n. 26, draws attention to the care of slaves: 'Evidence for the care of slaves comes from descriptions of farm life. Columella (*On Agriculture* 11.1.18; 12.1.6), for instance, insists that on an estate the *vilicus* ("steward") and his wife were to show special solicitation for sick slaves, and provide an infirmary (*valetudinarium*) where they could recuperate.' Often slaves were well trained and highly skilled in their areas of expertise and hence were considered essential for the maintenance of the household and its estate. See King, *Hippocrates' Woman*, pp. 164-70, for further nuances on this.

6. Stambaugh, *Ancient Roman City*, p. 135.

7. Just as *pharmaka* heals the bodies, so the religious tradition and its practices can bring healing and wholesome integration to the Earth. The human and the other-than-human intersect in the realm of religious healing.

8. J.S. Elliott, *Outlines of Greek and Roman Medicine* (London: Bale and Danielsson, 1914), p. 7. R. Gordon, 'The Healing Event in Graeco-Roman Folk-medicine', in P.J. van der Eijk, H.F.J. Horstmanshoff and P.H. Schrijvers (eds.), *Ancient Medicine in its Socio-Cultural Context: Papers Read at the Congress Held at Leiden University 13-15 April 1992* (Amsterdam: Rodopi, 1995), pp. 363-76 (365), makes the point also that many of the charms reported by Marcellus were for self-help by the patient. He goes on to ask the question 'Can that have been true of the tradition itself; or is it merely that the charms which were widely known and so available to the paradoxographical and herbalist traditions were those connected with illnesses and lesions generally considered treatable at home, by the head of the family?'

9. It has been noted earlier that except for the treatises on *Diseases of Women*, the Hippocratic corpus gives little attention to *pharmaka*.

10. Theophrastus refers to roots which are medicinal 'ῥιζῶν ὅσαι φαρμακώδεις' in the concluding paragraph of *Caus. plant.* 9.20.6.

11. J. Scarborough, 'The Pharmacology of Sacred Plants, Herbs, and Roots', in C.A. Faraone and D. Obbink (eds.), *Magika Hiera: Ancient Greek Magic and Religion* (New

York: Oxford University Press, 1991), pp. 138-74 (138), and he adds, p. 149, in relation to the ῥιζοτόμοι that they are 'a professional group of herbalists who collected medicinal roots and herbs, selling them at country fairs, hawking their virtues for pains and ailments of many kinds'. Even though the noun is gendered masculine, it may well have functioned as a collective noun to refer to both women and men rootcutters who had knowledge of roots and plants and their healing potential and who functioned as folk healers. Gordon, 'Healing Event', p. 374, includes 'wise women and herbalists' among its practitioners. I can find no indication in *Caus. plant.* 9.8.1-8 in which Theophrastus describes both the careful and magico-religious practices around the collection of plants and roots which specifically includes women among the ῥιζοτόμοι and I notice that Hort, the translator, renders the collective article as 'men'.

12. By way of example, see *Nat.* 24.92.143-48 for the citing of Glacias, Dieuches, Diodotus, and Hippocrates; 24.99.156-59, Pythagoras and Democritus; and passim for citing of male sources.

13. Scarborough, 'Pharmacology', p. 166 n. 38, notes similarly that 'almost all of the names of "herbalists" and experts on folk medicines (including matters of sexual nature), as given by Theophrastus, Pliny, Galen, and Athenaeus are those of men, not women'.

14. Kleinman, *Patients and Healers*, p. 50.

15. Homer, *Od.* 10.305.

16. This is developed in Chapter 1.

17. Scarborough, 'Pharmacology', pp. 145, and 166 n. 38, are two examples.

18. It should be noted here that similar powers are attributed to both Medea (Seneca, *Med.* 752-70) and Oenothea (Petronius, *Satyricon* 134).

19. For a brief discussion, see H.D. Betz, 'Introduction to the Greek Magical Papyri', in H.D. Betz (ed.), *The Greek Magical Papyri in Translation Including the Demotic Spell* . I. *Texts* (Chicago: University of Chicago Press, 2nd edn, 1992), pp. xli-lviii (xli). H.G. Kippenberg, 'Magic in Roman Civil Discourse: Why Rituals Could Be Illegal', in P. Schäfer and H.G. Kippenberg (eds.), *Envisioning Magic: A Princeton Seminar and Symposium* (Leiden: E.J. Brill, 1997), pp. 137-63 (157), gives the following examples of this: 'Hellenic laws dealt with magic in a similar way as the early Roman law had done. A woman of Lemnos named Theoris was condemned to death for *asebia*, because she had used drugs and incantations (Dem 25, 79-80). Also condemned to death was a priestess named Ninos (Dem 19, 281). She too is said to have made potions. Both women were indicted for poisoning (*pharmaka*). Probably both were punished for the damage they had caused, rather than for using magical devices.'

20. For a discussion of the issues involved in Apuleius' work, see A.F. Segal, 'Hellenistic Magic: Some Questions of Definition', in R. van den Broek and M.J. Vermaseren (eds.), *Studies in Gnosticism and Hellenistic Religions: Presented to Gilles Quispel on the Occasion of his 65th Birthday* (Leiden: E.J. Brill, 1981), pp. 349-75 (362-64).

21. Gordon, 'Healing Event', p. 363.

22. I have already noted Dioscorides' testing of results.

23. Gordon, 'Healing Event', p. 365 n. 12, makes the claim, citing as his source G.E.R. Lloyd's *Science, Folklore and Ideology*, that 'between Aristotle and Theophrastus on the one hand, and Pliny on the other, reference to information provided first-hand by hunters, root-cutters etc. dwindles to vanishing point'.

24. Gordon, 'Healing Event', p. 366.

25. This is the final point made by J. Scarborough, 'Adaptation of Folk Medicines in the Formal Materia Medica of Classical Antiquity', in J. Scarborough (ed.), *Folklore and Folk Medicines* (Madison: American Institute of the History of Pharmacy, 1987), p. 29.

26. Gordon, 'Healing Event', p. 373.

27. Interestingly, however, the few indicators of women in the world of folk healing in Theophrastus are in relation to the distinguishing of diseases particular to women as one finds in the Hippocratic and other gynaecological literature. See Theophrastus *Caus. plant.* 9.9.2: 'The root is used in childbirth, for diseases of women'. 9.9.3 makes reference to the use of cyclamen root 'as a pessary for women' and in 9.16.1, dittany is said to have many purposes but is useful 'especially for women in childbirth'. Pliny too makes reference from time to time to the 'diseases of women' – *Nat.* 26.40.151-163.

28. In Pliny, *Nat.* 21.1.1, he marvels at the beauty of blossoms in which Nature is 'in her most sportive mood, playful in her great joy at her varied fertility'. Later, at the beginning of 22.1.1 he reveals, however, that always his wonder is mixed with a perspective that sees the material or 'Nature's gifts' as 'created for the needs or pleasures of mankind'.

29. Aune, 'Magic in Early Christianity', *ANRW* 23.2, pp. 1507-557.

30. Schäfer and Kippenberg, *Envisioning Magic*, 'Introduction', p. xi. See also Segal, 'Hellenistic Magic', pp. 349-75.

31. Hippocrates, *Jusj.* 1.

32. This is emphasized by M.T. Compton in two articles, 'The Union of Religion and Health in Ancient Asklepieia', *Journal of Religion and Health* 37.4 (1998), pp. 301-12; and 'The Association of Hygieia with Asklepios in Graeco-Roman Asklepieion Medicine', *Journal of the History of Medicine and Allied Sciences* 57 (2002), pp. 312-29.

33. R. Garland, *Introducing New Gods: The Politics of Athenian Religion* (London: Gerald Duckworth, 1992), p. 134.

34. For a fuller summary, see L.R. LiDonnici, *The Epidaurian Miracle Inscriptions: Text, Translation and Commentary* (Texts and Translations, 36; Graeco-Roman Religion Series, 11; Atlanta: Scholars Press, 1995), pp. 5-14.

35. LiDonnici, *Epidaurian Miracle Inscriptions*, pp. 15-19. H. Avalos, 'Medicine', in E.M. Meyers (ed.), *The Oxford Encyclopedia of Archaeology in the Near East* (5 vols.; New York: Oxford University Press, 1977), III, p. 451, notes that '(c)ity states invested in the care of the chronically ill by building *asclepieia* and other healing temples'.

36. For an extensive study of the Athenian dedications and inventories, see S.B. Aleshire, *The Athenian Asklepieion: The People, their Dedications, and the Inventories* (Amsterdam: J.C. Gieben, 1989).

37. The Epidaurian narratives are available in full text in LiDonnici, *Epidaurian Miracle Inscriptions*, pp. 84-131. She notes, p. 42, in relation to the different types of text, that 'Epidauros is best known for narrative inscriptions, represented by the Iamata; Corinth lacks inscriptions but is rich in terra-cotta body-part votives, while Athens and Piraeus have many stone votive reliefs, without any text'.

38. Aleshire, *Athenian Asklepieion*, p. 45.

39. Aleshire, *Athenian Asklepieion*, p. 45, notes that the inventories of the Epistatai of Artemis Brauronia are 'exclusively or almost exclusively women'. R.S. Kraemer, *Her Share of the Blessings: Women's Religions among Pagans, Jews, and Christians in the*

*Greco-Roman World* (New York: Oxford University Press, 1992), p. 22, notes that except for offerings to Asclepius, most Athenian women's offerings were to female deities.

40. LiDonnici, *Epidaurian Miracle Inscriptions*, p. 49, notes that where names of home towns are included in inscriptions from Lebena, suppliants tend to come from the city itself or the neighbouring city of Gortyn.

41. LiDonnici, *Epidaurian Miracle Inscriptions*, pp. 50-82.

42. Kleinman, *Patients and Healers*, pp. 207-215.

43. I am using the numbering given by LiDonnici, *Epidaurian Miracle Inscriptions*, and quotations from the inscriptions will be her translation. These accounts can also be found in E.J. Edelstein and L. Edelstein, *Asclepius: A Collection and Interpretation of the Testimonies* (2 vols. In 1; Baltimore: The Johns Hopkins University Press, 1998 [1945]), pp. 220-29, §423 (*IG* IV, 1, nos 121-22). The numbers in brackets are those from the Edelsteins' translation.

44. LiDonnici, *Epidaurian Miracle Inscriptions*, p. 105 n. 15, points to the intensifier in this sentence which is difficult to translate but is intended to intensify the fact that Sostrata cannot walk.

45. LiDonnici, *Epidaurian Miracle Inscriptions*, p. 89 n. 10, where LiDonnici points out that the 'Iamata frequently use the preposition ἐκ before a woman's home town, but this does not occur with the names of men, who are simply described as being "of" a given place'. This is a subtle gender difference which recognizes the citizenship of the male and the more derivative status of the woman but the focus on healing obscures this.

46. There is a play in this narrative between ὄψιν which describes Ambrosia's encounter and ενύπνιον which describes the encounter between the blind and the lame and the god at which she scoffs. Both terms are used to describe suppliants' encounters in the Iamata-inscriptions.

47. In B21 (41), Erasippa is also given a phiale 'in which was a drug' (φάρμακον), and she is instructed to drink and then to throw up.

48. A1 (1); A2 (2); B5 (25); B11 (31); B14 (34); B19 (39); B22 (42).

49. There are a number of minor female healing deities, often associated with childbirth. Also within the family of Asclepius, one finds Epione, the wife of Asclepius, and Panacea, one of his daughters. Neither, however, seem to have a developed tradition like that of Hygieia, also daughter of Asclepius, although they do appear from time to time in iconographical and epigraphic representations of this family of healing deities.

50. In *Orphei Hymni* 67 (Edelstein and Edelstein §601), Hygieia is claimed as the 'wife' of Asclepius.

51. See Scholia in Aristphanem, *Ad Plutum*, 639 (Edelstein and Edelstein §278); and the several references in Pausanius, *Descr.* 8.31.1 (§639) and 2.2.3 (§746).

52. H. Sobel, *Hygieia: Die Göttin der Gesundheit* (Darmstadt: Wissenschftliche Buchgesellschaft, 1990), who has undertaken the most extensive study of Hygieia available to us today, notes on her opening page, p. 1, that, although Hygieia is often associated with Asclepius, she does not stand in subordination to him but in a parallel function ('nicht in untergeordneter, sondern in gleichberechtigter Funktion'). For her study of the literary and inscriptional material in relation to Hygieia, see pp. 5-8. G.D. Hart, *Asclepius: The God of Medicine* (London: Royal Society of Medicine Press, 2000),

p. 29, also notes that 'Hygieia became a partner in the practice of Asclepian temple medicine and achieved full divinity'.

53. Here I would agree with Compton, 'Association of Hygieia with Asklepios', p. 320, when he suggests that evidence of Hygieia as leader of a cult is rare but I think he makes too strong a claim for the 'rarity of her appearing alone'.

54. Aleshire, *Athenian Asklepieion*, pp. 11-12; and R.J. Coffman, 'Historical Jesus the Healer: Cultural Interpretations of the Healing Cults of the Graeco-Roman World as the Basis for Jesus Movements', in *SBLSP* 1993 (ed. E.H. Lovering; Atlanta: Scholars Press, 1993), p. 419.

55. Aleshire, *Athenian Asklepieion*, p. 12.

56. See Sobel, *Hygieia*, p. 8.

57. For an analysis of this representation, see Sobel, *Hygieia*, pp. 12-17.

58. See, for example, L.E. Roller, *In Search of God the Mother: The Cult of Anatolian Cybele* (Berkeley: University of California Press, 1999), pp. 9-19, who demonstrates how gender has shaped the study of female divine figures; and L. Goodison and C. Morris, 'Introduction. Exploring Female Divinity: From Modern Myths to Ancient Evidence', in L. Goodison and C. Morris (eds.), *Ancient Goddesses: The Myths and the Evidence* (Madison: University of Wisconsin Press, 1998), pp. 6-21 (14-19), who point to questions of power and authority and its representation in the divine and human communities and indicate the complexity of a study of ancient goddess figures.

59. Goodison and Morris, 'Exploring Female Divinity', p. 18.

60. T. Frymer-Kensky, *In the Wake of the Goddesses: Women, Culture, and the Biblical Transformation of Pagan Myth* (New York: Free Press, 1992), p. 25.

61. Sobel, *Hygieia*, p. 19.

62. Edelstein and Edelstein, *Asclepius*, §578. The text reads: 'I sadly fear that Philumena's sickness has become more serious: to you, Asclepius, and you, Health [Salus, Latin name for Hygieia], I pray that there may be none of this'.

63. See A.-F. Morand, *Études sur les hymnes Orphiques* (Religions in the Graeco-Roman World, 143; Leiden: E.J. Brill, 2001), p. 26, for the Greek text of these two hymns and Compton, 'Association of Hygieia with Asklepios', p. 319, for an English translation.

64. Compton, 'Association of Hygieia with Asklepios', p. 319.

65. Compton, 'Association of Hygieia with Asklepios', p. 322.

66. Sobel, *Hygieia*, pp. 66, 72.

67. Sobel, *Hygieia*, pp. 19, 71.

68. Compton, 'Association of Hygieia with Asklepios', p. 324

69. Compton, 'Association of Hygieia with Asklepios', p. 328.

70. R.E. Witt, *Isis in the Graeco-Roman World* (Aspects of Greek and Roman Life; London: Thames and Hudson, 1971), pp. 185-97, traces the healing tradition associated with Isis (and Serapis) from its Egyptian origins into the Greek and Roman worlds, claiming that incubation was associated with the temples of Isis as well as the Sarapeum, especially that of Alexandria.

71. S.K. Heyob, *The Cult of Isis among Women in the Graeco-Roman World* (EPRO, 51; Leiden: E.J. Brill, 1975), who demonstrates women devotee's participation in the cult of Isis as well as their roles among the priestesses, has not provided any specific link between healing women and Isis' healing role.

72. A more detailed study of this could be the focus of another research project.

73. This section, like the previous one, makes no attempt to survey Israel's health care system nor to engage all those scholars who have, indeed, undertaken such a study. In the context of this study, it seeks simply to continue the search for women healing in Biblical Judaism and the gendering of the health care system as it relates to women healing.

74. K. Seybold and U.B. Mueller, *Sickness and Healing* (trans. D.W. Stott; Biblical Encounters; Nashville: Abingdon Press, 1981), p. 105.

75. The translation being used is the New Revised Standard Version. The male gendering of the divine dominates the text even though the human community is rendered more inclusively in this translation.

76. Wells, *Language of Healing*, p. 104. As can be seen by these early examples and as demonstrated by Wells, the verb ἰάομαι characterizes this divine healing which is central to the LXX.

77. Avalos, *Illness and Health Care*, pp. 418-19. It should be noted, however, that Avalos, p. 245, recognizes also that in Israel's health care system 'Yahweh was the only healing deity that could be consulted, and consulting any other deity was a grave offense'.

78. T.C. Römer, 'Competing Magicians in Exodus 7–9: Interpreting Magic in the Priestly Theology', in Todd Klutz (ed.), *Magic in the Biblical World: From the Rod of Aaron to the Ring of Solomon* (JSNTSup, 245; London: T&T Clark International, 2003), pp. 12-22 (13).

79. Avalos, *Illness and Health Care*, p. 280.

80. Ilan, *Jewish Women in Greco-Roman Palestine*, p. 189.

81. Ilan, *Jewish Women*, p. 189. Attention has already been drawn to the fact that there is no explicit reference to women as midwives or physicians or exercising any of the healing arts in the corpus of the Second Testament.

82. Avalos, *Illness and Health Care*, pp. 251-53.

83. A.J. Bledstein, 'Was *HABBIRYÂ* a Healing Ritual Performed by a Woman in King David's House?', *BR* 37 (1992), pp. 15-31.

84. For a more extensive discussion of this aspect of Israel's health care system see Avalos, *Illness and Health Care*, pp. 260-77.

85. Avalos, *Illness and Health Care*, p. 265.

86. Avalos, *Illness and Health Care*, pp. 265-66.

87. One aspect that I have not covered above has been the many psalms which function as prayers for healing, demonstrating further that the temple and the cultus was the location of God's healing work (see Pss. 30.2; 38.3-8; 41.4; 103.3; 107.20; 147.3, by way of but a few examples).

88. Avalos, *Illness and Health Care*, p. 290, in light of not only Jer. 8.22 but also 46.11 and 51.8-9, suggests that Gilead 'was a center for medicinal resins such as "balsam"' and that the physicians of Gilead 'were famous for their knowledge of these medicaments'. A more extensive ecological reading would be informed through dialogue with R.H. Harrison, *Healing Herbs of the Bible* (Leiden: E.J. Brill, 1966).

89. R.E. Clements, *Wisdom for a Changing World: Wisdom in Old Testament Theology* (Berkeley Lectures, 2; Berkeley: Bibal Press, 1990), pp. 49-50, says that '(p)robably... there always had existed other practitioners of medicine, specialists in breaking spells

and overcoming powerful forms of magic which formed an ever-present alternative to the spartan aid of the official cultus'.

90. Avalos, *Illness and Health Care*, p. 298.

91. C.V. Camp, 'Understanding a Patriarchy: Women in Second Century Jerusalem through the Eyes of Ben Sira', in A.-J. Levine (ed.), *Women Like This: New Perspectives on Jewish Women in the Greco-Roman Period* (Early Judaism and its Literature, 1; Atlanta: Scholars Press, 1991), pp. 1-39.

92. See Camp, 'Understanding a Patriarchy' for further elaboration of this.

93. See E.A. Johnson, *She Who Is: The Mystery of God in Feminist Theological Discourse* (New York: Crossroad, 1992); J.E. McKinlay, *Gendering Wisdom the Host: Biblical Invitations to Eat and Drink* (JSOTSup, 216; Gender, Culture, Theory, 4; Sheffield: Sheffield Academic Press, 1996); and S. Schroer, *Wisdom Has Built her House: Studies on the Figure of Sophia in the Bible* (trans. L.M. Moloney and W. McDonough; Collegeville, MN: Liturgical Press, 2000) are among those who explore the female gestalt of the divine in the figure of Sophia/Wisdom. O. Keel and C. Uehlinger, *Gods, Goddesses, and Images of God in Ancient Israel* (trans. T.H. Trapp; Minneapolis: Fortress Press, 1998), provide the most extensive study of the imaging of the divine in Israel to date and the only link they offer, p. 339, to a female divine healer is that health may have been one of the areas of responsibility of the 'Queen of Heaven' to whom the women offer libations and cakes in Jer. 44.15-19.

94. Although she is said to save in Wis. 9.18, she is not named as Saviour as was Hygieia, nor is healing, as we have explored it in this work, a specific characteristic associated with her despite the influence of the religion of Isis on the characterization of Sophia. See Schroer, *Wisdom Has Built her House*, pp. 104-107.

## *Chapter 4*

1. Kleinman, *Patients and Healers*, p. 27.

2. Weissenrieder, *Images of Illness*, p. 35.

3. Mark 1.21-28, 29-31, 39, 40-45; 2.1-12, 15-17; 3.1-6, 10-12, 14-15, 20-27; 5.1-20, 21-43; 6.1-5, 7-13, 14-16, 53-57; 7.24-30, 31-37; 8.22-26; 9.14-29, 38-41; 10.46-52.

4. Mark 4.38 (disciples); 5.35 (some from the crowd); 9.17 (one of the crowd); 9.38 (the disciple, John); 10.17, 20 ('rich' man); 10.35 (James and John); 12.14 (Pharisees and Herodians); 12.19 (Sadducees); 12.32 (scribe); 13.1 (disciple); 14.14 (on Jesus own lips). Jesus does teach more explicitly in the temple in Jerusalem but this is depicted as a response to the challenges of his opponents (Mk 11.27–12.44).

5. Pilch, *Healing in the New Testament*, p. 71, claims that 'Mark presents Jesus as teacher-as-healer'. In terms of the Markan storytelling, it would seem that healer-teacher is a more accurate designation in that it places the emphasis on healing since stories of healing rather than teaching dominate the gospel.

6. A. Dawson, *Freedom as Liberating Power: A Socio-Political Reading of the ἐξουσία Texts in the Gospel of Mark* (NTOA, 44; Göttingen: Universitätsverlag Freiburg Schweiz/Vandenhoeck & Ruprecht, 2000), pp. 127-29, suggests that in this context ἐξουσία should be understood as freedom: 'Jesus is teaching with great freedom...Jesus exercised his freedom and taught differently from the traditional teaching of the scribes'.

7. Hippocrates, *Epid.* 1.11.12-15. 'The art τέχνη has three factors, the disease, the patient, the physician. The physician is the servant of the art'. Avalos, *Illness and Health*

*Care*, p. 104, points to the difficulty of being able to establish the reputation of itinerant healers. He notes Galen's concern that a wanderer is more likely to be an imposter. Since Jesus' healing is linked to his itinerancy as will be noted below, the need to establish reputation early in the narrative is essential.

8.  Wells, *Language of Healing*, p. 126.

9.  S.R. Garrett, *The Demise of the Devil: Magic and the Demonic in Luke's Writings* (Minneapolis: Fortress Press, 1989), pp. 5-9, discusses this in relation to the Lukan narratives of demon possession.

10. Garrett, *Demise of the Devil*, p. 6.

11. For an interesting example of a study of one particular healing story and the suggestions of a range of symbolic understandings within the health care systems of the Graeco-Roman world which may have informed interpretation, see J.G. Cook, 'In Defence of Ambiguity: Is There a Hidden Demon in Mark 1.29-31?', *NTS* 43 (1997), pp. 184-208.

12. Pilch, *Healing in the New Testament*, p. 69, concurs with such a reading as does Cook, 'In Defence of Ambiguity', p. 185. J.C. Thomas, *The Devil, Disease and Deliverance: Origins of Illness in New Testament Thought* (JPTSup, 13; Sheffield: Sheffield Academic Press, 1998), pp. 130-61, demonstrates that Mark does not generally equate illness and demon possession. Only in Mk 9.14-29, he suggests, is a physical infirmity explicitly attributed to a demonic spirit. He goes on, however, to suggest that a Markan audience may have brought a number of different interpretive scenarios to the healing of Simon's mother-in-law, one of which was that the fever was the result of demon possession.

13. King, 'Self-Help, Self-Knowledge, p. 141, refutes Lesley Dean-Jones' argument that there were twice as many male as female case histories in the *Epidemics* because women tended to consult traditional healers rather than professional healers on the basis of no evidence to support this. It is important for this study, however, to note that in the case histories of the *Epidemics*, in the inscriptions found in the Asclepieum at Epidauros as discussed in Chapter Three, and in the gospel narratives, accounts of women being healed are fewer than those of male healings.

14. M.R. D'Angelo, 'Re-membering Jesus: Women, Prophecy and Resistance in the Memory of the Early Churches', *Hor* 19 (1992), pp. 199-218 (202).

15. Wells, *Greek Language of Healing*, pp. 73-77, examines the use of Θεραπεύω in the Hippocratic corpus (See her Appendix 4, pp. 300-307), concluding that 'there is in the verb θεραπεύω and its cognate form the idea of continuous service, service performed with the express purpose of improving the health, and therefore the happiness, of the patient. It implies selfless and persevering care on an individual level, but does not, in and of itself, guarantee a cure.'

16. Wells, *Greek Language of Healing*, p. 136, also notes that in a teaching context Θεραπεύω meant '*to change one's way of life*' (emphasis is that of Wells).

17. Wells, *Greek Language of Healing*, pp. 62, 77, 101. See also LiDonnici, *Epidaurian Miracle Inscription*, pp. 96-97, A15; 100-101, B2; and 106-107, B9.

18. For a detailed analysis across the synoptics, see Wells, *Greek Language of Healing*, pp. 180-91.

19. BAGD, p. 798, where it is noted that this verb is found in the Hippocratic literature.

20. Wells, *Greek Language of Healing*, p. 62.

21. BAGD, p. 383.

22. C. Evans, ' "Who Touched Me?" Jesus and the Ritually Impure', in B. Chilton and C. Evans (eds.), *Jesus in Context: Temple, Purity, and Restoration* (AGJU, 39; Leiden: E.J. Brill, 1997), pp. 353-76 (353), says of Jesus in this context that he 'likened himself to a physician sent to heal the sick'.

23. Cook, 'In Defence of Ambiguity', p. 187, also makes this claim.

24. I will use the general terminology 'healing stories' to include both healing of physical illnesses and the driving out of demons or unclean spirits.

25. The only exception is 5.38 when Jesus enters Jairus' house specifically to heal (5.21-24a and 35-43 as context).

26. Kee, *Medicine, Miracle and Magic*, pp. 9-10, 21-25; and H. Remus, *Jesus as Healer* (Understanding Jesus Today; Cambridge: Cambridge University Press, 1997), pp. 4-6, 19.

27. G. Vermes, *The Changing Faces of Jesus* (New York: Viking Compass, 2000), pp. 252-63. See also Kee, *Medicine, Miracle and Magic*, pp. 81-83, and the much more extensively argued position of W.S. Green, 'Palestinian Holy Men: Charismatic Leadership and Rabbinic Tradition', in *ANRW* 19.2, pp. 619-47. Green demonstrates convincingly, that Tannaitic Judaism sought to shift power from the priests of the cult to the rabbis whose central activity was study, together with prayer and ritual observance. He points out that except for the traditions of Honi, the Circle-maker, no healing stories appear in the Mishnah. And while Hanina ben Dosa is considered a rabbi of the latter half of the first century, the redaction of stories of healing attributed to him belong to the period of the *Amoraim* according to Green.

28. This is most clear in an analysis such as that of Remus, *Jesus as Healer*, pp. 13-39. See also the painstaking analysis of John P. Meier, *A Marginal Jew; Rethinking the Historical Jesus* (3 vols.; New York: Doubleday, 1994), II, pp. 535-630, in which he discusses not only the lateness of the traditions of Honi and Hanina ben Dosa but also those of Philostratus' *The Life of Apolonius of Tyana*.

29. The only parallel of this piling up of story upon story of healing would be the tales or narratives of healing attributed to Asclepius on the stelae of his temple in Epidauros, but these are individual healing accounts and have not been incorporated into an extended narrative. See LiDonnici, *Epidaurian Miracle Inscriptions* and Aleshire, *Athenian Asklepieion*. Within the Hippocratic corpus, *Epidemics* has account after account of people suffering from illness and their cure or their demise. The purpose, however, is to describe the illness, its symptoms, progression and resolution. These narratives are not associated with a particular physician. It would seem therefore, that J.D.M. Derrett, 'Mark's Technique: the Haemorrhaging Woman and Jairus' Daughter', *Bib* 63 (1982), pp. 474-505 (475), is correct in claiming that 'the healing stories are not told in order to provide a list of the precise illnesses from which Jesus supplied cures. They are *not* a mini-case book!' (emphasis is that of the author).

30. Green, 'Palestinian Holy Men', p. 625.

31. This analysis does not place the Jesus of Christianity over against first-century Judaism in a supersessionist way but rather situates Jesus, the Jewish charismatic healer, in conflict with shifting bases of power within the socio-political reality of

Judaism. A health care system will always be situated within the social reality of its time that includes the political, cultural and religious.

32. This might be considered another example of the blurring of the lines between healing and casting out of demons.

33. Kleinman, *Patients and Healers*, pp. 207-209; 238-43.

34. See the variety of articles in C. Osiek and D.L. Balch (eds.), *Families in the New Testament World: Houses and House Churches* (Louisville, KY: Westminster/John Knox Press, 1997) and D.L. Balch and C. Osiek (eds.), *Early Christian Families in Context: An Interdisciplinary Dialogue* (Grand Rapids: Eerdmans, 2003). For a discussion of the variety of scholarly opinions on the provenance of the Markan gospel in recent scholarship, see F.J. Moloney, *The Gospel of Mark: A Commentary* (Peabody, MA: Hendrickson, 2002), pp. 12-13.

35. This is one of the critiques that I have already raised in relation to Pilch, *Healing in the New Testament*, and further examples will be detailed below. See also Malina, *The New Testament World*, pp. 117-48.

36. See M. Sawicki, 'Archaeology as Space Technology: Digging for Gender and Class in Holy Land', *MTSR* 6.4 (1994), pp. 319-48.

37. J. Økland, ' "*IN PUBLICUM PROCURRENDI*": Women in the Public Space of Roman Greece', in L. Larsson and A. Strömberg Lovén (eds.), *Aspects of Women in Antiquity: Proceedings of the First Nordic Symposium on Women's Lives in Antiquity* (Jonsered: Paul Astroms, 1998), pp. 127-41 (128).

38. E.M. Meyers, 'The Problems of Gendered Space in Syro-Palestinian Domestic Architecture: The Case of Roman-Period Galilee', in Balch and Osiek (eds.), *Early Christian Families*, pp. 44-69. Note also in this same volume R.P. Saller, 'Women, Slaves, and the Economy of the Roman Household', pp. 185-206.

39. The house is not only an important setting but also a significant concept within the Markan gospel narrative with οἰκία occurring 18 times and οἶκος 13 times. A number of these are associated with healing, either as the place of healing or the site to which the healed person returns (οἰκία – 1.29; 7.24; 14.3; and οἶκος – 2.1, 11; 5.38; 7.30; 8.26).

40. Many studies have contributed to the development of this picture but note in particular the evidence in Lefkowitz and Fant, *Women's Life*. Ilan, *Jewish Women*, p. 133, notes the exceeding caution needed in identifying women's quarters in dwellings in Palestine in the first century and that gender separation would have been a luxury of the rich.

41. M.F. Trainor, *The Quest for Home: The Household in Mark's Community* (Collegeville, MN: Liturgical Press, 2001), p. 25.

42. Sawicki, 'Spatial Management', p. 11.

43. S. Guijarro, 'The Family in First-Century Galilee', in H. Moxnes (ed.), *Constructing Early Christian Families: Family as Social Reality and Metaphor* (London: Routledge, 1997), pp. 42-65 (50-52).

44. Kleinman, *Patients and Healers*, p. 50.

45. Kleinman, *Patients and Healers*, p. 207, places 'attitudes of participants' as one of the *characteristics of interpersonal interaction* in his cross-cultural criteria.

46. Pilch, *Healing in the New Testament*, p. 67.

47. Trainor, *Quest for Home*, pp. 93-94, explores at least two scenarios or household

constructions that would explain why Simon's mother-in-law might be in his house. This has always been a puzzle to scholars but need not specifically concern us here.

48. Kleinman, *Patients and Healers*, p. 243.

49. In terms of Kleinman's categories, we do not have access to any of the explanatory models shared or otherwise between healer and client/patient. See Kleinman, *Patients and Healers*, p. 240.

50. Cook, 'In Defence of Ambiguity', pp. 184-208.

51. D.E. Garland, '"I Am the Lord Your Healer": Mark 1:21–2:12', *RevExp* 85 (1988), pp. 327-43 (333).

52. Hippocrates, *Morb.* 2.44, 45, 46, 47; *Aff.* 11 and 12, on the other hand, treat fevers that are considered illnesses in their own right.

53. Økland, 'Women in the Public Space', p. 138, demonstrates that '[t]he Roman house was not private by modern standards' and that domestic space was as much male space in the Roman world as female space in that it was the place where privacy among males could be achieved.

54. See Hippocrates, *Epid.* 3.140 (Case VI, the maiden daughter of Euryanax), 235-52 (Case XI, a Thasosian woman) and 253-68 (a maiden of Larissa) by way of demonstration.

55. Dean-Jones, '*Autopsia, Historia*', pp. 41-59, explores evidence in the Hippocratic literature of women's knowledge of their own bodies in a way not accessible to the male physician.

56. King, 'Self-Help, Self-Knowledge', p. 143.

57. Kleinman, *Patients and Healers*, pp. 207-208. In the next healing story, the leper obliquely names himself as 'unclean' and indicates that he believes that Jesus can make him clean (1.40); Jairus names his daughter as 'at the point of death' and communicates to Jesus his belief that if he comes and lays hands on her she will live (5.23); the father of the boy with the dumb spirit names and describes the symptoms of his son's illness (9.17-18); and at Jesus' invitation, Bartimaeus requests sight, an implicit indication of his being blind. Each of these supplicants with voice is male, but there are also stories in which the third person narrator describes male as well as female illnesses. The women's voices, however, have been silenced in relation to their illnesses. In some Markan accounts, therefore, the explanatory models are explicit and seem to be gendered in terms of a lack of women's voices.

58. LiDonnici, *Epidaurian Miracle Inscriptions*, p. 99, A18; p. 109, B 11.

59. Touch in other healing narratives is described by means of the more formal phrase ἐπιτίθημι τὰς χεῖρας and will be considered in the following section of this chapter (5.23; 6.5; 7.32; 8.23, 28).

60. Kleinman, *Patients and Healers*, pp. 208, 243.

61. The leper is sent by Jesus to the priest but simply to carry out the required ritual (1.43-44); the paralytic is sent to his house (2.11) as is the blind man of Bethsaida (8.26); and the Gerasene man is sent home to proclaim what Jesus has done and he begins to do this (5.18-20).

62. D. Krause, 'Simon Peter's Mother-in-law – Disciple or Domestic Servant? Feminist Biblical Hermeneutics and the Interpretation of Mark 1.29-31', in A-J. Levine and M. Blickenstaff (eds.), *A Feminist Companion to Mark* (Sheffield: Sheffield Academic Press, 2001), pp. 37-53.

63. Krause, 'Simon Peter's Mother-in-law', pp. 50-53.

64. E. van Eck and A.G. van Aarde, 'Sickness and Healing in Mark: A Social Scientific Interpretation', *Neot* 27 (1993), pp. 27-54 (45).

65. This is contrary to the reading of J. Dewey, 'Jesus Healings of Women: Conformity and Non-conformity to Dominant Cultural Values as Clues for Historical Reconstructions', *BTB* 24.3 (1994), pp. 122-31.

66. The Hippocratic text *Airs Waters Places* (passim) lays out in detail the effect of location on health. It is of interest for the gospel text under discussion that the diseases found in the first location isolated by the Hippocratic author resemble those in the Markan account: women are subject to excessive fluxes (ῥοώδεας) and children to the sacred disease which some commentators attribute to the daughter of Jairus (Hippocrates, *Airs Waters Places* 3.18-21, 21-23). I am not suggesting exolicit influence here but do draw attention to the ecology of healing functioning in the world of Greek and Roman medicine and the possible social and cultural intertext.

67. This is the one point at which one might argue that a gender distinction is made but as the investigation continues, it will be clear that there may be factors shaping the woman's actions other than gender.

68. Neither supplicant addresses Jesus by a title, but it should be noted that in v. 35 those who come to Jairus to announce the death of his daughter speak of Jesus as teacher. Again, teaching and healing are intimately linked in this Markan account.

69. Kleinman, *Patients and Healing*, p. 243.

70. See S. Haber, 'A Woman's Touch: Feminist Encounters with the Hemorrhaging Woman in Mark 5.24-34', *JSNT* 26.2 (2003), pp. 171-92 (187), and Evans, 'Who Touched Me?', p. 369, are just two examples of this approach.

71. Weissenrieder, *Images of Illness*, pp. 258-59.

72. Ilan, *Jewish Women in Greco-Roman Palestine*, p. 69.

73. Dean-Jones, *Women's Bodies*, pp. 47-48, suggests that 14 was the age at which a girl was thought 'capable of fulfilling the roles of adult women in marriage and motherhood' but that she may not yet have started to menstruate, with menarche not occurring until she was perhaps 18.

74. A. Wire, 'Ancient Miracle Stories and Women's Social World', *Forum* 2.4 (1986), pp. 77-84 (79).

75. For a much more detailed discussion of these texts, see King, *Hippocrates' Woman*, pp. 205-46. She critiques the history of interpretation of these texts in terms of hysteria. Her work needs to be brought into dialogue with Weissenrieder, *Images of Illness*, pp. 257-58, 264-67; and Derrett, 'Haemorrhaging Woman', pp. 481-85.

76. King, *Hippocrates' Woman*, p. 246.

77. If this is so, then she is the mirror image of the woman with the haemorrhage. For the woman, the flow of blood is excessive whereas for the young woman the normal flow of blood associated with the onset of menstruation is not occurring. For both there is dis-ease in their female bodies.

78. Ἐγείρω at .1; ., 11, 12; .; .7, 38; .1; .4, 16; .7; 1.9; 1.6; 1., 22; 1.8, 42; 16.6; and Ἀνίστημι at 1.35; 2.14; 3.26; 5.42; 7.24; 8.31; 9.9, 10, 27, 31; 10.1, 34; 12.25; 14.57, 60.

79. For a more lengthy discussion of stories of raising from the dead, see Meier, *A Marginal Jew*, II, pp. 773-88.

80. Ilan, *Jewish Women*, p. 69, a claim based on historical data.

81. M.-E. Rosenblatt, 'Gender, Ethnicity, and Legal Considerations in the Haemorrhaging Woman's Story: Mark 5:25-34', in I.R. Kitzberger (ed.), *Transformative Encounters: Jesus and Women Re-viewed* (Biblical Interpretation Series, 43; Leiden: E.J. Brill, 2000), pp. 137-61. See also C. Fonrobert, 'The Woman with a Blood-flow (Mark 5:24-34) Revisited: Menstrual Laws and Jewish Culture in Christian Feminist Hermeneutics', in C.A. Evans and J.A. Sanders (eds.), *Early Christian Interpretation of the Scriptures of Israel* (Sheffield: Sheffield Academic Press, 1997), pp. 121-40 (129); and Dewey, 'Jesus' Healings of Women', p. 128.

82. A.-J. Levine, 'Discharging Responsibility: Matthean Jesus, Biblical Law, and Hemorrhaging Woman', in D.R. Bauer and M.A. Powell (eds.), *Treasures New and Old: Recent Contributions to Matthean Studies* (SBLSymS, 1; Atlanta: Scholars Press, 1996), pp. 379-97.

83. On this aspect, see Fonrobert, 'Woman with a Blood-flow', p. 130. She goes on to say: '[t]he difference between *being touched and touching* is more significant than it seems' (author's emphasis).

84. S.J.D. Cohen, 'Menstruants and the Sacred in Judaism and Christianity', in S.B. Pomeroy (ed.), *Women's History and Ancient History* (Chapel Hill: University of North Carolina, 1991), pp. 273-99 (278).

85. Cohen, 'Menstruants and the Sacred', p. 279.

86. Fonrobert, 'Woman with a Blood-flow', p. 131.

87. Fonrobert, 'Woman with a Blood-flow', p. 134.

88. Fonrobert, 'Woman with a Blood-flow', p. 134.

89. Weissenrieder, *Images of Illness*, pp. 240-41.

90. Weissenrieder, *Images of Illness*, pp. 242-46.

91. King, *Hippocrates' Woman*, p. 221.

92. Soranus, *Gyn.* 3.43.

93. Weissenrieder, *Images of Illness*, p. 253, says in this regard that 'the number of weeks, months – or very occasionally years – are seen as signs of intensification of the illness and of the imminence of death. If a physician diagnoses a patient as being near death, the therapy is discontinued. The patient is already considered to be dead.'

94. Wells, *Greek Language of Healing*, pp. 182-83, says following her analysis of this text that 'Jesus was not only physically healing the man, he was giving him the opportunity for full spiritual participation in his community. Thus, in this way, σώζω as it is used here is holistic in meaning.' She sees the verb belonging to a 'network' of terms associated with healing, p. 191, developing the symbolic reality of healing and health.

95. Evans, 'Who Touched Me?', p. 368.

96. Only at the end of my research did I gain access to M.R. D'Angelo's article 'Gender and Power in the Gospel of Mark: The Daughter of Jairus and the Woman with the Flow of Blood', in J.C. Cavadini (ed.), *Miracles in Jewish and Christian Antiquity: Imagining Truth* (Notre Dame Studies in Theology, 3; Notre Dame: University of Notre Dame Press, 1999), pp. 83-109. She too studies these two healing narratives intertextually with medical and magical texts concluding that such a re-reading of these texts might point toward a sharing of spirit and power.

97. D. Flusser, 'Healing through the Laying-On of Hands in a Dead Sea Scroll', *IEJ* 7 (1957): 107-108.

98. J.-L. Chrétien, *The Call and the Response* (trans. A.A. Davenport; New York: Fordham University Press, 2004), pp. 4, 82, 84.

99. Chrétien, *Call and Response*, p. 84.

100. F.G. Downing, 'The Woman from Syrophoenicia and her Doggedness: Mark 7:24-31 (Matthew 15:21-28)', in G.J. Brooke (ed.), *Women in the Biblical Tradition* (Studies in Women and Religion, 31; Lewiston, NY: Edwin Mellen Press, 1992), pp. 129-49 (132, 135).

101. G.H. Twelftree, *Jesus the Exorcist: A Contribution to the Study of the Historical Jesus* (Peabody, MA: Hendrickson, 1993), p. 90.

102. S. Ringe, 'A Gentile Woman's Story Revisited: Rereading Mark 7.24-31', in A.-J. Levine and M. Blickenstaff (eds.), *A Feminist Companion to Mark* (Sheffield: Sheffield Academic Press, 2001), pp. 79-100 (87).

103. Ringe, 'Gentile Woman's Story', pp. 84-85.

104. G. Theissen, 'Lokal- und Sozialkolorit in der Geschichte von der syrophönik- ischen Frau (Mk 7 24-30)', *ZNW* 75 (1984): 202-225.

105. Theissen, 'Lokal- und Sozialkolorit', p. 213.

106. Hippocrates, *Morb. sacr.* 10.28-44; 1.1-2.46.

107. W. Cotter, *Miracles in Greco-Roman Antiquity: A Sourcebook for the Study of New Testament Miracle Stories* (London: Routledge, 1999), pp. 77-79.

108. The verb used in Tob. 3.17 in which healing and the freeing from demon posses- sion are linked is ἰάομαι.

109. See G. Theissen, *The Gospels in Context: Social and Political History in the Synoptic Tradition* (trans. L.M. Maloney; Edinburgh: T&T Clark, 1992), p. 79. This text includes an English translation of the German article cited earlier.

110. Kleinmann, *Patients and Healers*, p. 241.

111. See Theissen, *Gospels in Context*, pp. 62-65 for one summary. Ringe, 'Gentile Woman's Story', pp. 83-96 engages with a number of different studies.

112. Theissen, *Gospels in Context*, p. 75, nuances the possible layers of meaning and usage of such a saying.

113. In later re-tellings of this story, when struggles arose in the emerging Christian communities over whether the *basileia* message of Jesus characterized by healing and teaching could go beyond the confines of Israel, this story may have taken on many more layers of meaning as one finds in numerous commentaries and other studies.

114. See Firatli, *Les stèles*, Planche 35, Nos 139, 140, 143 and the commentary, pp. 96-97.

115. Avalos, *Illness and Health Care*, pp. 60, 111-13, 202-16.

116. I acknowledge here the permission granted by Orbis Books to include in this section material explored at greater length in my article 'The Pouring Out of Healing Ointment: Rereading Mk 14:3-9', in F.F. Segovia (ed.), *Toward a New Heaven and a New Earth: Essays in Honor of Elisabeth Schüssler Fiorenza* (Maryknoll, NY: Orbis Books, 2003), pp. 157-78.

117. We noted earlier that a stereotypical gendering of space – the *oikos* associated with women, the *polis* with men – was being renegotiated in the first century in Pales- tine as well as the Roman world more generally. For the shifts in women's participation in meals, see K.E. Corley, *Private Women Public Meals: Social Conflict in the Synoptic Tradition* (Peabody, MA: Hendrickson, 1993), pp. 24-79.

118. K.E. Corley, 'The Anointing of Jesus in the Synoptic Tradition: An Argument for Authenticity', *JSHJ* 1.1 (2003), pp. 61-72 (64).

119. Corley, 'Anointing of Jesus', p. 66.

120. In the Graeco-Roman world, as we have seen, one of the places where women's activity in healing was not a threat to the public gendered system was in the popular sector of the household. It was here women could function as care-givers, as midwives and perhaps even as professional doctors. It was their move into the public arena that was causing the renegotiation of gender and space, of public and private in which this story seems to participate. The house is, however, public space when the context for the *deipnon*.

121. There is nowhere in the LXX where any more than two of the words of the phrase 'alabaster jar of costly ointment of pure nard poured over the head' occur together and any occurrence of two in the same context is rare. Scripturally, the language is unique to this Markan story and its parallels in the gospels. *Alabastron* occurs only once – 2 Kgs 21.13. *Muron* designates the blend of sacred anointing oil in Exod. 30.22-33. It is not for anointing the human body but in Ps. 132.2 it is poured out over the head of Aaron. Judith anoints her body with *muron* before she goes to encounter Holofernes (Jdt. 10.3). *Muron* occurs in the same verse as *nardos* in Song 4.14 but not in the same phrase as in Mk 14.3.

122. See M.C. Howard, 'Athenaeus', *OCCL*, p. 70, and C.B. Gulick, 'Introduction', in Athenaeus, *The Deipnosophists* I (trans. C.B. Gulick; London: Henemann, 1951), p. xv. Corley, *Private Women*, pp. 24-66, notes the way in which the Romans took over the customs and etiquette of the Greeks in relation to public meals (*deipnon* and *symposium*).

123. Theophrastus, *Inquiry into Plants* (*De causis plantarum*), provides an excellent study of and appreciation of plants first and foremost in and of themselves and not according to their usefulness to the human community. Dioscorides and others stand in this same tradition which could be evoked in reading this story of ointment/oil of pure nard.

124. Theophrastus, *Caus. plant.* 9.7.2, links μύρον and νάρδος in the same paragraph in which he is discussing the medicinal value of these plant products and their combinations.

125. Just a little later in Athenaeus, *Deip.* 15.692a-c, there is quite an extensive discussion as to the way that anointing the head with oil or ointment during the drinking session that would follow the meal was efficacious for health because it prevented dryness and hence fevers. Also at the very beginning of Masurius' intervention, he draws in the ancient author Alcaeus who speaks of μύρον being poured (χευάτω) over the breasts which he then discusses as the place of the heart which is also comforted by sweet odours (Athenaeus, *Deip.* 15.687d-e). The discussion then moves to the heart as the place in the body where the 'more authoritative part of the soul resides', concluding that 'in agitation caused by fear you will find the heart beats most noticeably'. (Athenaeus, *Deip.* 15.687f-688a)

126. See B.J. Malina, 'The Individual and the Community – Personality in the Social World of Early Christianity', *BTB* 9 (1979), pp. 126-38, and its development by Pilch, *Healing in the New Testament*, pp. 106-11.

127. Such contrast is augmented during the passion narrative and made most explicit

by the absence of male disciples at the foot of the cross where the women, described in discipleship terms, remain present (Mk 15.40-41). For a discussion of their status as disciples see V. Phillips, 'Full Disclosure: Towards a Complete Characterization of Women who Followed Jesus in the Gospel According to Mark', in I.R. Kitzberger (ed.), *Transformative Encounters: Jesus and Women Re-viewed* (Leiden: E.J. Brill, 2000), pp. 17-24.

128. Wainwright, 'Pouring Out', p. 168.

129. BAGD, p. 529.

130. For a much more extensive discussion of women's association with death and mourning rituals, see K.E. Corley, *Women and the Historical Jesus: Feminist Myths of Christian Origins* (Santa Rosa: Polebridge, 2002), pp. 107-139; and C. Osiek, 'The Women at the Tomb: What Are They Doing There?', *ExAud* 9 (1993), pp. 97-107 (102-104).

## Chapter 5

1. LiDonnici, *Epidaurian Miracle Inscriptions*, p. 55.

2. H.L. Nelson, 'Resistance and Insubordination', *Hypatia* 10.2 (1995), pp. 23-40 (24).

3. The Markan proclamation is a little more complex, beginning with the fulfilment of a *kairos* or opportune time and an invitation to believe in the good news.

4. This is in contrast to the Markan narrative in which Jesus moves immediately from the calling of the four fishermen into his healing activity, beginning in the synagogue of Capernaum. For the Matthean summary passages, see 4.23-25; 8.16-17; 9.35; 11.2-6; 12.15-21; 14.14; 14.34-36; 15.29-31; 19.2; 21.14-15.

5. Nine of these are the healing of human diseases or infirmities and the tenth is the calming of the sea that may have been seen as a healing of disorder in the cosmos.

6. For a diagram of this see E.M. Wainwright, *Toward a Feminist Critical Reading of the Gospel According to Matthew* (BZNW, 60; Berlin: W. de Gruyter, 1991), p. 81.

7. E.-J. Vledder, *Conflict in the Miracle Stories: A Socio-Exegetical Study of Matthew 8 and 9* (JSNTSup, 152; Sheffield: Sheffield Academic Press, 1997), p. 27, especially n. 60, points to the general acceptance of this structure in Matthean scholarship.

8. While H. Moxnes does not use this terminology explicitly, he does situate what is narrated in these two accounts in first-century Galilee: 'When the brothers left that place, the effect was both that the livelihood of their household was threatened, and that their father was dishonoured and suffered a loss of authority. Moreover, they were called out of a very specific location into an uncertain task and into a movement rather than into a new place.' See H. Moxnes, *Putting Jesus in His Place: A Radical Vision of Household and Kingdom* (Louisville, KY: Westminster/John Knox Press, 2003), p. 56.

9. The reader has learnt in the interim that crowds follow Jesus (8.1), a scribe offers to follow (8.19) presumably as a disciple (μαθήτης) because 8.21 begins 'another of his disciples' and to this one Jesus offers the invitation to follow as in 4.19. The reader has encountered a group called οἱ μαθηταὶ gathering around Jesus on the mountain (5.1) and must fill in the gaps as to how this group which seems larger than the four summoned fishermen was formed. In 8.23 the two words μαθήται and ἀκολουθέω come together. A new named disciple, Matthew, is called to follow in 9.9 and the group οἱ μαθήται appear in 9.10 and 11. When encountering 'his twelve disciples' in 10.1, the

reader already has developed a sense of a significant group engaging with Jesus in his preaching/teaching and healing ministry beyond the crowds.

10. This data has led a number of scholars to explore the therapeutic aspects of this title. See L. Novakovic, *Messiah, the Healer of the Sick: A Study of Jesus as the Son of David in the Gospel of Matthew* (WUNT, 2.170; ed. J. Frey; Tübingen: Mohr Siebeck, 2003); and D.C. Duling, 'Matthew's Plurisignificant "Son of David" in Social Science Perspective: Kinship, Kingship, Magic, and Miracle', *BTB* 22 (1992), pp. 99-116.

11. See A.J. Saldarini, *Matthew's Christian-Jewish Community* (Chicago Studies in the History of Judaism; Chicago: University of Chicago Press, 1994), pp. 179-82, who recognizes both the model of the *theios aner* or 'holy man' and the biblical and rabbinic traditions of divine mediators as meaning-making systems for understanding the Matthean construction of Jesus the healer.

12. J.A Comber, 'The Verb THERAPEUO in Matthew's Gospel', *JBL* 97.3 (1978), pp. 431-34 (433), argues that the Matthean use of the verb θεραπεύω in the second half of the gospel distinguishes the response of the Jewish leaders from the Jewish crowd.

13. Pilch, *Healing in the New Testamen*, pp. 81-84, seeks the emic viewpoint in the Matthean healing narratives of Matthew 8–9, suggesting that all the stories have a boundary element. Pilch's recognition of boundaries is insightful but also very general as most healing stories are about boundaries.

14. The language used in Matthew's gospel is not the same as that which character-izes the Hippocratic corpus. Nor does it seem to acknowledge this world except in the parabolic saying of Jesus in 9.12: 'Those who are well have no need of a physician but those who are sick'. There is no reference to the haemorrhaging woman spending all that she has on physicians (cf. Mk 5.26).

15. Wells, *Language of Healing*, p. 139. This differs, however, from Pilch's notion of *symbolic healing* which addresses how the telling of stories of healing functions symbolically. See Pilch, *Healing in the New Testament*, pp. 32-34.

16. Kleinman, *Patients and Healers*, p. 207, lists 'time' as one of the 'characteristics of the interpersonal interaction' in his categories of analysis.

17. A.F. Segal, 'Matthew's Jewish Voice', in D.L. Balch (ed.), *Social History of the Matthean Community: Cross-Disciplinary Approaches* (Minneapolis: Fortress Press, 1991), pp. 3-37 (26-29).

18. Nelson, 'Resistance and Insubordination', p. 23.

19. Wainwright, *Feminist Critical Reading*.

20. For a more extensive discussion of this aspect of the Matthean account, see Wainwright, *Feminist Critical Reading*, pp. 184-85, 190.

21. In the telling of these stories of healing, the narrator is removed from the actual therapeutic encounters and so the telling of the story reflects the community's sym-bolic reality in relation to health and healing rather than that of Jesus and the recipients of his healing.

22. See Kleinman, *Patients and Healers*, pp. 207-208, for a brief description of ex-planatory models as they function within the categories of analysis being used in this project.

23. B.J. Malina and R.L. Rohrbaugh, *Social-Science Commentary on the Synoptic Gospels* (Minneapolis: Fortress Press, 1992), pp. 69-85, in relation to the healing stories of Matthew 8–9.

24. Wainwright, *Feminist Critical Reading*, pp. 181-82.

25. LiDonnici, *Epidaurian Miracle Inscriptions*, p. 55.

26. In Mk 5.23, the young girl is described as close to death and it is only after the healing of the woman with the haemorrhage that messengers come to Jairus to tell him that his daughter has died.

27. For a much more extensive coverage of the centrality and symbolic function of the metaphor of 'house' in Matthew's gospel see M.H. Crosby, *House of Disciples: Church, Economics, and Justice in Matthew* (Maryknoll, NY: Orbis Books, 1988).

28. Wire, 'Ancient Miracle Stories', pp. 77-84; and Demand, *Birth, Death, and Motherhood*, p. 11.

29. Numbers 19.14-20 provides the biblical basis for laws in relation to corpse contagion.

30. B.R. McCane, 'Is a Corpse Contagious? Early Jewish and Christian Attitudes toward the Dead', in *SBLSP* 1992 (ed. E.H. Lovering, Jr; Atlanta: Scholars Press, 1992), pp. 378-88 (380). Note that the ruler has come to Jesus rather than remaining to participate in the tumult being made by the crowd and the flute players of the mourning rituals (Mt. 9.23).

31. H. King in her study of women patients, 'Self-Help, Self-Knowledge, pp. 136-37, notes that, '[t]he whole point of the Hippocratic assertion of the norm of female ignorance and silence is to make it obvious why the Hippocratic doctor is so necessary: the whole point of Galen's emphasis on the absolute silence of the patient is to demonstrate his own brilliance in deducing what is wrong with her'. The gospel storytelling is likewise seeking to demonstrate the healing power of Jesus and hence there is a silencing of women healed and women's healing.

32. Matthew's gospel includes this term 62 times, Luke – 57 times, Mark – 7 times and John only 4 times. See also Wainwright, *Feminist Critical Reading*, pp. 197-98, for a closer analysis of this parallel.

33. King, *Hippocrates' Woman*, p. 92.

34. The ruler, on the other hand, speaks directly to Jesus and we learn his attitude to the healing for which he asks from his words spoken in direct speech in the narrative.

35. King, 'Self-Help, Self-Knowledge', pp. 135-48.

36. King, 'Self-Help, Self-Knowledge', p. 143.

37. BAGD, p. 798, for these possibilities within the semantic range of the verb.

38. J.J. Pilch, 'Reading Matthew Anthropologically: Healing in Cultural Perspective', *Listening* 24 (1989), pp. 278-89 (286).

39. Wainwright, *Feminist Critical Reading*, pp. 85-86, 186-87.

40. As well as drawing this conclusion from the study undertaken herein, I have also been informed in this insight by Levine, 'Discharging Responsibility', pp. 396-97.

41. See E.M. Wainwright, *Feminist Critical Reading*, pp. 98-116, 217-52; *idem*, 'A Voice from the Margin: Reading Matthew 15:21-28 in an Australian Feminist Key', in F.F. Segovia and M.A. Tolbert (eds.), *Reading from This Place*. II. *Social Location and Biblical Interpretation in Global Perspective* (Minneapolis: Fortress Press, 1995), pp. 132-53; and *idem, Shall We Look for Another?*, pp. 84-92.

42. The study of the parallel account in Mk 7.24-31 revealed the same lack of scholarly attention given to the demon possession by comparison with other such stories in Mark.

43. E.M. Wainwright, 'Not without my Daughter: Gender and Demon Possession in Matthew 15.21-28', in A.-J. Levine and M. Blickenstaff (eds.), *A Feminist Companion to Matthew* (Sheffield: Sheffield Academic Press, 2001), pp. 126-37.

44. See Wainwright, *Shall We Look for Another?*, p. 86, for a more extensive discussion of this aspect of the narrative.

45. Elsewhere I have argued that gender and ethnicity are intimately linked in this pericope when the focus was on the interaction between the Canaanite woman and Jesus. See Wainwright, *Feminist Critical Reading*, pp. 104-18. 244-47.

46. The imagery of Jesus as boundary-walker in this narrative has been developed in Wainwright, *Shall we Look for Another?*, pp. 84-92.

47. In the Markan label of the healed girl, there is a description of the demon having left the girl: καὶ τὸ δαιμόνιον ἐξεληλυθός (Mk 7.30).

48. The blind and dumb demoniac whom Jesus heals in 12.22, the one encountered subsequent to his first withdrawal as noted above, is likewise designated as healed by Jesus with the use of the verb θεραπεύειν but the new cultural label used in relation to him is that he 'spoke and saw'. The verb θεραπεύειν is descriptive of the work of Jesus rather than the state of the healed man.

49. No new cultural label is given to the two demon-possessed Gadarenes in Mt. 8.28-34.

50. See M.W. Dube Shomanah, 'Divining Texts for International Relations: Matt. 15:21-28', in I.R. Kitzberger (ed.), *Transformative Encounters: Jesus and Women Reviewed* (Leiden: E.J. Brill, 2000), pp. 315-28.

51. The new cultural label of the woman with a haemorrhage is time specific as is that of the Canaanite woman's daughter and the same phrase links the two – ἀπὸ τῆς ὥρας ἐκείνη.

52. See Wainwright, *Feminist Critical Reading*, pp. 126-28.

53. W. Houghton, 'The Pistic Nard of the Greek Testament', *Proceedings of the Society of Biblical Archaeology* 10 January (1888), pp. 144-46. See also J. Köbert, 'Nardos Pistike – Kostnarde', *Bib* 29 (1948), pp. 279-81.

54. A. Primavesi, *Gaia's Gift: Earth, Ourselves and God after Copernicus* (London: Routledge, 2003), p. 115.

55. Wainwright, *Feminist Critical Reading*, pp. 131-32.

*Chapter 6*

1. Remus, *Jesus as Healer*, p. 65.

2. J. Achterberg, *Woman as Healer* (Boston: Shambhala, 1990), p. 2.

3. Pilch, *Healing in the New Testament*, p. 98. N. Janowitz, *Magic in the Roman World: Pagans, Jews and Christians* (Religion in the First Christian Centuries; London: Routledge, 2001), p. 29, notes that this is characteristic of religious texts of the first century CE.

4. Kleinman, *Patients and Healers*, p. 44.

5. Garrett, *Demise of the Devil*, p. 37, notes that although the amount of narrative which deals with this struggle is 'small in quantity', it is 'mammoth in significance'.

6. See the extensive study of Twelftree, *Jesus the Exorcist* for much more detail than is possible here in relation to exorcism.

7. See one taxonomy in Weissenrieder, *Images of Illness*, pp. 305-306, who suggests that there is a sociological, a cultural-anthropological, and a psychological approach.

8. Garrett, *Demise of the Devil*.

9. Twelftree, *Jesus the Exorcist*.

10. B.J. Malina and J.H. Neyrey, *Calling Jesus Names: The Social Value of Labels in Matthew* (Foundations and Facets; Sonoma: Polebridge, 1988), pp. 1-32.

11. Malina and Neyrey, *Calling Jesus Names*, pp. 23-25.

12. Malina and Neyrey, *Calling Jesus Names*, p. 22.

13. Malina and Neyrey, *Calling Jesus Names*, p. 25, where G.P. Murdock is cited, *Theories of Illness: A World Survey* (Pittsburgh: University of Pittsburgh Press, 1980).

14. See Garrett, *Demise of the Devil*, p. 6, for this terminology.

15. Janowitz, *Magic in the Roman World*, pp. 1-2.

16. Malina and Neyrey, *Calling Jesus Names*, pp. 3-32, point to the struggle over authority between the Jewish communities under the rule of the Pharisees and the Jewish-Christian communities who give allegiance to Jesus and the resultant mutually exchanged labels of being in league with the power of the prince of demons.

17. See S.J. Noorda, ' "Cure Yourself, doctor!" (Luke 4:23): Classical Parallels to an Alleged Saying of Jesus', in J. Delobel (ed.), *Logia* (BETL, 59; Leuven: Leuven University Press, 1982), pp. 459-67.

18. It should be noted in passing here that the other definite Lukan use of ἰάτρος is in the proverbial saying regarding those needing a physician being the sick not the healthy (Lk. 5.31 exactly parallel to Mk 2.17 and Mt. 9.12). In some manuscripts the oblique reference to those who could not heal the woman with the haemorrhage (ἥτις...θεραπευθῆναι) is amplified by adding a phrase which begins with ἰατροῖς.

19. Wells, *Language of Healing*, pp. 160-61.

20. We saw in the previous chapter that ἰάομαι seemed to be used to designate ethnic healing in the Matthean gospel but this is not so in Luke because apart from its joint use with θεραπεύω, it is used in relation to the healing of the centurion's servant (7.7), the woman with the haemorrhage (8.47), the boy with the unclean spirit (9.42), the man with dropsy (14.4), one of the lepers (17.15), and the soldier whose ear is healed (22.51).

21. Weissenrieder, *Images of Illness*, p. 207 and see her n. 305 for a list of texts.

22. B. Witherington III, 'On the Road with Mary Magdalene, Joanna, Susanna, and Other Disciples – Luke 8:1-3', in A.-J. Levine and M. Blickenstaff (eds.), *A Feminist Companion to Luke* (Cleveland: Pilgrim Press, 2001), pp. 133-60 (133-34), discusses a similar question but from a different perspective.

23. C.B. Ubieta, 'Mary Magdalene and the Seven Demons in Social-Scientific Perspective', in I.R. Kitzberger, *Transformative Encounters: Jesus and Women Re-viewed* (Leiden: E.J. Brill, 2000), pp. 203-23 (215), likewise recognizes this passage as summary but she suggests that it hinges two sections together within the longer section 4.14–9.50.

24. Malina and Neyrey, *Calling Jesus Names*, p. 25.

25. E.A. de Boer, 'The Lukan Mary Magdalene and the Other Women Following Jesus', in Levine and Blickenstaff (eds.), *Feminist Companion to Luke*, pp. 140-60 (146 n. 16), argues for an alternative position, namely that the 'many others' of v. 3 are not healed, on the grounds of ἕπται πολλαί being 'coordinative to γυναῖκές τινες, Jesus and

the Twelve'. Scholarly opinion is divided and, as de Boer indicates, one or other position is often assumed rather than demonstrated. I would suggest, however, that given the use of πολύς in accounts of the healing of many (4.41; 7.21) that here too it reiterates that γυναῖκές τινες includes the 'many others' among those healed. See also the layout of the verse at the beginning of this section which demonstrates that the listing of the women including the 'many others' is like a parenthesis in the very long sentence.

26. See M. Zerwick and M. Grosvenor, *A Grammatical Analysis of the Greek New Testament* (2 vols.; Rome: Biblical Institute, 1974), I, p. 204, who say of the periphrastic pluperfect that it implies 'permanence'; and M. Zerwick, *Biblical Greek* (Scripta Pontifici Instituti Biblici, 114; Rome: Iura Editionis et Versionis Reservantur, 1963), pp. 98-99, §290.

27. It is rare for θεραπεύω to occur in the description of the healed state or, in Kleinman's terms, in the culturally manipulated label, except in summary passages when it is generally used in the active voice to describe the action of Jesus. See, however, Lk. 6.18.

28. BAGD, 495, column 1, gives the metaphoric use of the noun as 'torment, suffering...of bodily illness'. Its non-metaphoric usage means 'whips' or 'lashes'. The word is clearly intended to designate severe suffering not just disease.

29. Both readings are possible given the grammatical construction in the text. BAGD, 115, column 1, gives the meaning 'weakness' which the authors associate with bodily weakness. They link ἀσθένεια with πνεῦμα in 8.2 indicating that the weakness is caused by demons.

30. C. Ricci, *Mary Magdalene and Many Others: Women who Followed Jesus* (trans. P. Burns; Minneapolis: Fortress Press, 1994), p. 131. She concludes that '[s]ymbolically, the number seven expresses a complete period of time and the idea of totality itself'.

31. Within the gospels, see Mk 15.40, 47; 16.1-8; Mt. 27.56, 61; 28.1-10; Lk. 24.1-12 and Jn 19.25; 20.1-18. See also H. Hearon, *The Mary Magdalene Tradition: Witness and Counter-witness in Early Christian Communities* (Collegeville, MN: Liturgical Press, 2004), which studies the gospel traditions and J. Schaberg's monumental study, *The Resurrection of Mary Magdalene: Legends, Apocrypha, and the Christian Testament* (New York: Continuum, 2003).

32. K.L. King, *The Gospel of Mary of Magdala: Jesus and the First Woman Apostle* (Santa Rosa: Polebridge, 2003).

33. See M. Sawicki, 'Magdalenes and Tiberiennes: City Women in the Entourage of Jesus', in I.R. Kitzberger (ed.), *Transformative Encounters: Jesus and Women Re-viewed* (Leiden: E.J. Brill, 2000), pp. 181-206 (181-202). See also B.E. Reid, *Choosing the Better Part? Women in the Gospel of Luke* (Collegeville, MN: Liturgical Press, 1996), pp. 124-34.

34. Ubieta, 'Mary Magdalene', has already undertaken a social-scientific reading of Lk. 8.1-3. I will, however, introduce some new insights informed by the study of healing women, especially those encountered in Chapter 3 of this study who were accused of magic and demon possession.

35. Ubieta, 'Mary Magdalene', pp. 208-11, develops this aspect in greater detail than is possible here.

36. Gourevitch, *Le mal d'être femme*, pp. 113-28.

37. Drawing on the work of E. Dio-Bleichmar, Ubieta, 'Mary Magdalene', p. 214, acknowledges the clinical manifestations of hysteria but also examines its social function especially among women as a protest against gender roles and their consequent social injustices and inequalities.

38. S. Guijarro, 'The Politics of Exorcism: Jesus' Reaction to Negative Labels in the Beelzebul Controversy', *BTB* 29.3 (1999): 118-29, traces the accusations levelled at Jesus back to the context of the historical Jesus.

39. Guijarro, 'Politics of Exorcism', p. 122.

40. Malina and Neyrey, *Calling Jesus Names*, p. 22.

41. Guijarro, 'Politics of Exorcism', p. 124.

42. Schüssler Fiorenza, *In Memory of Her*, pp. 245-332; J.P. Hallett, 'Women's Lives in the Ancient Mediterranean', in R.S. Kraemer and M.R. D'Angelo (eds.), *Women and Christian Origins* (New York: Oxford University Press, 1999), pp. 13-34; J.F. Gardner, *Women in Roman Law and Society* (Bloomington: Indiana University Press, 1986); and K.J. Torjesen, *When Women Were Priests: Women's Leadership in the Early Church and the Scandal of their Subordination in the Rise of Christianity* (New York: HarperSanFrancisco, 1993).

43. In particular T.K. Seim, *The Double Message: Patterns of Gender in Luke and Acts* (Nashville: Abingdon Press, 1994); and Reid, *Choosing the Better Part?*

44. M.D. Hamm, 'The Freeing of the Bent Woman and the Restoration of Israel: Luke 13.10-17 as Narrative Theology', *JSNT* 31 (1987), pp. 23-44 (23), says in relation to another text, '[t]he author, surely, must have something else in mind. At a time when we are coming to appreciate Luke as an author who is in full control of his material, this narrative deserves renewed attention.' We can also apply Hamm's conclusions to this text.

45. Zerwick, *Biblical Greek*, p. 98, §290.

46. Guijarro, 'Politics of Exorcism', p. 123, says in relation to the accusers of Jesus that they 'try to assign him a new identity, a new self of a negative kind. They do this in order to neutralize his activity, which they perceive as negative.' The same could be said of these women healers. Their healing activity and art has been neutralized by this Lukan text.

47. There is a textual variant in this phrase: some texts contain the plural αὐταῖς while there are also significant witnesses to the singular of the pronoun αὐτῷ. B.M. Metzger, *A Textual Commentary on the Greek New Testament* (London: United Bible Societies, 1971), p. 144, suggests that the singular may be a correction made by Marcion and followed by others. Ricci, *Mary Magdalene*, pp. 156-58, discusses this at length arguing for the singular form and this is supported by R. Karris, 'Women and Discipleship in Luke', in Levine and Blickenstaff (eds.), *Feminist Companion to Luke*, pp. 41-43 (29). Ricci's argument, however, seems to favour an interpretation she wants to put forward rather than being grounded in textual analysis. I will, therefore, opt for the plural reading that has stronger attestation.

48. Seim, *Double Message*, p. 81, notes that it is not until Luke 12 onwards that the διακον-terminology is directed to the Twelve or disciples.

49. J.N. Collins, *Diakonia: Re-interpreting the Ancient Sources* (New York: Oxford University Press, 1990), pp. 111-15, and passim. This is in keeping with the cultural coding of patron/client and broker which the social scientific approach to New Testament

studies has uncovered which sees Jesus as broker between humanity and God. See H. Moxnes, 'Patron-Client Relations and the New Community in Luke–Acts', in J.H. Neyrey (ed.), *The Social World of Luke–Acts: Models for Interpretation* (Peabody, MA: Hendrickson, 1991), pp. 241-68, especially 257-60 for a perspective on Jesus as broker.

50. A number of studies have now demonstrated that first-century women of Asia Minor and elsewhere in the Roman empire, including Palestine, did have access to and independent use of resources. See Seim, *Double Message*, pp. 64-66 and various sections of Lefkowitz and Fant, *Women's Life*.

51. Seim, *Double Message*, p. 62, says that the addition of the phrase about resources 'alters the emphasis away from an actual meal situation and towards a more general sense of support and provision'. I would agree with her assessment of this.

52. This reading differs markedly from that of J.M. Arlandson, *Women, Class, and Society in Early Christianity: Models from Luke–Acts* (Peabody, MA: Hendrickson, 1997), pp. 162-65, who argues that the women of Lk. 8.1-3 surpass the Twelve because of their service.

53. E. Schüssler Fiorenza has developed this aspect of reading under what she calls a hermeneutics of re-membering and reconstruction. See for instance *Wisdom Ways: Introducing Feminist Biblical Interpretation* (Maryknoll, NY: Orbis Books, 2001), pp. 183-86, for her most recent articulation of this aspect of feminist biblical interpretation. She says (p. 185), that 'texts and injunctions that seek to censure or limit wo/men's behavior must be read as prescriptive rather than as descriptive of reality. If wo/men are forbidden from a certain activity, we can safely assume that they might actually have engaged in it so much that it became threatening to the kyriarchal order.'

54. D'Angelo, 'Re-membering Jesus', p. 202.

55. Simon will appear as a character in the narrative only at 5.1-11.

56. BAGD, 7890, column 1.

57. Both the Markan and Matthean accounts, as we have seen, simply use the participial form of the verb πυρέσσω together with a description of her lying down or paralysed in the Matthean account.

58. Pilch, 'Reading Matthew Anthropologically', p. 286.

59. Collins, *Diakonia*, p. 245, simply assumes on this as the necessary reading from his analysis of other intertexts without any analysis of the language in the context of particular gospels and their rhetorical purposes. Corley, *Private Women*, p. 121, after a more lengthy discussion, concludes that in the Lukan narrative when men serve it is seen as leadership but when women serve it is to wait on tables. Reid, *Choosing the Better Part*, p. 101, also accepts this as the dominant reading.

60. For an alternate reading against the grain of this text, see Reid, *Choosing the Better Part*, pp. 101-102.

61. Weissenrieder, *Images of Illness*, pp. 314-21, in particular p. 315.

62. Weissenrieder, *Images of Illness*, p. 328.

63. Hamm, 'Freeing of the Bent Woman', says 'the laying on of hands is not clearly indicative in this question (i.e., indicating healing rather than deliverance)'.

64. J. Nolland, *Luke 9:21-18:34* (WBC, 35B; Nashville: Thomas Nelson, 1993), p. 722, adds another dimension when he notes that one of the difficulties of this story is that 'the form of the material is thought to be caught between that of a miracle story and of a controversy dialogue'.

65. BAGD, 72, column 2, gives the literal meaning of the verb as 'rebuild, restore, lit., of a fallen structure'.

66. Note the suggestion earlier in the exploration of the healing of Simon's mother-in-law that the verb used in that account might suggest the severity of paralysis.

67. W. Carter, *Matthew and the Margins: A Sociopolitical and Religious Reading* (Maryknoll, NY: Orbis Books, 2000), pp. 123-25.

68. Carter, *Matthew and the Margins*, p. 124.

69. Hamm, 'Freeing of the Bent Woman', p. 28, suggests that 'virtually all of the LXX uses' of the verb used uniquely by Luke to describe the bent woman's standing straight up, ἀνορθόω, 'refer to the...restorative action of God'. He continues: '[i]t becomes plausible, then, that Luke employed the word at 13.13 with these LXX connotations in mind'.

70. Designated by the present participle.

71. Note that this reference to Satan in the controversy of 13.14-17 links this story back to the controversy over Jesus' power to cast out demons being attributed to Beelzebul (11.18).

72. Elizabeth Dowling, in her well-argued thesis, 'Taking Away the Pound: Women, Theology and the Parable of the Pounds in the Gospel of Luke' (PhD dissertation, Melbourne College of Divinity, 2005), points to the fact that although the narrative describes the woman praising God, we do not hear her voice.

73. See Reid, *Choosing the Better Part*, pp. 163-68, who demonstrates the two-edged nature of this story. Seim, *Double Message*, p. 41, includes this woman among those who are 'now included in the community of God from which they had been excluded or to which they had been granted only a very peripheral membership'. Her interpretation, when read through the lens of this study, indicates that the restoration is to membership but not to the full functioning of their healing role. E. Schüssler Fiorenza, 'Lk 13:10-17: Interpretation for Liberation and Transformation', *TD* 36.4 (1989), pp. 303-19 (311-19), proposes a liberating contextualization of Lk. 13.10-17 which differs from that emerging from this study but which does not contradict it.

74. See by way of example, Reid, *Choosing the Better Part*, pp. 144-62; Seim, *Double Message*, pp. 97-112; V. Koperski, 'Women and Discipleship in Luke 10.38-42 and Acts 6:1-7: The Literary Context of Luke–Acts', in Levine and Blickenstaff (eds.), *Feminist Companion to Luke*, pp. 161-96; and others in this same volume.

75. Schüssler Fiorenza, *But She Said*, p. 62.

76. Schüssler Fiorenza, *But She Said*, p. 68.

77. Seim, *Double Message*, pp. 81-88, demonstrates generally that the women who serve and who are designated by this language of idealization in the gospel are then 'excluded from the actual positions of leadership'. For Seim's study of Lk. 10.38-42, see pp. 97-112. In conclusion, p. 112, Seim makes a claim that resonates with what has emerged in this study. She says that 'leaders are to devote themselves to service. But the women who have served cannot become leaders'. I have claimed that leaders are to devote themselves to healing. But the women who heal not only cannot become leaders but need to be placed in need of healing before they can be identified with service which removes them from service which is active healing. They are relegated to women healed from the most severe possession and their service as healing women is rendered invisible.

78. E. Schüssler Fiorenza, *Bread Not Stone: The Challenge of Feminist Biblical Interpretation* (Boston: Beacon Press, 1984), pp. 20-22.

79. Schüssler Fiorenza, *Wisdom Ways*, pp. 148-51.

80. Schüssler Fiorenza, *Wisdom Ways*, p. 150.

81. Dowling, 'Taking Away the Pound', argues that the women's public voice is taken away and this would render the woman of voice and of confrontation unacceptable to the Lukan story-telling.

82. For a discussion of shared or different sources, see Corley, *Private Women*, pp. 122-23, who suggests an original shared chreia.

83. E.R. Thibeaux, ' "Known to Be a Sinner": The Narrative Rhetoric of Luke 7:36-50', *BTB* 23 (1993), pp. 151-60.

84. Seim, *Double Message*, pp. 90-91, considers that such a depiction points to the woman being a prostitute. Reid, on the other hand, *Choosing the Better Part*, pp. 115-18, warns against too easy an assumption in this regard because the type of sin is not named.

85. Such an interpretation is informed by Thibeaux, 'Known to Be a Sinner'.

86. I have chosen not to explore the healing of the barrenness of Elizabeth in the first chapter of Luke's gospel as it does not appear to come within the Lukan thematic developed in this chapter. Similarly, I have not considered the widow of Nain as a woman healing as it is her son whose physical life is restored. I recognize, however, that this is certainly a story of restoration which encompasses the mother but as with Elizabeth, it does not fit within the strong Lukan thematic explored above.

87. Reid, *Choosing the Better Part*, p. 142, notes the Lukan removal of three verbal links between the woman and Jesus that have been discussed in the study of the healing women of Matthew's gospel and Jesus.

88. Only a few witnesses include the reference to physicians presumably to bring the Lukan text into agreement with Mark. See Metzger, *Textual Commentary*, p. 145.

89. Anzaldúa, *Borderlands/La Frontera*, pp. 78-79.

# BIBLIOGRAPHY

Achterberg, Jeanne, *Woman as Healer* (Boston: Shambhala, 1990).

Albert, Maurice, *Les médicins grecs à Rome* (Paris: Hachette, 1894).

Aleshire, Sara B., *The Athenian Asklepieion: The People, their Dedications, and the Inventories* (Amsterdam: J.C. Gieben, 1989).

Alexander, Loveday, 'Luke's Preface in the Context of Greek Preface-writing', *NovT* 28 (1986): 48-74.

—*The Preface to Luke's Gospel: Literary Convention and Social Context in Luke 1.1-4 and Acts 1.1.* (SNTSMS, 78; Cambridge: Cambridge University Press, 1993).

Alic, Margaret, *Hypatia's Heritage: A History of Women in Science from Antiquity to the Late Nineteenth Century* (London: Women's Press, 1986).

Allbutt, T. Clifford, *Greek Medicine in Rome: The Fitzpatrick Lectures on the History of Medicine Delivered at the Royal College of Physicians of London in 1909–1910* (London: Macmillan, 1921).

André, Jacques, *Être médecin à Rome* (Paris: Société d'Édition 'Les Belles Lettres', 1987).

Anzaldúa, Gloria, *Borderlands/La Frontera: The New Mestiza* (San Francisco: Aunt Lute Books, 1987).

Archer, Léonie J., Susan Fischler and Maria Wyke (eds.), *Women in Ancient Societies: An Illusion of the Night* (New York: Routledge, 1994).

Arlandson, James Malcolm, *Women, Class, and Society in Early Christianity: Models from Luke–Acts* (Peabody, MA: Hendrickson, 1997).

Athenaeus, *The Deipnosophists* (trans. Charles Burton Gulick; LCL; London: Heinemann, 1927-41).

Aune, David E., 'Magic in Early Christianity', *ANRW* 23.2.1507-57 Part 2, *Principat* 23.2 (ed. Wolfgang Hasse; Berlin: W. de Gruyter, 1980).

Avalos, Hector, *Illness and Health Care in the Ancient Near East: The Role of the Temple in Greece, Mesopotamia, and Israel* (Atlanta: Scholars Press, 1995).

—'Medicine', in Eric Meyers (ed.), *The Oxford Encyclopedia of Archaeology in the Near East* (5 vols.; New York: Oxford University Press, 1997), III, pp. 450-59.

—*Health Care and the Rise of Christianity* (Peabody, MA: Hendrickson, 1999).

Balch, David L., and Carolyn Osiek (eds.), *Early Christian Families in Context: An Interdisciplinary Dialogue* (Grand Rapids: Eerdmans, 2003).

Betz, Hans Dieter, (ed.), *The Greek Magical Papyri in Translation Including the Demotic Spells.* I. *Texts* Chicago: University of Chicago Press, 2nd edn, 1992).

Bledstein, Adrien Janis, 'Was *HABBIRYÂ* a Healing Ritual Performed by a Woman in King David's House?', *BR* 37 (1992), pp. 15-31.

Blum, Jeanne Elizabeth, *Woman Heal Thyself: An Ancient Healing System for Contemporary Women* (Shaftesbury: Element, 1995).

Brooke, Elisabeth, *Women Healers through History* (London: Women's Press, 1993).

Camp, Claudia V., 'Understanding a Patriarchy: Women in Second Century Jerusalem through the Eyes of Ben Sira', in Amy-Jill Levine (ed.), *Women Like This: New Perspectives on Jewish Women in the Greco-Roman Period* (Early Judaism and its Literature, 1; Atlanta: Scholars Press, 1991), pp. 1-39.

Carter, Warren, *Matthew and the Margins: A Sociopolitical and Religious Reading* (Maryknoll, NY: Orbis Books, 2000).

Cato, Marcus Porcius, *On Agriculture* (trans. William Davis Hooper; Cambridge: Harvard University Press, 1936).

Chrétien, Jean-Louis, *The Call and the Response* (trans. Anne A. Davenport; New York: Fordham University Press, 2004).

Clark, Gillian, *Women in Late Antiquity: Pagan and Christian Life-Styles* (Oxford: Clarendon Press, 1993).

Clarke, Adele E., and Virginia L. Olesen, 'Revising, Diffracting, Acting', in Adele E. Clarke and Virginia L. Olesen (eds.), *Revisioning Women, Health, and Healing* (New York: Routledge, 1999), pp. 3-48.

Clements, Ronald E., *Wisdom for a Changing World: Wisdom in Old Testament Theology* (Berkeley Lectures, 2; Berkeley: Bibal Press, 1990).

Coffman, Ralph J., 'Historical Jesus the Healer: Cultural Interpretations of the Healing Cults of the Graeco-Roman World as the Basis for Jesus Movements', in *SBLSP* 1993 (ed. Eugene H. Lovering; Atlanta: Scholars Press, 1993), pp. 412-43.

Cohen, Shaye J.D., 'Menstruants and the Sacred in Judaism and Christianity', in Sarah B. Pomeroy (ed.), *Women's History and Ancient History* (Chapel Hill: University of North Carolina Press, 1991), pp. 273-99.

Cohn-Haft, Louis, *The Public Physicians of Ancient Greece* (Northampton, MA: Department of History of Smith College, 1956).

Cole, Susan G., 'Could Greek Women Read and Write?', in Helen P. Foley (ed.), *Reflections of Women in Antiquity* (New York: Gordon and Breach, 1981), pp. 230-45.

Collins, John N., *Diakonia: Re-interpreting the Ancient Sources* (New York: Oxford University Press, 1990).

Comber, Joseph A., 'The Verb THERAPEUO in Matthew's Gospel', *JBL* 97.3 (1978), pp. 431-34.

Compton, Michael T., 'The Union of Religion and Health in Ancient Asklepieia', *Journal of Religion and Health* 37 (1998), pp. 301-12.

—'The Association of Hygieia with Asklepios in Graeco-Roman Asklepieion Medicine', *Journal of the History of Medicine and Allied Sciences* 57 (2002), pp. 312-29.

Conkey, Margaret W., and Joan M. Gero, 'Tensions, Pluralities, and Engendering Archaeology: An Introduction to Women and Prehistory', in Joan M.Gero and Margaret W. Conkey (eds.), *Engendering Archaeology: Women and Prehistory* (Oxford: Basil Blackwell, 1991), pp. 3-30.

Conrad, Lawrence I., Michael Neve, Vivian Nutton, Roy Porter and Andrew Wear (eds.), *The Western Medical Tradition: 800 B.C.–1800 A.D.* (Cambridge: Cambridge University Press, 1995).

Cook, John Granger, 'In Defence of Ambiguity: Is There a Hidden Demon in Mark 1.29-31?', *NTS* 43 (1997): 184-208.

Corley, Kathleen E., *Private Women Public Meals: Social Conflict in the Synoptic Tradition* (Peabody, MA: Hendrickson, 1993).

—*Women and the Historical Jesus: Feminist Myths of Christian Origins* (Santa Rosa: Polebridge, 2002).

—'The Anointing of Jesus in the Synoptic Tradition: An Argument for Authenticity', *JSHJ* 1.1 (2003): 61-72.

Cotter, Wendy, *Miracles in Greco-Roman Antiquity: A Sourcebook for the Study of New Testament Miracle Stories* (London: Routledge, 1999).

Coyle, J. Kevin, and Steven C. Muir, *Healing in Religion and Society, from Hippocrates to the Puritans: Selected Studies* (Lewiston, NY: Edwin Mellen Press, 1999).

Crosby, Michael H., *House of Disciples: Church, Economics, and Justice in Matthew* (Maryknoll, NY: Orbis Books, 1988).

D'Angelo, Mary Rose, 'Re-membering Jesus: Women, Prophecy and Resistance in the Memory of the Early Churches', *Horizons* 19 (1992), pp. 199-218.

—'Gender and Power in the Gospel of Mark: The Daughter of Jairus and the Woman with the Flow of Blood', in John C. Cavadini (ed.), *Miracles in Jewish and Christian Antiquity: Imagining Truth* (Notre Dame Studies in Theology, 3; Notre Dame: University of Notre Dame Press, 1999), pp. 83-109.

Dawson, Anne, *Freedom as Liberating Power: A Socio-Political Reading of the ἐξουσία Texts in the Gospel of Mark* (NTOA, 44; Göttingen: Universitätsverlag Freiburg Schweiz/Vandenhoeck und Ruprecht, 2000).

Daysh, Zena, 'Foreword: Human Ecology and Health in a Global System', in Morteza Honari and Thomas Boleyn (eds.), *Health Ecology: Health, Culture and Human-Environment Interaction* (London: Routledge, 1999), pp. xv-xviii.

de Boer, Esther A., 'The Lukan Mary Magdalene and the Other Women Following Jesus', in Amy-Jill Levine, and Marianne Blickenstaff (eds.), *A Feminist Companion to Luke* (Cleveland: Pilgrim Press, 2001), pp. 140-60.

Dean-Jones, Lesley, '*Autopsia, Historia* and What Women Know: The Authority of Women in Hippocratic Gynaecology', in Don Bates (ed.), *Knowledge and the Scholarly Medical Traditions* (Cambridge: Cambridge University Press, 1995), pp. 41-59.

—*Women's Bodies in Classical Greek Science* (Oxford: Clarendon Press, 1996).

Demand, Nancy, *Birth, Death, and Motherhood in Classical Greece* (Baltimore: The Johns Hopkins University Press, 1994).

—'Monuments, Midwives and Gynaecology', in P.J. van der Eijk, H.F.J. Horstmanshoff and P.H. Schrijvers (eds.), *Ancient Medicine in its Socio-Cultural Context: Papers Read at the Congress Held at Leiden University, 13-15 April, 1992* (Atlanta: Rodopi, 1995), pp. 275-90.

—'Women and Slaves as Hippocratic Patients', in Sandra R. Joshel and Sheila Murnaghan (eds.), *Women and Slaves in Greco-Roman Culture: Differential Equations* (London: Routledge, 1998), pp. 69-84.

Derrett, J. Duncan M., 'Mark's Technique: The Haemorrhaging Woman and Jairus' Daughter', *Biblica* 63 (1982), pp. 474-505.

Dewey, Joanna, 'Jesus' Healings of Women: Conformity and Non-Conformity to Dominant Cultural Values as Clues for Historical Reconstruction', *BTB* 24.3 (1994), pp. 122-31.

Diprose, Rosalyn, *The Bodies of Women: Ethics, Embodiment and Sexual Difference* (London: Routledge, 1994).

Dowling, Elizabeth Victorina, 'Taking Away the Pound: Women, Theology and the Parable of the Pounds in the Gospel of Luke' (PhD dissertation, Melbourne College of Divinity, 2005).

Dowling, Melissa Barden, 'Vestal Virgins: Chaste Keepers of the Flame', *Arch* 4 (2001), pp. 42-51.

Downing, F. Gerald, 'The Woman from Syrophoenicia and her Doggedness: Mark 7.24-31 (Matthew 15.21-28)'. in George J. Brooke (ed.), *Women in the Biblical Tradition* (Studies in Women and Religion, 31; Lewiston, NY: Edwin Mellen Press, 1992), pp. 129-49.

Doyal, Lesley, *What Makes Women Sick: Gender and the Political Economy of Health* (New Brunswick: Rutgers University Press, 1995).

Dube Shomanah, M.W., 'Divining Texts for International Relations: Matt. 15.21-28', in Ingrid Rosa Kitzberger (ed.), *Transformative Encounters: Jesus and Women Re-viewed* (Biblical Interpretation Series, 43; Leiden: E.J. Brill, 2000), pp. 315-28.

duBois, Page, *Sowing the Body: Psychoanalysis and Ancient Representations of Women* (Chicago: University of Chicago Press, 1988).

Duling, Dennis C., 'Matthew's Plurisignificant "Son of David" in Social Science Perspective: Kinship, Kingship, Magic, and Miracle', *BTB* 22 (1992), pp. 99-116.

Ebron, Paulla Tsing, and Anna Lowenhaupt, 'In Dialogue? Reading across Minority Discourses', in Ruth Behar and Deborah A. Gordon (eds.), *Women Writing Culture* (Berkeley: University of California Press, 1995), pp. 390-411.

Edelstein, Emma J., and Ludwig Edelstein, *Asclepius: A Collection and Interpretation of the Testimonies*, I and II ( (2 vols. in 1; Baltimore: The Johns Hopkins University Press, 1998 [1945]).

Ehrenreich, Barbara, and Deidre English, *Witches, Midwives and Nurses: A History of Women Healers* (London: Writers and Readers Publishing Cooperative, 1973).

—*Complaints and Disorders: The Sexual Politics of Sickness* (London: Writers and Readers Publishing Cooperative, 1976).

Elias, Jason, and Katherine Ketcham, *In the House of the Moon: Reclaiming the Feminine Spirit of Healing* (London: Hodder and Stoughton, 1995).

Elliott, James Sands, *Outlines of Greek and Roman Medicine* (London: Bale and Danielsson, 1914).

Elvey, Anne, 'Leaf Litter: Thinking the Divine from the Perspective of Earth', in K. McPhillips (ed.), *What's God Got to Do with It? Essays from a One Day Conference Exploring the Challenges Facing Feminism, Theology, and the Conceptions of Women and the Divine in the New Millennium, August 2nd 1999, Sydney University* (Hawkesbury: Humanities Transdisciplinary Research Unit, University of Western Sydney, 2001), pp. 59-68.

—'Earthing the Text? On the Status of the Biblical Text in Ecological Perspective', *ABR* 52 (2004): 64-79.

Evans, Craig A., ' "Who Touched Me?": Jesus and the Ritually Impure', in Bruce Chilton and Craig A. Evans (eds.), *Jesus in Context: Temple, Purity, and Restoration* (AGJU, 39; Leiden: E.J. Brill, 1997), pp. 353-76.

Fatum, Lone, 'Women, Symbolic Universe and Structures of Silence: Challenges and Possibilities in Androcentric Texts', *ST* 43 (1989), pp. 61-80.

—'1 Thessalonians', in Elisabeth Schüssler Fiorenza (ed.), *Searching the Scriptures*. II. *A Feminist Commentary* (New York: Crossroad, 1994), pp. 250-62.

Feldman, Christina, *The Quest of the Warrior Woman: A Path of Healing, Empowerment and Transformation* (San Francisco: Aquarian, 1994).

Finkler, Kaja, *Women in Pain: Gender and Morbidity in Mexico* (Philadelphia: University of Pennsylvania Press, 1994).

Firatli, Nezih, *Les stèles funéraires de Byzance Gréco-Romaine, avec l'édition et l'index commenté des épitaphes par Louis Robert* (trans. A.N. Rollas; Paris: Librairie Adrien Maisonneuve, 1964).

Flusser, D., 'Healing through the Laying-On of Hands in a Dead Sea Scroll', *IEJ* 7 (1957): 107-108.

Fonrobert, Charlotte, 'The Woman with a Blood-Flow (Mark 5.24-34) Revisited: Menstrual Laws and Jewish Culture in Christian Feminist Hermeneutics', in Craig A. Evans and

James A. Sanders (eds.), *Early Christian Interpretation of the Scriptures of Israel* (JSNTSup, 148; SSEJC, 5; Sheffield: Sheffield Academic Press, 1997), pp. 121-40.

Fox-Genovese, Elizabeth, 'Literary Criticism and the Politics of the New Historicism', in H. Aram Veeser (ed.), *The New Historicism* (New York: Routledge, 1989), pp. 213-24.

French, Valerie, 'Midwives and Maternity Care in the Greco-Roman World', in Marilyn Skinner (ed.), *New Methodological Approaches to Women in Antiquity* (Lubbock: Texas Tech University Press, 1987), pp. 69-84.

Frymer-Kensky, Tikva, *In the Wake of the Goddesses: Women, Culture, and the Biblical Transformation of Pagan Myth* (New York: Free Press, 1992).

Gaetens, Moira, *Imaginary Bodies: Ethics, Power and Corporeality* (New York: Routledge, 1995).

Gardner, Jane F., *Women in Roman Law and Society* (Bloomington: Indiana University Press, 1986).

Gardner, Jane F., and Thomas Wiedemann, *The Roman Household: A Sourcebook* (London: Routledge, 1991).

Garland, David E., '"I Am the Lord your Healer": Mark 1.21-2.12', *RevExp* 85 (1988), pp. 327-43.

Garland, Robert, *Introducing New Gods: The Politics of Athenian Religion* (London: Gerald Duckworth, 1992).

Garrett, Susan R., *The Demise of the Devil: Magic and the Demonic in Luke's Writings* (Minneapolis: Fortress Press, 1989).

Goodison, Lucy, and Christine Morris, 'Introduction. Exploring Female Divinity: From Modern Myths to Ancient Evidence', in Lucy Goodison and Christine Morris (eds.), *Ancient Goddesses: the Myths and the Evidence* (Madison: University of Wisconsin Press, 1998), pp. 6-21.

Gordon, Richard, 'The Healing Event in Graeco-Roman Folk-Medicine', in P.J. van der Eijk, H.F.J. Horstmanshoff and P.H. Schrijvers (eds.), *Ancient Medicine in its Socio-Cultural Context: Papers Read at the Congress held at Leiden University 13-15 April 1992* (Amsterdam: Rodopi,1995), pp. 363-76.

Gourevitch, Danielle, *Le mal d'être femme: La femme et la médicine dans la Rome antique* (Réalia; Paris: Société d'Édition 'Les Belles Lettres', 1984).

Green, William Scott, 'Palestinian Holy Men: Charismatic Leadership and Rabbinic Tradition', *ANRW* 19.2.619-647. Part 2, *Prinipat* 19.2 (ed. Wolfgang Haase; Berlin: W. de Gruyter, 1979).

Grosz, Elizabeth, *Volatile Bodies: Toward a Corporeal Feminism* (St Leonards: Allen and Unwin, 1994).

Guijarro, Santiago, 'The Family in First-Century Galilee'. in Halvor Moxnes (ed.), *Constructing Early Christian Families: Family as Social Reality and Metaphor* (London: Routledge, 1997), pp. 42-65.

—'The Politics of Exorcism: Jesus' Reaction to Negative Labels in the Beelzebul Controversy', *BTB* 29.3 (1999), pp. 118-29.

Habel, Norman C., 'The Challenge of Ecojustice Readings for Christian Theology'. *Pacifica* 13 (2000): 125-41.

—(ed.), *Reading from the Perspective of the Earth* (The Earth Bible, 1; Sheffield: Sheffield Academic Press, 2000).

Haber, S., 'A Woman's Touch: Feminist Encounters with the Hemorrhaging Woman in Mark 5.24-34', *JSNT* 26.2 (2003), pp. 171-92.

Hallett, Judith P., 'Women's Lives in the Ancient Mediterranean'. in Ross Shepard Kraemer and Mary Rose D'Angelo (eds.), *Women and Christian Origins* (New York: Oxford University Press, 1999), pp. 13-34.

Hamm, M. Dennis, 'The Freeing of the Bent Woman and the Restoration of Israel: Luke 13.10-17 as Narrative Theology', *JSNT* 31 (1987), pp. 23-44.

Hands, A.R., *Charities and Social Aid in Greece and Rome* (London: Thames and Hudson, 1968).

Hanson, Ann Ellis, 'Hippocrates: *Diseases of Women 1*', *Signs* 1 (1975), pp. 581-82.

Haraway, Donna Jeanne,, 'Situated Knowledges', in Donna Jeanne Haraway, *Simians, Cyborgs, and Women: The Reinvention of Nature* (London: Free Association, 1990), pp. 183-202.

—*Simians, Cyborgs, and Women: The Reinvention of Nature* (London: Free Association, 1990).

—*Modest_Witness@Second_Millenium. FemaleMan©_Meets_Oncomouse*™: *Feminist and Technoscience* (New York: Routledge, 1997).

Harrison, R.H., *Healing Herbs of the Bible* (Leiden: E.J. Brill, 1966).

Hart, Gerald D., *Asclepius: The God of Medicine* (London: Royal Society of Medicine Press, 2000).

*Heal*, http.//encarta.msn.com/dictionary_/heal.html (accessed 30 March, 2001).

*Heal*, http.//dictionary.reference.com/search?q=heal (accessed 23 June, 2005).

Hearon, Holly, *The Mary Magdalene Tradition: Witness and Counter-Witness in Early Christian Communities* (Collegeville, MN: Liturgical Press, 2004).

Heyob, Sharon Kelly, *The Cult of Isis among Women in the Graeco-Roman World* (EPRO, 51; Leiden: E.J. Brill, 1975).

Hippocrates, *Airs Waters Places* (trans. W.H.S. Jones; LCL; London: Heinemann, 1923).

—*Epidemics I and III* (trans. W.H.S. Jones; LCL; London: Heinemann, 1923).

—*The Oath* (trans. W.H.S. Jones; LCL; London: Heinemann, 1923).

—*The Sacred Disease* (trans. W.H.S. Jones; LCL; Cambridge: Harvard University Press, 1943).

—*In the Surgery* (trans. E.T. Withington; LCL; Cambridge: Harvard University Press, 1944).

—*Epidemics II, IV, V, VI, VII* (trans. Wesley D. Smith; LCL; Cambridge: Harvard University Press, 1994).

—*Fleshes* (trans. Paul Potter; LCL; Cambridge: Harvard University Press, 1995).

—*Physician* (trans. Paul Potter; LCL; Cambridge: Harvard University Press, 1995).

Homer, *Odyssey Books 1–12* (trans. A.T. Murray, revised by George. E. Dimock; LCL; Cambridge: Harvard University Press, 1995).

—*Iliad Books 1–12* (trans. A.T. Murray, revised William F. Wyatt; LCL; Cambridge: Harvard University Press, 1999).

Honari, Morteza, 'Health Ecology: An Introduction', in Morteza Honari and Thomas Boleyn (eds.), *Health Ecology: Health, Culture and Human-Environment Interaction* (London: Routledge, 1999), pp. 1-34.

Houghton, William, 'The Pistic Nard of the Greek Testament', *Proceedings of theSociety of Biblical Archaeology* January 10 (1888), pp. 144-46.

Howard, M.C., 'Athenaeus', in M.C. Howard (ed.), *The Oxford Companion to Classical Literature* (Oxford: Oxford University Press, 1989), p. 70.

Hurd-Mead, Kate Campbell, *A History of Women in Medicine: From the Earliest Times to the Beginning of the Nineteenth Century* (Haddam: Haddam Press, 1938).

Ilan, Tal, *Jewish Women in Greco-Roman Palestine* (Peabody, MA: Hendrickson, 1996).

Jackson, Ralph, *Doctors and Diseases in the Roman Empire* (London: British Museum Publications, 1988).

Janowitz, Naomi, *Magic in the Roman World: Pagans, Jews and Christians*.(Religion in the First Christian Centuries; London: Routledge, 2001).

Jantsen, Grace M., *Power, Gender and Christian Mysticism* (Cambridge: Cambridge University Press, 1995).

Jex-Blake, Sophia, *Medical Women: A Thesis and a History* (Edinburgh: Oliphant, Anderson and Ferrier, 1886).

John, Mary E., *Discrepant Dislocations: Feminism, Theory and Postcolonial Histories* (Berkeley: University of California Press, 1996).

Johnson, Elizabeth A., *She Who Is: The Mystery of God in Feminist Theology* (New York: Crossroad, 1992).

Johnstone, Steven, 'Cracking the Code of Silence: Athenial Legal Oratory and the Histories of Slaves and Women', in Sandra R. Joshel and Sheila Murnaghan (eds.), *Women and Slaves in Greco-Roman Culture: Differential Equations* (London: Routledge, 1998), pp. 221-35.

Joshel, Sandra R., and Sheila Murnaghan, 'Introduction: Differential Equations', in Sandra R. Joshel and Sheila Murnaghan (eds.), *Women and Slaves in Greco-Roman Culture: Differential Equations* (London: Routledge, 1998), pp. 1-21.

Karris, Robert, 'Women and Discipleship in Luke', in Amy-Jill Levine and Marianne Blickenstaff (eds.), *A Feminist Companion to Luke* (Cleveland: Pilgrim Press, 2001), pp. 21-43.

Kee, Howard Clark, *Medicine, Miracle and Magic in New Testament Times* (SNTSMS, 55; Cambridge: Cambridge University Press, 1986).

Keel, Othmar, and Christoph Uehlinger, *Gods, Goddesses, and Images of God in Ancient Israel* (trans. T.H. Trapp; Minneapolis: Fortress Press, 1998).

King, Helen, 'Agnodike and the Profession of Medicine', *Proceedings of the Cambridge Philological Society* 32 (1986), pp. 53-77.

—'The Daughter of Leonides: Reading the Hippocratic Corpus', in Averil Cameron (ed.), *History as Text: The Writing of Ancient History* (London: Gerald Duckworth, 1989), pp. 11-32.

—'Self-Help, Self-Knowledge: In Search of the Patient in Hippocratic Gynaecology', in Richard Hawley and Barbara Levick (eds.), *Women in Antiquity: New Assessments* (London: Routledge, 1995), pp. 135-48.

—'Beyond the Medical Market-Place: New Directions in Ancient Medicine', *Early Science and Medicine* 2.1 (1997), pp. 88-97.

—*Hippocrates' Woman: Reading the Female Body in Ancient Greece* (Cambridge: Cambridge University Press, 1999).

King, Karen L., *The Gospel of Mary of Magdala: Jesus and the First Woman Apostle* (Santa Rosa: Polebridge, 2003).

Kippenberg, Hans G., 'Magic in Roman Civil Discourse: Why Rituals Could Be Illegal', in Peter Schäfer and Hans G. Kippenberg (eds.), *Envisioning Magic: A Princeton Seminar and Symposium* (Leiden: E.J. Brill, 1997), pp. 137-63.

Kitzberger, Ingrid Rosa (ed.), *Transformative Encounters: Jesus and Women Re-viewed* (Biblical Interpretation Series, 43; Leiden: E.J. Brill, 2000).

Kleinman, Arthur, *Patients and Healers in the Context of Culture: An Exploration of the Borderland between Anthropology, Medicine, and Psychiatry* (Berkeley: University of California Press, 1980).

—*Writing at the Margin: Discourse between Anthropology and Medicine* (Berkeley: University of California Press, 1995).

Köbert, J., 'Nardos Pistike - Kostnarde', *Bib* 29 (1948), pp. 279-81.

Koperski, Veronica, 'Women and Discipleship in Luke 10.38-42 and Acts 6.1-7: The Literary Context of Luke–Acts', in Amy-Jill Levine and Marianne Blickenstaff (eds.), *A Feminist Companion to Luke* (Cleveland: Pilgrim Press, 2001), pp. 161-96.

Korpela, Jukka, *Das Medizinalpersonal im Antiken Rom: Eine Sozialgeschichtliche Untersuchung* (Helsinki: Suomalainen Tiedeakatemia, 1987).

Kraemer, Ross Shepard, *Her Share of the Blessings: Women's Religions among Pagans, Jews, and Christians in the Greco-Roman World* (New York: Oxford University Press, 1992).

Krause, D., 'Simon Peter's Mother-in-law-Disciple or Domestic Servant? Feminist Biblical Hermeneutics and the Interpretation of Mark 1.29-31', in Amy-Jill Levine and Marianne Blickenstaff (eds.), *A Feminist Companion to Mark* (Sheffield: Sheffield Academic Press, 2001), pp. 37-53.

Kudlien, Fridolf, *Der Griechische Arzt im Zeitalter des Hellenismus: Seine Stellung in Staat und Gesellschaft*, VI (Abhandlungen der Geistes- und Sozialwissenschaftlichen Klasse; Mainz: Akademie der Wissenschaften und der Literatur, 1979).

Kühn, C.G., *Caludii Galeni Opera Omnia* (Hildersheim: Georg Olms, 1965).

Lamphere, Louise, Helena Ragoné and Patricia Zavella, *Situated Lives: Gender and Culture in Everyday Life* (New York: Routledge, 1997).

Laquer, Thomas, *Making Sex; Body and Gender from the Greeks to Freud* (Cambridge: Harvard University Press, 1990).

Lefkowitz, Mary R., and Maureen B. Fant, *Women's Life in Greece and Rome: A Source Book in Translation* (Baltimore: The Johns Hopkins University Press, 2nd edn, 1992).

Lerner, Gerda, *Why History Matters: Life and Thought* (New York: Oxford University Press, 1997).

Levine, Amy-Jill, 'Discharging Responsibility: Matthean Jesus, Biblical Law, and Hemorrhaging Woman', in David R. Bauer and Mark Allan Powell (eds.), *Treasures New and Old: Recent Contributions to Matthean Studies* (SBLSymS, 1; Atlanta: Scholars Press, 1996), pp. 379-97.

Levine, Amy-Jill, and Marianne Blickenstaff (eds.), *A Feminist Companion to Luke* (Cleveland: Pilgrim Press, 2001).

Liddell, Henry George, and Robert Scott, *A Greek-English Lexicon* (New York: American Book Company, 18th rev. edn, 1897).

LiDonnici, Lynn R., *The Epidaurian Miracle Inscriptions: Text, Translation and Commentary* (Texts and Translations, 36; Graeco-Roman Religion Series, 11; Atlanta: Scholars Press, 1995).

Lionnet, Françoise, *Postcolonial Representations: Women, Literature, Identity* (Ithaca, NY: Cornell University Press, 1995).

Lipinska, Mélanie, *Histoire des femmes médicins depuis l'Antiquité jusqu'à nos jours* (Paris: G. Jacques, 1900).

Littré, E., *Oeuvres Complètes d'Hippocrates*, VIII (10 vols.; Paris: A.M. Hakkert, 1961).

Lloyd, G.E.R., *Science, Folklore and Ideology Studies in the Life Sciences in Ancient Greece* (Cambridge: Cambridge University Press, 1983).

Low, Alaine, and Shoraya Tremayne, 'Introduction', in Alain Low and Shoraya Tremayne (eds.), *Sacred Custodians of the Earth?: Women, Spirituality and the Environment* (New York: Berghahn, 2001), pp. 1-20.

Malina, Bruce J., 'The Individual and the Community-Personality in the Social World of Early Christianity', *BTB* 9 (1979), pp. 126-38.

—*The New Testament World: Insights from Cultural Anthropology* (Louisville, KY: Westminster/John Knox Press, rev. edn, 1993).

Malina, Bruce J., and Jerome H. Neyrey, *Calling Jesus Names: The Social Value of Labels in Matthew* (Foundations and Facets; Sonoma: Polebridge, 1988).

Malina, Bruce J., and Richard L. Rohrbaugh, *Social-Science Commentary on the Synoptic Gospels* (Minneapolis: Fortress Press, 1992).

Mattern, Susan P., 'Physicians and the Roman Imperial Aristocracy: The Patronage of Therapeutics', *Bulletin of the History of Medicine* 73 (1999): 1-18.

McCane, Bryon R., 'Is a Corpse Contagious? Early Jewish and Chrsitian Attitudes toward the Dead', in Eugene H. Lovering Jr (ed.), *SBLSP* 1992 (Atlanta: Scholars Press, 1992), pp. 378-88.

McClain, Carol Shepherd, 'Reinterpreting Women in Healing Roles', in Carol Shepherd McClain (ed.), *Women as Healers: Cross-Cultural Perspectives* (New Brunswick: Rutgers University Press, 1989), pp. 1-19.

McKinlay, Judith E., *Gendering Wisdom the Host: Biblical Invitations to Eat and Drink* (JSOTSup, 216; Gender, Culture, Theory, 4; Sheffield: Sheffield Academic Press, 1996).

Meier, John P., *A Marginal Jew; Rethinking the Historical Jesus*, II (3 vols.; New York: Doubleday, 1994).

Mellor, Mary, *Feminism and Ecology* (Cambridge: Polity Press, 1997).

Metzger, Bruce M., *A Textual Commentary on the Greek New Testament* (London: United Bible Societies, 1971).

Meyers, Eric M., 'The Problems of Gendered Space in Syro-Palestinian Domestic Architecture: The Case of Roman-Period Galilee', in David L. Balch and Carolyn Osiek (eds.), *Early Christian Families in Context: An Interdisciplinary Dialogue* (Grand Rapids: Eerdmans, 2003), pp. 44-69.

Moloney, F.J., *The Gospel of Mark: A Commentary* (Peabody, MA: Hendrickson, 2002).

Morand, Anne-France, *Études sur les hymnes Orphiques* (Religions in the Graeco-Roman World, 143; Leiden: E.J. Brill, 2001).

Moxnes, Halvor, 'Patron-Client Relations and the New Community in Luke–Acts', in Jerome H. Neyrey (ed.), *The Social World of Luke–Acts: Models for Interpretation* (Peabody, MA: Hendrickson, 1991), pp. 241-68.

—*Putting Jesus in His Place: A Radical Vision of Household and Kingdom* (Louisville, KY: Westminster/John Knox Press, 2003).

Nelson, Hilde Lindemann, 'Resistance and Insubordination', *Hypatia* 10.2 (1995), pp. 23-40.

Nolland, John, *Luke 9.21-18.34* (WBC, 35B; Nashville: Thomas Nelson, 1993).

Noorda, S.J., ' "Cure Yourself, Doctor!" (Luke 4,23): Classical Parallels to an Alleged Saying of Jesus', in Joel Delobel (ed.), *Logia* (BETL, 59; Leuven: Leuven University Press, 1982), pp. 459-67.

Novakovic, Lidija, *Messiah, the Healer of the Sick: A Study of Jesus as the Son of David in the Gospel of Matthew* (WUNT, 2.170; ed. J. Frey; Tübingen: Mohr Siebeck, 2003).

Nutton, Vivian, 'Healers in the Medical Market Place: Towards a Social History of Graeco-Roman Medicine', in Andrew Wear (ed.), *Medicine in Society: Historical Essays* (Cambridge: Cambridge University Press, 1992), pp. 15-58.

Okely, Judith, *Own or Other Culture* (London: Routledge, 1996).

Økland, Jorunn, ' "*IN PUBLICUM PROCURRENDI*": Women in the Public Space of Roman Greece', in Lena Larsson and Agneta Strömberg (eds.), *Aspects of Women in Antiquity: Proceedings of the First Nordic Symposium on Women's Lives in Antiquity* (Lovén, Jonsered: Paul Aströms Förlag, 1998), pp. 127-41.

Ortner, Sherry B., *Making Gender: The Politics and Erotics of Culture* (Boston: Beacon Press, 1996).

Ortner, Sherry B., and Harriet Whitehead, *Sexual Meanings: The Cultural Construction of Gender and Sexuality* (Cambridge: Cambridge University Press, 1981).

Osiek, Carolyn, 'The Women at the Tomb: What Are They Doing There?', *ExAud* 9 (1993), pp. 97-107.

Osiek, Carolyn and David L. Balch (eds.), *Families in the New Testament World: Houses and House Churches* (Louisville, KY: Westminster/John Knox Press, 1997).

Parker, Holt T., 'Women Doctors in Greece, Rome, and the Byzantine Empire', in Lillian R. Furst (ed.), *Women Healers and Physicians: Climbing the Long Hill* (Lexington: University Press of Kentucky, 1997), pp. 131-50.

Paton, William Roger, and Edward Lee Hicks, *The Inscriptions of Cos* (Oxford: Clarendon Press, 1891).

Phillips, V., 'Full Disclosure: Towards a Complete Characterization of Women who Followed Jesus in the Gospel According to Mark', in Ingrid Rosa Kitzberger (ed.), *Transformative Encounters: Jesus and Women Re-viewed* (Biblical Interpretation Series, 43; Leiden: E.J. Brill, 2000), pp. 17-24.

Pilch, John J., 'Understanding Biblical Healing: Selecting the Appropriate Model', *BTB* 18 (1988), pp. 60-66.

—'Reading Matthew Anthropologically: Healing in Cultural Perspective', *Listening* 24.3 (1989), pp. 278-89.

—*Healing in the New Testament: Insights from Medical and Mediterranean Anthropology* (Minneapolis: Fortress Press, 2000).

Pitt-Rivers, Julian, *The Fate of Shechem or the Politics of Sex: Essays in the Anthropology of the Mediterranean* (Cambridge: Cambridge University Press, 1977).

Plato, *The Republic*, I (trans. Paul Shorey; LCL; Cambridge: Harvard University Press, 1982).

—*Theaetetus* (trans. Francis MacDonald Cornford; New York: Liberal Arts Press).

Pleket, H.W., *Epigraphica*. II. *Texts on the Social History of the Greek World* (Leiden: E.J. Brill, 1969).

Pliny, *Natural History: With an English Translation in Ten Volumes* (trans. W.H.S. Jones; Cambridge: Harvard University Press, 1951).

Plumwood, Val, *Feminism and the Mastery of Nature* (London: Routledge, 1993).

—*Environmental Culture: The Ecological Crisis of Reason* (Environmental Philosophies; London: Routledge, 2002).

Pollard, Tessa M., and Susan Brin Hyatt, 'Sex, Gender and Health: Integrating Biological and Social Perspective', in Tessa M. Pollard and Susan Brin Hyatt (eds.), *Sex, Gender and Health* (Cambridge: Cambridge University Press, 1999), pp. 1-17.

Pomeroy, Sarah B., *Goddesses, Whores, Wives, and Slaves: Women in Classical Antiquity* (New York: Schocken Books, 1975).

—'Plato and the Female Physician (Republic 454d2)', *AJP* 99 (1978), pp. 496-500.

Primavesi, Anne, 'Ecology and Christian Hierarchy', in Alaine Low and Soraya Tremayne (eds.), *Sacred Custodians of the Earth? Women, Spirituality and the Environment* (New York: Berghahn Books, 2001), pp. 121-39.

—*Gaia's Gift: Earth, Ourselves and God after Copernicus* (London: Routledge, 2003).

Pringle, Rosemary, *Making Some Difference: Women in Medicine* (Griffith University: Uniprint, 1996).

—*Sex and Medicine: Gender, Power and Authority in the Medical Profession* (Cambridge: Cambridge University Press, 1998).

Rajan, Rajeswari Sunder, and You-me Park, 'Postcolonial Feminism/Postcolonialism and Feminism', in Henry Schwarz and Sangeeta Ray (eds.), *A Companion to Postcolonial Studies* (Oxford: Basil Blackwell, 2000), pp. 53-71.

Reid, Barbara E., *Choosing the Better Part? Women in the Gospel of Luke* (Collegeville, MN: Liturgical Press, 1996).

Remus, Harold, *Jesus as Healer* (*Understanding Jesus Today*; Cambridge: Cambridge University Press, 1997).

Ricci, Carla, *Mary Magdalene and Many Others: Women Who Followed Jesus* (trans. Paul Burns; Minneapolis: Fortress Press, 1989).

Ringe, Sharon, 'A Gentile Woman's Story, Revisited: Rereading Mark 7.24-31a', in Amy-Jill Levine and Marianne Blickenstaff (eds.), *A Feminist Companion to Mark* (Sheffield: Sheffield Academic Press, 2001), pp. 79-100.

Robbins, Vernon K., *Exploring the Texture of Texts: A Guide to Socio-Rhetorical Interpretation* (Harrisburgh, PA: Trinity Press International, 1996).

Robert, Louis, 'Index Commenté', in Nezih Firatli, *Les stèles funéraires de Byzance Gréco-Romaine, avec l'édition et l'index commenté des épitaphes par Louis Robert* (trans. A.N. Rollas; Paris: Librairie Adrien Maisonneuve, 1964), pp. 131-89.

Roller, Lynne E., *In Search of God the Mother: The Cult of Anatolian Cybele* (Berkeley: University of California Press, 1999).

Römer, Thomas C., 'Competing Magicians in Exodus 7-9: Interpreting Magic in the Priestly Theology', in Todd Klutz (ed.), *Magic in the Biblical World: from the Rod of Aaron to the Ring of Solomon* (JSNTSup, 245; London: T&T Clark International, 2003), pp. 12-22.

Rosenblatt, Maire-Eloise, 'Gender, Ethnicity, and Legal Considerations in the Haemorrhaging Woman's Story: Mark 5.25-34', in Ingrid Rosa Kitzberger (ed.), *Transformative Encounters: Jesus and Women Re-viewed* (Biblical Interpretation Series, 43; Leiden: E.J. Brill, 2000), pp. 137-61.

Rushton, K.P., 'The Parable of John 16.21: A Feminist Socio-Rhetorical Reading of the (Pro)creative Metaphor for the Death-Glory of Jesus' (PhD dissertation, Griffith University, 2000).

Saldarini, Anthony J., *Matthew's Christian-Jewish Community* (Chicago Studies in the History of Judaism; Chicago: University of Chicago Press, 1994).

Saller, Richard P., 'Women, Slaves, and the Economy of the Roman Household', in David L. Balch and Carolyn Osiek (eds.), *Early Christian Families in Context: An Interdisciplinary Dialogue* (Grand Rapids: Eerdmans, 2003), pp. 185-206.

Sargent, Carolyn, and Caroline B. Brettell, *Gender and Health: An International Perspective* (Upper Saddle River: Prentice Hall, 1996).

Sawicki, Marianne, 'Archaeology as Space Technology: Digging for Gender and Class in Holy Land'. *MTSR* 6 (1994), pp. 319-48.

—'Spatial Management of Gender and Labor in Greco-Roman Galilee', in Douglas R. Edwards and Thomas McCollough (eds.), *Archaeology and the World of Galilee: Texts and Contexts in the Roman and Byzantine periods* (Atlanta: Scholars Press, 1997), pp. 7-28.

—'Magdalenes and Tiberiennes: City Women in the Entourage of Jesus', in Ingrid Rosa Kitzberger (ed.), *Transformative Encounters: Jesus and Women Re-viewed* (Biblical Interpretation Series, 43; Leiden: E.J. Brill, 2000), pp. 181-206.

Scarborough, John, 'Adaptation of Folk Medicines in the Formal Materia Medica of Classical Antiquity', in John Scarborough (ed.), *Folklore and Folk Medicines* (Madison: American Institute of the History of Pharmacy, 1987), pp. 21-31.

—'The Pharmacology of Sacred Plants, Herbs, and Roots', in Christopher A. Faraone and Dirk Obbink (eds.), *Magika Hiera: Ancient Greek Magic and Religion* (New York: Oxford University Press, 1991), pp. 138-74.

Schaberg, Jane, *The Resurrection of Mary Magdalene: Legends, Apocrypha, and the Christian Testament* (New York: Continuum, 2003).

Schäfer, Peter, and Hans G. Kippenberg (eds.), *Envisioning Magic: A Princeton Seminar and Symposium* (Leiden: E.J. Brill, 1997).

Schaffer, Kay, 'Colonizing Gender in Colonial Australia: The Eliza Fraser Story', in Alison Blunt and Gillian Rose (eds.), *Writing Women and Space: Colonial and Postcolonial Geographies* (New York: Guilford Press, 1994), pp. 101-120.

Schönfeld, Walther, *Frauen in der Abendländischen Heilkunde: Vom klassischen Altertum bis zum Ausgang des 19. Jahrhunderts* (Stuttgart: Enke, 1947).

Schroer, Silvia, *Wisdom Has Built her House: Studies on the Figure of Sophia in the Bible* (trans. Linda M. Maloney and W. McDonough; Collegeville, MN: Liturgical Press, 2000).

Schüssler Fiorenza, Elisabeth, *Bread Not Stone: The Challenge of Feminist Biblical Interpretation* (Boston: Beacon Press, 1984).

—'Lk 13.10-17: Interpretation for Liberation and Transformation', *TD* 36.4 (1989), pp. 303-19.

—*But She Said: Feminist Practices of Biblical Interpretation* (Boston: Beacon Press, 1992).

—*In Memory of Her: A Feminist Theological Reconstruction of Christian Origins* (New York: Crossroad, rev. edn, 1992).

—*Jesus – Miriam's Child, Sophia's Prophet: Critical Issues in Feminist Christology* (New York: Continuum, 1994).

—*Sharing her Word: Feminist Biblical Interpretation in Context* (Boston: Beacon Press, 1998).

—*Rhetoric and Ethic: The Politics of Biblical Studies* (Minneapolis: Fortress Press, 1999).

—*Wisdom Ways: Introducing Feminist Biblical Interpretation* (Maryknoll, NY: Orbis Books, 2001).

Segal, Alan F., 'Hellenistic Magic: Some Questions of Definition', in R. van den Broek and M.J. Vermaseren (eds.), *Studies in Gnosticism and Hellenistic Religions: Presented to Gilles Quispel on the Occasion of his 65th Birthday* (Leiden: E.J. Brill, 1981), pp. 349-75.

—'Matthew's Jewish Voice', in David L. Balch (ed.), *Social History of the Matthean Community: Cross-Disciplinary Approaches* (Minneapolis: Fortress Press, 1991), pp. 3-37.

Seim, Turid Karlsen, *The Double Message: Patterns of Gender in Luke and Acts* (Nashville: Abingdon Press, 1994).

Seybold, Klaus, and Ulrich B. Mueller, *Sickness and Healing* (trans. Douglas W. Stott; Biblical Encounters; Nashville: Abingdon Press, 1981).

Sharp, Sharon A., 'Folk Medicine Practices: Women as Keepers and Carriers of Knowledge', *Women's Studies International Forum* 9 (1986), pp. 243-49.

Skeggs, Beverley, *Formations of Class and Gender: Becoming Respectable* (London: Sage, 1997).

Sobel, Hildegard, *Hygieia: Die Göttin der Gesundheit* (Darmstadt: Wissenschftliche Buchgesellschaft, 1990).

Soranus, *Soranus' Gynecology* (trans. Owsei Temkin; Baltimore: The Johns Hopkins University Press, 1991).

Spivak, Gayatri Chakravorty, 'Can the Subaltern Speak?', in Patrick Williams and Laura Chrisman (eds.), *Colonial Discourse and Post-Colonial Theory: A Reader* (New York: Harvester Wheatsheaf, 1993), pp. 66-111.

Stambaugh, John E., *The Ancient Roman City* (Baltimore: The Johns Hopkins University Press, 1988).

Stark, Rodney, *The Rise of Christianity: A Sociologist Reconsiders History* (Princeton, NJ: Princeton University Press, 1996).

Tempkin, Owsei, *Hippocrates in a World of Pagans and Christians* (Baltimore: The Johns Hopkins University Press, 1991).

Theissen, Gerd, 'Lokal- und Sozialkolorit in der Geschichte von der Syrophönikischen Frau (Mk 7 24-30)', *ZNTW* 75 (1984), pp. 202-25.

—*The Gospels in Context: Social and Political History in the Synoptic Tradition* (trans. L.M. Maloney; Edinburgh: T&T Clark, 1992).

Theophrastus, *De Causis Plantarum* (trans. Benedict Einarson and George K.K. Link; LCL; Cambridge: Harvard University Press, 1976).

—*De Causis Plantarum* (trans. Benedict Einarson and George K.K. Link; LCL; Cambridge: Harvard University Press, 1990).

—*De Causis Plantarum* (trans. Benedict Einarson and George K.K. Link; LCL; Cambridge: Harvard University Press, 1990).

Thibeaux, Evelyn R., ' "Known to Be a Sinner": The Narrative Rhetoric of Luke 7.36-50', *BTB* 23 (1993), pp. 151-60.

Thomas, John Christopher, *The Devil, Disease and Deliverance: Origins of Illness in New Testament Thought* (JPTSup, 13; Sheffield: Sheffield Academic Press, 1998).

Torjesen, Karen J., *When Women Were Priests: Women's Leadership in the Early Church and the Scandal of their Subordination in the Rise of Christianity* (New York: Harper SanFrancisco, 1993).

Trainor, Michael F., *The Quest for Home: The Household in Mark's Community* (Collegeville, MN: Liturgical Press, 2001).

Trible, Phyllis, *God and the Rhetoric of Sexuality* (OBT; Philadelphia: Fortress Press, 1978).

Twelftree, Graham H., *Jesus the Exorcist: A Contribution to the Study of the Historical Jesus* (Peabody, MA: Hendrickson, 1993).

Ubieta, Carmen Bernabé, 'Mary Magdalene and the Seven Demons in Social-Scientific Perspective', in Ingrid Rosa Kitzberger (ed.), *Transformative Encounters: Jesus and Women Re-viewed* (Biblical Interpretation Series, 43; Leiden: E.J. Brill, 2000), pp. 203-23.

van der Eijk, P.J., H.F.J. Horstmanshoff and P.H. Schrijvers (eds.), *Ancient Medicine in its Socio-Cultural Context: Papers Read at the Congress on Ancient Medicine Held at Leiden University, 13-15 April, 1992* (Atlanta: Rodopi, 1995).

van Eck, E., and A.G. van Aarde, 'Sickness and Healing in Mark: A Social Scientific Interpretation', *Neot* 27 (1993), pp. 27-54.

Veeser, H. Aram, 'Introduction', in H. Aram Veeser (ed.), *The New Historicism* (New York: Routledge, 1989), pp. x-xvi.

Vermes, Geza, *The Changing Faces of Jesus* (New York: Viking Compass, 2000).

Vledder, Evert-Jan, *Conflict in the Miracle Stories: A Socio-Exegetical Study of Matthew 8 and 9* (JSNTSup, 152; Sheffield: Sheffield Academic Press, 1997).

Wainwright, Elaine M., *Towards a Feminist Critical Reading of the Gospel according to Matthew* (BZNW, 60; Berlin: W. de Gruyter, 1991).

—'A Voice from the Margin: Reading Matthew 15.21-28 in an Australian Feminist Key', in F.F. Segovia and M.A. Tolbert (eds.), *Reading from this Place. II. Social Location and Biblical Interpretation in Global Perspective* (Minneapolis: Fortress Press, 1995), pp. 132-53.

—*Shall We Look for Another? A Feminist Rereading of the Matthean Jesus* (Maryknoll, NY: Orbis Books, 1998).

—'Not without my Daughter: Gender and Demon Possession in Matthew 15.21-28', in Amy-

Jill Levine and Marianne Blickenstaff (eds.), *A Feminist Companion to Matthew* (Sheffield: Sheffield Academic Press. 2001), pp. 126-37.

—'The Pouring Out of Healing Ointment: Rereading Mark 14.3-9', in Fernando F. Segovia (ed.), *Toward a New Heaven and a New Earth: Essays in Honor of Elisabeth Schüssler Fiorenza* (Maryknoll, NY: Orbis Books, 2003), pp. 157-78.

Weissenrieder, Annette, *Images of Illness in the Gospel of Luke: Insights of Ancient Medical Texts* (WUNT, 2.164; Tübingen: Mohr Siebeck, 2003).

Wells, Louise, *The Greek Language of Healing from Homer to New Testament Times* (BZNW, 83; Berlin: W. de Gruyter, 1998).

Wilkinson, John, *The Bible and Healing: A Medical and Theological Commentary* (Grand Rapids: Eerdmans, 1998).

Winkler, John, 'The Constraints of Eros', in Christopher A. Faraone and Dirk Obbink (eds.), *Magica Hiera: Ancient Greek Magic and Religion* (New York: Oxford University Press, 1991), pp. 214-43.

Wire, Antoinette, 'Ancient Miracle Stories and Women's Social World', *Forum* 2 (1986): 77-84.

Witherington III, Ben, 'On the Road with Mary Magdalene, Joanna, Susanna, and Other Disciples – Luke 8.1-3', in Amy-Jill Levine and Marianne Blickenstaff (eds.), *A Feminist Companion to Luke* (Cleveland: Pilgrim Press, 2001), pp. 133-60.

Witt, R.E., *Isis in the Graeco-Roman World* (London: Thames & Hudson, 1971).

Wyke, Maria (ed.), *Gender and the Body in the Ancient Mediterranean* (Oxford: Basil Blackwell, 1998).

Zerwick, Maximilian, *Biblical Greek* (Scripta Pontifici Instituti Biblici, 114; Rome: Iura Editionis et Versionis Reservantur, 1963).

Zerwick, Max, and Mary Grosvenor, *A Grammatical Analysis of the Greek New Testament*, I (2 vols.; Rome: Biblical Institute Press, 1974).

# INDEX

## INDEX OF REFERENCES

### OLD TESTAMENT

CLASSICAL

INSCRIPTIONS

INDEX OF NON-BIBLICAL NAMES

Printed in the United States
91679LV00001B/175-222/A